# DEAR BILL

## THE CORRESPONDENCE OF WILLIAM ARTHUR DEACON

EDITED BY
JOHN LENNOX AND MICHELE LACOMBE

# Dear Bill

## The Correspondence of William Arthur Deacon

UNIVERSITY OF TORONTO PRESS
Toronto Buffalo London

Toronto Buffalo London
Printed in Canada
Reprinted in 2018
ISBN 978-1-4875-7693-6 (paper)

Printed on acid-free paper

---

**Canadian Cataloguing in Publication Data**

Deacon, William Arthur, 1890-1977
Dear Bill

Includes index.
ISBN 0-8020-2624-9

1. Deacon, William Arthur, 1890-1977 – Correspondence.
2. Critics – Canada – Correspondence. I. Lennox, John Watt, 1945-
II. Lacombe, Michèle. III. Title.

PS8025.D4A4 1988 C818'.5209 C88-093990-7
PR9183.D4A4 1988

---

FRONTISPIECE William Arthur Deacon in the early 1930s. Thomas Fisher Rare Book Library

This book has been published with the help of a grant from the Canadian Federation for the Humanities, using funds provided by the Social Sciences and Humanities Research Council of Canada. Publication has also been assisted by the Canada Council and the Ontario Arts Council under their block grant programs.

For Clara

# Contents

# Preface

PREPARING A SELECTION of William Arthur Deacon's correspondence raises a few unique questions and imposes several less unique choices. The major editorial challenge posed by the letters to and from Deacon is not what to include but what to exclude. We have compiled a collection of correspondence rather than only letters from Deacon in order to present both sides of a number of literary and professional friendships and associations, highlighting the ideas and personalities of the individuals who confided to Deacon their day-to-day plans and preoccupations. These entries account for most of the correspondence and within this parameter the emphasis falls as much on the dynamics of the exchange as on Deacon's own concerns and opinions. Although his interests, indeed his entire leisure time, were taken up with the needs of writers, he would have been the first to insist that his concerns were subordinate to and generally indistinguishable from theirs.

No other examples exist in Canadian literary scholarship of one critic's correspondence with many writers. Desmond Pacey's *The Letters of Frederick Philip Grove* (1976) and Carl Ballstadt, Elizabeth Hopkins, and Michael Peterman's *Susanna Moodie: Letters of a Lifetime* (1985) are both outstanding examples of editions of one writer's collected letters. Bruce Whiteman's *A Literary Friendship: The Correspondence of Ralph Gustafson and W.W.E. Ross* (1984) presents a two-way correspondence. Our aim has been to offer a sampling of characteristic and significant exchanges between 1920 and 1960. The letters we have selected have been reprinted in their entirety; there has been no attempt to aim for greatest coverage through excerpted passages, since excerpts, no matter how judicious, are inevitably elliptical and invariably stripped of context and significance. Moreover, to have included complete correspondences, like those with Emily Murphy, Gabrielle Roy, or Hugh MacLennan – all outstanding from start to finish – would have meant devoting several hundred pages to individuals at the expense of other, equally important exchanges. Such complete correspondences with 'mainstream' figures would, in any event, ignore recent revisions of the Canadian literary 'canon' and of our notions of canonicity.

Any selection of this kind is the product of editorial judgment. Our aim has been to present a selection which reflects, however imperfectly, what we consider to be the primary value and fascination of the complete Deacon correspondence: the account – inclusive and comprehensive – of the dynamic and often difficult development over a forty-year period of different aspects of our literary and cultural history. To do so, as this correspondence reveals, is to include exchanges from a wide variety of correspondents – major, minor, obscure, and forgotten – with whom Deacon kept in touch over a lifetime. A chronological arrangement is dictated by this historical bias; such an arrangement, we hope, also conveys something of the narrative energy and the sense of discovery inherent in the massive Deacon Collection itself.

We have attempted to balance clarification of content against readability by keeping annotations and other editorial interventions as brief and unobtrusive as possible. Deficient punctuation, capitalization, underlining, and related bibliographical inconsistencies have been corrected, except where such corrections detract from the idiosyncratic style and flavour of the originals – as in the letters of Laura Goodman Salverson, Kate Ruttan, James D. Gillis, Gabrielle Roy, and Germaine Guèvremont, for example. Interpolations in square brackets have been added where the sense of a letter or a sentence requires, and [sic] is used only to indicate apparent inconsistencies or errors. Explanatory notes are placed at the end of letters and provide factual or contextual information required for an understanding of references; a few allusions could not be located or explained, even after much searching, and they remain unannotated.

Other editorial changes have involved the vertical spacing and horizontal ruling of margins for salutations, addresses, and signatures; the elimination of redundant information from addresses; the spelling out in full of street addresses and provinces; the standardizing of dates; the standardizing with a comma of Deacon's variable punctuation of salutations. While every effort has been made to ensure the accuracy of transcription of the letters in this volume, responsibility for any existing errors rests solely with the editors. For the most part, we have used Deacon's unsigned carbon copies of his letters; in the rare cases where originals were kept or located, we have followed the convention of the unsigned letter. Since virtually all Deacon's letters were written in Toronto, we have not included the typed or letterhead address; exception has been made for the few letters written in Winnipeg prior to his move to Toronto in April 1922.

Readers who wish to know more about the entire Deacon correspondence or about the original letters selected for publication can refer to a copy of DEAKDEX, the computerized inventory to the Deacon MS Collection, which catalogues all letters in four separate lists: by correspondent, by date, by subject of letter, and by type of correspondent (such as poet, novelist). The Deacon Collection itself is housed in the Thomas Fisher Rare Book Library, University of Toronto.

*Dear Bill* marks the final stage of a long-term research project that began in the summer of 1977, produced a biography and index in 1982, and now results in this volume of correspondence. An undertaking of this kind could not have been realized without enormous support and good will from many quarters and individuals, among them the Social Sciences and Humanities Research Council of Canada, the Thomas Fisher Rare Book Library and the Robarts Library of the University of Toronto, and York University. The SSHRCC provided initial research funding and, later, John Lennox's leave fellowship in 1985–6. Richard Landon, Head, Thomas Fisher Library, and Rachel Grover, also of the Fisher Library, made access to the Deacon Papers a priority and, with Robert H. Blackburn, former Chief Librarian, University of Toronto, arranged for the Deacon Project to be given spacious headquarters in the Robarts Library. This was an incalculable advantage for the completion of our work and a much-appreciated gesture of inter-university co-operation.

Throughout the work on this project, we have been the beneficiaries of the support and interest of William Deacon's family, especially his son-in-law Lloyd Haines and his granddaughter Charity Haines. Their co-operation from the beginning has meant a great deal. The exchanges contained in the present volume would not have seen the light of day were it not for the permission of Deacon's correspondents, their heirs, and executors. Our gratitude is extended to the following people: John S. Aylen, Constance Beresford-Howe, Earle Birney, Mrs Ethel Brown, Morley Callaghan, Robert Choquette, Susan K. Creighton, Esmée de la Roche, Jean-Marcel Duciaume, Imogen Knister Givens, J. King Gordon, A. Leonard Grove, Louise Guèvremont-Gentiletti, Molly Costain Haycroft, R. Martin Kenney, the late A.R.M. Lower, T.M. MacInnes, Grace Woodsworth MacInnis, Mrs Lewis MacIsaac, Hugh MacLennan, Miss V. Macpherson, W.O. Mitchell, Bruce Mowatt, Peter C. Newman, the late Viola Pratt, Al Purdy, Thomas Raddall, Leon Rhodenizer, Lady Joan Roberts, Beth Pierce Robinson, Sinclair Ross, the late Gabrielle Roy, George Salverson, B.D. Sandwell, Dorothy MacDonald Taylor, and Margaret Coulby Whitridge.

Others who contributed to our work were our research assistants Christina Cole, Anne Comer, Ruth Panofsky, and Jeanette Seim Lynes, who displayed considerable expertise in the art of tracking down obscure references. To York's Secretarial Services, especially its supervisor Patricia Cates and Grace Baxter, word processor extraordinaire, we are grateful for the care and patience in typing and revising endless drafts of the correspondence manuscript.

Gerald Hallowell, our editor at the University of Toronto Press, has worked with us on this project from the beginning and has always provided expert advice and encouragement. We thank him for these and for his constant interest in the possibility of a volume of correspondence. We are also grateful to Jean Wilson, who read the correspondence typescript and once again proved the efficacy of a sharp editorial eye.

The person who has been most instrumental to the completion of this project as a whole is Clara Thomas. Her work as co-author of the biography and her support during preparation of the present volume have been crucial. Our debt to her goes beyond words and always will.

JOHN LENNOX AND MICHÈLE LACOMBE

# Introduction

'I WANT TO BE an anonymous herald, announcing the great ones.' When William Arthur Deacon wrote to John Garvin about his literary ambitions in 1921, he responded to a query for 'a few particulars' about himself with a thousand-word epistolary essay. Aware of his weaknesses as well as his strengths, Deacon nevertheless took his role as herald very seriously and told Garvin that his contribution to the growth of Canadian letters would be as a catalyst rather than as a creative writer or 'a critic with a foot rule.' Deacon soon became a reader's reviewer and a writer's critic – directing his reviews to the general readership he was trying to create and addressing the writer's concerns more directly in his private correspondence. *Dear Bill: The Correspondence of William Arthur Deacon* is concerned with the critic in this latter capacity, as literary advocate and letter-writer extraordinaire; the letters in it have been selected and arranged as much to set forth the style and ideas of Deacon's correspondents as to reveal his own beliefs and personality.

*William Arthur Deacon: A Canadian Literary Life* (1982) recorded the professional life and work of a man who, fuelled by his own Methodist background and an overlay of the idealism of theosophy, blended his ambition, talents, and nationalistic fervour into a lifelong mission to encourage and promote Canadian writers and their works. This volume is, in part, a companion to the biography. Out of a total of approximately 13,000 letters, this selection is designed to show how Deacon and his correspondents shared concerns which reflected factors important to the evolution of our cultural history: the constant encouragement of our writers, the growth of their professional confidence, the creation of a readership, and the co-operation of a publishing network. Much of the rhetoric of Deacon and his generation, stressing an idealistic belief in 'national consciousness,' for example, inevitably has been superseded. Nevertheless, Deacon's understanding of what was essential to Canada's cultural autonomy – a strong community of creative individuals who debate common interests with each other and their audience – remains as valid a goal now as it was in his day.

When John George Bourinot published *Our Intellectual Strength and Weakness* in 1893, he idealized our literature in its present and future role as graceful ornament to a civilized nation. Thomas Guthrie Marquis, in his chapter for *Canada and Its Provinces* (1913), wrote pragmatically of English-Canadian literature as one more factor in the gross national product; in the same volume Monseigneur Camille Roy, writing of French-Canadian literature, saw it as an important element in holding Quebec true to itself. Deacon's correspondence reveals the persistence of these goals and beliefs. Beset by the difficulties and reversals of the Depression years, Deacon in 1934 wrote a Christmas letter to Henry Weeks, a young Canadian friend contemplating doing university studies in the United States:

> The new conditions are going to be too complicated for us. Mine is a Euclidian mind; I don't really understand Einstein ... You young fellows will have to go into it [the future]; and plan a new life by dealing familiarly with factors quite beyond me ... I shall quit what I humorously style my 'public life' (meaning my private interest in public affairs) and you chaps must go on lit only by your own creative thinking ...
>
> I have a word of advice for you, however; and that is to think highly of faith. Not only to keep faith, but to realize the sterility of cynicism, and the fertility of belief, which is positive ... This is not merely an economic matter, or a political one, or religious: it is everything at once – one of the turning points of history and the greatest of recorded history ... For God's sake prepare for it with all that is in you. Learn at that great University. Learn from the nimble-minded Americans. Then come back where you belong and dig in as and where it seems good to you or as circumstances permit ...
>
> Don't be negative; don't be afraid; and don't be restricted. Realize that you can influence destinies in a big way. When forms are breaking up and a new order is sorting itself out, a man can accomplish in one lifetime what would normally take a hundred lives of first rate talent.

Perhaps because Deacon himself felt that he was working in an age where centuries' worth of growth occurred in a single lifetime, largely due in his case to the impact of World War I, the foregoing effectively summarizes his, and earlier, generations' belief in Canadian literature as finally coming of age. For Deacon, this maturation was linked with much larger developments whose parameters were as vague as they were significant. In his concern about the future of Canada, Deacon – like Lorne Pierce, his authors and their audience – voiced his beliefs in the nineteenth-century rhetoric of material and spiritual progress. Unlike Pierce, he tempered these with an essentially modern iconoclasm and sense of realism. The difference between Deacon and the next generation of critics, mostly academic, is that his view of himself as an iconoclast was essentially populist in nature, revising rather than radically departing from nineteenth-century ideals. Deacon's 'newness' and contribution resided not in his aesthetic – his desire for so-called realism was really more of a taste for the romantic and didactic than for modernism – so much as in his politics, that is, his thorough understanding and wholesale critique of colonialism, expressed in his desire for native forms, regional themes, and cultural self-recognition. His dreams and hopes have since been met by the establishment of the Canada Council, the Social Sciences and Humanities Research Council of Canada, provincial granting agencies, and by the growth of the media and of the university community at home and abroad. The letters reflect several transitional stages in this gradual process, making them important as cultural documents far beyond the personalities of the individuals involved, although in many cases these continue to intrigue the reader.

Deacon did not remain alone in recognizing and fighting obstacles to the growth and recognition of Canadian writers and writing. In *On Canadian Poetry* (1943) E.K. Brown outlined the problems of establishing Canadian literature as he saw them; his words are still relevant in the economically strained 1980s. Geographically and therefore economically, book publishing and book-selling were plagued, then as now, by great distances; psychologically, Canadian culture was marked by a colonial mentality scarcely a generation removed from that implicitly examined in George Parker's *The Beginnings of the Book Trade in Canada* (1985). As a member of the forward-looking graduate faculty at the University of Chicago, Brown had been in the forefront of the struggle to make American literature a respected academic discipline in the United States. He knew that the Canadian situation was similar and inevitably affected by the historical time-lag which marked other aspects of our development.

Deacon arrived on the scene in the early 1920s, two decades before the publication of Brown's book, with a prejudice against academics which he never lost, stemming in part from his impressions of Pelham Edgar during his years at Victoria College (1907–9). Deacon turned elsewhere for his models, to literary journalists like Christopher Morley, cultural commentators like H.L. Mencken, and literary historians like Van Wyck Brooks, all critics of broad cultural interests who nurtured American writers or who contributed to their belated recognition. The critics and men of letters who influenced Deacon read literature as a revelation of cultural and historical transformation and saw themselves as contributing to this process. Figures such as Edmund Wilson and Maxwell Perkins, the greatest of a dying breed of professional critics, essayists, and editors, shared in the United States the territory which, in Canada, Lorne Pierce and Deacon addressed with more modest pretensions but with undying enthusiasm in the face of limited publishing resources and a small readership.

The short-term fate of Deacon's expectations was a common one for the kind of prophet and forerunner he deemed himself to be. Many of the first generation of 'professional' academics in the Canadian field in the 1940s and 1950s were embarrassed by his zeal and misunderstood his unstinting faith in writers' potential. If Deacon's praise was naïve and uncritical by some standards, it was not indiscriminate. A new generation of scholars and critics, in what is now a relatively stable and confident community of letters, is in a better position to recognize and reassess Deacon's place and contribution as a broadly based cultural promoter and commentator.

Deacon's early correspondents were the audience to whom he first defined his role and beliefs. Writing to Tom MacInnes on 4 December 1922, Deacon stated that he was '"among' newspapermen, but not 'of' them.' He went on to insist that 'I am not a journalist as the term is generally understood but a literary critic. This is a species of vertebrate rare in the Dominion. I am a very rotten specimen, I admit, but with that philosophic imprudence characteristic of me I saw that Canada needed a critic – an official appreciator –

more than anything else, and I sprang to fill the office till a better man can be found.' As a reviewer-critic, he constantly defined his role as one of 'reasoned admiration' in which he was the middleman, using his powers of judgment to create an evaluation of the text that would bear the stamp of his individuality. The dynamic complement to such reviewing is found in the letters, where he felt free to indulge his strong personality and creative impulses, providing his literary friends with a focus for their arguments. Deacon's quirky intellect and letter-writing persona impelled writers to voice their own worries, struggles, and triumphs, sometimes clarifying thoughts for the first time in the process of articulating them. At the same time, correspondence helped to satisfy Deacon's own more modest but equally compelling ambitions as writer, and some of his best and most characteristic work emerges from the letters he wrote in the course of his forty-year career.

When Deacon bought his first typewriter in 1919 and began his massive correspondence, keeping copies of most of the letters he sent as well as the replies he received, he was still in Winnipeg. Ostensibly he was a lawyer with the firm of Pitblado, Hoskin; in reality, the writing for which he had begun intensive self-training was speedily moving to the forefront of his ambitions. He was submitting essays to many journals in Canada and the United States, and was honoured in the spring of 1921 to be named assistant literary editor, without pay, for John W. Dafoe's *Manitoba Free Press*. Through the influence of Winnipeg friends and of B.K. Sandwell, at that time editor of *The Canadian Bookman*, Deacon left the Canadian mid-west for Toronto in 1922 to serve as literary editor of *Saturday Night*. He immediately launched a serious and responsible exploration of Canadian letters that he was to continue for the rest of his life. His reviews during his six years at *Saturday Night*, and his column of literary news, gossip, and humour, 'Saved from the Waste-Basket,' brought him dozens of correspondents. He wrote to them at length, looking forward to hearing of their literary concerns and ambitions, and at the same time looking back, for his own morale's sake, to the friends and advisers of his Winnipeg years: above all to Judge Emily Murphy, his 'mother in the craft,' first mentor, confidante, and life-long friend, and to another early friend and sponsor, W.T. Allison of the University of Manitoba, who reviewed widely and published, under the pseudonym 'Ivanhoe,' critical essays for the *Winnipeg Tribune*.

The overall picture of the Canadian literary scene in the 1920s given by the correspondence is one of great optimism, activity, and variety. Contrary to an often repeated myth, it was not particularly difficult to be published, as a perusal of publishers' advertisements in the press of the time will show. On the contrary, critical voices sounding from the pages of the young and aggressively intellectual *Canadian Forum*, founded in 1920, denounced the Canadian publishing scene as far too soft and undiscriminating. Ryerson Press, under Lorne Pierce, was in the forefront of the field, but McClelland and Stewart, Macmillan, Musson, Thomas Nelson, Longmans, Dent, and Thomas Allen were all publishing and advertising Canadian writers. In the fall of 1925 Graphic Press, based in Ottawa, was formed in a bold attempt to sustain an exclusively Canadian publishing house and was especially close to Deacon's heart. It lasted for only seven years, but during that time managed to produce eighty books, including Frederick Philip Grove's *A Search for America* (1927) and Deacon's own *Poteen* and *The Four Jameses* (1927), as well as several books under the imprints of Ariston and RU-MI-LOU.

What was difficult, of course, was to sell the books in a country as vast and as sparsely supplied with readers and bookstores as Canada. Only the barest handful of Canadian writers made a good living from their work and among these Mazo de la Roche, after the success of her prize-winning *Jalna* in 1927, was perhaps pre-eminent. It was inevitable that the categories of 'popular' and 'serious' writing, defined by the fledgling Canadian Authors' Association as 'professional' and 'amateur,' would be mutually exclusive, with the association responding to the economic concerns of the former much more than to the critical needs of the latter. Among editors, Lorne Pierce was the outstanding patron of Canadian writers; like Deacon, he was one of the few people who could and did bridge the growing gap between literary journeymen and genuine artists. He was a gentle, highly literate, and enthusiastic man of letters who had a characterictically strong sense of mission. Hired by Ryerson in 1920, he encouraged young poets through his institution of the Ryerson chapbooks in 1925. Ryerson launched writers like Grove, E.J. Pratt, and Deacon himself and initiated The Makers of Canadian Literature series in the 1920s.

Ryerson imprints were very often extremely handsome productions, designed and illustrated by such artists as F.H. Varley, C.W. Jefferys, and Thoreau Macdonald. Pierce, however, did not have the editorial skills of an Alfred Knopf, much less of a Maxwell Perkins. Like writers everywhere, his writers were a touchy lot, and unlike Deacon he did not have the personality or the literary authority to dominate them or to help them much with the structuring of their works. Many of the Ryerson publications of his time cry out for rigorous editing, particularly fiction, for Pierce was more at home with poetry and essays than with fiction. Deacon was occasionally hired as a free-lance reader of fiction manuscripts for Ryerson, Macmillan, and Graphic, but soon found that he could not spare the time to write his characteristically detailed responses for a nominal fee.

The frenzied and optimistic activity of the decade, the sense that Canadian literature was at last finding its feet, were reflected in various histories of literature from Ray Palmer Baker's *A History of Canadian Literature* (1920) to Lorne Pierce's *An Outline of Canadian Literature* (1927). Vernon Rhodenizer's *A Handbook of Canadian Literature* (1930) complemented his radio lectures in Nova Scotia, for which book lists appeared in the Halifax newspapers. Related concerns and hopes had also been expressed in 1921 by the founding of the Canadian Authors' Association. First begun by a small group of professional writers, including B.K. Sandwell and Stephen Leacock, for the purpose of trying to improve Canadian copyright legislation, the CAA quickly attracted a large membership. One hundred and ten people attended its founding convention in Montreal in the spring of 1921; Sandwell's *Canadian Bookman* became its official organ in 1921–2. Like *The Bookman*, the CAA soon was an important focus for national literary activity, and its annual conventions and branch activities served as the rallying-ground, both social and professional, for many writers at this time. Deacon was a charter member of the Winnipeg branch and for decades a vociferous supporter of the association, rising through the presidency of the Toronto branch (1937–9) to become national president from 1946 to 1948. With the successful establishment of the Association came communal lobbying power. Anticipating the work of the Writers' Union, the CAA soon became vocal on many other issues besides copyright – contracts, royalties, and the need for Canadian literary prizes; to its credit, it also' made a sincere and prolonged effort to welcome French-Canadian writers to the group.

Of course, the intense activity and optimism of the twenties did not entirely erupt from a wasteland. Pelham Edgar of Victoria College had long been a leading voice in the encouragement of first-class work among Canadian writers. One of his protégées, Marjorie Pickthall, had achieved a good deal of publishing success between 1913 and her death, at age thirty-nine, in 1922. Among Deacon's correspondents, John Garvin, then regarded as one of Canada's leading men of letters, was known as an editor and anthologist; Charles G.D. Roberts, Duncan Campbell Scott, and Tom MacInnes, poets of radically different styles, audiences, and accomplishments, had long been read with interest; E.J. Pratt and Wilson MacDonald had recently emerged as popular poets. B.K. Sandwell, editor, teacher, and journalist, knew enough about Deacon and of the literary climate and periodical press of Canada to recommend that Deacon be hired by *Saturday Night*.

As the 1920s began, Pratt was in the first stages of his career as a poet; he and Deacon renewed the acquaintance they had first formed as students at Victoria College and became firm friends and correspondents. Roberts, acknowledged as the 'old chieftain' or 'father' of Canadian literature, especially after his return to Canada in 1925, loved and guarded his position somewhat jealously. For readers, Bliss Carman came next in line, while Wilson MacDonald saw himself as the new rival for 'kingship.' None of Deacon's critical judgments is as obviously open to question as his choice, for a time, of MacDonald as 'the genius of the bunch.' MacDonald's popularity was fostered by poetry readings and reading tours which were as much a phenomenon in the 1920s as in the 1960s. Many schoolchildren heard Roberts, Carman, and MacDonald, all of whom were tireless readers, travellers, and self-promoters. Pratt also undertook a trip to the West and, later in the decade, Grove toured as well.

The overwhelming bulk of the correspondence of the 1920s is with individual writers at all stages and ages. Mazo de la Roche worked hard at her writing and was extremely protective and professional about it, while maintaining a façade of lady-like dilettantism. Laura Goodman Salverson, who badly wanted more knowledge of her craft, felt herself culturally stifled in Port Arthur, where she lived with her husband and son, and was convinced of her ineptitude in English because her mother tongue was Icelandic. She was, however, a woman of talent and determination, as Deacon recognized, and her correspondence is bittersweet, a record of ambitions and potential only partly realized.

When Arthur Phelps wrote of his enthusiasm for Grove's *Over*

*Prairie Trails* (1922), Deacon became, and remained, a staunch adviser and supporter, much involved in the anti-censorship fight when *Settlers of the Marsh* appeared in 1925, and busy with the arrangement of funds and speaking engagements for Grove's 1928 and 1929 reading tours. He was quick to recognize the power of Grove's writing, as his *Saturday Night* review of *A Search for America* (1927) demonstrates, and two decades later he was the one who personally carried the Governor-General's Award for *In Search of Myself* (1946) to the ailing and embittered Grove at his home near Simcoe, Ontario. The paucity of Grove letters is one of the Deacon Collection's mysteries: the numbers of them that must at one time have existed have dwindled to a mere five.

One of the most eager and serious of the writers who sought communication with Deacon was Raymond Knister. Calling Deacon, with politically astute yet obvious sincerity, 'the Dean of Canadian Letters,' Knister initiated an exchange that lasted until his tragic drowning. Deacon did not really understand the modernist movement, but he was eager to learn, applauding Knister's appearance in *This Quarter*, encouraging him in criticism, and urging him to write novels. It was Knister who asked Deacon in 1926 if he knew Morley Callaghan; at that time he did not, but he made a point of getting in touch with Callaghan from whom, as from Knister, he was eager to learn.

In some ways the most revealing correspondents are the less well-known professionals and would-be professionals with their concerns about the craft of writing, their eagerness for constructive advice, and their universal problems with publishers, publicity, royalty payments, and the technicalities of book production. The literary Paris and France that Deacon knew superficially as the place where Knister and Callaghan had been successful in placing their early stories, came to life in a more comic and bizarre way in his correspondence with Francis Dickie, an expatriate Canadian who wrote the 'Letter from Paris' column for *Saturday Night*. Dickie's tales of woe and of his unorthodox way of life were a constant source of entertainment for Deacon and vied in eccentricity with his brief but intense and one-sided correspondence with the redoubtable Kate Ruttan, whom Deacon had contacted in the course of preparing *The Four Jameses* (1927).

By the time Deacon was able to initiate periodic literary supplements to *Saturday Night* in 1925, he had assembled a network of writers and academics all across the country who were delighted and honoured to review for him. Understandably, he congratulated himself on his centrality to Canadian literary life; understandably too, he was disgruntled by A.J.M. Smith's publication of 'Wanted: Canadian Criticism' in *The Canadian Forum* of April 1928, the month of his own dismissal from *Saturday Night* following several years' battles with its conservative contributing editor, Hector Charlesworth. Smith was in the vanguard of the movement to academicize Canadian literary studies; then as now, however, as Robertson Davies has succinctly written in *The Well-Tempered Critic* (1981), 'Canada as she really is, and Canada as seen through the eyes of our professors, are two very different places' (147). Deacon insisted that he was never ready to trust 'the professor' to nurture Canadian writers as he did, nor to promote the reading and study of their works, but there were exceptions to his suspicions. Sherwood Fox, professor of classics and dean of arts at the University of Western Ontario in the mid-1920s, hoped to give Deacon the chance to present a series of lectures on Canadian literature. The opportunity never materialized, although their initial exchange of letters initiated a long-standing correspondence. Another exception was Vernon Rhodenizer of Acadia University, whose course in Canadian literature was already well established, and who was a pioneer in presenting it from Halifax as a radio series in 1928–9. He and Deacon enjoyed mutual trust and stimulating correspondence, debating, among other matters, the relative merits of realism and romance in the writings of Grove and de la Roche. Despite occasional and short-lived disagreements, Pratt remained a loyal friend and supporter.

When Deacon was fired from *Saturday Night* in 1928, his popularity with readers and writers was undiminished, and his ambitions, particularly forh the literary supplement, were boundless. However, in his pursuit of both readers and a forum for the discussion of Canadian writing, he could be and often was arrogant and insubordinate. In any case, his place was wanted for Horace Sutton ('Hal Frank'), the nephew of *Saturday Night*'s publisher, Margaret R. Sutton. With valuable connections supplied by friends across the country, Deacon soon assembled a string of newspapers for whom he wrote weekly literary columns. By 1930 he knew that his lifeline was his work with *The Mail and Empire* of Toronto; with the onset of the Depression, *The Mail and Empire* pushed him out of specialized literary journalism as his exclusive domain into the broader fields of political, educational, and public affairs, whose issues encompassed Deacon's widening interests. With the worsening of the Depression and the international situation, many of his new correspondents came more and more to be men intensely concerned with large social and political issues.

Two events acted as catalysts for Deacon in this orientation: the publication of his own utopian work *My Vision of Canada* (1933) and the institution in 1932 by the YMCA of the Canadian Institute on Economics and Politics at Geneva Park on Lake Couchiching, which he attended in 1935 and to which *The Mail and Empire* made him special correspondent in August 1936. The new correspondence with political and academic activists like A.R.M. Lower, who seems to have agreed fully with Deacon's unorthodox beliefs as a nationalist, and the more phlegmatic J.S. Woodsworth, whose intelligence and political integrity Deacon admired, is indicative of the critic's expanding interests in this eventful decade. These men wrote with a sense of the extreme urgency of national and international crisis; their correspondence illuminates many of the concerns of Canada's best minds in that period of tension and growing crisis.

The 'Dirty Thirties' generated their share of eccentric but effective visionaries: for a time Deacon wrote at considerable length to Father Athol Murray, founder of Notre Dame College (now an affiliate of the University of Regina), which operated out of abandoned boxcars in Wilcox, Saskatchewan. Murray and Deacon represented for each other a hope for sanity and a thrust towards peace; but war came inexorably and, like many other pacifists, Deacon was swept up by its inevitability. For a while, however, Murray's college was for Deacon what *My Vision* was for Murray, a glimmer of hope and idealism in a sombre and treacherous decade. Although Deacon thought of himself as a socialist, like Murray he was too much of a maverick to be part of any political party, as he admitted to Woodsworth; however, in the 1930s he continued to champion a vision of a pacifist and nationalist Canada which, in its idealism and energy, places him at the very heart of that socialist decade's millenarian thrust.

Deacon's circle of literary friends and correspondents continued to grow in the thirties. He challenged Grey Owl, who had risen quickly to international fame with *Pilgrims of the Wild* (1934) and *Tales of an Empty Cabin* (1936), about his alleged Indian background, instituting one of the most interesting of all correspondences. Lovat

Dickson, a publisher and Grey Owl's biographer, has said that the long letter of 10 May 1935 is Grey Owl's first record of his legend and self-vindication. Georges Bugnet, a French immigrant to Rich Valley, Alberta had responded to Deacon's long and favourable review of the translation (1929) of Bugnet's first novel *Nipsya* (1924). Despite their differences of opinion, Bugnet was happy to find such appreciation in an English-speaking reviewer, and openly discussed his writing and his convictions about French Canada in his letters. Bugnet and Grey Owl were two of many friends who contributed to the national scope and comprehensiveness of Deacon's *Literary Map of Canada* (1936), illustrated by Stanley Turner, a unique project which, with the failure of Deacon's hope for a collection of essays of social criticism tentatively entitled 'Open Minds,' provided its author with a means of playful diversion.

For health reasons, Deacon had been declared unfit for service in World War I. In 1939 he was too old to enlist, but he became Deputy Administrator of the Wartime Prices and Trade Board's newsprint-rationing division. Since late 1936 he had been literary editor of *The Globe and Mail*, his 'Fly Leaf' column as popular a feature for both writers and readers as 'Saved from the Waste-Basket' had been in the 1920s. His wife Sally took over the management of the *Globe*'s book page for the war's duration, though Deacon was based in Toronto and continued to be in charge of format and, to a large extent, its content. It was an exciting time for Canadian writers, despite the tragedies and worries of the war: these years saw the publication of Sinclair Ross's *As for Me and My House* (1941), Hugh MacLennan's *Barometer Rising* (1941) and *Two Solitudes* (1945), Earle Birney's *David and Other Poems* (1942), and, eventually, Gabrielle Roy's *Bonheur d'occasion* (1945), all novels and poems which represent a serious advance and a maturity not seen since the early work of Grove, Callaghan, and Pratt.

Deacon's correspondence slackened during the busy war years, but the writers who were published then are among our best and they were anxious, as writers always have been, to find and cherish a knowledgeable critic and friend. Among new correspondents of the 1940s and 1950s, Thomas Raddall, Hugh MacLennan, and Gabrielle Roy wrote frequently and at length, and remained friends well after Deacon's retirement in 1960. A highly entertaining correspondence of this period is Raddall's, its tone a man-to-man sharing of concerns in writing and publishing and, on Raddall's part, the skill of a born story-teller which makes every letter a tale in itself. MacLennan and Dorothy Duncan, his wife, found the world of Canadian letters a desert and were delighted and heartened by their warm relationship with Deacon. Like him, they distrusted what they saw as academics' high-handed appropriation of literary discussion and they responded eagerly and candidly to a bookman with whom they could sustain an open-handed literary friendship in which common interests ranged over literature in general, specific writing problems and successes, and the vagaries of publishing, cutbacks, royalties, and reviewing.

Through MacLennan, Deacon first learned of Gabrielle Roy's *Bonheur d'occasion*. Very shortly, Deacon and Roy became firm friends – he a kindly, always appreciative reader and business adviser to her, and she a shy and hesitant young woman, somewhat overwhelmed by her first success, and grateful for a solicitous mentor who was also a former Manitoban. Like Pierce, Deacon had always had a special interest in the writers of French Canada since the early 1920s, when for a time they had been part of the Canadian Authors' Association. He felt, therefore, increasingly fortunate when he began corresponding with Germaine Guèvremont in the spring of 1946. The excitement in discovering new writers and developments in literary French Canada is palpable in the letters of the immediate post-war period.

This broadening of interest was accompanied by a growing consolidation and eventual regrouping of writers and their interests within the literary community itself, not without the usual pitfalls and disagreements. The Governor-General's Awards, established by the CAA in 1936, codified its criteria with a set of rules and procedures in the formation of an Awards Board in 1944. Sponsored by the CAA, *The Canadian Poetry Magazine*, established in 1936 under Pratt's editorship, was directed briefly by Earle Birney from 1946 to 1948. Birney's publishing of modernist verse alienated many of the CAA's members and executive, but before he resigned in anger Birney had shown the vigorous quality of contemporary Canadian poetry, proof of which appeared elsewhere in *Preview, First Statement, Contemporary Verse*, and *Northern Review*.

When Deacon became National President of the CAA in 1946, his mood, and that of the association, was one of overwhelming optimism. During his tenure he struck and guided committees that obtained significant income tax privileges from Ottawa, drew up a standard book contract to protect writers from exploitation by certain publishers, and issued, in the *The Bookman*, special bulletins on copyright information. After fifteen years of depression and war Deacon, like his generation, expected great advances in all things Canadian, including the final stage of a growing climate of acceptance for writers and their works. Correspondence from 1945 to 1948 is vast, much of it to do with the CAA and its all-embracing concerns for our literature. As a literary journalist, however, Deacon was still haunted by the insecurity of his profession; he carried enduring scars from his *Saturday Night* débâcle of 1928 and from the brief, but shattering, two-week hiatus in his employment by *The Globe and Mail* after George McCullagh founded it in 1936. Nevertheless, in these immediate post-war years his anxieties were subordinate to his and his correspondents' hope for a renewal of energy and interest in Canadian writing. On the whole, the younger generation shared his confidence and enthusiasm. Earle Birney was a temporary recruit; Deacon had greatly admired *David and Other Poems* (1942) and was eager to draw the poet into the work of the CAA. Constance Beresford-Howe, almost a generation younger than Birney, was more amenable to advice from a solicitous senior critic, as was the naïve and ebullient aspirant Margaret Coulby, to whom Deacon gave blunt but warm-hearted attention in response to queries about becoming a writer.

The post-war years also saw yet another stage in the academic institutionalization of Canadian literature. Professors such as Claude Bissell and Robert McDougall of the University of Toronto, Malcolm Ross of Queen's University, Desmond Pacey of the University of New Brunswick, and Carl Klinck of the University of Western Ontario gradually came to dominate the field. With the Report in 1951 of the Massey Commission on National Development in the Arts, Letters and Sciences, the literary community was poised for change. The CAA, which had acted as Canada's largest and most influential writers' organization and lobby group for three decades, was no longer nearly as representative as it once had been. The eventual establishment of the Canada Council in 1957 entailed, among other things, the official consolidation of the Governor-General's Awards Board as an adjudicatory body completely independent of the association. However, the formation of the Canada Council paradoxically put into practice in 1959 two causes close to Deacon's heart: the attaching of a $1000 cash prize to each award and the inauguration, within the Governor-General's Awards, of prizes for work in French.

Deacon's fear was that the growing role of the university in the realization of shared goals would deepen the rift between the intelligent reader and the professional critic, who together shared and influenced the growing field of Canadian writing. He understood how professional writers, who candidly expressed their opinions to him, moved uneasily beside the growing numbers of academic critics, the two camps often betraying mutual misunderstanding in a relationship which continues to be both fragile and fruitful. However, he could not have foreseen the university's unprecedented role in expanding the present and future readership for Canadian authors, nor did he imagine the degree to which many of our writers would be associated with academic institutions, especially following university expansion in the 1960s. To the bitter end, Deacon heroically and articulately deplored the creation of any official cultural hierarchy, although he also persisted in reducing the danger of cultural hegemony to a simple conflict between 'popular' and 'obscure' writing. We should respect him for the former, and understand the latter as we situate him within the larger context of our literary development.

Through the 1950s the correspondence reflects more and more Deacon's status as an established figure and his talent for critical judgment and advice. Invariably, this role as critic and adviser was gratefully acknowledged above and beyond the respect due to the elder statesman he had become. One young and enthusiastic correspondent of this last period was Peter Newman, in whom Deacon saw great promise. Newman was one of many who was happy to express his thanks for Deacon's support in his early writing years. Thomas Costain, the best-selling novelist and editor at Doubleday, was able to show his appreciation in promoting a contract between George Nelson of Doubleday Canada and Deacon for a history of Canadian literature and a volume of memoirs, neither of which was completed. The mid-1950s and the mid-1960s brought two brief and unexpected correspondences linking Deacon's early work with the future assured by the younger writers he had always supported and promoted. In 1956 James D. Gillis, one of the subjects of *The Four Jameses*, wrote a letter of appreciation following a much-delayed first reading of Deacon's book. Ten years later, the poet Al Purdy was requesting Deacon's signature on a prized copy of *The Four Jameses*.

When he reluctantly retired in 1960 at seventy years of age, many of Deacon's old correspondents reversed their customary roles: where he had supported, encouraged, and advised for so long, now they in their turn steadfastly heartened him. Old publishing friends, Lorne Pierce, Jack McClelland, and George Nelson among them, urged him to write both his memoirs and a history of Canadian literature. The two were often awkwardly and necessarily intertwined in fact and memory; however, until the failure of Deacon's health and memory in the mid-sixties, George Nelson of Doubleday gave him the staunchest editorial support and advice. Friends of long standing like Lorne Pierce and Hugh MacLennan and newer writers like Peter Newman wrote moving testimonials to him about his importance to their work. Deacon suffered the prolonged ravages of Altzheimer's Disease from about 1967, when his correspondence ends, until his death in 1977; by the mid-1960s he knew, however, that Canadian literature was established in many of the ways he had worked for.

The main thrust of the entire Deacon Collection, as of this selection, reveals how no academy, no professional group, and no granting system, however necessary and beneficial, can entirely take the place of the nurturing of our writers by good reading, honest criticism, and personal encouragement through failures as well as successes, through bad times as well as good. Deacon had a talent for friendship which matched his enthusiasm and patience for a wide circle of correspondents. He became and remained for forty years one focal point in Canadians' recognition of themselves, their culture, and their heritage.

# Chronology

April 1890
William Arthur Deacon born in Pembroke, Ontario, the son of William Herbert Deacon (1856–90) and Sarah Annie Davies (1862–1948)

24 December 1890
Death of William Herbert Deacon. Sarah Annie and her infant son move to Valleyfield, Quebec, to live with her mother and her Methodist clergyman father; in 1892 they all move to Chambly

1895
Deacon's grandfather retires with his family to Stanstead, Quebec

September 1901
Enters Stanstead College, a Methodist co-educational school

June 1905
Matriculates from Stanstead, having won Eastern Townships Bank Silver Medal

1905–7
First-year McGill courses at Stanstead

Summer 1907
Job as a fire-ranger at Temagami Forest Reserve; returned to this job in summers of 1908 and 1909

September 1907–May 1909
Victoria College, Toronto

Fall 1909
Does not return to Victoria, but begins working as Assistant Editor for *Monetary Times of Canada*

1910–11
Assistant Office Manager, Ontario Power Company, Niagara Falls

1911–13
Time-keeper and later salesman at Manitoba Bridge and Iron Works owned by his uncle, Thomas Russ Deacon

30 June 1913
Marries Edna Gladys Coon in Weston, Ontario

1913–14
Involved in real estate and contracting

1914
Applies to and is accepted as student by the Law Society of Manitoba. Moves to Dauphin to article under Frank E. Simpson

1916
Tries to enlist, but rejected on health grounds; he and Gladys become theosophists

1917
Leaves Simpson for Pitblado, Hoskin in Winnipeg

1918
Meets Mrs Sarah (Sally) Townsend Syme at Theosophical Society; LL B from University of Manitoba; spends summer in New York being treated for nervous collapse; sworn in as attorney

Spring 1921
Deacon and Gladys separate; WAD named Honorary Assistant Literary Editor of *The Manitoba Free Press*; becomes charter member of Winnipeg branch of the Canadian Authors' Association

April 1922
Leaves Pitblado, Hoskin

May 1922
WAD and Sarah move to Toronto and Deacon begins working for *Saturday Night* on 29 May

1923
*Pens and Pirates* (Ryerson). Birth of William Herbert on 21 July

1924
*Peter McArthur* (Ryerson)

1925
Birth of Deirdre on 26 February; first 'Literary Section' in *Saturday Night* on 28 November

1926
*Poteen* (Graphic). Birth of Mary on 17 July

1927 *Four Jameses* (Graphic)

1928
Fired from *Saturday Night* on 3 April and immediately begins national syndication of weekly book reviews; becomes literary editor of *Mail and Empire* on 19 September

1931
*Open House*, with Wilfred Reeves (Graphic)

1933
*My Vision of Canada* (Ontario Publishing Company)

1936
*Literary Map of Canada* (Macmillan). Dropped as literary editor with sale of *Mail and Empire* on 21 November, but reinstated by *Globe and Mail* on 2 December

1937–9
President, Toronto Branch, Canadian Authors' Association

1940
*Here Comes the Censor* (Macmillan)

November 1942–December 1945
Deputy Administrator, Wartime Prices and Trade Board paper-rationing section, Toronto

1944–9
Chairman, Governor-General's Awards Board

1946–8
National President, Canadian Authors' Association

October 1951–March 1952
Ryerson lectures on Canadian literature

1953
*The Four Jameses*, revised edition (Ryerson)

14 December 1960
Involuntary retirement from *Globe and Mail*, but agrees to continue 'Fly Leaf' columns

1961
Retirement dinner at King Edward Hotel in Toronto on 11 January; signs contract with Doubleday in September for history of Canadian literature and for book of memoirs

6 July 1963
Last 'Fly Leaf' appears

5 March 1969
Sally dies

1974
Reissue of revised edition of *The Four Jameses* (Macmillan) with an introduction by Doug Fetherling

5 August 1977
Death of William Arthur Deacon

# DEAR BILL

# THE CORRESPONDENCE OF WILLIAM ARTHUR DEACON

3 November 1921

To Tom MacInnes[1]

650 McDermot Avenue
Winnipeg
November 20, 1921

Dear Mr. MacInnes,

Trying out a new machine – forgive errors. It's a Corona, the Lizzie of the typewriter world. O! How I love a real machine!

Well, Sir, your piece in SATURDAY NIGHT[2] came out yesterday – much abbreviated, I fancy. I send you one copy under separate cover, a second is in my drawer awaiting your more particular instructions as to address, and a third is in my 'MacInnes' file, available for emergency, and if possible to be kept there as data for further 'MacInnes' articles. It sure hit at the right moment, and your prose is lucid enough. I hope it does some good.

Bliss Carman is making a tour of the West and getting good money for lectures. His main lecture here got him $375.00 and the University gave him $100.99 (no, no, not the odd cents – that's this damn machine) for a short talk to the undergrads. This Canadian Literature movement means melon cutting for established writers and I hope you get in on it. Wait till that collected edition comes out! Say, I hope you are going to leave in 'Walt Whitman.' It's a good poem and you owe it to Walt. You know you do. For Lord's sake make this a complete edition. A purchaser does not have to read them all but some of us would be very glad to.

Today I finished my 'Janey Canuck'[3] for *Free Press* publication December 31st. Yours was the first, you know, of a series to extend over two years, and which I hope later to bring out in book form. I write for them every month but they only take four of these special introductions annually. You will be interested to know that my piece on you, representing 1% of my published work for the last three years has brought me more recognition than anything else. So you may be disappointed in the rest of my work. I spoke at the University lately and a sweet little senior introduced me as 'famous (!!!) for my essays on modern poetry.' I have been larfing ever since. I believe Dunsany[4] was right when he wrote 'The Assignation.' Fame said to the poet: 'I will meet you in the graveyard back of the workhouse in a hundred years.'

I hope that hotel at Hongkong is large enough to accommodate the mail I have been sending you, and that you are not too bored reading it all.

Most Cordially Yours,

1 Thomas Robert Edward MacInnes (1867–1951) was a Canadian poet, lawyer, and entrepreneur who had participated in the Yukon gold rush and who was for several years a journalist in China, where he also launched and oversaw construction of the Canton Street Railway System between 1919 and 1922. Among his volumes of romantic poetry, the best known were *A Romance of the Lost* (1908); *Lonesome Bar: A Romance of the Lost and Other Poems* (1909); *In Amber Lands* (1910); *Rhymes of a Rounder* (1913), and *A Fool of Joy* (1918). Deacon had planned to write a book about him in Ryerson's Makers of Canadian Literature series, but the project was never realized. Nevertheless, in the twenties Deacon did voluntarily assume some of the management of MacInnes's literary affairs, arranged for the publication of his complete poems by Ryerson in 1923, and even for a time had MacInnes as a house guest when the older man found himself temporarily destitute. An inveterate letter writer, MacInnes composed his missives directly on the typewriter, his speed as a typist contributing to their considerable length and breezy tone.

2 MacInnes's letter to the editor ('The Front Page,' 19 November, p 2) advocated 'a policy of live and let live' between the Americans and the Japanese on the eve of the world arms conference in Washington.

3 Emily Gowan Ferguson Murphy (1868–1933), feminist, judge, and author, wrote under the pseudonym 'Janey Canuck,' which Deacon affectionately used when writing the woman whose early and formative influence led him to call her his 'mother in the craft.' Of her many books, it is *The Black Candle* (1922), an indictment of the opium trade in Canada, and the projected novel on the same subject, never finished, that she discusses with Deacon in her letters. Appointed in 1916 as the first female police magistrate in the British Empire, Emily Murphy became even more well known when in 1932, with four other women including Nellie McClung, she appealed the famous *Persons* case to the Privy Council in Westminster and won. That decision reversed an earlier ruling and concluded that women were legally persons under the British North America Act and were thus entitled to hold senior government posts. Deacon's article, 'A Study in Nom de Plumage,' introducing Emily Murphy, first appeared in *The Winnipeg Free Press*, and subsequently in *The National Pictorial*.

4 Edward John Moreton Drax Plunkett, Lord Dunsany (1878–1959), popular Irish poet, story-teller, and playwright, whose romantic style and theosophical beliefs had great appeal for Deacon and MacInnes at this time.

## From John Garvin[1]

Federal Finance Corporation
Limited
1605 Royal Bank Building
Toronto, Ontario
November 22, 1921

Dear Mr. Deacon:

I have read your comprehensive article on six anthologies[2] in *The Canadian Bookman* for December, with much interest and pleasure, and I thank you very sincerely for your generous reference to *Canadian Poets*.

As you do not include my second anthology, *Canadian Poems of the Great War*, and as it contains short biographies of 73 Canadian Poets and much of their best war verse, I am curious to know why it was excluded from your article. Is it possible you have not seen this work? One of the best critics in London, England, declared it to be 'A great book.'

Unfortunately *Canadian Poets of the Great War* does not include Wilfred Campbell's war verse, nor that of Stead.[3] The owners of the copyrights, The Musson Book Company, refused permission. The publisher of Norah Holland's[4] war poetry also refused. But all the other worth-while poets are there.

As I like to have some biographical knowledge of every Canadian writer of ability, and as I am not familiar with your past record, will you be so kind as to send me a few particulars? You seem to have come into prominence quite recently, or else my observation has not been as keen as it should have been. You are certainly doing good work now with your pen, and for that reason I should like to know more about you.

Arrangements have not yet been concluded with a publisher to bring out a complete edition of Tom MacInnes's poems, but I hope to have this matter settled within a few days.[5] As soon as I know definitely, you and MacInnes will hear from me.

We are having a most interesting Canadian Authors' Week in Toronto.

Very truly yours,
John W. Garvin

1 John William Garvin (1859–1935) was a writer and anthologist, best known for his editorship of *The Collected Poems of Isabella Valancy Crawford* (1905), *Canadian Poets and Poetry* (1916, 1926), and *Canadian Poems of the Great War* (1918). In 1921 he was President and Editor of the Radisson Society of Canada Limited, which published the series Master-Works of Canadian Authors.
2 'A Guide to the Anthologies,' reprinted in *Poteen* (1926), is a survey, incorporating charts and statistics, of the major collections of Canadian poetry available in print. Deacon concluded that Garvin's *Canadian Poets* was the best of the recent anthologies.
3 Robert James Stead (1880–1959), novelist, poet, and publicity agent for Canadian Pacific Railways and then for the Department of Immigration; he is best known for his prairie novel *Grain* (1926). Wilfred Campbell (1858–1918), whose work is sometimes included with that of the 'Confederation Poets'
4 Canadian poet (1876–1925) and first cousin to W.B. Yeats. *Spun Yarn and Spindrift* was published by Dent of Toronto in 1918.
5 *Complete Poems of Tom MacInnes* did not appear until 1923, when it was published by Ryerson.

---

## To B.K. Sandwell[1]

900 Bank of Hamilton Chambers
Winnipeg
November 24, 1921

Dear Mr. Sandwell,

I have just come in from hearing Arthur L. Phelps[2] lecture on Canadian Poetry at the library. He had a copy of *The Bookman*, graciously referred to my little article,[3] and urged the audience to subscribe. This is the third of the Book-week series, Tuesday – Dr. John Maclean on Books of Travel, Wednesday – Professor Chester Martin on History of Western Canada, Thursday – Phelps, Poetry, Friday – Mrs. Ruth Cohen (Sheila Rand) Canadian novelists.[4]

Well Phelps' verbal advertisement for you was the last straw. I have been getting ready to write you for several days. This week I have read *The Bookman* from cover to cover, in odd moments, usually last thing before going to bed. I consider it great stuff (barring one article which you will please proceed to forget for the moment). And I want to tell you so frankly. I suppose it is ten years since I read any magazine entire. I take *The New York Times* to which I contribute occasionally, and I never read more than four articles in any one issue, sometimes less.

And in my humble judgement the outstanding pieces were the work of the Editor. No contributions in this issue are in the same class with yours. You would have been interested if you could have seen me reading the Norwood thing.[5] I grinned from end to end as much as my pipe would let me, and chuckled with delight over the finesse with which you handled it. You got safely across without sacrificing anything. I sure do admire that skill, and hope some day to emulate it.

The way you handled Sir Andrew in re Hemon[6] was also delightful. That brings me to something I want to say but which you need not answer. You, I think, are writing with a 'new freedom.' When *The Bookman* started and I was asked for my opinion, I expressed general satisfaction, but pointed to the list of the advisory committee and their numerous academic degrees. 'I fear,' I said, 'that these letters create a surplus ballast, that is almost sure to sink the ship.' My guess is that you found yourself under too much restriction, and I see (or imagine) a new tone here that is going to improve *The Bookman* 100%. Pardon the freedom of expression I have allowed myself herein, but I simply had to voice my appreciation.

Finally, I understand perfectly why I appear on the cover. My piece is the only one that purports to be general survey of Canadian Literature, or any considerable portion thereof. It was therefore fitting for Book-week but I am not getting a swelled head over it because I realize perfectly that it is not criticism, nor literature in itself but just a simple little plain statistical article happily suited to the occasion of publication.

1 Journalist, author, teacher, and man of letters, Bernard Keble Sandwell (1876–1954) was the editor of *The Canadian Bookman* (1919–21) at the same time as he was a member of the Department of Economics at McGill University (1919–23). He went on to become Head of the Department of English at Queen's University (1923–5) and subsequently spent the longest period of his working career as editor of *Saturday Night* (1932–51). A founding member in 1921 of the Canadian Authors' Association, Sandwell published several of Deacon's early articles in *The Canadian Bookman*. During his years at the Montreal *Herald* (1905–11), where he worked as drama critic and associate editor, he had known Frederick Paul, who left the *Herald* in 1909 to become editor of *Saturday Night*. It was Sandwell who in 1922 recommended that Paul hire Deacon.

2 Arthur Phelps (1887–1970). Professor of English at Wesley College, later United College, Winnipeg (1921–45); contributor to the literary sections of *The Manitoba Free Press* and *Saturday Night*. Through their literary interests and shared summers at Bobcaygeon in the twenties, he and Deacon became friends.

3 'Anthologies of Canadian Verse' in *The Canadian Bookman* for December 1921 was an early version of the longer essay eventually published in *Poteen* (1926).

4 John MacLean (1851–1928), missionary and educator who wrote about the Indians

of the Canadian West; Chester Martin (1882–1958), historian, author of *Lord Selkirk's Work in Canada* (1916) and other books and at this time with the Department of History, University of Manitoba; Ruth Cohen, Winnipeg journalist (1913–23) who used the pseudonym 'Sheila Rand.' After moving to England, she wrote a weekly 'Letter from London' column for Deacon's book page under the pseudonym Wilhelmina Stitch.

5 An unsigned review of Robert Norwood's poetic biblical drama *The Man of Kerioth*, in *The Canadian Bookman* for July 1920. The reviewer briefly calls attention to Norwood's 'fresh and unconventional' treatment of biblical material. Robert Winkworth Norwood (1874–1932), a clergyman and poet, was the subject of the first volume in the Makers of Canadian Literature series (1923) by Albert Durrant Watson.

6 Sir Andrew Macphail (1864–1938) was professor of the history of medicine at McGill (1907–37), founder and editor of the McGill *University Magazine* (1907–20), author, and translator of the first English version of *Maria Chapdelaine* (1921), which was followed by William Hume Blake's translation in the same year. Deacon alludes to Sandwell's anonymous article, 'The Three Sisters Chapdelaine,' in the *Bookman* for December 1921, a critical preface to excerpts from the original text and the two translations by Macphail and Blake. Sandwell thought the Macphail translation too literal.

---

## To John Garvin

Suite 3 – 650 McDermot Avenue
Winnipeg
November 27, 1921

Dear Mr. Garvin,

Your favor of the 22nd is before me, and I am puzzled to know just how I ought to reply. My instinct is to be non-commital and polite and to shield myself from scrutiny behind a solid wall of reserve – for various reasons, not the least of which is that my little reputation has far outrun the merits of my published performance, thanks to the C.A.A. and fortuitous circumstances generally. It really makes me feel uncomfortable. Of course I can discount your implication that I have 'come into prominence' on the grounds that I was writing about your work in such a way that you were bound to be hit in the eye. I spoke to the undergrads of the U. of M. lately and was highly amused when I was introduced as one 'famous' for this and that. Of course it was merely a break [sic] of a sweet little senior who wanted to gush a bit – But these things are getting to be too damn frequent for comfort. Phelps lectured the other night at the library on Canadian Poetry, and treated my anthology article as though it were an important utterance! So, after thinking things over I decided to be frank with you, and write you a long chatty letter, telling you enough about myself, and my literary endeavors so that you need never worry any more about my possibilities as a dark horse. I'll give you the facts and you can scratch the name of Deacon out of your list of 'possibilities.'

The 'ten lost years' as I call them ended with my graduation in Law from the University of Manitoba (LL.B.) in 1918. Then I determined that my boyhood dreams would become the serious goal of my life. So I started to write, and one of the first things I turned out was an appreciation of John Cowper Powys, written in the heat of a first enthusiasm, and having in it something of the pent-up fires of the preceding 10 years. This I sent to my friend Dr. Chas. W. Colby,[1] and he had it inserted in *The University Magazine* for April 1919. I would be glad to have you read this piece as it is fairly representative of one side of me. Having other literary heroes – Masters, Dunsany, Cabell I got down to hard work, and produced a book 'In Fame's Antechamber' containing full length studies of these men and their works.[2] I could never get a publisher. It was the usual heartbreak. Henry Holt,[3] for instance, kept the MS. a year and never read it. My friend Emslie called on the supposed reader, Mr. Bristol, and got it back. B. 'It's no good.' E. 'I think it is clever and timely, and would have a sale. Have you read it?' B. 'No. I don't have to read it. I know it's no good'. And Henry Holt stole my title, and presented it to another author writing a similar kind of work. I have had the satisfaction and chagrin of seeing my opinions arrived at slowly by one leading critic after another, until now the originality of the thing is no more. Cabell – then a most obscure writer – has since been 'made' by the suppression of [his novel] *Jurgen*, and he is now writing inferior stuff and everyone knows, or pretends to know, him. Bierstadt, author of *Dunsany the Dramatist* has recanted in *The Theatre Magazine*, and taken up the position I took two years previously.[4] Oh well! Oh hell, eh? What's the use? That MS. sits on my shelves and it is going to cost somebody real money before it ever gets out of my front door again.

Then I have done a good few essays – the ones of lesser value get published, the few things I am satisfied with get bound up once a year and join 'Fame's Antechamber.' My first appearance in *The Canadian Bookman* was in July 1920, with an article written a year before, after I had spent three months in New York. I think you would like that, though it is pretty light. Sandwell published a little biography at the back.[5] In it is all I care to give out of a personal nature. My life has been much more adventurous than those facts indicate, but ...

As an example of my work in the essay I would call your attention to 'The Headpiece' (650 words) in *The National Pictorial*, Windsor Ont. In her speech here at a C.A.A. luncheon, Janey Canuck, with her usual blarney, referred to it as 'a classic of Canadian prose that will go down in the permanent literature of the country.' Janey's a dear, and those were sweet words but I think the essay would appeal more to her than to the majority of critics. However, frankly, I do consider it as good work as I have ever done, and am willing to be judged by it. The *Pictorial* has just moved to 81 Victoria St. Toronto, and their files will doubtless be open to you. The September issue, by the way.

I contributed to *The Canadian Nation*[6] till it died of Malnutrition, and my 'Killing the Sheriff' in the issue of April 3rd, 1920 and my 'Local Talent' – November 1920, you would perhaps like. I don't know. I get very sick of my pieces, even 'Fame's Antechamber' I sometimes think is a lot of rubbish, in a bombastic style.

I had some fun this fall when I broke into *The New York Times Supplement* with an attack on Richard Le Gallienne's statement of Matthew Arnold's opinion of Keats.[7] Mr. Le Gallienne was kind enough to reply, but made a weak defence by asserting that he didn't say it. He did.

Odd things of mine get published elsewhere, the only place I am a regular is *The Manitoba Free Press Literary Supplement* for which I write every issue, and which has brought me more recognition than anything else. Some of these articles and reviews are absolutely worthless and the MacInnes thing is about the best of the lot. Mr. Dafoe, the Editor in Chief and Mr. Roberton the editor of *Supplement*[8] are very much pleased with me, and they pay me well but my chief motive in doing it is to get known a little so some publisher will take pity on me and bring out a volume of collected essays. So far they are not a bit interested. I am an ardent nationalist and make it a rule to write for a Canadian audience, and I submit everything to Canadian periodicals first, even though that means a heavy financial sacrifice sometimes. I earn a good living at Law, and will not either submerge myself in the American Literary Movement or write at the dictation of a Canadian editor. I shall wait till there is a Canadian market. Also, because I want very much to drop Law and devote myself entirely to literary criticism and essay work. I have made it a rule that they have to pay me. I insist jealously on my status as a professional writer, and being a lawyer I have no false modesty about seeing that I get my price. Consequently I am much better paid for my contributions than most Canadian writers of my class. I am always absolutely sincere, not only in my opinions but in the quality of workmanship. I always do my best. I work very hard. I spend time and money to fit myself for my work, and see no reason why I should not be paid by the public which enjoys my work. All I want is a moderate living. The joy of my work is sufficient luxury for me, but the bread and butter must come. Until it does I am doomed to work at Law 7 hours daily and literature another 7.

My anthology article is a mere bundle of statistics, with a snap judgment or two on the books so that people might first be shamed into buying one of them and second, make a semi-intelligent choice. I do not consider it to be an important pronouncement, though what I said was perfectly sincere, as far as it went. It was written a year ago, and a friend who knows me well said 'It's dull enough to get into print.' At that time I did not know of *Poems of the Great War*, such is the state of bookselling in this town. Some time later I bought it. My piece was already in Sandwell's hands. I feared to add to the length of the article, and also considered it a timely book rather than one of permanent value like *Canadian Poets*. You will pardon my frankness. War poetry has been a nightmare to me – most of it. Your book was a revelation. Up to that time I had marked three war poems as worth remembering – 'In Flanders Fields,' 'The Soldier' by Brooke and 'Draw the Sword, O Republic' by Masters in *Towards the Gulf*. Your book contains many notable pieces, and is by far the best collection of war poetry I have seen. It confirms my opinion, expressed to the University here, that our poetic achievement during the past 25 years has not been surpassed in quality or quantity by any country with whose literature I am familiar. I regret exceedingly that this collection was not mentioned in my article, as it may create a wholly unfair impression in the mind of the reader. Especially is this true on account of the publicity which came as a complete surprise to me. I had thought that the current *Bookman* would be full of general surveys of Canadian Literature, and that my little dull piece would be one of the minor features of the issue. I was amazed to see my name on the cover, and to find that it had awakened serious interest. Phelps took me down a peg in his lecture by saying that lawyerlike I had gone at it mathematically, implying that my literary perceptions were astray, or wholly wanting. Poor boy! he is one of the 150 I had to treat with silence. I am particularly fond of minor poets, and am amused that so many of them are now sore at me.

And that brings me to an important point. I aim to be an essayist, and a very special kind of critic. I have found in my own little group that I have a certain power of transmitting literary enthusiasms. By reading and discussing modern works I often fire my friends with love for an author. I seek therefore to be an introducer and an interpreter, rather than a critic with a foot rule. I have discovered that many people need to be shown the excellencies of a book before they can see them for themselves. It is to show them that I write pieces like MacInnes. I want to be an anonymous herald, announcing the great ones. And because of my national bias I want to announce our own men to Canadian readers. I think there should be a place for me in the Canadian Movement. I hope I shall be able to serve it. As Canadian essayists can be counted on the fingers of one hand I hope that there will be a chance for me to get out the things which I am writing and shall write so long as I can navigate a pen. If they won't sell, on the shelf they go! And so long as I am producing I am more or less content that they should sit there until such time as I am devoting myself wholly to my chosen lifework. When the spirit moves me I work at my novel, though this is an opus in the nature of a joke. I think I shall prove to my own satisfaction that I cannot write fiction. Anyway it is a side-issue and at best part of my effort to find a public on whom I can ultimately foist my essays.

To my biography you would add that my war record is 'unfit.' It is an important point but a delicate one. I have the army doctor's rejection written across my application in 1916. One of Gen. Hughes' staff of doctors prevented me getting in by a side door by telling me that I would do my country a greater service by going into the back lane and committing suicide than by taking the offered commission; that I would never stand the training in Canada, let alone that in England, and it was a foregone conclusion that I would die before I got to France. Now I am a pretty husky cuss, and look the picture of manly vigor. Well, you know, you can't say anything about a thing like that, only if you are going to be the historian of the modern movement, and if you are going to ever say anything about me, it is as well that you should know the facts. I would like to leave this on record, in the archives you seem to be collecting.

Finally, if you are still reading, and haven't gone to sleep, I want to thank you for your kind letter. I am not any more prominent than I am famous. I am an obscure writer, laboring faithfully to produce literature, and seemingly fated to get only inferior work into print at this stage of the game. I append a copy of Janey Canuck's letter to me on the occasion of the MacInnes piece appearing. She is a MacInnes authority you know. I value it – treasure it – being human. She says I may publish it. *The Free Press* wanted to, but I refused permission because I felt her warm Irish heart had run away with her judgment. If you read 'John Cowper Powys' and 'The Headpiece' you will be able to form a fair idea of my youthful exuberance, and general incapacity.

In the anthology piece I tried to imply a decided preference for *Canadian Poets* without unfairness to the other collections. I like it best because it is most in harmony with my own predilections for that modern spirit which is so largely the legacy of Whitman and which, as I see it, is rapidly revolutionizing civilization. Mr. Dafoe's wonderful speech before the Canadian Club here yesterday on the Washington conference might as readily have come from the lips of either Whitman or Christ. The world's salvation lies that way, and I am a little whooper-up for the great prophets of all time, but particularly for the living ones. If Sandwell is satisfied with the Edward Carpenter piece[9] I recently sent him you will see well enough what ideals I stand for.

Now let this be a lesson to you never again to ask an author, particularly a shy one, to spill out his heart to his typewriter on a Sunday afternoon. With profuse apologies for boring you, with this intensely personal, though I trust not egotistical, recital, I am,

Cordially yours,

1 Colby (1865–1955), a clergyman, taught English and history at McGill (1893–1910) and was a personal friend of Deacon and his mother through mutual affiliation with Stanstead College. Dr Colby took over the editorship of the *McGill University Magazine* from Sir Andrew Macphail in 1920.

2 Never published, it studies the writings of John Cowper Powys (1872–1963), the English critic and poet; Edgar Lee Masters (1868–1950), the Chicago poet; James Branch Cabell (1879–1958), American author of Arthurian fantasy novels; and Lord Dunsany.

3 American publisher and man of letters (1840–1926); president of Henry Holt & Co. of New York from 1873 until his death. He does not appear to have published a book borrowing Deacon's title.

4 Edward Hale Bierstadt (b. 1891), whose *Dunsany the Dramatist* appeared in 1917

5 'Manhattan, The Book-Buyer's Heaven' was reprinted in in *Pens and Pirates* (1923).
6 Edited by D.M. LeBourdais from 1919 to 1921, it was subtitled 'A National Journal Devoted to Constructive Canadian Thought,' and was published in Ottawa.
7 In a review of *The John Keats Memorial Volume,* issued by the Keats House Committee, and of *Poems,* the Keats anthology edited by T.J.C. Sanderson (31 July 1921, pp 4–5), Le Gallienne quoted Arnold as ranking Keats with Shakespeare. Deacon responded with the context for Arnold's remark (28 August 1921, p 13), and Le Gallienne replied in a subsequent review (25 September 1921, p 3) that it had never occurred to him to place Keats and Shakespeare on an equal footing.
8 John Wesley Dafoe (1866–1944), journalist, editor, author, prominent liberal intellectual, and Canadian nationalist. He was editor-in-chief of the *Manitoba Free Press* from 1901 until his death and instituted its literary supplement in 1921. His best-known book is *Canada: An American Nation* (1935). Thomas Beattie Roberton (1879–1936), journalist and author, joined the *Manitoba Free Press* in 1918 and became editor of its new literary supplement in 1921. *T.B.R.: Newspaper Pieces* (1936), published shortly after his death, won the first Governor-General's Award for non-fiction.
9 Deacon's article on Carpenter (1844–1929), the English theosophist and poet who borrowed heavily from the thought of Walt Whitman, appeared in *The Canadian Theosophist* of February 1921.

---

## From B.K. Sandwell

703 Drummond Building
Montreal
November 28, 1921

*Anthologies*

Dear Deacon

(We are all brothers: let us drop titles).

(The printers are as usual keeping me waiting for letterheads).[1]

Your letter has naturally exalted me much. But my 'new freedom' is merely the result of a gradual learning of what the public will stand *from me* & from *The Bookman*. I have always had a very strong 'sense of my audience.' It is not a quality that makes great prophets or founders of great religions; but I fancy it is a useful quality in the editor of a review. It is true that in the September number I was only editor & in December I was proprietor; but I do not think that made much difference; the 'new freedom' was coming on gradually with the growing public appreciation of the *C.B.* Neither the owners nor the Editorial Committee ever interfered with me in the slightest degree. – I have not yet collected in cash the new capital which has been promised me, so you may have to wait a few weeks for your cheque, but it will arrive. – Norwood takes it very amiably. Sir Andrew I have not yet heard from.

Gratefully yours,
B.K. Sandwell.

1 The letterhead – 'Community Players of Montreal' – included the logo and listed the executive committee of the organization for the 1920–1 season.

---

## From Tom MacInnes

Kwongtung Tramway Company Limited
[Hong Kong]
December 20, 1921

Dear Mr. Deacon

I was very glad indeed to get your letters of the 7th and 20th last month. I love the three authors you mention, altho I have only made acquaintance with part of their work. *The Gods of Pagana*, which I read over and over, and *The Tents of the Arabs* and *The Gods of the Mountain*, which I saw very well presented here by students of Hongkong University two years ago, constitute my knowledge of Dunsany. The students who played were nearly all Chinese, with a few Siamese, Indians, and Parsees. Their English is well modulated, with the delightful Oriental-Oxford accent which one so often hears among the educated Eurasians, Chinese, and the Macinese (natives of Macao half Portuguese, half Chinese, half Malay, and nobody knows what the other half may be – very mediaeval Catholics) who attend the University here. I read over and over again *The Crock of Gold* and *The Demi Gods*, and that is all I know of James Stephens.[1] One work of A.E.[2] I have read – the only one – and much appreciate the parts of it which I can understand: *The Candle of Vision*. I am glad that your own affairs are looking brighter, and hope you will hold your ground and fight to a victory just where you are. There is no better country than Canada to be in today. I do not know if I told you anything in my last letter of my troubles here with the Canton Government, and certain others. I sent the details to Dickie,[3] because he has such a number of papers apart from his Sunday School circle – papers of financial importance in the United States with very wide circulation – that my intention to hit certain Canton politicians can best be served by showing them up at the places where they are endeavouring to secure loans to finance their campaign against Pekin.[4] They will not win. If they concentrated their efforts on cleaning up their own southern Provinces, and promoting industrial enterprises and suppressing pirates and bandits they would receive more sympathy from the white population out here. The pirates are getting worse all the time. Mrs. MacInnes and I were going up the West River to Wuchow two weeks ago on a Chinese boat officered by British officers, but we postponed our trip, owing non-arrival expected funds. Just as well, as the boat was pirated just beyond Sanshui, and all passengers stripped. The most daring piracy recently however occurred last week, a ship sailing from Shanghai to Hongkong, under British officers, was attacked. The pirates got away with $120,000. I will enclose newspaper clipping giving you the story, also of another attempted piracy on West River in which the pirates got the worst of it.

My article to *Saturday Night* was, as you surmised, much abbreviated. Maskee – it was enough as it was. Thanks very much for sending the copy to me, it contained news of special interest both to my wife and myself.

As to joining the C.A.A. I do not think I will. I might have done so in Vancouver when they formed a branch there, but the night they gave the inaugural dinner I got drunk – drunk before I got to the Club you understand, because at the dinner itself no liquor was served. I certainly had intended to keep sober that night, at least until after the dinner and meeting was over, but – well, accidents will happen. And sometimes for the best.

You ask for a snapshot of me. I will send you one from Canton when I go up there next week – have a friend there with a camera. It will be up to ate, if you want to use it. As to Garvin not sending you one: well, I told Garvin I did not want my picture in the *Collected Poems*, so it may well be that he has none to send you. After all the verse is the thing, not the mug of the writer. You ask me to retain my poem on Walt Whitman for the Collected Edition. The reason I leave it out, together with a few others, is that they jar, they discord, with the tone of the other poems. And I want nothing *American* or *English* in my book. I write for the Canadian who will appear I hope, and hold our land, the end of this century and following.

I am financially worried, as usual, and also my wife is in poor health. However maybe my fairy godmother will appear before very long and tell us what to do to get out of our troubles, or will bring something to us. She should – today is the thirty-fourth anniversary of our marriage. She enjoyed helping me in a little affair here the other night. A brother of an old client of mine, Wong Kee Kit of Vancouver, is in business here as a Chinese banker, and possible dealer in opium. He lives in a nice house half way up the Peak, and when he was going home about ten days ago in his private chair, just after leaving his shop in Wing Lok street a man stepped quickly up to the side the chair, and drove at him with a dagger. I think he intended driving it through his throat, but, perhaps owing to the swaying of the chair, his aim miscarried, and the dagger went through the cheek bone and into the mouth. The assailant escaped, and Ki Tong was taken to hospital. Next day his brother, Kee Kit, who is here on a visit, came to me and said he could get no satisfaction from the police, and wanted me to get him a lawyer, and protection, also to stir up an investigation. You must understand there is a triple body of police here, all under the Captain Superintendant of Police, British, Indian, and Chinese. Everywhere the Chinese, whether official or private, find a way to impose their system of squeeze. I consulted the head of a firm of solicitors here, a very fine old man and great lawyer, whom I have known for several years. He detailed one of his men to investigate. This man speaks English, Portuguese and Chinese with equal fluency. Next day Kee Kit came and told me that a friend of the man detailed to investigate had come to him and said: give us $6,000 and you will have police protection, and an investigation made. If you do not then proceedings will be taken to banish your brother forever from the Colony. Off I go to the head of the firm to demand an explanation. Genuine surprise expressed. Man detailed sent for. Seeing us together, he gave this explanation: Kee Kit must have misunderstood: they did not demand $6,000, but the other side, that is the side which backed the attempted assassination, said they would spend $6,000 in order to get Ki Tong banished. Reason given was that a profit of $70,000 had recently been made on opium smuggled into the Colony – only the Government is allowed to import or sell opium for smoking in the Colony – and that this sum was to be divided in proportion of 40 to 60, and Ki Tong had the money in his safe and refused to make a division at present. So it was decided to kill him. Also the Police had decided to banish Ki Tong from the Colony soon as he came out of Hospital. A warrant for his arrest and detention and deportation was already made out, and was at the central police station. This I verified for myself. I asked why, if the police knew so much about the $70,000 profit made on the opium and other details of the gang of alleged smugglers, why did they not take action before, why did they wait for a murder to be committed, why were they refusing an investigation, why were they not trying to find those implicated in the attempted murder, why were they taking action only against the man stabbed. A shrug of the shoulder, the Colony a queer place, depths beyond depths in Chinese intrigue, Ki Tong had better submit to arrest and a decree of banishment without any investigation. Well, came the afternoon that Ki Tong was ready for discharge from hospital; also came the Chinese police to arrest him. No warrant. He was taken to Westpoint Sub-station. Through the influence of solicitors I secured his release until morning, owing his weak condition, and said we would bring him to the chief police station in morning and surrender him for deportation, or the police could take him at his residence early in the morning. His family furnished private guards in meantime. An hour after Kee Kit came to the hotel and said his brother was much afraid of being detained the next day, that he would be kept in prison a week or more before he was taken to ship for deportation, that the Chinese police would beat him till he agreed to pay money, and also that on his surrender other large fees would be demanded. My wife, with better wit than the rest of us said: The Canton boat leaves at ten o'clock tonight; they will not expect him to leave his house tonight; you go back, put him in European clothes with a soft hat drawn over his face toward the wounded cheek; we will be waiting in an auto at a certain place at half past nine; slip him quietly out of the house on foot and come to the auto; we will have two rooms and tickets for the boat; you go on at the last minute before sailing; we go on board with you, and then leave. So you escape the squeeze, the publicity of the banishment proceedings, and consequent loss of face. And it was all carried out just that way: I knew the British police inspector on the wharf and stopped to chat a moment with him, while my wife went forward talking to Ki Tong. The Chinese police and Indian police, seeing him with a European lady, did not stop to question or search him, as they often do with all Chinese passengers, being on the outlook for arms and opium. Ki Tong is now safe in his rich home in Canton; some people here are very angry; what may yet follow I do not know. But it was an incident;

and the old solicitor, to whom I told it all, agreed that it was wisely done.

Well, I must be going.

Best regards to you and yours –
Tom MacInnes

P.S. Just as leaving was asked to remain meet Chinese official from Canton in town to see me. So will pass the time typing a few more words. This A.E. that you speak of: he is great in spots – at least in the spots where I can understand him. But I fear he is something of a Sein Fein [sic]. I wish God would drown them all – body and bones – and all of their class and mentality.

Have just read over what I have written in preceding pages, and you may think me inconsistent when I leave out Walt Whitman from my collected edition and leave in Edgar Allan Poe, having said something foolish about not wanting anything American or English in my book. Well, in defence would say: Poe was not an American in any sense but accident of birth. He was a Latin poet, one of the greatest who ever took up his pen. He has no more relation to the modern one hundred per cent Amurrican than the Chinese official whom I await has to me. Americans before their civil war, before the time of Walt Whitman, I had some sympathy with, even tho my forebears in Canada had to fight them off our line. Hawthorne, Washington Irving, and their crowd – they are a million miles above the bragging, discordant, free verse, jazz drunk commercial pens that claim to represent American literature today. Maybe in this matter I cannot see straight being so disgusted with what I have seen of the workings of the Rockefeller-Baptistmissionary intrigues in China to control.

My man is announced – so long – T.M.

1 Stephens (1882–1950) was an Irish lyric poet and story-teller motivated by nationalistic sentiments.

2 Pseudonym of George William Russell (1867–1935), the Irish theosophist and poet-essayist associated with the revival of the 1890s

3 Francis Dickie (1890–1976) was for a time popular Canadian nature writer who achieved a short-lived reputation with his wilderness stories in books such as *The Master Breed* (1923) and *Umingmuk of the Barrens* (1927). His Heriot Bay retreat on Quadra Island, BC, was burned out in 1926 and Dickie exiled himself to Paris where he wrote an expatriate 'Letter from Paris' commissioned by Deacon

for *Saturday Night*. A freelance journalist who contributed to *Maclean's, The Western Home Monthly*, and other journals for over forty years, he, like Tom MacInnes, was one of Deacon's 'Causes' and enjoyed playing the role of the 'lost generation' writer.

4 A clipping of Dickie's article about MacInnes' difficulties in tramway building is preserved in the MacInnes correspondence. By 1921, civil government in China had disintegrated and internal war pitting North (including Peking) against South (including Canton) for control of China was endemic.

---

## From Emily Murphy

11011 – 88th Avenue
Edmonton
August 10, 1922

My dear William:

I must hasten to congratulate you on the *splendid* work you are doing on *The Toronto Saturday Night*, and on the vast amount of space they are allotting to you. Apart from this opportunity for self-expression, it means real shekels, and a contented mind. Whoever sent you to Toronto did you a real service. Isn't that right Boy?

I am getting *The House of Souls*.[1] One absolutely must read it after your review. Your pen was tingling when you wrote that. You always seem to summon up the exact words for the subject. This is evidently the result of your reading classics as well as the modern stuff. At any rate, you have O'Donovan[2] beaten in five hundred ways, and have become a valuable asset to your paper. Stay with it everyday. It means a lot to Canadian literature to have these reviews.

I was telling Mrs Madge Macbeth[3] about you last night, and she said she had already met you. It was at some party at Ottawa at which Hopkins Moorehouse[4] was also present. She will see you on her way through Toronto. I told her, too, about your salvaging the W.P.B.,[5] and of the tea party at the Macdonald. So you think we ought to have 'a feast of season.' William, I'd say something right here only I'm afraid you would put it down again, and then I'd be in sorry trouble. Oh well, you remember the story Jacobs[6] tells in one of his books about a sailor saying to his pal, 'Matey, I must go and do some 'ead work now!' 'Oh?' queries the pal, 'what with?'

I contend I am right in this stand. Didn't a Toronto writer say awhile ago in Port Arthur, that none of her clan had any genius. We haven't William, we haven't, *but think of her telling it*. Canadian authors might have deceived the public awhile longer if she had only been less candid and more discreet.

Mrs Macbeth and I also had a conversation about *The National Life* and she has asked me to write at once to Miss Kennedy[7] along the lines I suggested. She will do so as well. Miss Kennedy is such an exceptionally fine woman, it would be a thousand pities to see her fail in an endeavor into which she has put so much thought, energy and money. Besides, we need the paper. I am glad you are advising her on the matter.

I spoke to two booksellers about putting the reviews [Deacon's criticism] on sale but they both said the same thing – 'The booksellers supply us with the material, and the public get it in the papers,' or words to this effect. I don't know if Eastern booksellers are equally materialistic, but it is really quite hard to work up literary enthusiasm even in 'the trade.' I am hoping their admittance to the Author's Association may instil a love of letters into some of them. A man who loves literature ought really to be a better bookseller.

I know you are anxious to be off to your reviews, so will make an obeisance to '*Candide*' – my profound respects, Sir Knight – and wish you continued good fortune.

As ever, sincerely,
Emily F. Murphy

1 A collection of novellas published in 1906 by Arthur Machen (1863–1947), popular British author of occult fiction

2 Under this name, Peter Donovan (b. 1884), author of several books of humour, was Deacon's predecessor at the book pages of *Saturday Night*.

3 Madge Hamilton Lyons MacBeth (1878–1965), journalist, novelist, and feminist. *The Land of Afternoon* (1924) is her fictional parody of Ottawa life; *Shackles* (1927) is a novel about women's domestic bondage.

4 Arthur Herbert Joseph ('Hopkins') Moorhouse (b. 1882), journalist, politician, and author of a book on the co-operative farmer's movement in the West as well as several novels

5 'Saved from the Waste-Basket' was Deacon's weekly column of literary news in *Saturday Night*'s book page.

6 William Wymark Jacobs (1863–1943), English author of a series of humorous books about sailors and dockworkers

7 Grace E. Kennedy was president of the National Review Publishing Company, which from 1921 issued the Toronto monthly *National Life*.

## To Emily Murphy August 15, 1922

Dear Janey,

Thanks about Miss Kennedy. She is, as you say, just the type of person we want as a leader in Canadian journalism. I write in her paper, by the way under several aliases, appearing twice at least in each issue, but of course my anxiety about her exceeds my petty interests.

Allen[1] sent me a folder about the book but the book itself has not come yet. When it does – oh what a chance to spank you.

*The House Of Souls* is Black Magic – fouler than the sewers of hell. Of course not one in ten thousand will see what is in there as I, an occultist, did. My review was the result of the clash between my literary conscience and my moral conscience. It is quite evident to me that the author knew quite well what he was doing, and writes from knowledge – camouflaging a little here and there, so as to make it appear idle superstition.

Now Janey you mustn't spoil me with all this blarney. Of course I like it, but principally because it comes from you, and you know better than anyone else, except a few close friends, what I am about. Some of them are puzzled – some just think I am crazy – but you *know*, have seen right into me, and have understood precisely what I am trying to do. My patriotism is very deep and sincere. I think I can do a tremendous work by just being plain honest, saying what I think. Some of the insincere, biased, and sometimes openly dishonest reviewing that goes on in this country makes me plain sick.

Also you have been shrewd enough to guess – what few others have – viz. that my literary ambitions are serious and far-reaching. I am just beginning. It remains to be seen how far my people will stand for a homegrown prophet. Of course if there is no room for me I shall go to London or New York. I am willing to live for my Country but not die for it. You're no use to anyone when you're dead, and if I find I have reached my limit here and am stagnating I shall move on in self-preservation.

I am just on a small salary as a trial for six months, till December 1st. Everyone is so appreciative and nice that I think they will keep me on. It remains to be seen what they will do for me in the line of real pay. We can talk over that when you come.

Everything is going as well as can be expected. Subscribers are expressing themselves as satisfied, and the owner[2] is impressed with the response of the public to my efforts. If you and other good friends don't flatter all the sense out of me I'll get along all right.

Thanks for the book-store canvass. I didn't mean reviews so much as essays like 'The Angels.'[3] I *love* the essay, and the publishers believe that Canadians won't read essays, so I just thought I would try a little private distribution – more for advertising than anything else – get them used to the name.

The special articles on page 2 are causing considerable talk. Mr. Paul dined the other night with Walter Curry (Crown Prosecutor here for 15 years) and Mr. Barr a prominent manufacturer and the present Atty-Gen.[4] They were all highly complimentary and hoped the public would get real excited and do something to remedy conditions. Paul is consequently pleased with me.

I work slowly so have to work long hard hours – all the time in fact but I am so happy in my work and in my little home that I am putting on flesh.

The person 'who sent me to Toronto' – who was it? Well, at bottom, it was my dear Sarah and my love for her. I won't give you details now – but when you come you can hear all about it – if you promise not to steal what is going to be my first novel ...

And that same dear Sarah is very anxious that you stay with us when in Toronto.

Yes I was at Madge MacBeth's house. I imagine she is a splendid business agent – for Madge MacBeth – but I don't think she is any use to us – She has had all her idealism (if she had any) knocked out of her long ago. She is much *too hard*.

And now a fond adieu. You were a perfect dear to write me all these things. I am awfully tired tonight. We have just gone to press and I had to have my pages re-set three times before I was satisfied with them. The compositors and make-up men are awfully nice and patient with me, but I guess I tried them sorely today.

With best love from us both – Gratefully

Sarah says to add from her that she has read the folder and is 'just crazy to see the book.'

1 Deacon is referring to the Toronto publishers of *The Black Candle* (1922), her study of the opium trade in Canada.
2 Harold Gagnier (1873–1922), Toronto entrepreneur who made his money in trade journal publications, had bought *Saturday Night* in 1906. On his death in October 1922, ownership passed to his holding company Consolidated Press Limited, and its new president, Margaret R. Sutton.
3 An essay first published in *Saturday Night*, 29 July 1922 and included in *Pens and Pirates*
4 Charles Frederick Paul (1866–1926) was Editor-in-Chief of *Saturday Night* from 1909 until his death. An American, Paul came to Montreal to work for the *Star* in 1896, where he remained until moving to *Saturday Night*. He hired Deacon in 1922 on the basis of a recommendation from B.K. Sandwell, whom Paul knew from his Montreal days. Walter John Barr (1855–1930) was a Toronto jeweller, stockbroker, and patron of the arts. The Attorney-General of Ontario in 1922 was the Honourable William Edgar Raney (1859–1933).

---

## From E.J. Pratt[1]

Bobcaygeon, Ontario
Monday morning
[September 1922]

Dear Billy,

Would you like to run up to Bobcaygeon on a holiday for one, two, three or four days as your time would permit? Art Phelps and wife have just left for Winnipeg. My wife and bairn are in Toronto and I am left alone in my cottage for one whole week ending Sept 23rd. I have just shot two wild black ducks less than an hour ago. What am I going to do with them? They won't keep till my return and I can't eat them all by myself. Could you run up early in the week. The train leaves Toronto 9.05 AM and 5 PM, and leaves Bobcaygeon 6.45 AM and 2.45 PM. So good connections. Great sleeping here out in the open air and thoroughly screened in. Not a footstep day or night to disturb dreams. I have a little garden containing, at present, sweet corn, beans, tomatoes, squash and so on, all clamouring for your stomach. An open fireplace with pine stumps! Evening smokes! Fresh cream! Bass!!

Can you come? J.V. MacKenzie had arranged to come but was suddenly called to New York and so had Ernie McCullogh,[2] but he had, likewise, to cancel the trip.

If you can make it let me know by wire – Ned Pratt, Bobcaygeon, and I will meet you, with canoe, at the station. Bring some of your stuff with you while away an evening. Enjoyed 'Angels' very much and several other articles.

Sincerely
Ned Pratt

1 Edwin John Pratt (1882–1964) established himself as one of Canada's finest narrative poets from the publication of *Newfoundland Verse* (1923) with Ryerson Press. A professor of English at Victoria College, University of Toronto, from 1920 to 1953, Pratt had known Deacon since their undergraduate days at Victoria, where both were members of the class of 1911. Although they had their differences of opinion, their friendship endured throughout their adult lives, cemented by common career and family concerns dating from the early 1920s.
2 A personal friend, no relation to the newspaper publisher George McCullagh. John Vernon McKenzie (1919–63), associate editor of *Maclean's Magazine* (1919–26)

---

## To B.K. Sandwell[1] September 22, 1922

My dear Sandwell,

When you were in the office yesterday I had not read 'English Realism to a Canadian,' in the September *Bookman*. I have done so today and would like to commend you, as editor, and Mr. MacDonald,[2] as writer. This is the sort of thing that *The Bookman* should print; it gives food for thought, and it represents a Canadian viewpoint. I say this the more readily because I do not agree with the conclusions of the writer. The deep-seated liking of the natural Canadian for the romantic in fiction, I admit, and commend, believing that while this depressing English realism is natural to an Englishman, and therefore right and wholesome for him, that it is not the next step on the evolutionary path for the Canadian. I think our trend towards idealism, like all other national traits, should be developed – subject to a severe criticism, which will rid us of sentimentality. But to destroy national ideals is to destroy this nation. We have to complete our course as a nation – and we are far from having completed it – before we can safely start that tearing-down process which will result in the cosmopolitan view. Foreign influences we get in plenty; and they are helpful, within limits. But while in our national babyhood we need the sheltered atmosphere of a strong insularity, and if we do not have it there will surely be precocity, followed by premature decadence. Knowing me as you do, you will know how warped my opinions are on all subjects and how little attention to pay to my remarks. But do not forget what I started out to say, namely that we want more articles like this which deal with phases of our national mental development.

Cordially yours,

1 In Deacon's handwriting at the top left-hand corner of this letter is pencilled 'Not sent, file NOTE for Essay.'

2 Adrian MacDonald's article argued that psychological realism in the English novel had created a fresh and 'unlaboured' style and was intellectually stimulating.

---

## From Lorne Pierce[1]

The Ryerson Press
Toronto
October 16, 1922

My dear Mr. Deacon:–

When Arthur L. Phelps was in town, just before returning home, he left a large envelope of your MSS[2] with me to look thru.

I took almost a whole day off to read them. After my slight acquaintance with you in Winnipeg, and my even better acquaintance with you as Candide in *Saturday Night*, I felt that in reading them I was in happy session with an old friend.

Several of your pieces I found very delightful. 'The Head Piece' was a very clever bit of satire. You have a wonderful gift in this line, and one that will make you a powerful foe. I should imagine, however, that you have a sufficient fund of good natured humor to preserve a healthy sweetness of mind which is, after all, essential to the highest art.

'Tom MacInnes' is a fine sample of literary criticism. You ought to attempt more along this line. If there is one thing we need more than another in this Canada of ours it is a new school of literary criticism. Some of the old twaddle peeled off by our college professors is enough to kill the trade. The recurring urbanities and futilities of Canadian Authors' Book Week will presently see us inundated with more log-rolling bees and sloppy soft drink criticism. We've got to commence farther back and score up with such goods as you have delivered here.

'Free Verse' is not so good, but gives a suggestion of that happy balance you can preserve between the IS and AIN'T of the business of criticism, the positive and the negative functions of the art.

I have already taken up too much of your time. I just want to drop a wee word of encouragement. You have already made a real place for yourself in Toronto. It is a staid town in many ways, and sometimes acts a little dour and all that, but there is a warm heart beating for the man who kicks out. You have a real daring literary fist, and you will certainly command a hearing, and some respect even from the Calvinists and the 'millionaire Methodists' you like to lambaste. To borrow one of the quotations you make in one of the screeds I should say that you might even now hire a painter to decorate your front door with the legend:

> 'Living trimly by my wit.'[3]

May we not get together someday and have a real chat? I shall leave it to you to set the time. We have a sort of a place here to eat, but I suggest we agree on a rendezvous and then agree as to the day.

With best wishes for your unlimited success, I am,

Very sincerely yours,
Lorne Pierce

1 Lorne Pierce (1890–1961) was first adviser (1920–2) and then editor (1922–60) with Ryerson Press, working to promote the publication of an increasing number of Canadian books. In 1923 he launched the Makers of Canadian Literature series – monographs on various English-Canadian and French-Canadian writers that combined biography, critical appreciation, and a brief selection of the writer's work. In 1926 he established the Lorne Pierce Medal, awarded by the Royal Society of Canada for distinguished service to Canadian literature. It was Ryerson which published Deacon's first two books, *Pens and Pirates* and *Peter McArthur*, the latter in the Makers series. Pierce's own works include *Our Canadian Literature* (1922), an anthology which he co-edited with Albert Durrant Watson; *An Outline of Canadian Literature* (1927), a survey of the literatures of French and English Canada; and *William Kirby: The Portrait of a Tory Loyalist* (1929).

2 Published by Ryerson as *Pens and Pirates* (1923)

3 This line is taken from the last stanza of Tom MacInnes's poem 'Ballade of Detachment.'

## To Lorne Pierce October 16, 1922

Dear Dr. Pierce,

I'll lick your boots for the kind words you emit about my little essays. For perfectly selfish reasons I am crazy to be friends with the publishers – Yea I want to get a book out. I have been writing for years and years and have a whole bagful of essays like the Headpiece and like Tom MacInnes. Every year I get my MSS bound up and stick it on the shelf. How I have prayed for the funds to finance even a chapbook.

Now – between ourselves – I want to explain my attitude towards the books I review. I do not say things that people may consider me clever. I am just plain honest, and go to print with all my prejudices on my head. I do not, in fact, like to be sarcastic or biting. But often my space forbids my patting elaborately on the head that which ought to be kicked in the pants, and consequently where I would like to be gently deprecatory I have to be more brusque than I like. I love good books.

Next – a tip – why does your house send me only inane novels? Don't you see that every week I review some solid book of importance? Send me a damn good theological book once in a while. I see for instance that you are agents for *The Outline of Science.*[1] Now if you invested say $12.00 by sending me that I would feel justified in giving you space that would cost you $400.00 to $500.00 as advertising. I suppose I should not tell you but I have even advised some of my readers who write in here for tips that they should get it. Now I don't know what else you have on your list, but please try to think of *Saturday Night* as a place where a weighty volume will likely get consideration – and space. Of course I cannot promise anything definite. Your books will have to take their chance, but the American publishers such as Crowell and Boni and Liveright tumbled themselves to what I was doing and now send me all their more important books. I would hate to see the Canadian publishers left out altogether from the premier position each week. Forget I told you this, but if you want to experiment, it might pay you. I notice too that my Canadian issues now going to press for Bookweek do not contain a single Ryerson title. I am sorry. The space is gone – but surely to Heaven, you published some Canadian books this fall didn't you? WHY KEEP IT SO SECRET?

It would give me the greatest pleasure to have lunch with you when and where you say. Make the hour suit your convenience, and pick me up here if you will, any day. Except Tuesdays. Shall we say Wednesday? I am like the kid who was asked to visit his Uncle 'sometime,' and replied: 'Sure. When?'

Cordially,

1 Published in 1922, written by Sir John Arthur Thomson (1861–1933)

---

## From Mazo de la Roche[1]

89 Collier Street
Toronto
March 16, 1923

Dear Mr. Deacon,

At Lady Willison's tea[2] I kept my eyes open for a tall young man with the airy dignity that should become Candide, but, as I did not discover you, I came to the conclusion that, like myself, you were a shy person addicted to lurking in corners. At any rate, the only interesting person I met there was Merrill Denison[3] whom I had for some time been wanting to meet.

I see by *Saturday Night* that there is a probability that you will review my novel *Possession*. Someway, before you read it, I want to tell you that I lived on just such a farm as Grimstone for years, so that I know the life whereof I write. I have tried with all the power that is in me to depict the life on this farm, in that warm belt of Western Ontario, where on a fine day the spray of Niagara is visible. I have tried to reproduce something of the mingling of the old and new world beneath the roof of Grimstone, and to give the feeling of the sensuous fullness of the summer there.

Some of the happiest, and, by far the most tragic, years of my life were spent there, so that I have a sort of passionate sensitiveness about the book that you may understand. I gave two years to the writing of it and wish I could have given more.

Since this note is written to Candide the critic, and not to Candide, the Play Boy of the Waste-Basket, I think I can rely on him not to refer to it on that page.

Most sincerely,
Mazo de la Roche

1 Mazo de la Roche (1879–1961) was on the point of publishing her first novel, *Possession*, in 1923 when she began her correspondence with Deacon. With the appearance of the immensely successful *Jalna* in 1927, she acquired an international literary reputation which was sustained by the continuing publication of the popular Whiteoak novels.

2 Rachel Wood Turner (d. 1925), first wife of Sir John Willison (1856–1927), at this time dean of Canadian journalists. She is not to be confused with Marjorie MacMurchy, writer and journalist, who became the second Lady Willison in 1926. In 1925 Sir John Willison founded *Willison's Monthly*, a public affairs journal which ceased publication in 1929.

3 Author and dramatist (1893–1975), Denison wrote early realistic plays which were collected and published as *The Unheroic North* (1923). He served as artistic director and playwright at Hart House Theatre, University of Toronto, during the 1920s and was, with Deacon, a theosophist and member of the Toronto Writers' Club.

---

## To Mazo de la Roche March 17, 1923

Dear Miss de la Roche,

It was good of you to write me, and I appreciate your confidences. In general I very much prefer knowing as little as possible of the author and the history of his book before I commence reading. I like to judge literary work on its own merits – or rather get my impressions without the obstacle of preconceived ideas, for of course to 'judge' contemporary work is foolish. The judgments are so apt to be reversed. In this case I trust your intuition. Doubtless you were right to approach me, though nothing usually makes me quite so hostile as a request for a favorable review – no matter how subtly the appeal may be conveyed. I shall try to see that you are exempt from the penalty I usually impose unconsciously.

At the tea I met Merrill Denison. We arrived together and stayed together till some woman – evidently you – got him away from me. Then I paid my respects to Mrs. Garvin and came away. You probably missed me through looking for too young a man. My friend,

Miss [Jean] Graham, teases me about my youth because I am younger than she, but there is nothing like the age difference she has doubtless led you to suppose. It is really some time since I played with a rattle. So next time you look for me keep your mind fixed on an oldish gentleman with a bay window in front. I hope you look soon, and have better luck next time.

Sincerely,

---

## From Lorne Pierce

The Ryerson Press
Toronto
May 1, 1923

Dear Mr. Deacon:–

You will be glad, I know, to receive the first volume to be printed of the Makers of Canadian Literature Series.[1] It is just fresh from the press. I hope that you are pleased with it. The other volumes will be uniform in style and general arrangement. I think that you will agree with me that Dr. Watson[2] has established a high tradition here.

I am hoping that we may have your copy for the volume on Peter McArthur[3] in time for publication this Fall. Will you kindly let me know well in advance what copyright material you will require in order that there may be no delay from this end?

The French section is already complete in outline, and only some four volumes remain to be definitely assigned in the English section; but there is no immediate hurry about these. An active campaign of advertising will be carried out in the immediate future. I hope by this Fall to have a complete prospectus of the entire Series which will appear in the leading magazines.

Any suggestions which you may have to offer for the improvement of the Series will be gladly received.

Thanking you for your most cordial cooperation in this enterprise, I am,

Yours very sincerely,
Lorne Pierce

1 A series of brief, appreciative monographs about individual authors edited by Pierce and Victor Morin. Eleven volumes appeared between 1923 and 1926; the twelfth and final volume was published in 1941.

2 Albert Durrant Watson (1859–1926) was a Toronto author, physician, occultist, and poet who published *Robert Norwood* (1923) as the first volume in the Makers of Canadian Literature series. He and Pierce had previously collaborated on the anthology *Our Canadian Literature* (1922).

3 Journalist, humorist, writer (1866–1924) who became well known for his rural columns, which appeared regularly in *The Globe* and *The Farmer's Advocate*. Deacon's *Peter McArthur* appeared in 1924 as part of the Makers of Canadian Literature series.

---

## To Lorne Pierce May 3, 1923

Dear Dr. Pierce,

Many thanks for your letter of the 1st instant, and copy of *Robert Norwood* by Dr. Watson, both of which came to me a few minutes ago. I think that the little volume is dignified and attractive – could not possibly be more so. I think it exactly in keeping with the idea behind the series, and in itself very artistic. I do not care quite so much for the color gray as used on the dedication and title pages, but doubtless you have tried out all the alternatives, and have arrived at the best possible decorative scheme. As to contents, I have not yet had time to read the book, but shall do so at once. I am looking forward to the experience with pleasure.

I had hoped for an opportunity to explain to you in person my reasons for delay with the McArthur book. I do not like to fail to keep promises, but if I had had more experience in writing books I doubt if I would have promised you my copy by June 15th. As it is, I have been hampered in ways I did not expect. Mr. McArthur seems incapable of telling a plain tale of what he has done with his life. I had to give up my cross-examinations as I saw he did not like being held down to unvarnished facts delivered in their proper chronological sequence. His son and I are now trying to draft a skeleton biography between us. Then too Mrs. Deacon has not been well and as I am even newer at the baby business than at authorship, I have been worried. I was also wanting to see this first volume and see what kind of a thing was expected of me. I had thought this would be out before Xmas last, and hesitated to let my work take too definite shape until I saw a sample. I feel now I have something more to work on, and hope interruptions will be less frequent. I greatly appreciate the honor you have done me in entrusting a book to me, and want to meet your requirements in every way. And I am very sorry that I cannot live up to the understanding we had about the date for delivery of MS. In this I feel I have broken my contract, and if you wish to entrust the work to more reliable hands you are free to do so. If I am to be allowed an extension, I shall not let anything interfere with production. As Blake says – I will not rest, nor stay my hand,

Till I have built Jerusalem
In England's green and pleasant land.

As to Mr. McArthur's copyrights there will be no difficulty, as he has made it a rule never to have anything of his copyrighted anywhere, and he has never signed any agreement with any publisher. He assures me you are free to use anything.

While you are kind enough to flatter me by asking for suggestions, I feel it would be a presumption in me to make any, even if any occurred to me, which is not the case. I would like, however, to express my confidence in the undertaking. The Chronicles of Canada have proved exceptionally popular,[1] and I expect this series will be welcomed by an even wider public. I believe your sales should run to half a million within the next ten years. In view of the sales of *The Book of Knowledge* and the Chronicles, this is not as extravagant as it sounds. I think you will go slowly at first, but will gain momentum with every fresh volume added, and when the series stands complete it ought to be the best selling thing ever put out in Canada. And for the cause of popularizing Canadian Literature, the work is, of course, unique, and must prove useful and instructive to the whole reading public.

Am I right in naming the price as $1.25? and should I say anything at this time about your plans for other bindings?

I shall be glad to know what you decide to do about the McArthur book, and whether, in case I am to go on, it would be possible to obtain fall publication if the MS. comes in later than June 15th. If so, what is the dead-line date?

Yours truly,

1 A series of thirty-two historical monographs, edited by historian G.M. Wrong and

librarian H.H. Langton and published by Glasgow, Brook and Company of Toronto between 1914 and 1916

## To Raymond Knister[1] May 3, 1923

Dear Mr. Knister,

I am sorry we did not get more of a chance to chat, but I hope that you will come to Toronto again sometime when we have greater leisure. Your kind words quite bowled me over, as I am not aiming at virtuosity at all, but at simplicity. From a brother reviewer, yours was high praise indeed, and I am sure quite unmerited. Between ourselves, I am very anxious to see a more free, genial and honest discussion of books than has been possible in the past. I think we have all been too much afraid of each other and ourselves; and all I want to do is to converse frankly on literary matters. If we all say what we really think right out in meeting, I believe contemporary literature will benefit more than through any other single agency. Trusting that we shall get better acquainted later, I am,

Sincerely yours,

1 Raymond Knister (1891–1932) was an early modernist poet, novelist, and short-story writer whose work was published during the 1920s in avant-garde literary magazines such as *The Midland*, *Poetry*, and *Voices*, and in the Paris reviews *This Quarter* and *transition*. He edited *Canadian Short Stories* (1928), the first of its kind, and published a rural novel, *White Narcissus* (1929), along with several posthumous works, among them *My Star Predominant* (1949), a fictionalized biography of Keats.

## To E.J. Pratt May 3, 1923

My dear Ned,

It was most thoughtful of you to send me this autographed copy [of *Newfoundland Verse*], which I value highly. I shall treasure it against my old age, when I shall be poverty-stricken, and too old to work. Then in a moment of dire need I may sell it – a genuine first edition Pratt – to some wealthy library for a few thousands to see me through the last years. So your act is not only courteous; it is generous, and for those thousands I thank you with all my heart.

I hear the most encouraging reports of your sales, and begin to think that your pipe-dream of royalties may have something in it after all. We sold one to John Coffin of Calgary. Do you know him? He says that Newfoundland will never be part of Canada – would have everything to lose and nothing to gain. He evidently hails from down your way.

With best regard to Mrs. Pratt, and hopes for a pleasant summer in which you may regain your health fully, and a couple of bucketfuls more of thanks, I remain,

Ever cordially yours,

---

## From E.J. Pratt

25 Tullis Drive
Toronto
Friday noon
[May 1923]

Dear Bill,

The Review[1] tended to rest on my collapsed heart more effectively than digitalis. What impressed me more favourably than anything else was the expression of your own critical integrity where side by side with your own valued appreciation you were not backward in stating an adverse judgment upon inferior work.

It's your intellectual candour no less than your literary insight that is making your column live to-day. Put the petrol on us and apply the match when necessary. There is a lot of dead timber to be consumed. God himself has special uses for flames, and a self-complacent poet makes excellent roasting material.

Thanks Bill, anyway, old thing, for the generous space you gave the volume in your paper. It was more than I deserved.

I am lying on my back in bed and may have to remain here for two more weeks – slow heart convalescence after flu. But anytime you and your beloved wife feel like straying up this way for an evening chat – and let us hope it will be very soon – the door is wide open. There is still a little sherry left and a humidor for John Cotton[2] and a *great deal* of welcome.

Ned

1 Deacon's review of *Newfoundland Verse* appeared in *Saturday Night*, 21 April 1923, and praised Pratt's maturity, strength, and beauty despite the unevenness of the collection.
2 Pratt's characteristic humour and love of word play bring together references linking Deacon to the famous and persuasive New England Puritan clergyman (1584–1652); the popular John Cotton tobacco products of the 1920s, which recall Deacon's own love of pipe tobacco and his earlier comment on Pratt's 'pipe dream of royalties'; and the pun on John Coffin, who had bought a copy of *Newfoundland Verse*.

---

## From Raymond Knister

Blenheim, R.R. 1
Ontario
May 10, 1923

Dear Mr. Deacon:

I was very glad to have your letter, following as it did the opportunity of telling you personally how much I liked your reviews. It may interest you to know that it was partly the spirit of emulation aroused by reading some of your work which led me into reviewing. There is no perceptible resemblance in our styles, and I fear you need be under no anxiety on that score: it will be a long time before I approach a book with the graceful ease you display. Nor do we always agree in our ratings – or beratings – of this or that author, which is refreshing ... Wasn't it Goethe in his *Conversations* who said that when we say what we actually think we automatically became brilliant – if it wasn't, we'll say it should have been! That must have been what I meant when I told you that your criticism was brilliant.

But as you will have seen, you should have considered before writing me that you were laying yourself open to the necessity of receiving and at least returning my mss. I occasionally try my hand at a short story, and this one happens to be of moderate length,[1] so I simply had to try it on *SATURDAY NIGHT*. It's a gross libel perhaps on any living Middle-West novelist, and I hope that I myself will never in my proper person write with such a style. One editor wrote that it was 'after' Henry James, before I'd read his later work. I hope it will not be too boring. Thanking you for your letter.

Yours very truly,
Raymond Knister.

1 The title of the story is unknown.

---

## From E.J. Pratt

25 Tullis Drive
Toronto
Monday [June 1923]

Dear Bill,[1]

Off to Chicago tomorrow. I have lost a cheque for $30 somewhere, and have wondered whether I left it in my inside pocket of the coat put into the suitcase over the kitchen door. Cheque made out by *Maclean's Magazine* in my favor. It was attached to a note by a clip and is inside of an envelope. I may have left it in my coat (black with white pin stripe). There are two suitcases strapped up on top. Would you mind opening them up and examine the coat. If you find it send it to Vi 25 Tullis Drive. If you can't find it there it may be on one of the shelves in the living room. If not there I guess I may have lost it in transit as I had my coat off in train. Hope you are having a good time. Get all the rest you can.

Love to all
Ned

1 Deacon was staying at Pratt's cottage.

---

## From Raymond Knister

Blenheim
Ontario
September 18, 1923

Dear Mr. Deacon:

This is to thank you for your very pleasant comment on my article on 'The Canadian Short Story' in the *Canadian Bookman*, in your 'Waste-Basket' of last week. Commendation from such sources is especially to be valued; for isn't it (not to become Freudian!) to deserve commendation, considerably at least, that one chooses to write?

I want too to hail you as dean of Canadian reviewers, on the appearance of your collected volume, *Pens and Pirates*. Unlike most deans your prospect is good of surviving many years to enjoy the distinction. Congratulations.

But this letter must serve a third purpose, for I have some Scotch blood in my veins. The Sir John Suckling poem reminded me of some poems I'd been writing in a similarly antique vein. I'm enclosing two for possible use. Others perhaps later, if they return [from] editorial bournes. My published poems are as yet few, a group of seven in December *Midland*,[1] though *Poetry*[2] and *American Poetry Magazine*[3] have each accepted one.

Very truly yours,
Raymond Knister

1 *The Midland* was an Iowa City literary magazine (1915–33) which specialized in the work of American writers from the West. Knister was a member of its editorial staff in 1923–4.
2 The Chicago magazine edited by Harriet Monroe
3 Probably refers to the American Literary Association's Milwaukee publication, issued from May 1919

---

## To Raymond Knister September 20, 1923

Dear Mr. Knister,

You are very rash. Suppose you don't like it? For I had the pleasure of autographing your review copy yesterday, and same should be in your hands by now. And I would appreciate a review by you if you think the book is worth one. In fact I think I am more curious to see what you will say than any of the others. I can tell almost to a hair's breadth how every one of the older men are going to jump. Their positions are defined and they will stay within the walls they have built. But you are still a free man, and liable to do anything, and may be counted on to speak plain and like the sergeant's wife 'tell 'em true.' Go to it. Ease your mind, and don't mind my feelings. I'm nerved up to take some severe punishment, for I know it's coming. Some of them have just been laying for me – and I guess I deserve the spanking I'll surely get.

I'm afraid you are in a minority of one about the dean business – much as I appreciate your good will and support. However if you manage to elect me by your own acclamation, I can only retaliate by offering you the highest chair on the faculty – the chair of Truth and Good Sense. Don't ever leave it, even if they rotten-egg you. I really think Canadian reviewing has improved in candor and sincerity and plain downright honesty since I began here 18 months ago. I do not take all the credit by any means, though I helped of course. Ruth Cohen (Sheila Rand) of Winnipeg, yourself and several other of the newer voices – Merrill Denison for instance – are all striving for the same thing that I am. And between us we are making some slight impression on the old method of flattering the publisher and the author, and leaving the books almost unread and wholly unconsidered. (This for your private ear).

Now about your poems. The editor-in-chief [Frederick Paul] buys all outside material for the whole paper, and he has an inflexible rule against paying for poetry. This is used as 'fillers' – principally in the women's section. They are scalped or taken from anthologies, and in rare cases a poet of standing for some personal reason wants his work in the paper and makes us a gift of something. Knowing my own fondness for poetry, you will understand how I feel about this. I always decline offered material because I do not think it fair to take a poet's product without pay, any more than to take coal without pay. Even if you offered these gratis, the decision would not rest with me but with the women's editor. And if I were you I would try to sell them to *The Canadian Home Journal*, *The Canadian Magazine*[1] or *Ainslie's*[2] – who have good taste. I like 'Still Young' very much, and you will see from *Pens and Pirates* how much I too admire the work of the Caroline School.

Finally, I want to reiterate my apologies for not reading your former MS. I work about 16 hours a day as it is, and if I started to grant requests for private criticisms (they are always coming in) I could not get through in 60 hours per diem. I'm dreadfully sorry but I have to be ruthless here.

Hope you get some fun out of *P & P*. There are no strings on you. Flay the deuce out of me![3]

1 *The Canadian Magazine* (1893–1939) was a Toronto periodical which published Canadian fiction, poetry, book news, and articles of general interest. Edited from 1906 to 1925 by Newton Faul MacTavish (1877–1941), journalist and nationalist, it was taken over in 1925 by Maclean Publications, which issued it until its demise.

2 Published under various names from 1897 to 1926, it had by 1923 evolved into 'a magazine of clever fiction,' publishing the best-known British and American writers. Under Street and Smith, it achieved a circulation of 250,000 before merging with the *Far West Magazine*.

3 Knister's brief review appeared in January 1924 and described the 'chief impor-

tance' of *Pens and Pirates* as 'its defining an awakening literary consciousness in Canada' (*The Midland*, 10,1, 63).

---

## From Laura Goodman Salverson[1]

2111 – 14A Street West
Calgary
March 31, 1924

Dear Mr. Deacon:

I have long wanted to express my appreciation for your interest in my book [*The Viking Heart*]. May I hope that you believe me sincere in having wanted only to give a little picture of what my countrymen did in Manitoba – and that none but myself could have obtained these true experiences of the pioneers?

Because of your helpful review[2] I feel indebted to you and every reviewer – feel it incumbent upon me that I try to improve and be worthy of this faith in my effort.

Therefore I would like to lay before you this vindication of myself as regards Mrs. Reeve's attack.[3] She makes herself safe from the law by hiding behind an anonymous attack but has left no stone unturned to have this *Bookman* letter brought before me, and admitted to my husband that it was I she referred to.

May I trust that you will allow time and my future actions to prove the integrity of my character?

Sincerely Yours,
Laura Goodman Salverson

1 Laura Goodman Salverson (1890–1970) is best known for *The Viking Heart* (1923), a novel about the Icelandic pioneering experience in Manitoba. Her autobiography, *Confessions of an Immigrant's Daughter* (1939), won the Governor-General's Award for non-fiction. Her novel, *The Dark Weaver* (1937), won the fiction award, but it was *The Dove of El-Djezaire* (1933), based on the Icelandic sagas, which represented her developing interest as a writer of historical romances rather than of realistic fiction about prairie immigrants. Encouraged by Austin McPhail Bothwell (1885–1928), a Regina teacher and writer who spurred Salverson to write *The Viking Heart*, which she dedicated to him and his wife, she gradually overcame her fear of criticism as a Canadian writer whose mother tongue was not English. After Bothwell's sudden death, she more and more confided her hopes, frustrations, and opinions on numerous topics to Deacon in her characteristically idiomatic prose style.

2 In *Saturday Night*'s 'The Bookshelf' of 17 November 1923, Deacon praised *The*

*Viking Heart* for partaking 'of the good qualities of both the realistic and historical novel.'

3 The March 1924 number of *The Canadian Bookman* contained a letter signed by Winifred Reeve (pseud. Onoto Watanna, b. 1879), the Calgary author of romantic novels with oriental and western Canadian backgrounds. Reeve, who described Salverson as 'a certain author [who] had her first book published during the last Fall season,' claimed that Salverson, for 15% of her royalties, had hired 'a certain "critic"' to write and place favourable reviews. She further claimed that in private conversation, the 'certain author' had defended her actions. In her letter to Deacon, Salverson enclosed a carbon copy of her rebuttal to *The Canadian Bookman* in which she listed twenty-two newspapers which had carried reviews of *The Viking Heart*. In June 1924 the *Bookman* published a sworn affidavit from Austin Bothwell, Salverson's 'critic,' to the effect that there had been no payment, agreement, or contract between Laura Salverson and himself. Reeve herself had, in fact, published a highly laudatory review of *The Viking Heart* in the Calgary *Albertan* on 13 November 1923.

---

## To Laura Goodman Salverson

April 4, 1924

Dear Mrs. Salverson,

I was surprised to hear from you in connection with Mrs. Reeve's *Bookman* letter. As I remember it, the criticism was directed at some reviewer who was supposed to have accepted a 15% interest in the book as pay for certain services. Possibly the critic might feel the need of clearing himself from the imputations, but certainly there is no reason for you to worry.

Let this be your certificate – if you want one – that I was in no way bought, and my opinions were independently arrived at from reading *The Viking Heart* and from my previous knowledge of literature. I consider your novel the best Canadian story of 1923; and I have already said so in *Saturday Night*, in the *Literary Review* of *The New York Evening Post* (for March 29th, 1924) and in a public address delivered before the Canadian Literature Club, Toronto, January 10th, 1924 on Canadian Literary Production of 1923. No one familiar with my writings will ever accuse me of being bribed by you to say so.

Do not worry too much about this. In the long run people are going to judge your book on its merits, and quite without reference to Mrs. Reeve's charges.

And I do not wish to be on record as expressing any opinion as to the ethics of the case from your agent's standpoint. If he became a partner in the book, and then published apparently disinterested reviews praising the book – particularly if he used pen-names – there are those who will suspect that he was influenced by his financial interest in the book's success. As to whether such charges are justified, I do not propose to discuss. It is a matter that can be left with the gentleman in question. If you feel that publicity is necessary, *The Canadian Bookman* is the proper journal to use. My present intention is to make no reference to this in the columns of *Saturday Night.*

Sincerely yours,

This letter is personal. I do not want you to show it to any third party whomsoever, as I do not wish to be drawn into the controversy. You are free to quote the first two paragraphs only.

WAD.

---

## From Laura Goodman Salverson

2111 – 14A Street West
Calgary
[April 1924]

Dear Mr. Deacon:

I believe you have misunderstood my purpose in writing you – please believe that I had no intentions of drawing you into any controversy nor have I used the names of any reviewer. I only disliked having you think me party to this cheap publicity game, a thing I would never do and even if I would which my purse would not allow.

All I have done is to send that list of reviews to *The Bookman,* reviews by persons unknown to me and hence beyond the shadow of doubt. However Mr. Bothwell's honor is not a thing under suspicion – his word is as good as any man's. And never have I seen an article from him, unless his name appears with it.

However this is not the matter under discussion; let me add only this: that I shall take no liberties with your name nor any other. I may refer to magazines & papers but not to persons. If it were at all possible I should let this matter drop. I have tried to ignore it but

Mrs. Reeve insists upon taking my silence for fear and has twice published ridiculous things in the paper here. I do not intend to begin a woman war of gossip but neither will I be accused of theft and say nothing *but* I shall leave the battle to wiser heads than mine.

I would return your letter – were I not afraid of appearing angry. You must believe me honest in saying I shall not use it, so there this matter ends.

Sincerely yours,
Laura Goodman Salverson

---

## From Raymond Knister

THE MIDLAND
Iowa City, Iowa
May 14, 1924

Dear Mr. Deacon:

I have wanted before to thank you for the fine tribute you gave my story, 'The Loading,' a few weeks ago.[1] Assuredly it is gratifying to see the thing getting the comment it is, so long after my writing it, and after offering it to most magazines on the continent. I am (almost) tempted to write more short stories. Meanwhile I continue to work on a novel.

I am sending you a copy of our latest number, containing verse of mine. My somewhat literal rurality hurts me here too on the marketing side, but *Poetry, Voices,*[2] and *The American Poetry Magazine* have either printed or accepted a few.

Spring finds me with exile's fever, and I am thinking of return – perhaps to Toronto, next winter. The problem is largely economic with me, but I dare say it is little harder to supply my simple wants in one place than in another.

I have hoped to see you at the Annual Meeting of the Authors' Association, but I don't even know whether it is provided this year that workers for newspapers and magazines are given gratuitous railway tickets.

Trusting that you are continuing the good fight, and with best wishes for the same (particularly that it won't end too soon)

Sincerely yours
Raymond Knister

1 'Raymond Knister Exciting Attention' (*Saturday Night*, 12 April 1924) commented on 'the quality of Mr. Knister's art in narrative' and deplored Canadians' ignorance of his work in the face of American enthusiasm.
2 A poetry magazine established in New York in 1921 by its editor, Harold Vinal

---

## To Raymond Knister June 4, 1924

Dear Mr. Knister,

First let me thank you for *The Midland*. I read your verses with interest, as indeed I read all your work. Though you do not ask for criticism I am going to take my life in my hands (or rather our friendship, which I value) and say that I find something lacking in these poems. And the lack, so far as I can place it, is want of tonal harmony: I see the pictures, follow your thought, but your words do not sing themselves to me out loud. My eye and mind are responsive, but my ear is not caught. Now that is probably because there is something the matter with my ear, but I know you will take the slight objection in the friendliest spirit (in which of course it was voiced). And I would be a false friend to you if expressly or tacitly I told you I was overcome by these verses. My feeling is essentially one of indifference because I cannot *hear* them.

Far different was my reaction to your Campbell article in June *Queen's Quarterly*.[1] By God, man, you've rung the bell! I am sure that the posterity of a century hence, when remembering the death of Wilfred, will quote some part, and a large part, of your critical essay. It is immense, just hits the nail on the head, and is thoroughly sane, well-informed and fair. It shows you as more mobile emotionally than anything else of yours I have seen. To the best of my memory it is the best critique by a Canadian of a Canadian that I have ever seen. Assuredly, it is time for you to be the Dean – if we can pry Morgan-Powell[2] loose from the job. I am not joshing: you have inaugurated a new era in Canadian criticism. I have read your article with great profit, and I agree with everything you say about his work. As I was reading, Professor Archibald MacMechan[3] of Halifax walked into my office (he is another Dean by the way, holding sway over the Maritime Provinces for a generation). We discussed you; or rather I told him about you and we discussed the article. He was delighted, and pointed out that 'The Mother,' to which you refer, is an almost straight steal from Sir Walter Scott's notes to, I think, 'The Lay of the Last Minstrel' – anyway you can trace it easily in the notes of the complete Scott. This information is the property of A.M. and his discovery is not for us to make public – unless he dies without doing so. I note you speak of Campbell's dipping his cup in other men's pails. Here is your proof. Make a note of it, and get it exact.

I was sorry not to see you at Quebec. We had a good time. I could not find out anything for you about the Hamilton paper though a friend promised to look it up for me. Of course I want to see you back in Canada, but openings for lit'ry gentlemen, are, if anything, fewer than ever, and I do not know of anything at all that would pay even your room rent. Even the cheaper type of journalists are out of jobs in great numbers, and they are always in greater demand than high class ones. Still, if you move, keep in touch with me please. I have *Stories from the Midland*[4] on my desk, but in the rush have not had time to read and review it yet. But I will. With sincerest congratulations on the finest piece of work of yours I have ever seen,

Cordially yours,

1 'The Poetical Works of Wilfred Campbell' (XXXI, 4, 435–49) reviews Campbell's posthumous collection. Knister's critical assessment takes into account Campbell's personal and aesthetic beliefs, viewing him as a poet-prophet of the Victorian era.
2 Stanley Morgan-Powell (1867–1962). Editor and book reviewer for the *Montreal Star* (1908–46) and promoter of Canadian literature
3 The Dalhousie University professor (1862–1935) remembered for *Headwaters of Canadian Literature* (1924)
4 An anthology compiled by John Towner Frederick (b. 1893), founder-editor of *The Midland*, which published the book in 1924

---

## To Emily Murphy

The Police Court
Edmonton
August 14, 1924

My dear William

I am enclosing you a snap taken in my garden on Sunday – under my own vine and birch tree. It doesn't show that 'nifty roll,' the Star speaks of, and which you declare to be an actuality.

That is all right William – just an outward and visible sign of an inward and spiritual pliability. Every P.M. who is any good should lie easy to both sides, (with just a tilt, you understand, towards the Police).

I was down at the Provincial Jail to-day and the Superintendent Blythe and the Deputy Minister of Public Works were with me. I was making a report on conditions at the jail for the Social Service Council of Canada.

In the death cell, old Picarello[1] had drawn a picture of the hangman on the wall – 'a downcast hangman who had no job' he said, but the hangman got the job alright. It must have been a grim satisfaction to that official as he bound 'Pic' and bound him up to know that he had 'Finis' up his sleeve.

At any rate, as I saw this crude attempt at authorship, it seemed that Pic reached back from outer darkness and appeared to be a very human fellow after all. There was a friend of mine who wrote a book called *Pens and Pirates*, and he knows the ropes, if not from a mariner's standpoint, at least from that of the literary man. May he never know the hangman's!!!!!

The Warden told me that he never expected to be executed (I mean Picarello) till that very last moment. When the Warden entered his cell, he fainted – it was a couple of hours before daylight – for he knew the hangman was right there.

The Warden tells me that the death watch is changed every four hours because this official must never take his eyes off the condemned man. If left longer the watchman's eyes get heavy and he falls asleep. Don't you think this is almost as bad as execution – to be observed for every instant? This alone, might drive a man to murder. There's a story here alright. Maybe, I'll introduce it in my book. I haven't written anything at it since last Spring, being very busy and unduly inclined to festive occasions.

Superintendent Wm. Blythe was borne on the jail farm over 50 years ago when it was the headquarters of the Mounted Police. He was a bugler in their band, as a boy, and lately was appointed the Superintendent. Yet, there are people who think this country is about 15 years old. He is a lusty, likeable fellow and has a wife who makes a wonderful dinner. Our waiter who came and stood at the dining room door with a [tray] upon which Madam laid the dishes from the table, was a gentleman convicted for a breach of the new liquor act in Alberta, but I pretended I didn't see.

In one of the cells I talked with a man who is to die on August

30th for killing his child in a fit of rage. He wasn't a murderer to me, and I don't think he is either. I have written the Minister of Justice [Hon. Ernest Lapointe] (but no one knows not even the prisoner) saying this should be culpable homicide under 261 of the Code, and that the sentence should be commuted to life imprisonment.

He and his wife were lovers as boy and girl and lived on adjoining farms in the States. He came here 11 years ago, and went to an arid district. In all that time, he never had a crop and I think his nerves broke under the strain, and so he destroyed what he had been trying to protect. It must be so for he is loved by his relatives, and even by his neighbours.

I didn't cry – only the men with me. It would be foolish to bid him be strong and then be weak myself. And I told him too, about all the strong young men alive to-day who would die before him – in the next 6 weeks, and of what Sir Walter Scott said,

> 'Come he slow, or come he fast,
> It is but death that comes at last.'

He is quite a fine looking man but his hair has turned white this last month or so, and his hands were clammy as I held them in mine.

I told the Hon. the Minister of Health [H.S. Béland], at Ottawa that I have sent two people to the Asylum because they 'waited for the rain' but that city folk could not comprehend this tragedy. I asked him to try hard to grasp it. I feel sure this is just another case, as exemplified in a man.

There are two women in the Fort awaiting trial for murder, but I could not stand anymore. One is watched all the time by the girl convicts, because she has attempted suicide by hanging on two occasions, and nearly succeeded.

Do you remember those lines in *Eugene Aram*:[2]

> 'A thousand times I groaned,
> The dead had groaned but twice.'

Don't show this to Sarah, it would sadden her. I don't know why God lets me look into hearts like these. Maybe, He knows I need it to keep my balance true. I often feel it would, otherwise, be quite easy to fly without even a propeller. It must be the altitude here that causes this.

Always affectionately,
Janey Canuck.

1 Emil Picariello (b. 1880) was accused and convicted of the shooting murder of a police constable in Coleman, Alberta, on 21 September 1922. Picariello was executed on 2 May 1923.
2 Highly popular romance published in 1832 by E.G. Bulwer-Lytton (1803–73)

---

## From Raymond Knister

Blenheim, R.R. 1
Ontario
February 16, 1925

Dear Mr. Deacon, –

As you see, I have returned to the Land of the Maple. Left Iowa City in June, and stayed from then until the end of October in Chicago. I did some writing there for *Literary Review* of *The Evening Post* and reviews for *Poetry* (one I note is contained in the Feb. issue of the latter). Several times I have decided to review no longer but to confine myself to my unremunerative stories; but I met Sandburg and others in Chicago & other notables in Iowa, so that I have been trying to think of a Canadian magazine which might care for a series of articles on Mid-western writers.

Though I know that *Saturday Night* rarely prints stories, I am venturing to submit my most lately completed one. Can't say what I think of it myself (now) unless that perhaps it is too brittle. But if you read it yourself, I shall appreciate any comment.

In *Boston Transcript* for Dec. 6. I note that O'Brien[1] did not agree with *The Bookman* man about 'The Loading,' on which you so generously commented. Gave it two stars. But put 'The Strawstack' (*Can. Forum*. Oct. 1923.) on the Roll of Honor for 1924. I think this is the first time it's happened to a Canadian story in a Canadian magazine. Don't know whether it's included in the volume or not. Between you & I, O'Brien's wrong, I think. 'The Loading's' the better tale.

I fear I haven't thanked you for your letter about the Campbell article. It's immensely heartening to find some one among lit'ry people who *really* cares for that sort of thing more than I do. And there's no one from whose typewriter I'd rather have had such words about it. As to the poems, – the risk was nil. If you don't like them, or anything of mine, never hestitate to say so. No, they don't sing. I was rather overruled in their inclusion, as others I had seemed to me better.

What's new in Toronto? I learned that Lauriston[2] nearly came to doin's in his column with you, anent Stringer's *Empty Hands* (or *Unseeing Eyes*?)

Sincerely yours,
Raymond Knister

P.S. – Did you ever do that review of *Stories From The Midland*?
R.K.

1 Edward Joseph Harrington O'Brien (1890–1941). Editor of annual collections and yearbooks of American and British short stories
2 Victor Lauriston (1881–1973). Writer and journalist with *The Chatham News*, remembered for his *Inglorious Milton* (1934), a comic treatment of the small-town writer. Deacon carried on a friendly correspondence with Lauriston, who chided him both publicly and privately for his parody-review of *Empty Hands* by Arthur Stringer, 'What a Canadian Has Done for Canada,' which appeared in the 19 July 1924 issue of *The Literary Review* of *The New York Evening Post*. Stringer (1874–1950) is remembered for *Prairie Wife* (1915), the first novel in his prairie trilogy, a romantic series which has often been heralded for its 'realism.'

---

## To Raymond Knister February 19, 1925

Dear Mr. Knister,

Thank you very much for 'Elaine,'[1] which I have read with a great effort to understand it. Though I read part of it twice I am not altogether sure that I get your meaning wholly. Now of course this admission indicates how dense I am, entering on the old fogey class in fact, but from what I have learned about the perspicacity of our readers I feel sure that they will understand it less than I do. They are not used to subtlety; and I have been surprised to find how frequently they miss the purport of my bluntest remarks. Therefore I am afraid we should only puzzle them with literary caviar like this story of yours, and I am consequently returning it with profound regrets.

*The Canadian Forum* is the only magazine I can think of that pays at all and would be anxious to secure your articles on the mid-western writers. As you know I have no appropriation for buying material of any kind for the little department I operate: my salary is supposed to cover all editorial expense on those pages. But why confine yourself to a Canadian market? Surely *The Bookman* or *N.Y. Times* would be glad to get them and would pay you more for one than the whole series would bring you in Canada. I have severed my last tie with Canadian periodicals – apart from *Saturday Night* – and am selling my whole output among a half dozen N.Y. editors.

Yes, I published a review of *Stories from the Midland* in conjunction with *Country People* some months back – whenever it came out – but as we never save extra copies I'm afraid I cannot send you one. I mentioned your story.[2]

Lauriston threatened to chew me up over Stringer, but I begged him not to. I have no wish to heap further ridicule on Stringer, and if Lauriston punched me hard enough to do A.S. any good I would probably be forced to reply. So I asked him to drop it, and apparently he has granted my request. Nor do I care much if he thinks I was afraid of him: A.S. knows better.

Well, I am glad in a way you are back here, but only if you are happy in your environment; and for long I felt that you were destined to leave us permanently. I am glad to see men stay but I realize opportunities are few for the native scribe, and I think a man does best to follow his admirations and sympathies. I have an idea you might like New York and would do well there if you could establish one or two connections before migrating. I am sorry our contacts have been so few that I feel I cannot be of much practical help, and that you are rather at a loose end and need some sort of a hand up that in the nature of things I am not in a position to give. However I am much interested in your work, shall follow it with pleasure and trust we may some day get better acquainted.

Very truly yours,

1 'Elaine' was published in 1925 in the inaugural number of *This Quarter*.

2 'Progress of the Scriptorial Art in Iowa,' WAD's review of *Stories from the Midland*, and 'Down on the Farm,' his review of Ruth Suckow's novel *Country People*,

both appeared on 26 June 1924. Deacon admits that he was 'trained in the wrong school' to appreciate the subtleties of the new realism, and praises the Midwestern writers' ability to create atmosphere. Knister's 'Mist-Green Oats,' about 'the revolt of an educated farmer's son at the drudgery of farm labor,' was included in the collection.

---

## To Sherwood Fox[1] May 4, 1925

Dear Dean Fox,

I suppose you saw the masterpiece on page 5 last issue. Kindly omit flowers.

Really, I don't know what prompted me to open the subject of lecturing in Can. Lit., but it must have been the fact that I seem to be about the only person who has made any extended study of the subject and is not lecturing on it. Nearly all Canadian universities, as you know, have courses or half courses. Logan,[2] who started the movement, is a newspaperman at Halifax and goes down to Acadia twice a year to deliver a series of lectures. Thinking of him gave me a picture of myself spending weeks in London on the same errand. The advantage would be that I could deliver one a week, and you could start your course with only five lectures a year, if you wished, though I think ten would be better – five in the fall and five in the winter; and of course this could be expanded at any time. It does seem rather a shame that graduates should leave college without any instruction at all in the literature of their own country.

At many colleges seniors are offered short courses in contemporary English Lit. Edgar[3] lectures on Conrad, Hardy etc; and it was this and not 'modern' Eng. Lit. I had in mind. We all spend some time getting over the notion that literature with a capital L ended with Tennyson, or whatever man comes last in the text book. A needed sense of continuity is built up, I think, by introducing the student to the best of the living writers. One could speak on the Irish Renaissance, on Moore, Galsworthy, Meredith, the Free Verse movement, the return to the lyric and all that. Perhaps that is being done. If not – runs my dream – why not deliver two lectures on each of the days? – one on Can. Lit. and one on contemporary writers. At least, how dashed convenient and pleasant for me!

As you imply, all this is in the future; and your requirements might call for a very different type of lecturer; but I would so enjoy trying to instil an intelligent appreciation for these things into young minds that I hope somewhere sometime I will get a chance at such congenial work. Though my journalism often verges on the vulgar tricks of the vendor of patent medicines, the intent of my work is educative; and the core of it is the development of taste and the literary enthusiasms. I just thought it would do no harm to take you into my confidence in case your increasing needs should sometime make it possible for me to be of use.

Sincerely yours,

1 William Sherwood Fox (1878–1967) was a professor of classics, dean of arts (1919–27), and president (1927–47) of the University of Western Ontario. His books include *'T Ain't Runnin' No More* (1946), an ecological study of the beauty and exploitation of the Aux Sables River in southwestern Ontario; *The Bruce Beckons* (1952), an extended description of the landscape and history of southern Ontario's Bruce Peninsula; and his autobiography, *Sherwood Fox of Western* (1964).

2 John Daniel Logan (1869–1929) was a professor of English first at Dalhousie and then at Marquette University, Milwaukee, Wisconsin, and was co-author, with David French, of *Highways of Canadian Literature: A Synoptic Introduction to the Literary History of Canada (English) from 1760 to 1924* (1924).

3 Oscar Pelham Edgar (1871–1948), Professor of English at Victoria College, University of Toronto, and author of *Henry James* (1927) and *The Art of the Novel* (1933)

---

## From E.J. Pratt

Victoria College
Toronto
May 4, 1925

Dear Bill,

Just came back from London where I gave an address and reading on Newfoundland. As you haven't a phone I thought I'd drop you a line to tell you how much they appreciated your visit. After the address they whisked me off to the home of Grace Blackburn[1] where a number of the London Branch of the CAA had gathered. I never experienced more kindness anywhere; and we got talking about you and your work. Miss Fiddler (I think that's how you spell it) said you held them spell-bound for 2 hrs, Grace Blackburn wanted to be most warmly remembered to you and Seaborn (the Doctor)[2] said that Fox's appreciation amounted to enthusiasm. You must have had an extraordinary good time, even better than you thought. They told me how you stayed over on the following day missing train after train. Miss Denham intended answering your letter but there was sickness or something in the family at the time that pressed her for time. All thought your visit was well worth while for them & your treatment of Peter [McArthur] a crackerjack of exposition. A more magnetic and charming personality than Grace Blackburn I have rarely met. Thought I would just tell you. In haste.

Ned

1 Victoria Grace Blackburn (d. 1928), London resident whose war novel *The Man Child* was published posthumously in 1930. She worked for many years for the London *Free Press* and wrote under the pseudonym 'Fan-Fan.'
2 Probably Edwin Seaborn (1872–1951), a professor of medicine at Western

---

## To E.J. Pratt

May 5, 1925

Dear Ned,

I'll remember you to my dying day as one who is always doing thoughtful and kind things. Thanks awfully. You were quite right about the warmth of the London people; that is why I could not be sure how well they really liked me. And in your modesty you said not one word about how you did nor even what you talked on. Never mind, I'll write Jennie Fidlar.

Once more in your debt –

---

## From Sherwood Fox

University of Western Ontario
May 7, 1925

Dear Deacon:

Your article pleased me very much. Its frankly journalistic style will probably attract and hold the attention of far more readers than the type of article any one of us would write who are closely associated with the University and its problems.

Apparently you are not aware that every other year we give a course of two hours a week throughout the year in Canadian Literature. It is designated English 33. It is given in 1925–26 and not in

'26–'27. The person in charge of this course is our Assistant Professor, W. Cliff Martin, one of our own graduates who recently returned to us with a doctor's degree in English from Cornell University. I hope, however, that this course is not our *Ultima Thule.*

Yours very sincerely,
W. Sherwood Fox
Dean, University College of Arts

---

## From Wilson MacDonald[1] August 1, 1925

Dear Bill:

I am returning ballot. I support Mrs. Osborne in deference to Duncan Campbell Scott, and Marjorie MacMurchy in preference to Katherine Hale.[2]

Leslie Ried [sic] is the possessor of a good literary style but if he is admitted Callahan[3] [sic] and a host of others should be.

Am enjoying myself here although I had it out openly with Roberts last night and warned him that he must have something to say or cease writing.

As Charles G.D. Roberts I love him – as Major Roberts I despise him and told him so. As a comrade he is however as delightful as ever.

This week is poet's week. I wish you were here. I feel that you and Pratt alone have a part in the vision I have caught.

As ever,
Wilson

1 Wilson Pugsley MacDonald (1880–1967), romantic poet whose work was influenced by the verse of Walt Whitman and the mystical doctrines of theosophy. MacDonald enjoyed great national popularity in the 1920s; *Out of the Wilderness* (1926) was to become a popular bestseller.

2 Marian Francis Osborne (1891–1931), author of Macmillan chapbooks, whose *Sappho and Phaon, a Lyrical Drama* would be published by them in 1926; Duncan Campbell Scott (1862–1947), the Confederation poet whose *Collected Poems* would be published by McClelland in 1926; Marjorie MacMurchy Willison (d. 1938), the journalist; Amelia Beers Warnock (1878–1956), wife of John Garvin, and

whose latest Ryerson chapbook was *Morning in the West* (1923), issued under her pseudonym, Katherine Hale

3 Leslie Hartley Reid (b. 1896), novelist, whose *The Rector of Maliseet* (1925), *Saltacres* (1927), and *Trevy, the River* (1928) were all published by Dent in London; MacDonald is referring to Morley Callaghan the novelist and not Francis Callaghan the poet.

---

## To Wilson MacDonald August 4, 1925

My dear Wilson,

Thank you for your letter. I myself am voting for only three of the six candidates. What I fear is that others will treat the ballot as a mere form and vote carelessly for all six instead of using proper discretion. I quite agree that Reid is yet no fit member.

I was much amused at your report of talk with Roberts. I think we should not forget that our whole generation owes him a considerable debt for his pioneer work. He has done a great deal not only in setting standards but in encouraging Lampman and others, and I do think considerable respect should be shown his seniority. I truly think too that his urbanity has a very timely lesson for us younger men; and I want his visit to be as pleasant as may be. Whether he is past his usefulness is beside the point. In his time he broke trail, and if younger men are going farther that is but natural and right and should not in any way detract from the respect we show him. I believe it would be unfortunate if you had any breach with him. He is, after all, our guest, as well as the ancient chief; and if his lordship of 45 years must end – as all reigns end – I want his retirement from the throne to be orderly and decent, and without hard feelings anywhere.

As to his ability to steer the barque of Canadian literature at this time, I feel that if he tries that he is going to find there are a lot of factors he is not counting upon. His visit has certainly been a stimulus to literature in Canada. He's a fine lion. But as for trying to twist the movement to suit his judgment, or whim, or convenience, I think he had much better leave things alone. From all I have seen of him I think he is willing on the whole to do this. Just once or twice have I noticed a desire to take a hand in the game. If you don't rouse him up he will depart amiably in a month or so and we shall all have a fine memory of his genial and inspiring presence.

I think TIME will read him the plain truths you burn to tell him and if you leave it to Time we shall all be happier. He is by [no] means thin skinned; but you have a way of saying sharp things that often sting – the more in proportion as they are true; and I do hope you have not insulted him, though from your letter I fear the beans are spilled.

Tom MacInnes stayed at my house for ten days and is now at Pratt's cottage in Bobcaygeon. We bought a long article from him that is on front page financial this week.[1] Arthur Hawkes interviewed him for Star 'Spotlight,' and he has received another better bit of publicity that I shall tell you about later. I fancy when he goes west he will not be back here for some years, perhaps never, and I do wish it could have been arranged that he go and read at the [Muskoka] Assembly this month. I suppose there is no chance now. When Roberts met him in my office he was rather patronizing – just a little – which was a pity, for Roberts knows only *The Fool of Joy*, and that not well; and so knows nothing of the music of 'Amber Lands,' 'Arbor Arabesque,' 'Fey' &c, which put him as a technician in the lyric above Roberts or Carman, in my view. I so enjoyed having him as a house guest, as did Mrs. Deacon also; and love his unaffected simplicity, and have a greater respect than ever for his powers as poet and thinker. Too bad we did not know in time to work the Assembly, Poetry Society and Writers Club. Still, he is so thoroughly the gentleman that I guess maybe he is just as well off away from the Assembly where he might be treated as inferior in calibre to Carman and Roberts; and with things breaking rather badly for him financially I would not want him submitted to any snobbery.

This letter is, of course, entirely confidential. Wanted to back you up in case you are suffering from competition; and to remind you that your own reputation is secure, and will remain so it you do not alienate people by saying unkind things. I am no toady myself as you know, but I think a balance may be struck between an outspokenness that wounds needlessly and a silence that allows the truth to become apparent in an impersonal way. The best of luck, and give my kind regards to the Staples and Roberts. I omit Carman because he (like Fred Jacob)[2] is 'scarcely a casual acquaintance.'

Cordially,

1 Tom MacInnes's article, 'Canada's Opportunity in the Orient,' about China as a

future market for Canadian wheat, appeared in *Saturday Night*'s Financial Section, p 7, on 8 August.

2 Fred Jacob (1882–1928), Toronto critic and writer, author of *The Day before Yesterday* (1925), a novel set in small-town Ontario. Deacon succeeded him in 1928 as literary editor of *The Mail and Empire*.

---

## To W.T. Allison[1] October 26, 1925

My dear Allison,

Thank you for contribution received,[2] which makes you the first writer whose copy I have actually accepted in my new capacity of editor. You touched this off in just the right spirit, and although I should hack out 100 words I do not see how it can be done – the piece is so complete as it stands.

I may tell you in confidence that we are dropping $500 on this number, despite some rather large ads from the trade. If next fall we can make ends meet, we shall turn the thing into a quarterly the beginning of 1927, and enlarge it to a monthly as soon as possible.

It is my idea to furnish a medium whereby the abler Canadian critics may talk with the utmost candor, and to which the reader may turn for vigorous expressions of opinion from many minds: difference of viewpoint between the several writers will be the keynote. Besides independence of thought, I am striving for tolerance, a comprehensive survey, sound criticism and good writing. I am satisfied that with proper support from authors and the trade we can turn out something as fine in its way as the *International Book Review*,[3] and trust I am taking the tide at the flood and can steer my ship safe to port. With the support now being given *The Canadian Bookman* we should be able to finance it.

As president of the C.A.A.[4] you might keep in mind that our function is national, and that the prestige and wide high class circulation of *Saturday Night* is at the disposal of the Canadian writers and book interests; and that I am having a hard time convincing our business dept. as to the wisdom of my policy and it is up to the authors to get behind me, and to everybody concerned to support us. Perhaps you might impress the Ass'n with the fact of our consistent friendliness to the native author, who has always got a show here, and who will be given a better one once the new publication is firmly on its feet.

It was most kind of you to speak as you did of my own efforts. But I cannot go it any farther alone, and from now on shall be dependent upon the rest of you. For your present help and for your goodwill thanks. Cheque will go forward later. My regards to Wade[5] and the boys generally.

Cordially,

1 William Talbot Allison (1874–1941) was a professor of English at Wesley College, Winnipeg, from 1910 to 1920 and subsequently at the University of Manitoba from 1920 until 1939. Appointed literary editor of *The Winnipeg Tribune* in 1920, he wrote under the pseudonym 'Ivanhoe' and also reviewed books for Deacon in *Saturday Night*. Allison gave a great deal of literary encouragement to Deacon in his Winnipeg days and in the years following his move to Toronto.

2 Allison's review of Gilbert Parker's *The Power and the Glory* appeared in the first 'Literary Section' feature of *Saturday Night*, issued 28 November 1925. During his years at *Saturday Night*, Deacon produced six other literary sections: 2 October 1926; 4 December 1926; 12 March 1927; 1 October 1927; 26 November 1927; 17 March 1928.

3 The popular New York journal which purchased eight general review articles by Deacon between 1924 and 1926. In fact, Deacon's literary sections were more closely modelled on another New York publication, *The Saturday Review of Literature*.

4 From 1925 to 1927

5 H. Gerald Wade, a reporter for the *Western Municipal News*, taught extension courses for United College in Winnipeg during the 1920s.

---

## From Raymond Knister

Northwood
Ontario
October 27, 1925

Dear Mr. Deacon:

Hail! I have noted your articles in the *American Mercury*, *International Book Review*, etc. What did I say about the Dean, two years ago?

This Literary Supplement sounds interesting. Of course I'll be glad to write the review. But I have no copy of *Green Bush*.[1] Are you doing Walter Muilenburg's *Prairie* (Viking Press) and Ruth Suckow's new one?[2]

That 'Elaine' story you feared your readers would not comprehend was printed in the Spring Number of *This Quarter*, Paris. It was to print more of mine in the Summer Number, but I haven't heard of that. Probably they are defunct. Still I got a check out of them, and did better than with an essay on Katherine Mansfield which was accepted by *Phantasmus,*[3] Pittsburg. The magazine cashed in promptly. This is to warn you in time. *The Midland* printed a brace of poems, and *Voices,* N.Y. carried a loo line poem, 'After Exile' in its October number.

Minor matters, involving but a few pages. It seems the best I can do is sit here and write novels until one is printed, – possibly even thereafter. However I am hoping to contrive to get to Toronto in the Winter and hear music and see an odd play; also to amend our brief meeting.

Sincerely yours,
Raymond Knister

1 The second novel, published that year, by John Towner Frederick (b. 1893), editor of *The Midland*

2 Suckow (1892–1960), minor American novelist, short story writer, and member of the Iowan school of realists, had just published *The Odyssey of a Nice Girl* (1925).

3 A short-lived monthly (May–August 1924), reviewing critical and creative writing, edited by J.G. Edmonds

---

## From Francis Dickie

The Firs, Heriot Bay
British Columbia
November 8, 1925

My dear Deacon: –

I got your card regarding *The [American] Mercury*[1] and ordered copy from town, which arrived a couple of mails ago. As it is many moons since I wrote you, this is just a line to say I read the article with considerable admiration. It is a really masterful marshalling of material, and personally I could not find myself not in agreement with any of your statements. It is a pleasure too to see you breaking into the *Mercury;* I know none of the Canadian cognoscenti who have done it, or, are there any Canadian such? Outside yourself and one or two others who do not contribute to my knowledge, I know very few.

There is very little to tell you. We had a very bad time of it this summer. Forest fire swept down on us on a five mile front. Burned practically the whole island. Leaving an awful desert except in spots. I had all my library and a few light portable belongings on a raft for two days, anchored off my place in a howling north wind accompanying the flames. We had a desperate fight to save the house and an acre or so around it, but aided by a Forestry crew and a high pressure pump run by a gasoline engine of great power we won out. It is one of the worst ordeals of my life. Lost a number of books, the waves were so high they kept breaking over the big raft. Fortunately I had a big raft made some time ago to transport fir bark on and it came in handy at the needed moment.

This is a tragic land, this B.C., already it is beginning to show signs of the ruthless, wanton and absolutely uncaring looting of the big timber interests. Only thirty years since they started logging, yet for a hundred miles in every direction around me the country is become a barren waste. But what can one do. It is like trying to make a living writing sincere words.

Well, old chap, next year is the convention at Vancouver. You better make plans to come. As things stand now I will be here, so you can lay out to come back with me after convention for a week.

This will be all just now,

With best regards,
Fraternally yours,

P.S. Re my article on Canadian realism.[2] As you did not write me you could use it, I let *The Bookman* have it. They are sorely in need of stuff, but I seldom have time to do gratis stuff. I had my little rap at Stringer, much he cares, I guess. Prostitution and blatant mediocrity such as he has descended to always pay.

Francis Dickie

1 'The Annexation of Canada,' an article which contradicted Mencken's request for a favourable treatment of the subject, appeared in *The American Mercury* in November. The article was reprinted in *Poteen*.

2 'Realism in Canadian Fiction,' *Canadian Bookman*, VII, 10 (October 1925) 165. The article deals with the lack of and need for realistic writing.

## To Francis Dickie

November 20, 1925

Dear Mr. Dickie,

Thanks for your good letter. I am quoting over half of it in my Waste-Basket. It is in the woods that a letter can be written. I have been up till 2 a.m. every night for two weeks or more getting out the first Literary Section to *Saturday Night* – the 4th section – and this is the first note I have written in a month. Thanks for the invitation, but if I can get West at all it is a cinch that I shall have to race out and back. I am sending you a copy of the Section, and hope you will appreciate the amount of work I have done to create this thing from the editorial and advertising ends right down to the mechanical and circulation. It is a pity you live so far away that hasty assignments are out of the question. However, I wanted you to know the new thing in the Canadian literary heavens; and hope you can assist later in some way. There is plenty of time. A magazine which does not pay contribs is no use to us writers. Why support *The Bookman*? I don't even subscribe to it. The first rule I made for my magazine was that I would *buy* not beg material. Give me your support; and when I learn to edit a magazine I'll give you one worth supporting.

Cordially,

## From W.T. Allison

Department of English
University of Manitoba
Winnipeg
January 15, 1926

Dear Deacon,

Ever since the publication of your book supplement, I have been intending to write to you to send my warm congratulations but you know how hard driven I am all the time and how difficult it is for me to sandwich any correspondence into the day's work. I am making a bee this morning and I hope I am not too late to send my congratulations. I do hope you will be able to carry out your ambitious project. I know you will please and at the same time educate your readers – they need it, the education I mean – in this delightful way. I am very much discouraged about my annual supplement. The publishers have been very mean about it. The advertising this year almost reached the vanishing point, so I am seriously thinking of discontinuing this yearly toil. In all the eight years I have been issuing it only one publisher, Frank Appleton,[1] has ever written me a line of appreciation. As the *Saturday Night* is a Toronto publication, you will fare better. The publishers in your city are easterners. Like so many other people in Toronto, they do not give more than a passing thought to western Canada. I hope a real live publishing firm will spring up in Winnipeg some day and wake them up.

The main reason why you are doing such splendid work on *Saturday Night*, putting so much verve into your work, especially into your waste-basket column, which I always read with ever so much pleasure, as I am sure all your readers do, is because you had a western training.

I hear that *The Canadian Magazine* has gone under. It was about time! MacTavish was never cut out for an editor but I did enjoy his volume of Ontario essays, and his *History of Canadian Art* is a well-written book and beautifully printed.[2]

Bliss Carman is lecturing here at the university and is having a good time, a daily audience of 400. His seminar classes are attended by 125, mostly students. Pretty good for the wild and woolly! I understand that only a score attended his seminars at McGill and only half a dozen in cultured Toronto! I believe there is a keener interest in poetry out here where the crude west begins than in the effete, Pelham-Edgarized east.

Poor Bliss is being dined (not wined) and feted sumptuously in Winnipeg. He will be a very tired man when his train pulls out for Saskatoon!

Ever yours with best New Year's wishes,
W.T.A.

1 Franklin F. Appleton (1893–1951), Toronto publisher and supporter of Canadian writers. As manager of William Collins, he promoted that firm's publication of many Canadian books, among them Hugh MacLennan's *Barometer Rising* (1941).

2 *Thrown In* was published in 1923 and *The First Arts in Canada* in 1925.

---

## From Lorne Pierce[1]

Toronto
March 25, 1926

My dear Mr. Deacon;-

Some misunderstanding seems to have arisen in regard to the Lorne Pierce Medal of the Royal Society of Canada. It is inevitable, perhaps, that there should be a good deal of comment. As the facts are few and simple, there ought to be no occasion either for rhapsody or for picayune criticism.

For some years the conviction has been growing in my own mind that the Royal Society of Canada might well usurp some of the functions of the French Academy. Being a body of eminent scholars with an international standing, its imprimatur upon the work of the author should carry weight. Without presuming to immortalize anyone, its official recognition and approval would achieve three things:
(i) It would provide the highest literary distinction which a Canadian might hope to win from his countrymen.
(ii) The result of the award would be salutary in that, by holding up the best we had achieved as a nation, a premium would be placed upon excellence. In a country so young as Canada this positive appraisal of our literature has many obvious advantages.
(iii) Finally, such recognition would, in all probability, recommend the author to the more generous attention of those at home and abroad.

Of course there are other ways of honouring our authors. Nothing can take the place of a sympathetic understanding of those who are after all the real master builders of the state. The Royal Society of Canada in accepting the medal have merely followed the traditions of learned societies in every part of the world.

The conditions of the award are clearly set forth in the *Report of Council* of the Royal Society of Canada, for the year 1924–25.

1. The medal shall be known as the Lorne Pierce Medal of the Royal Society of Canada.
2. It shall be awarded to Fellows of the Royal Society of Canada or others

who are citizens of Canada, who shall have accomplished some achievement of especial significance and conspicuous merit. Literary criticism dealing with Canadian subjects shall receive prior consideration in this award over critical works which have not for their subject Canadian themes.
3. The award shall be made for works in either French or English. It is not intended that the medal shall necessarily be awarded annually, but only when an outstanding contribution has been made to Canadian Literature.
4. The award shall be made by a Committee consisting of the President of the Society, ex-officio, the Presidents of the English and French Sections of the Society, and one representative chosen by each of these two Sections of the Society. The President of the Society shall be the Convenor of the Committee which shall hold office until the close of the next succeeding annual meeting, at which meeting it shall present its report.
5. If in any year no award shall be made, an additional medal or medals may be awarded in succeeding years under the conditions stated in paragraph 2.
6. The presentation of the medal to the Society will take place at the annual meeting

One thing, perhaps, may need clarifying. The medal will be awarded to those who have made some significant contribution to imaginative, critical, or historical literature in Canada. The award may be made to an author for some single and unusual achievement; but more frequently the Royal Society of Canada will follow the precedent of the Academy of France or the Nobel Foundation and take into consideration the general excellence of an author's entire contribution to our Literature.

The obverse of the medal represents the sister cultures of Canada united in solicitude for the best of all possible art. The reverse contains an inscription in Latin which reads: 'In recognition of his outstanding contribution to Canadian Literature the Royal Society of Canada confers upon (author and year) its highest honours.'

Very sincerely,
Lorne Pierce

P.S. My very own! I want to set this thing right. A good deal grave & gay continues to be said in regard to the L.P.M. Perhaps you will care to give this space. I am writing two or three others.

L.P.

1 This letter, except for the postscript, was published in *Saturday Night*'s literary section on 10 April 1926.

---

## From Laura Goodman Salverson

2111 – 14A Street West
Calgary
[April 1926]

Dear Mr. Deacon:

I have been wanting to drop you a line for months but never had the courage – but crime will out! So then, let me thank you for the many kind things you have said of *V.H.* and the many unkind things you have left unsaid of my new book[1] which I suspect does not appeal to your taste.

Believe it or not, I have not troubled to read the press notices simply because I knew that a story of Idealism would not appeal to a public which looks upon itself as modernised and 'free' and all that sort of rot, but I had the silly desire to write up my old father in Stephen because it's something of a miracle to have an aged parent these days who still believes in beauty and loveliness of mind, that in fact 'as a man thinketh in his heart so is he.' There was a time when father's ideas used to worry us not a little especially when we were low in the larder and thin as to shoe leather, but I am just learning to appreciate what his dreams added to a hard and colorless life.

But I meant only to thank you for your kindness, not because of my work in the *V.H.* but because it is my humble belief that you are the only critic in Canada who endeavors to do for our Canadian letters what Anatole did for France – tell the truth even if it hurts! And if you will recall Anatole took a nip out of Zola for his extreme realism, for all his wit Anatole did not prefer the gloomy outlook to the cheerful nor deem it superior.

Is it too conceited in me to suppose you may be interested to know that I have at last done a real book? What I think a real book! An historical novel on the life of that great adventurer Leif the Lucky – *The Lord of the Silver Dragon* I've called it and it represents five years hard work in research and ancient languages. Until this story I've been sticking to character stuff just to avoid the danger of letting my plot do all the work as is so often the case in the historical romance. Now I hope to be off at last in my own field and if this falls flat I may as well fold up my wings and die for I do not intent to write sex stuff nor to do a series of *Viking Hearts*. My good friend Austin Bothwell tells me that at last I have done something better than *V.H.* so perhaps I may still hope. Sometimes I feel like a small David without a slingshot when I come up against my many enemies – mostly they are prepositions. Oh, the hateful little words! How many hours they have tormented me and how many times they have held up the whole show as it were. So you see I need time; but I mean to make good.

Sincerely
L.G. Salverson

1 *When Sparrows Fall* (1925) dealt with Icelandic and Norwegian settlement in a city resembling Duluth, Minnesota.

---

## To Laura Goodman Salverson

April 26, 1926

Dear Mrs. Salverson,

Thank you for your very kind letter. You are most sympathetic, and consequently understand pretty much what I am trying to do. For that I am grateful. But we evidently do not wholly know one another yet. You seem to be under the delusion that my taste is all for fierce realism, the sordid; whereas I am extremely idealistic, and dote on pleasant books. What I admire most of all is what I call artistic integrity, hence my devotion to *The Viking Heart*. As I saw it, you achieved a great reality because these things were very real to you, and you wrote of them with passion – a restrained passion, the more powerful in its restraint. For I believe in the law of indirections (my own name for it) by which what is in a writer gets out more effectively often if he tries to hold it back. I think you tried to write *V.H.* with utter simplicity, and unemotionally; and it came out as intense, throbbing drama. I think that whole book vital with the finest sort of idealism. When a writer sets out to write a beautiful book, he often overshoots and it becomes silly and mawkish. If his heart is pervaded with beauty, and he picks a sodden subject, the beauty will come out in spite of him. Nothing is sadder to me than a writer trying to be funny: the only humor worth while is that which comes of itself, cannot be repressed. To tell the truth I did not read your second novel entire. I can only read one book in 40 that reaches me, and I glanced through this and to me it looked weak and machine-made beside the other, so I did not go any farther. I have to be pretty eager to read a book before it is worth my while to do so, because so many big, important ones must go unread every week, and my readers suffer for my errors in judgment. Had I read it, I might have thought more highly of it than I did after half an hour with it. Pelham Edgar was severe with your poetry[1] – not at my suggestion, but with my silent approval. I do not think verse your proper medium. I am delighted to hear that you have a book you are proud of, also that you have sense enough not to try to repeat *V.H.* I am glad this new book deals with matters familiar to you and unfamiliar to most of the rest of us. If I may presume to give advice, always write out of your own particular knowledge, and from the heart. Do not imitate popular successes – that is if you want to create literature. Finally let me repeat what I have said so often in public, that your *Viking Heart* marks the beginning of a finer novel in Canadian literature, and if you never wrote any more your place would be secure. With best wishes –

1 'Four Books of Verse,' which contained Edgar's negative comments on Salverson's *Wayside Gleams* (1925), appeared in *Saturday Night*'s first Literary Section on 28 November 1925.

---

## From Francis Dickie

The Firs, Heriot Bay
British Columbia
September 22, 1926

My dear Deacon: –

Thanks very much for your letter and picture. I have been very unwell all summer, and put off writing you from day to day. But in view of possible radical change in my life, am going to write you fully.

As you know no writer in Canada has gone through more hardship and slaved and toiled more than I to write the worth while things I want to do, and at the same time live. Free lancing is the hardest game in the world, and doubly hard in Canada. I came out to the wilderness and hewed a place for myself, and I have got two big books written that satisfy me; as for the countless thousands of words of pot-boilers, well it was necessity. But I have at last reached a time when I must get out of the wilderness for a while at least, perhaps for ever. I do not know. Had it not been for my long illness dragging since last November and the consequent financial drain, I would have been in good shape to go along with my fiction. But I am forced to a change for the present. And so I plan to do the wildest thing of all: I expect to go to France, to Paris. I have very little money, but I have adventured before. If I go hungry in the end, well it will be no new thing. I believe the beauty, the art, the change of scene may stir me. I am telling you all this because you are a kindred spirit, one of the few I have met in Canada that feels for literature more than how much it will bring you. The beauty of a phrase, the cadence of words, a thought well said, awakes a responsive echo within you. So you will understand and feel with me in this moment of high adventure.

While I am there I will of course continue to write, and it occurred to me that in that world of art, of books and people, I will find many a paragraph that would fit in with your policy. Naturally, I will need to make all the money I can, and so I make the suggestion of sending you from time to time what I think would meet with your approval. Will you be interested in seeing it? It will give me courage to know.

I wish I could tell you all that I have gone through, and all my plans and dreams for worth while books. What a pity the great cash rewards go to wheat brokers etc. But there is no space now, and we have only one boat a week and I am perilously straining the time. You will consider this confidential, but as I expect to sail very soon, perhaps you will find time to write me by return mail. Rest assured anything I send you will be worth while; but that goes without saying. You didn't by any chance happen to see the *Haldeman/Julius Quarterly*[1] for October? They featured me. Have you seen a magazine in book form called *The American Parade*[2] ... good stuff. I don't have a chance to see the *Saturday Night*. Did you use something about me? Oh vanity, all is vanity, but I would like to have the clipping if it's not too late for you to find a copy.

Goodbye. If my Paris venture fail, and I don't feel like returning to the wilderness, perhaps you will see me in Toronto, if you do I know you'll extend the old kindly hand as you did to Tom Mac-

Innes and many another wanderer. I will say goodbye, old chap. Would you dare Paris with $300.00? What a game.

All this, I tell you, of course, for your secret heart.

Very sincerely
Francis Dickie

1 Founded and edited by Emanuel Haldeman-Julius (1889–1951), an American freethinker and writer. It was a forum in defence of atheism and materialism. Haldeman also began printing his famous 'Little Blue Books' in 1919 while editing this socialist weekly in Girard, Kansas.
2 *American Parade* was a quarterly edited by Haldeman-Julius, which merged with the *Haldeman/Julius Quarterly* in 1929; at various times before this, the editor used the two titles interchangeably.

---

## To Francis Dickie September 28, 1926

Dear Dickie,

I was very much touched with your writing me at this crisis in your career. Unfortunately I do not feel I know you well enough to advise definitely; but I know how suddenly these changes are apt to come about, and wish you good cheer and a brave heart in the experiment in Paris. I know what it is to step off the end of the plank, and not know where your foot is going to land. Sometimes I've struck rotten going, sometimes good; but – I'm still *going*. What conditions are in France I haven't the ghost of an idea; but God bless you, and may it be the turning point to success as my leaving law and coming to Toronto as a free lance writer in 1922 was the craziest and most successful move I ever made. Thank God you have no kids: your wife is able-bodied, and you can surely pick up a living. You are quite right in using every avenue and connection you can to get you revenue even if the jobs are tiny: one thing leads to another in writing more than in any other profession.

As far as *Saturday Night* goes, I have no say whatever in purchasing copy; if I had we might talk business as it would be useless to do in the present circumstances. For my regular Bookshelf page I must write my material not buy it. For the Literary Section, which appears infrequently, I am the main guy. In the copy I am sending you, you will see Sheila Rand's 'London Gossip.' That is to be an almost permanent feature. I cannot run one from Paris every time; and I do not want you to *copy* hers; but under 'A Letter from Paris' I could use a little stuff. Make it bright but not slangy. My suggestion is it shall not depend so much on anecdote as hers does, but take the form of a letter that I, or any other bookish person, would enjoy from a friend, a literary friend, in Paris. Make your first one 650 words long (*only*) and then we'll talk plans. It must be good, old man, even if you have to fall back on describing the bookshops along the Seine. If in doubt send me alternatives, or write overlength with clear indications of what paragraphs can be cut out so it will just fit 650. Of course I prefer you to know what is good and send me copy ready for the printer. I pay 1¢ a word only but I do pay; and $6.50 is a few meals, and that Section is good publicity for yourself. I want your first letter by November 10th, so I can get our artist Comfort[1] to do a heading. Then send me your Paris address as soon as you have one, and I'll try you out on book reviews from time to time. I'll send the books from here, and you follow instructions as to length of review and time to get article to me. This is not much but all I can offer definitely. But don't forget that essayette called 'A Letter from Paris' at 650 words neat.

I should think that you could pick up many an item that would suit Charlesworth,[2] but you will have to do that on spec. Remember this. Make your things as short as possible. 500 or 600 words have ten times the chance of acceptance that 1,000 or 1,200 has. For big stories 1,500 is our ideal length; nothing over 2,500 ever goes. Send illustrations wherever possible – one or at most two. But try to get hold of pithy things that you can boil down into the 500 word length. As soon as Charlesworth has accepted a few of these little ones he'll regard your longer efforts more favorably. Send them to him not me. Do not try to rival the cable news services.

I had intended the halftone of your study for the present Section, but later decided to use drawings only; so ran your photo in the regular Bookshelf.

1 Charles Fraser Comfort (b. 1900), Canadian artist who worked in commercial design (1925–38) and later served as Senior Combat War Artist (1943–6) and as Director of the National Gallery of Canada (1960–5). In the mid-1920s, he did pen-and-ink sketches at $1.00 each for Deacon's *Saturday Night* literary supplements.

2 Hector Willoughby Charlesworth (1872–1945), journalist, author, associate editor (1910–25), and then editor-in-chief (1925–32) of *Saturday Night*, and first chairman of the Canadian Radio Broadcasting Commission (1932–6)

From Lorne Pierce

233 Glen Grove Avenue West
Toronto
October 1, 1926

Dear Deacon:

I have just finished reading *Poteen* and wish to congratulate you on your book.

First: The book is well made, and again you are in luck.

Next I think you are striking a fine stride. Old friend *Pens & Pirates* I think is a better book, but your power is steadily growing. If you keep this up you will land into the group of essayists who must find mention in any future appraisal of our literature. If the sonnet is the touchstone of poetry, most assuredly the essay is the shibboleth to the fair land of prose.

I think you would have done well to leave out one or two. Whitman, for eg. and give him a go like your 'Carpenter' in a later vol.[1] Also 'Stringer.'[2] It is about the best lambasting I have seen done. It entirely pleases me – but in a book of essays, in this book, it doesn't seem to fit. You give the bounder too much immortality. Possibly also – 'Safe for Democracy.'[3] You could do this superbly in a longer article. You didn't touch the real high spots, besides there is something in making it 'safe' – at least for youngsters. In the unabridged authorized you have a hopeless tangle for a juvenile reader. Besides the miasma of words drives the majority of adults away. It is a case of comparative importance – and lust isn't supremely important.

You have mentioned my own name so frequently and so kindly that I would prefer saying no more. However I myself long for candid and pointed criticism. What I have said here is final and between friends.

Marjorie Pickthall died in Vancouver, and was 39 years old 1883–1922.

As I am contemplating a new ed. of *Our Can. Lit.* I would prize a suggestion from you, as to how it could be improved. How would you find its 'range'? 'Adequacy'? What 'peaks' are missing? This section is interesting to me. Garvin will buy you a silk hat for it, and, on the whole, what you say is quite true. Can. Lit. owes much to *Can. Poets.*

Your book deserves to be well and widely received. I covet for you increasing felicity in a magic realm where none but the royalty of letters may presume to enter.

Cum gratia
Lorne Pierce

1 The two essays in question are 'The Cult of Whitman' and 'Edward Carpenter: A Major Prophet.'
2 Arthur John Stringer, journalist, poet, and prolific popular writer, was the author of, among others, crime thrillers, the script for the American film *The Perils of Pauline* (1914), and the trilogy *The Prairie Wife, The Prairie Mother*, and *The Prairie Child* (1915–21). His sensational adventure tale of the Canadian North, *Empty Hands* (1924), was hilariously parodied by Deacon in 'What a Canadian Has Done for Canada,' an essay that first appeared in 'The Literary Review' of *The New York Evening Post* (19 July 1924) and was anthologized in *Poteen* (1926), published not by Ryerson but by Graphic Publishers of Ottawa.
3 'Making the Bible Safe for Democracy' deals with the efforts of Protestant fundamentalists to make the Bible respectable by expunging passages that might give offence to the innocent young reader.

---

## From Duncan Campbell Scott

108 Lisgar Street
Ottawa
October 1, 1926

My dear Deacon,

I have been enjoying my own copy of *Poteen*. Our new publishing firm[1] has made a nice book. I admire your lively & seemingly spontaneous style. You tell me you write with care & difficulty but one does not have that impression in the reading. I have always been a great admirer of Whitman and I approve of your essay. There is probably not a trace of his influence in my own work but long before I began to write Whitman had given me strength in the way you describe – I had most of *Leaves of G[rass]* by heart. Carpenter I don't know as well but of course I do appreciate his work. Your articles on our Literature are well done & will be useful. In the original meaning 'Poteen' is illegal stuff and the flavour & power of your brew is quite as stimulating as most unlawful things.

Many congratulations.

Yours truly
Duncan C. Scott

1 Established in 1924 as exclusively Canadian publishers, Graphic Publishers of Ottawa also printed Deacon's *The Four Jameses* (1927). Deacon corresponded extensively with them, urged the publication of F.P. Grove's *A Search for America* (1927), and supported the appointment of Grove as reader and adviser (1929–31). The firm went into receivership in May 1932 after having published approximately eighty Canadian books.

---

## To Duncan Campbell Scott October 4, 1926

Dear Dr. Scott,

It was characteristically thoughtful of you (a) to buy my book and, (b) write me such a flattering letter. It is doubly appreciated because to all intents and purposes you are the only surviving member of the Group of '61 who counts, and when our tradition is so short it is inspiring to know that you are watching, and friendly to our efforts. Lampman, Pauline Johnson[1] and Campbell are dead; Canon Scott[2] does not bulk very large; Roberts and Carman are mere shadows of their former selves, and have not only ceased to be producers but seem to be losing in personal prestige. You alone are active, and in possession of undiminished powers that I believe will not forsake you for 20 years to come. In a way you seem more of my generation than of theirs. I am awfully glad you have been so kind to Wilson [MacDonald]: it has meant a lot to him, and he was really worth it.

Between ourselves, I account for the non-setting of your sun by the fact that you have popularity still ahead of you. These others had their day, and have ceased to be: you have never had your day, and you won't cease to be until you have. That is coming, starting, I believe with the issue of your *Complete Poems* this fall, a book with which I am going to wrestle very seriously. Sometime this month my next semi-annual article will appear in the *Saturday Review of Literature* (N.Y.) and therein you will see how eagerly I look forward to having your works – at present I have only three or four odd volumes and your things in the anthologies – can't get your blinking stuff for love nor money. With this book, and the decline of your old partners, you should take the headship of Canadian letters. I think that will happen – tacitly. Wilson [MacDonald], I verily believe, is the greatest poet the country has yet produced, but he is like myself in the junior ranks, and no man for a leader anyway. To look to Roberts any longer is idle. Your big book coming at this time hastens recognition of a position that was yours anyway by force of gravity. And, if my opinion counts for anything, the leadership could not be in better hands – hands more kindly or freer from the deadening influence so often emanating from a senior writer whose prestige is dominant. As it is, we younger men need you very badly to keep an eye on us, and sort of hold the fort until we are entitled by experience to command ourselves. For myself, it will give me the greatest satisfaction to look to you as the chief and living symbol of Canadian literature for as many decades as you will be good enough to take an interest. Wilson in particular needs your steadying hand, and wise encouragement. I wish, too, you could find a way to urge Pratt to a higher type of creation than at present engrosses him. Of course I quite realize I haven't begun 'to write' yet. But I am grateful for the chance to get my hand in on this 'prentice work.

The Lampman article[3] I put in this week's paper today; and gave an advance copy to Musson as they wanted to quote me in their English advertising. May I thank you sincerely for the new figure you have made of him? And I shall keep that masterly 'Introduction' before me as a model when I am faced with similar jobs.

As to the modus operandi of *Poteen* – the first draft of 2 of them, 'Annexation' and 'Censorship,' were dashed off at a sitting each, as fast as my pen would work; but the rest was hammered out a word at a time as usual, and even in the first 2 pieces polishing and revision went on steadily right up to the page proof stage. But I must not keep you listening all day. Thank you again. Rest assured that no compliment I can receive will mean as much to me as your letter.

Sincerely and respectfully –

1 Popular Canadian poet (1862–1913) who impressed late Victorian audiences with her Mohawk presence onstage during years of touring Canada and England

2 Frederick George Scott (1861–1944), Anglican clergyman and romantic poet whose work was sometimes associated with the Confederation group. He was the father of the poet F.R. Scott (1899–1985).

3 'The Enhanced Lampman,' Deacon's review of *Lyrics of Earth*, edited and introduced by Scott, appeared in *Saturday Night* on 9 October 1926.

## To Lorne Pierce

October 5, 1926

Dear Pierce,

Many and heartfelt thanks for your kind letter approving of *Poteen*. In the circumstances your interest is doubly appreciated.

Your suggestions are valuable, especially in the matter of leaving out material, because you know it is my plan to carry forward the better things into later collections and pitch out the weak or merely timely items. At present, there is something in here to annoy everybody and it is amazing just what is pleasing who. E.g. Duncan Campbell Scott wrote me a warm note saying he was particularly struck by the Whitman piece, which he thought perfect, or words to that effect. I put in the Carpenter with diffidence, expecting to be reviled as a lunatic, but out of a sense of personal indebtedness to Carpenter – I did it out of loyalty; and behold – many folks like it! ... Apart from everything else, the book was shuffled together in somewhat of a hurry.

Thanks for correcting me on Miss Pickthall's age. Will have this changed in the third edition – the second is already on the press, and so we are too late to do anything at the moment.

As to *Our Can. Lit.*, I am in a difficult position, because the matter is extremely delicate. What I do not like is the Watson influence – the sweet and innocuous being preferred to the virile. You, alone, would not have picked what he influenced you to pick. I know, for example, that you think as I do that Callaghan's 'Golden Dagger' is the biggest thing, the best thing, in *The Reed and the Cross*;[1] and yet you and Watson put in your anthology some pretty verse about a violet or some bluebells or something tame. Of course, if you are aiming at the schools, you have taken the wise course; but if you are aiming to make the best Can. anthology for man's use, I'd try for sterner stuff. And then, when you have so little space, should Callaghan be in at all? Perhaps, but I'm darn sure Jimmy MacDonald[2] holds no such place in Can. Lit. as to entitle him to position, even if he has done some nice verses. Garvin pulls some awful bones, puts in some trash; but he gets some forceful things too, and Dr. Watson was not the right man to guide you to the forceful and compelling – the strong. Of course I do not imply there are not good *and suitable* things in your anthology; but just the same, you'll make a better one all by yourself. The steady improvement from edition to edition has been gratifying – and instructive.

Best wishes –

1 Francis Callaghan (b. 1902), minor lyric poet; Deacon had met him through theosophy in Winnipeg and wrote a foreword to *The Reed and the Cross* (Ryerson 1923), praising 'the rare music of his lyrics, and the genuinely Celtic skill of his cadenced lines.'
2 Deacon is confusing the name – John J. MacDonald – and pseudonym – James MacRae – of one of Canada's 'dear bad poets,' celebrated in *The Four Jameses* (1927).

---

## From Duncan Campbell Scott

Deputy Superintendent General of Indian Affairs
[Ottawa]
October 20–25, 1926

My dear Deacon,

I was sorry not to be at the P.E.N[1] Dinner but I found it quite impossible to leave; my Minister[2] is going West tomorrow and there is much to arrange. I was touched by yr ltr of Octr 4.

I am interested in you & Wilson & Pratt and the young men who are doing something just as I am in modern art in general. My mind keeps its eager curiosity of youth and I have never felt predisposed against new ideas or forms. In dealing with the group of writers born circa 1860 – I notice a tendency to establish a formal association of the individuals with the acknowledged head of C.G.D.R. This idea is quite erroneous. We were living far apart – A.L. & I were here & W.W.C also. After a time A.L.'s association with C.G.D.R. was not close. In the early days they corresponded and Roberts was at all times helpful & enthusiastic over anything that was done by any of us. But there was no acknowledged chieftainship nor was there any assumption of such a position by Roberts. I don't like to see this notion hardening into a tradition. We were working then as we are working now, far apart. That is the curse of our literary life, if we can be said to have one. All the aids that come with association and all the immense help that flows from an established tradition are wanting and our country is so huge &

unformed that we may never have them. But we shall have to keep on, and get what we can out of life & transmute & transfigure it as we are able. I have many plans in my head which I hope to be able to work out. Invention is not quite dead yet & the old tree may continue to bear fruit, a sort of November crop, you know. Our present day of rain & sodden leaves makes one think of November and the close of the year. I have just written a line to our Wilson MacDonald not particular or discursive but very much to the point. I may be in T- on Nov. 1–2 at the King Ed.

Yours ever truly,
Duncan C. Scott

1 Acronym ('poets, editors, novelists') for the pacifist, London-based international writers' association created in 1921 by Amy Dawson Scott

2 The Honourable Charles Stewart was Minister of the Interior, Mines, and Indian Affairs in the cabinet of Mackenzie King from September 1926 to June 1930.

---

## From B.K. Sandwell

42 Saint Mark Street
Montreal
January 14, 1927

Dear Deacon:

Who is Morley Callaghan, who has a piece of prose in the last *This Quarter* (the esoteric art magazine in Paris) on the life of a burlesque chorus-girl in Toronto, and is there described as a resident of Toronto who has not hitherto published? Was there not a Callaghan who did a highly temperamental book of young verse?[1] Anyhow, this chorus-girl thing is worth looking into. 'Re-Joyce greatly, ye daughters of Erin.'

My mind is again working freely, and my body fairly so.

It is not true that E.J. Pratt is the whole spirit of Canadian poetry. He is the Pratt's Motor Spirit. (See ads in *Punch*.) ... My love to Hector-Apollos[2] ('Paul planted, Apollos watered, but the Lord giveth the increase' – I quote from memory, my Bible being in storage in Kingston.) ... Send me a book to review.

Yours for Can-Lit.
B.K.

1 Sandwell is confusing the novelist Morley Callaghan (b. 1902) with the poet Francis Callaghan.
2 Hector Charlesworth

---

## From Wilson MacDonald

January 29, 1927
80 Granville Street
c/o Andrew Merkel

Dear Bill:

I have suffered terribly with my stomach and teeth during this trip and my correspondence is away behind.

I had 800 to hear me in Wolfville and the largest audience of the season in Truro.

I told Andy[1] to send you the clippings which I suppose he did.

I attacked Bush's[2] article in *The Dalhousie Review* and The Kings students roared when I pointed out mistake after mistake in this ass's construction of sentences.

In one place he says: 'his illusions were partly those of optimism, partly those of a scientist.'

If that isn't mixing 'metaphors' I don't know what is.

In the first sentence of the article there is a mistake in English.

Mrs. Tufts[3] was glorious. Andy Merkel is just what you described him to be – a good fellow when sober but he is terribly quarrelsome when drunk.

McMechan told his class he wouldn't cross the road to hear me and then said 'sleight of hand.'

Then when the hypocrite saw how everyone else in Halifax was receiving me he arranged a big reception for me at his home and I refused point blank to go and my refusal had all Halifax laughing.

I find a lot of bitterness here toward *Saturday Night* front page but you are held in high esteem.

Dr. MacFarlane of Dalhousie English Dept. has been loyal. He told me he marvelled at my long-suffering and said 'I would have punched Roberton for an article like the one in *The Free Press*.'

The girls in the province are the finest anywhere. I will have a lot to tell you on my return and sometimes grow lonesome for a chat with you.

With love to yourself and
Mrs. Deacon
Wilson

P.S. Enclosed find cheque for bills. W.M.

1 Andrew Doane Merkel (1886–1954), poet and Atlantic chief of the Canadian Press, to which he belonged from its formation in 1917 to his retirement in May 1946. He wrote volumes of historical verse, including *The Order of Good Cheer* (1946), and was a prominent member of the Song Fishermen, a Halifax-based club for amateurs of poetry.
2 Douglas Bush (1896–1983) was educated at the University of Toronto and Harvard (PHD 1923), and was at this time an English instructor at Harvard. 'Charles W. Eliot, of Harvard,' in *The Dalhousie Review* for January 1927, may have angered MacDonald because he still smarted from Bush's incidental derogatory comments about his verse in 'Making Literature Hum,' *The Canadian Forum* (December 1926), an article criticizing the CAA and Canadian Book Week for stressing quantity before quality.
3 Evelyn Tufts (née Smith), a native of Truro, Nova Scotia, was the wife of ornithologist Robie Tufts of Wolfville, NS. She wrote book reviews for the Halifax *Herald* and later was its Ottawa correspondent, becoming a life member of the Parliamentary Press Gallery. One of Deacon's favourite correspondents, she also wrote reviews for his literary section, characteristically preferring Joyce's *Ulysses* to Salverson's Viking romances.

---

## To Wilson MacDonald February 3, 1927

Dear Wilson:

I am happy to have your letter of the 29th, and know you have been well received in Eastern Canada. Mrs. Tufts wrote me how much they enjoyed your visit in Wolfville. Virginia cried all the way back from the station after you had left. If you have a minute, write them a letter – just a note.

Your account of the MacMechan contretemps was delightful: both of you acted entirely in character; and the comedy was rich. Of course you have made a lifelong enemy of the Professor. Nobody would forgive you for being made ridiculous over the rejection of a social invitation. Your habit of 'getting even' is amusing; but you must lay a good deal of the opposition to you to just such tricks.

Mrs. Tufts tells me that you think I should have attacked Roberton for his article about you. Attack him yourself, Son: In the first place it's not my funeral. In the second, he was equally nasty to me – possibly worse. And lastly, Brother, there isn't one case in a hundred where an author gains anything by 'going after' a reviewer. When we publish books, we've got to be prepared for a certain amount of punishment – some of it unjust, just as some of the praise is unjust – and the best thing to do about it is forget it. If you are not prepared for a good deal of abuse, don't publish books – especially books that matter.

What I am really writing you about is to give you a friendly piece of advice, if I may presume that far. As soon as your really important lectures are over in Nova Scotia, come home. Don't stick around waiting for little third class engagements. You go as a celebrity: everybody rushes to see the celebrity. Appear; collect your money; and disappear; so leaving the road open to return in a year or two years and repeat the whole thing with bigger crowds, etc. When you stay week after week in a section of the country, you lose for all time the glamor of the illustrious visitor. Just think this over, and don't repeat the mistakes of others. Familiarity with a good man does not breed contempt; but it takes away the burning desire to pay $1 to look at him.

I am deep into work on the March Literary Section, and having, as usual, the devil's own time making everything come out even. Do you want any space? Or will you be back in time to look after it?

I was talking to Frank McDowell[1] of the C.N.R. today and he wants you to read 'Muskoka' over the Radio, and me to introduce you. He wants to know when you will be back. I don't imagine there is any fee in it; but it is mighty good publicity, and if I were you I should like to stand in well with that Road, without too much thought of cashing in hastily on the friendship. Incidentally this radio reading is linked up with something else McDowell and I have in mind for the joint benefit of the three of us, but which I don't want to go into in a letter. Just don't turn it down till you are back and we've gone over it a bit.

Wishing you all luck,

P.S. Of course don't budge if you have something well worth staying for. But it would have to be mighty good to compensate you for staying a long time in one small city, which will inevitably have the effect of lengthening the time before you are invited there again as the prize ox at substantial fees.

W.A.D.

1 Franklin Davey McDowell (1888–1965) was the author of *The Champlain Road* (1939), an historical romance about the destruction of the Jesuit Huron mission,

which won the Governor-General's Award for fiction. As a CNR publicity man, McDowell helped provide railway passes for touring authors.

---

## From Francis Dickie

permanent address:
c/o The Canadian High Commissioner
Paris
Villa Nelle
St. Jean Cap-Ferrat
Alpes Maritimes
April 18, [1927]

Dear Deacon: –

Your letter reached me just the day before I left Paris, and warmed my heart. You don't know how much your splendid comradeship has cheered me in these last months when ill-health, depression born of overwork has made life so great a battle. I am glad you liked the stuff from Paris. With me it was largely a question of selection of what to send you there is so much.

Paris is a marvellous place, but the winter was unusually long this year, and unusually bad. And I worked very hard to no very great effect, I am afraid, though time will tell. I had quite a few interesting meetings. Sherwood Anderson had dinner with me one night, and spent the evening in my apartment, and I met a number of painters of talent. But I really shouldn't have been working at all, and finally I went to a specialist who told me to get out of Paris for awhile, if I valued my health. A friend of mine, Lyon Mearson, formerly managing editor of MacFadden's True Romances, has a villa near Monte Carlo, and had invited us down. So we left Paris on the 10th. And so here I am this Monday morning sitting on the terrace with the Mediterranean at my feet, the bay of Nice just around the corner, Monte Carlo seven miles on the other side. Last week we went to the Russian Ballet held in the theatre of the Casino at Monte Carlo, and between the acts I played roulette. Plenty of color. Just beyond where I am staying, Somerset Maugham has his magnificent villa, and Frank Harris lives six miles away at Nice. He is a friend of mine host, and Harris comes often. He is coming this week to dinner, so I will have a chance to talk all evening with one of the outstanding figures in modern literature. In the meantime I have been reading the first two volumes of his Autobiography,

*My Life and Loves.* It will rank in the annals of Anglo-Saxon literature as the most unique of autobiographies. It is unlike anything you ever read or even dreamed of. It treats of sex as no writer in any language has ever done. Rabelais and Brantome are Sunday school yarns. Quite aside from the sex, however, it is a remarkable story. Harris has known everybody that was anybody in the literary and financial life of Europe in the last fifty years.

I am glad you liked the Napoleon story. I spent a day in the Rodin museum in Paris recently. Words fail really to do justice to it. Some of his things moved me more than even the great works of the ancient Greeks in the Louvre.

I have a copy of Joyce's *Ulysses.* But it is hard reading. I don't know whether I am going to like it or not. I feel there are a thousand things I could write you, but already the day is half fled, and I must get along.

Thanks for your advice about the October issue. I will send you a story about 1st of September. Perhaps a review of Harris' two books might interest you.

I met Madge Macbeth in Paris. We had dinner together a couple of times. She went on to Rome. Frank Packard[1] came into Paris just a couple of days before I left. But I do not know him personally, and as nothing he has ever written appealed to me, I did not bother looking him up. I am afraid that is rather snobbish, is it not?

Did I tell you in my last letter that Hodder & Stoughton were bringing out a book of short stories of mine? I told them to send you advance copy. As for art, for writing, well I don't know, Deacon: You know those words of Baudelaire:

> To bear so vast a load of grief, thy courage Sisyphus, I crave,
> My heart against the task is brave,
> But art is long and time is brief!

And writing worth while things leads not to dollars.

And when you see the people promenading on the Boulevard des Anglais at Nice, and Monte Carlo, you marvel at it all, particularly me, who had just come from wandering around some of the worst streets in Paris where life crawls so thickly you can hardly move on the sidewalks, and life that is so pitifully poor!

Goodbye, for just now. I am afraid this is a horribly hit or miss, incoherent sort of letter, but it comes from my tired heart, such as it is. I have no plans. With best regards.

Very, very sincerely
Francis Dickie

1 Frank Lucius Packard (1877–1942), Canadian author of popular thrillers

---

## To Kate Ruttan[1] June 10, 1927

Dear Mrs. Ruttan,

I am very much interested in your father's poetry but have not been able to find out anything about him except that he was a successful cheese manufacturer, and prominent in the Liberal Party. Miss Janet C. McKellar, Librarian of Ingersoll, kindly suggested that you might be good enough to supply me with a little information about his life. I hope this is not asking too much, and enclose a few questions together with stamped self-addressed envelope for your convenience. If there is anything further you care to tell me about your Father, I shall be greatly obliged.

For many years I have made a study of the work of Canadian writers, and am now trying to collect full and accurate information about the lives of our older poets, as I fear if this is not done now it may be next to impossible to obtain proper records in another fifty years, or even in less time.

Thanking you for your kind help, I am,

Sincerely yours,

1 The irrepressible and eccentric daughter of an equally irrepressible and eccentric father – James McIntyre (1827–1906), the celebrated 'cheese poet' of Ingersoll, Ontario – Kate Ruttan (1858?–1928) was a poet and retired school teacher living at LaVallee, Rainy River District, Ontario. The author of *Rhymes, Right or Wrong, of Rainy River* (1926), she was consulted by Deacon for biographical information about McIntyre for *The Four Jameses* (1927). Deacon's humorous tribute to the four worst poets of Canada – James Gay, James McIntyre, James D. Gillis, and James MacRae – was first published by Graphic Press in 1927. A Canadian classic, it was republished by Ryerson in 1953 and by Macmillan in 1974.

## From Kate Ruttan

La Vallee, Ontario
June 20, 1927

Dear Mr Deacon,

I herewith enclose my original poems.[1] Two years ago I took tenders from Lindsay Warder for Six Hundred & something doll. & from Orillia *Times* for Five Hundred Dol. per thousand. I accepted Orillia *Times* at $500 per M. I am sold out nearly. I travelled 3 mos. last winter among my scholars of Auld Lang Syne a selling same. I could not sell many more but as a widow & orphan & daughter of Jas. McIntyre 40 yr's a Free Mason & 50 yr's an Odd Fellow & Caledonian Bard to boot, I wish you would make me an offer to publish another, M or 500 you selling the books to Odd Fellow & Masonic Lodges & paying me for the privilege in cash. Of course they would have to be published under my own name Kate McIntyre Ruttan. I can not furnish any money to publish same, but you give me the fame, & sell the same, to your Masons & Odd Fellows.

Do please make me an offer, & publish some of my poems in your *Saturday Night*, especially my verses on my dear dead daddy. Here's one to Winnipeg *Tribune*, who were always hauling him over the coals & he 21 yr's beneath the sod.

> Kate McIntyre Ruttan in her Daddy's Defence.
> Let him rest, a worthy Briton
> Why should you his poor corpse sit on
> Why should you discharge your wit on,
> His true tetrameter,
> He had the sparrrk o' nature's fire,
> Whilk Scottish poets a' desire,
> Poetic license ruled his lyre,
> And heart's diameter.

Have you a kind Christ like notion to advertise me in *Saturday Night*, & publish my book for you to sell.

Please make me an offer quick – how much you will give me for privilege of printing it & you to sell it for your selves, *but* must be under my own name, Kate McIntyre Ruttan, to give *Me* the *fame.* I would not give up *my* claim to the fame for a million of money.

I don't mind telling you my daddy's age &c but always remember, Ladies do not like to be reminded & the vote is no good to them for they won't own they're old enough to vote till they're too old & too feeble to travel to the polls.

Write quickly & fully. Some of my references are to Dr Marion,[2] Ottawa. Jas. Mathieu M.P.P. Toronto or Fort Frances, Ont. Peter Heenan, Ottawa (Minister of Labor). Dr D.C. McKenzie, Fort Frances. Editor Elliott, Times, Fort Frances, Ont. W.H. Clarke, Campaign Manager, Fort Frances, Ont. Wm Pilkey, Clerk of the Court, Fort Frances, Ont. Bank of Commerce, Fort Frances, Ont.

Kate McIntyre Ruttan

1 *Rhymes, Right or Wrong, of Rainy River* (1926) published by The Times Printing Company of Orillia, Ontario
2 Séraphin Marion (b. 1896), author and archivist, at this time French editor at the Public Archives of Canada (1926–53)

---

## From Kate Ruttan

1927 JUN 21 PM 8:46
LAVALLEE ONT

WA DEACON

EDITOR SATURDAY NIGHT TORONTO ONT

DO NOT PUBLISH YEAR OF BIRTH HE WAS UNIVERSALLY BELOVED DIED 1906 HIS FACTORYS FOUNDATION FELL FROM THAMES TORRENT COFFINS CASKETS CARD TABLES PIANOS PIANOLAS BEDS BUNKS ETC SAILED DOWN RIVER THAMES WILL WRITE TONIGHT AWAIT MY LETTER BURNT UP FLOODED DOWN KATE RUTTAN.

---

## From Kate Ruttan

La Vallee, Ontario
Rainy River District
[21 June 1927]

Dear Deacon,

We do not say Mister Shakspeare, Mister Byron, Mister Bobbie Burrrrrns, Mister Cow-per &c, so why do you allow a plebian patronymic in front of your noble name. You're the 3rd or 4th

Ecclesiastic in the realm. 1. Pope. 2. Archbishop. 3. Bishop. 4th. Deacon. Say was there once a clever 'Model' man in our Ingersoll School. 'Be' you this Model master or be you or be-est thee a boy of he? Say please don't publish date of Daddy's *birth*. It will hurt me very much. But you can say he died in 1906 (just 21 yr's ago). Say, don't be in a hurry. I can get a wonder acc. of his life inside a week. Also he was the bright & shining star of Ingersoll Literary Society, attended a Night School for Elocution, & taught (unofficially,) the boys, how to 'spout.' 'Spout' was his own word for 'declaiming or elocution or harangue.' One morn at six he heard the crack of doom & the crash of worlds. His 3 story steam furniture factory fell, (note 3 f's). 'Apt alliterations artful aid.' Foundation of furniture factory fell & sailed down to River Thames. Coffins, caskets, cupboards, card tables, chairs, pianos, pianolas – all commingled in confusion worse confounded. Also he was previously burned out. He wrote me his true townsmen collected Six Hundred Dollars for him that mournful morn. He was the loveliest man on earth.

Can you make me a good offer to publish my poems – under my own name? as I have not one dollar left for the purpose, but wish you to publish same paying me a generous cash price & giving me the *fame of my own name*. I should think at your royal instigation. Freemasons (he was forty years one) & Odd fellows (he was fifty years one & drew his last breath in Sanitarium as he was being presented in Town Hall with Illuminated Address for his 50th Anniversary of same) should do something wonderful for me & make me their mascot.

Please write at once & write fully.
'Great Expectations.'

In the depths
Kate Ruttan

---

## To E.J. Pratt

August 25, 1927

Dear Ned,

What have you got in the way of a short poem that would do in the Literary Section? Something not less than eight lines, and not over sixteen – with twelve preferred if in three quatrains, or fourteen or sixteen if without breaks for stanzas? Four quatrains is about the limit in length. Of course one or two lines can often be adjusted typographically. I can tell better when I see the material. I just give you these lengths to suggest that I want something to fill a space about what a sonnet would need in type, though, other things equal, I should not choose a poem in sonnet form.

Your various friends, including your publisher,[1] have been telling me about your long poem, 'The Iron Door,' that is to appear in book form this autumn. Why did you not mention it to me? If you do not want me to know what you are doing, I shall immediately assume ignorance again, and not mention it in any way – and excuse me for being aware of it. But I was thinking: Is there not in that somewhere a passage of a dozen lines or so that might be lifted out and published as a fragment in the Section in advance of the book? It would be a good announcement for the book. There would be just enough of it to rouse anticipation, not enough to satisfy curiosity. Of course I have not seen this poem; but from general familiarity with long poems I should guess that there must be somewhere in it some passage that would suit my present needs, and might, at a pinch, stand alone.

If not, what else have you? As you know I have always wanted you to submit something; and now, in view of your various books and coming trip west, I feel it is the right moment for you to appear in the sacred pages as poet. What have you?

Bearing in mind your lecture trip, I am not sure that you desire to do a review this time; and have not laid a book aside for you. If I am wrong, tell me. If you cannot or will not let me have appropriate verse, I fear I shall have to ask you to do a review, because I want you in there in some capacity; and if you want to do both, and have time for the review also, I do not see that using a poem in the same issue necessarily debars you as a critic.

Please let me know at once, and speak your mind freely. Love to Vi and Claire –

1 *The Iron Door* was published by Macmillan in 1927.

From E.J. Pratt

Bobcaygeon, Ontario
August 27, 1927

My dear Billy,

Your letter came this afternoon and I greatly appreciate your kindness and consideration. It was your good old self that was writing. I have been looking into some short poems to select one for your supplement but most of them possess a tragic cast that would unfit them for your bright columns. You remember I submitted a few of them last year and you decided quite rightly – with my concurrence – that they were somewhat too sombre. I intend, in the future, (this of course as the mood strikes me) to indulge the lighter lyrical moments. I am, however, submitting one called 'Cherries' not yet published in any form, nor offered for publication, but read at my recital last winter, which might fit in, but I am not sure of the length of its lines and stanzas as being adjustable to your space. If it does not so fit, feel perfectly at ease in sending it back, as I will understand.

I would like to deal with 'The Iron Door' at some length. You remember in a couple of conversations last spring, once in a walk down to your office, and again at a dinner with Burpee[1] that I had in mind the construction of a poem different from anything I had ever done. The theme came to me at the time of my mother's death last December. It originated in a dream where my mother, who was a woman of the profoundest faith in the life to come, was standing before a colossal door – the door of Death – and expecting without any fear of denial whatsoever, instant and full admission into the future state where she believed other members of her family had already entered. This was the nucleus of the poem. From there I elaborated it into a general conception of the problem of Immortality, starting with the feeling of despair and apparent inevitability which faces one at a grave-side. That is, from a particular experience, I tried to universalize the idea. In front of the door are gathered a vast multitude and a number of individuals emerge who present their cases to the unseen warders, or god or the governor of the Universe whoever he may be, demanding some information of what is going on, on the other side. All but one – the last – are drawn from persons I had known in life. The last one, to my mind, sums up the problem, partly biological, partly environmental, of injustice and inequality in the moral order, and she presents the case in its glaring enigma.

The first case is that of the naive simplicity of a child who relies upon a father to unravel the knots. The second is that of a rugged seaman who with a stark sense of justice asks the 'unknown admiral' if the great traditions of the service might be fairly assumed to prevail on the washes of the hinter sea, if such a sea might be assumed to exist. There is no cringing in this attitude whatsoever; he feels he has the right to ask and to demand it. The third – that of my own mother – represents a large number of people who believe implicitly in the essential soundness of the heart of the Universe and who impute to God only the same fair principles which they realize in their own honest natures. The next is a young man who gave up health and prime and life in a futile attempt to save an unknown life when there was not a human eye to stimulate or encourage the sacrifice. Then two more speak. One a searcher after beauty in all its forms in this life who is puzzled that Death should apparently negate the value of the quest; and another, a searcher after truth – a Hardyesque type (or Bertrand Russell type) – who meets with disillusion at the end, yet exhibits a noble stoicism when faced with what looks like extinction. Then comes the last with the most poignant and tragic appeal.

In order to make the psychological contrast as sharp as possible I put in a stanza or rather section describing the desolation of the world at this point – to give edge and relief to what follows. To my mind it would be a cardinal artistic and moral blunder to end it in complete gloom. The setting I think requires the conclusion, but I did not feel, on the other hand, that the requirements would be met by anything like a conventional heaven, harps or angels or such outworn paraphernalia. The only demand I make is that there shall be life and light with continued life effort on the other side. Hence I never see inside the door. I only judge by the reflection of the faces of human beings and by certain sounds which intermittently break through, that there are vast stretches beyond. I do not aim at solutions. I only wanted to give an imaginative and emotional interpretation of what I feel myself because I have never done anything which put the same compulsion on me for expression. I do not know if I thoroughly succeeded. I simply wrote as I felt.

The reasons why I did not give you more details on any scheme are vaguely these. I only finished it a few days before I left for Bobcaygeon, that is in its entirety. The general conception was submitted to Macmillans who decided that they would publish it on the first draft. A few of my friends were interested in it and asked for a reading which I gave. They were somewhat enthusiastic about it and urged immediate publication with some changes of lines etc. I did not hand it to you at the time – though I would dearly love to have done so – because of a natural reticence against appearing to influence a reviewer and I know how you must be embarrassed with authors coming to your office in advance of publication. I wanted you to make up your own judgment independently and I am writing this tonight because of your kindly interest expressed in your letter today. I had a very few typed copies, two of which went to the publisher's. In fact this one which I now send to you is the only one I have left and I gladly give it to you. The poem is in the galleys and I am not in immediate need of it. As for a section in the Supplement, I scarcely think a dozen lines could be taken out independently, though if some introduction could be given the sections from – *And at this darkest moment as I dreamed* to 'how lights & shadows leaped upon the dial' might conveniently be inserted. This of course at your own discretion.

Regarding the itinerary the developments are these. Nearly all the Canadian Club branches have ratified the arrangements of the Executive, though I am not yet in possession of the completed programme with dates etc. That will be in a few days and I can let you have a copy. I start on the 11th of September beginning with Chapleau, going to Keewatin, Winnipeg, Edmonton, Olds, Calgary, Revelstoke, Vancouver, Victoria, Kamloops, Moose Jaw, back to Winnipeg and other towns intervening & the trip is exclusively under the sponsorship of the Can. Club though in some cases the Authors' Branches have cooperated. The C.P.R. made out the itinerary and have granted transportation both for myself and Vi. I get back the first week in October. It is a poetry recital (my own).

So that's that, old boy. I expect to be in Toronto about the 6th and will see you.

The book appears sometime in late September in two editions, a limited autographed of 100 copies selling at 2.50 and a trade of 1.25. 1000 copies.

With best to yourself, Sal & family from Vi & me.

Ned Pratt.

P.S. The rush in September will probably prevent me from reviewing a book for the Section but I will be ready for the next one if you wish it.

N.

1 Lawrence J. Burpee (1873–1946) was a historian, anthologist, and secretary (1912–46) for Canada of the International Joint Commission, a Canadian-American regulatory body established in 1909 to arbitrate disputes involving land and water boundaries along the common frontier of the two countries. He is primarily remembered for his book on the history of exploration in Canada, *The Search for the Western Sea* (1908).

---

## To B.K. Sandwell November 14, 1927

Dear Sandwell,

Wilson MacDonald, whom Merrill Denison has aptly named the world's most imperfect guest, will be with you on Thursday; and it may be as well to forewarn you. In a sense you will be held responsible for his atrocities, and you will naturally hold me responsible for not telling you so here goes.

He is an anti-prohibition fanatic. He likes a good drink of strong liquor, but he only takes one on an occasion, one per diem.

Though himself approaching 50 years of age, he objects to associating with older people – particularly women. He does not like to associate with married people, particularly married women. That is why he hasn't been at my house in years. He desires to be perpetually surrounded by virgins from 16 to 21 years of age, and they must be pretty. He can relish a dozen to twenty of these at a time. Fear not. He will not copulate with them, but simply likes to play around with pretty girls – very much his inferiors in age and brains. The ideal entertainment is a dance at which only the undeflowered are present, and he is the only male.

He is a strict vegetarian.

He objects to everything that is set before him in the way of food – particularly dainties, and tells you how bad they are for you to eat, and what a healthful diet consists of and how well he can cook. (He does, in fact, everything well – he is the best tennis-player, skier, skater, poet, dramatist, piano player, watch-repairer etc., ad infin.)

His pet antipathy just now is Roberton of the Wpg. *Free Press* who knocked his book (I admit the article was spiteful and unfair) but still if you don't want a tirade of 3 hours keep off critics and reviewers.

Underneath it all he is a most sweet and lovable chap; only until one knows all his prejudices getting on with him for even a few hours is an almost unbearable strain. I speak as his best friend. I curse him out every six months or so and vow never to speak to him again, but I always do. He's a dear soul, who has lived too much to himself, that's all. I don't say it is up to you to provide either the one drink or the 20 virgins, but guessed you might be preparing some little treat, and it would be as well not to have it consist in a platter of roast pork with a 250 pound matron to talk to him while he eats.

Treat him as you like. I have just warned you. Step easy, and don't contradict him, even when he insists the moon is made of green cheese –

---

## From Charles G.D. Roberts

The Marlborough
Winnipeg
April 27, 1928

My dear Deacon –

I have just heard from Gerald Wade & Allison that you are leaving *Saturday Night*. I feel that it is a calamity. The loss to *Saturday Night* I consider incalculable. And unless you speedily find another suitable vehicle for the expression of your personality, the loss to Canadian literature will be very grave. I feel rather dismayed.

Every warmest good wish to you.

Ever yours
Charles G.D. Roberts[1]

I expect to be back at the good old Ernescliffe about the 3rd or 4th, & shall hope to see you right speedily.

1 Deacon's friendship with the Confederation poet (1860–1943) began after Roberts's return to Canada from Europe in 1925, from which time he reigned in Toronto as 'the father of Canadian literature.' He undertook a trans-Canada tour in 1925, was awarded the first Lorne Pierce Medal in 1926, and was knighted in 1935.

It was with Roberts in mind that Deacon urged and supported the creation of the Canadian Writers' Foundation in 1931.

---

## To Charles G.D. Roberts April 30, 1928

My dear Roberts,

It was most generous of you to write me from Winnipeg, particularly when you imagined me hard hit. As a matter of fact I am not quite as helpless, nor my prospects quite as hopeless, as is thought in certain quarters. I admit readily I am no millionaire, and I have to re-establish myself; but that, I think, is within the bounds of possibility. When I see you we can go into things more fully.

*Saturday Night*'s loss, as you are good enough to term it, is *Saturday Night*'s concern, and none of mine. I haven't one minute to worry over their fortunes, nor any feeling in the matter.

Unfortunately your note from Vancouver came in too late for me to get mention in the paper of the conclusion of your course. Naturally I would have liked to note this historic event, but this felicity was not permitted me. And as you were en route I could not reply to tell you the circumstances.

Trusting you have had a pleasant time, and signal success as well; and thanking you sincerely for this welcome token of your good will, I remain,

Faithfully yours,

---

## From Georges Bugnet[1]

Lac Majeau
Alberta
January 30, 1930

Dear Sir,

Your article on my book *Nipsya* just reached me. – (No, I do not live, and never lived, in Quebec, save for a few days.)

So far, you are the only one who gives me (in the first part of your study) some kind of explanation why *Nipsya* may be compared with *Maria Chapdelaine*.

Louis Hémon's masterpiece fell into my hands when I was writing the last part of *Nipsya*. Then, I had to murder poor Bonhomme

LaJeunesse. Why? Because, in *Maria Chapdelaine*, I found the long drawn illness of the old lady getting a little tiresome. It gave me the idea to try and do better. By the way, the *real* Bonhomme (81 years old) had really and recently died (pneumonia, too) and **he did walk** to his bed twenty minutes before his death. In my book, I did not insist on the twenty minutes. Life, in books, to be accepted as 'life as it is' must not be too accurately true to facts.

Outside of this plain case of murder, Hémon came too late to influence me. Of course, I noticed that, having chosen a somewhat similar phase in Canadian life, we accidentally spoke of the same things, as many other authors meet. When I read *your* comparison I perceived the deeper analogies. Your judgement, I think, is fairly sound.

For all that, my opinion is that *Maria Chapdelaine* is far above *Nipsya*. It has the best mark of genius: greatness and simplicity.

Can critics be criticized? – My book a product of imagination because Mabigan had never seen such a display of *red* northern lights? – Well, I have lived in Mabigan's country since 1905. I happened to be one of the very few who saw such a display (in November 1918 – may have been the signature of the armistice in the skies). Most Albertans have never seen one. But we have plenty of the usual and some of the unusual kind (see *Nipsya* again).

Re the historic side, we Westerners would welcome a little more sympathy from our Eastern fellow-citizens. Western history has, so far, been written mostly by Easterners with prejudiced minds. An impartial historian will never use the words: Riel rebellion. – Riel was not a rebel. Was he an 'insurgent'? Even this is debatable. Our grandsons will call him a great patriot, a misunderstood genius.

As to the soundness of judgment on the part of the Métis, I wish an Easterner would come and get stuck in a mudhole for half a day somewhere in central Alberta. Maybe he would understand why the Métis objected to have the land divided in squares with geometrical road allowances. We, who have to foot the bill, spending millions upon millions, we do catch the point.

In *Nipsya* the purely historical part has only been pointed out because I feared that, by stressing it, it would crush the heroine.

But what I am after is that, again, life in books must not stick to facts. Had I painted in Vital a man of Riel's type, a Métis not only deeply but madly religious, with intellectual power and intensity of patriotism equal to Riel's, most readers (and critics) would have thought or said that the author was perfectly crazy. So I tried to draw a portrait of Vital from a milder but not very uncommon type. Moreover, I suppose I wrote the book with an unconscious feeling that most of my readers would be French Catholic people.

I decided to write the 'Author's Note' about Vital after a discussion of his character with my skilful and pretty translator[2] and with Mr. A.B. Watt, editor of *The Edmonton Journal*, who both objected to Vital's 'sermons.' Mrs. Woodrow, with my consent, shortened them a bit here and there.

Thanking you for your high appreciation, I pray you, dear sir, to believe me

Sincerely yours
Georges Bugnet

P.S. – If you deem it useful, you are at liberty to publish this in part or whole, correcting my English where it is too bad.
P.S. again. – I have just received *The Canadian Bookman*. – T.G. Marquis[3] says: 'Nothing finer in Canadian literature has been done than the chapter entitled "The Voyageur's Last Adventure".' So Hémon's influence was, after all, rather useful.

1 A poet and novelist, Georges-Charles-Jules Bugnet (1879–1981) emigrated from France to western Canada in 1905. His works include *Nipsya* (1924), 'a tale of the Northwest Rebellion,' and *La Forêt* (1935), a story of pioneer hardship. From 1924 to 1929 he was editor-in-chief of *L'Union*, a magazine published in Edmonton and western Canada's most important French-language periodical.
2 Constance Davies Woodrow (1899–1937), minor poet. The English translation of *Nipsya* appeared in 1929.
3 Thomas Guthrie Marquis (1864–1936), journalist, novelist, and popular historian

## To Georges Bugnet

February 6, 1930

My dear Mr. Bugnet,

You are doubtless right in all you say. I trust you did not think me unsympathetic, nor that I was accusing you, by implication, of imitating Hemon. The truth is, I admire *Nipsya* very much, and enjoyed it thoroughly. As I saw it, it follows a certain well defined French tradition in a clarity obtained by the isolation of the theme from all extraneous matters and circumstances. I believe this to be a perfectly permissible way of writing; but I also believe that it contains a danger. While it serves to throw the essentials into high relief, it is devoid of shading that may be vital, and is certainly lifelike – such as we find in the haphazard, or random, selection (or non-selection) of matter in typically English writers like Dickens. I quite agree that his work is not good as to design nor clarity; but I think it recreates life, and is seldom artificial. My own ideal in the novel lies midway between these two opposite ideals.

Thank you for telling me about the living originals from which you worked. That is most valuable commentary.

Probably I misunderstood the exact style of the northern light display in the book. In northern Ontario, and central Manitoba, at points far south of Edmonton, I have more than once seen displays that seemed to me, in recollection, to tally with the one you described in color and so forth; and most of my life has been spent indoors. Therefore I assumed that such displays could not be rare in Alberta. But this is a mere detail.

You must forgive one of the English Protestant tradition, who was brought up in the Province of Quebec, for weariness with the veneration with which the habitant has been treated in Canadian literature for the past ten years. We are faced with two to six volumes each season which pour unstinted adulation on the habitant. We English-Canadians, so far as we know the French-Canadian, like him and respect him. But we are not ourselves angels, and we suspect that the French Canadian is not one either – a man with a little different cultural background (not so different, it is all European after all), a different language and a different religion (but both French and English are now more than racial languages; they are universal languages. And I understand that the two branches of Christianity both worship God in the person of his Son, Jesus.) It seems to us that you French are a trifle over sensitive, ready to suspect us of holding you in contempt where no such idea is in our heads; and of any indications of a willingness to laugh at your own foibles, as we make fun of ourselves, we see not a trace.

This has very little to do with *Nipsya*, but explains, perhaps why I mention with impatience the growing myth of the flawless habitant, which is not a good thing – in my opinion – to draw both races together. The national cause demands that we stand together. To do this we must know one another, and avoid what may irritate the other. The French Canadian fears that the day may come when the English Canadian may try to deprive the Frenchman of his language and religion. I do not believe it. In 40 years I have *never* heard such a proposal discussed. We have fanatics, certainly; but I am sure that not one in a thousand of English Canadian Protestants would dream of interfering with the religion and language of the French Canadian. Try to rid your people of this idle fear. The French Catholic minority has nothing to fear from us; but we need each other's help in developing this country, and in the constitutional problems that face us. Do impress upon those of your race in Canada that we may be culpably ignorant about you, and criminally indifferent; but we are not a menace to you – in any respect whatsoever.

It was not my intention to speak with disrespect of Riel. I used the word rebellion because we English always use that word. For myself, the rebel may be either a good or bad man; he is just the man who is actively opposed to the government – say, an unofficial opposition. We English have magnificant rebels in our history of whom we are very proud. In Canada, we always speak of the Rebellion of 1837 (here in Ontario) by William Lyon Mackenzie; yet we enshrine him among our great men, and always think of him with gratitude for having won us certain political liberties. Yet we still call him a rebel and believe he was one – a most praiseworthy rebel.

At this time it would be a splendid thing to get out a biography of Riel, about whom we English know very little. If you have done one in French, can it not be translated; and if you have not done one, will you not write his life to appear simultaneously in French and English? I can assure you of considerable interest among us English.

Thank you for writing to me. Be assured that I admired your book very much, and still believe that from some viewpoints it is better than *Maria Chapdelaine*, from others not quite so good. And please remember that the day of hostility between the French and English in Canada is past forever, or rather that whatever misunderstandings there may be in the future will only be due to mutual ignorance – the ignorance that it is your business and mine, as writers, to dispel forever.

Yours very cordially,

## From Georges Bugnet

Lac Majeau
Alberta
February 17, 1930

Dear Sir,

My first letter must have been rather misleading. Of course, my English is not as clear as my French.

No. I never suspected you of accusing me of plagiarizing Hémon.

Re: French tradition of clarity – v.s. Dickens' way of writing, this is a hard question to answer. Going to the bottom of it, I'm inclined to believe that there is a good deal of difference between the Anglo-saxon and the French minds. Taking the novel, an Englishman will prefer to see plenty of action, outward life, even down to its little pecularities. French people prefer the inward analysis, and do not care much for many details. Regarding plays, same thing. Shakespeare is greatly admired in France, but Molière pleases us far more. Why? Because with much less action, outward action I mean, with practically no colours, he paints human characters so powerfully that you recognize them everywhere and everyday around you. The Tartuffes, the Harpagons, etc., fill the world, in every nation.

I said 'he paints.' Yes, after all, I might make another comparison: between a novel (or a play) and another art: sculpture. I do believe that the Greek canons of sculpture are the most perfect. And here again we find elimination of small details, idealized humanity.

The conclusion of these rambling considerations? Probably that your ideal in the novel would please everybody, myself included, – but who is going to write that perfect novel?

As you see, when writing letters I go too fast, jumping over words – no time for details and even niceties – rather blunt – naked ideas – shame on me!

No, I hold no brief for the French-Canadian habitant. I do not even know him (the Quebec kind, I mean). I'm a Frenchman (from France) turned into a Canadian, a No. 1 hard Western Canadian. – I perfectly agree with you about the race and religion question. For five years I have been preaching – when editor of *L'Union*[1] – to all Albertan-French people, exactly the same ideas you preach me in your letter. (But I did like your preaching and am going to show it to a few friends – English Protestants – as there is a good deal of belief, here, in Alberta, that Ontarioans are mostly fanatics.) Only, when I preached, myself, to my French flock (38,000 people) I placed the blame on themselves, because, I said, if our English-speaking fellow-citizens ignore you, this is due to your own silence, your own 'stand-aloofness,' (is that an English word?) your own lack of confidence in yourselves.

I may add that they understood this, and that, I believe, nowhere more than in Alberta English-speaking and French-speaking Canadians understand each other and work with each other in better unison, to-day. Outside of Alberta, well, you know, minorities are always hypersensitive.

Re: Riel – it is this way. A *rebel*, in proper English, I believe, is a man who revolts against established authority, accepted government. In 1869 there was no established government in Manitoba or the Territories. Hence, the word 'rebellion' appears to me a quiproquo [sic], and rather misleading. Would you say that, in the Great War, France 'rebelled' against Germany? – No? – Well, for Riel and his people they were exactly in the same case as the French of 1914 – or rather of the French of 1429 in Joan of Arc's times, part of their country having already been taken from them.

Yes, I would like to write Riel's history. But, to live, I have to farm, and my farm is miles away from any library and documents. I might have turned into a passable writer, if leisure had been granted me. Leisure, alas, is a rare fortune in my life. Perhaps, if I can bring Carrier[2] to sign a contract, on *Nipsya*, a fair contract, it might help me to give more of my time to literary efforts. But it looks as if Carrier wants to keep 'the whole cheese' to himself.

Do believe, dear sir, that I appreciated your article; and your letter, very much. I have a proneness to discuss vehemently. Do not take me more seriously than I do myself. I am somewhat disdainful of human reason, my own included. Hence my dogmatic ways: trying, I suppose, to convince myself as much as the audience (or is it : auditors?)

Thankfully yours,
G.B.

A little post-scriptum – re: the perfect novel.

As far as I know every reviewer found *Nipsya* a fairly good book. The other day, I heard differently.

We had a meeting of the school-board, of which I am a kind of permanent secretary-treasurer (12 years on the job).

I offered to sell a copy of *Nipsya* for the school library, so that anybody could read it in the district without having to buy it.

But one of the 3 trustees had already bought one, and he said:

'I don't think this book is worth $2.50. It looks a big book 'cause they used thick paper. But it has less than 300 pages, and the writing is not any too small. Besides, I did not get much kick out of it.'

The two other trustees (Swedish) looked at each other doubtfully.

I did not insist, did even keep a very serious face.

For all I knew, the majority of the ratepayers might have blamed the school-board for squandering $2.50 on a book with no kick in it.

Lucky I've not written *Maria Chapdelaine*, ain't I? I would have got it worse, surely. – But I must admit that I never met with such originality in literary criticism.

It gave Mrs. Bugnet and me unending laughs, for days, every time it recurred in our minds.

What say you about using this standard of criticism for the next book you have to appreciate?

G.B.

1 The last issue of *L'Union* appeared on 19 April 1929.

2 Louis Carrier (1898–1961) was a journalist, lecturer, publisher, and collector of Canadiana. He established Mercury Press in 1928 and published books under the imprint of Louis Carrier and Company, with offices in Montreal, New York, and Paris. Carrier and Company specialized in translations into English of French-Canadian books for foreign markets.

---

## From Mazo de la Roche

Seckington
Winkleigh
North Devon
March 12, 1930

Dear Bill,

Your article 'Whiteoaks in England'[1] arrived yesterday. It reminded me that your delightful letter of 21st January is still unanswered.[2] It is one of those letters answered many times in imagination while, in actuality, I reply to dozens less interesting. I get so many letters from strangers and, when I have saved up a dozen or so, I set to work answering them. They are such kind letters, full of appreciation and praise, but after I have spent an evening in replying to them – I can't tell you how depressed I feel. I have the strangest sensation of being nothing but a shadow – making signs to other shadows, somewhere out in the dark.

Speaking of letters from strangers, I should like to tell you in confidence, that, though I have had letters from England, the United States, Australia, Germany and India about WHITEOAKS, I have had only *one* from Canada. That was an anonymous letter upbraiding me because the family at Jalna are 'not pure-minded, *clean* Canadians!' After the scores of beautiful letters from strangers of other countries this came rather as a jolt. What is there about that word 'clean' that is so repulsive?

I have liked your articles on *Whiteoaks* so very much. You have the gift of saying the right thing in the right way. You don't give with one hand and take away with the other. Some one sent me a Montreal magazine with that bit about the river and the lake. I am proud of it as you were.

I don't believe you need worry about my 'writing new stuff with money in view.' My imagination simply won't stand forcing. Also there is something in my disposition which rebels at authority – even the authority of my public. To illustrate this let me tell you that I spent the summer and early autumn writing something that I am quite sure my American publishers looked on as rather a waste of my time. Indeed one of the heads of the company wrote imploring me – 'Not to go down any by-paths.' This was a life of the Scottish terrier I had for thirteen years. I wanted to write it and write it I did! Now I have a cable from the American publishers to tell me how pleased they are with the MS. 'A lovely picture,' they call it. Well, that is very nice, but my own way came first.

I am now working on the third book of the *Whiteoak* trilogy. I am going to stay here in Devon until July working on it. Then, I expect, I shall finish it in Canada. I am stuck here immovable – each day like the day before. We had an invitation to spend a week in a delightful house in London to see the Italian pictures. Do you think I could go? This week I am invited up to see a play. Do you think I can go? No, I simply can't budge. I have no appetite. A change would do me a world of good. But that inexorable something in me won't let me move. One thing I have promised to do is to visit Clemence Dane[3] near Axminster but that is quite near. And, by Heaven, if I could get out of that I would!

That adorable little Bill! I should like to see him. Mrs. Deacon told me the children's names one day over the telephone. Bill's anxiety over your 'lasting' may irritate you but your anxiety that I should 'last' is very touching to me. Why, when I read your letter, I got up and walked about the room – to think that some one over there should be worrying about me. I guess you are right about my weaknesses, and your advice seems good. My only trouble now is rheumatism, my nerves are pretty fit. It is very prevalent here in Devon.

You suppose Caroline[4] 'is still with me.' Still with me! Do I breathe? Do I live? Have I not made away with myself? Yes, she is still with me! To think that she hates you is to wrong the most generous mind I have ever known.

As ever sincerely
Mazo.

Our excitements are – an occasional political meeting, drinking tea with naval officers, and following the Hunt in a motor car. The other day I stood on a high bank with a dozen other followers, and only one man beside *myself* saw the fox, far below, escape across a red ploughed field while the hounds still bayed in the wood for him & I was *proud*!

M.

Write again.

1 The article, describing de la Roche's success in England, appeared in *The Mail and Empire* on 1 February 1930.
2 This letter is missing from the Deacon Collection.
3 Pseudonym of Winifred Ashton (1888–1965), popular British novelist and feminist writer, among whose works is the play *A Bill of Divorcement* (1921)
4 Caroline Louise Clement (1888–1972) came to live with Mazo de la Roche's family at a very early age. A distant relation who was described as de la Roche's 'cousin,' she became Mazo's life-long companion.

## To Mazo de la Roche April 18, 1930

Dear Mazo,

The populace is celebrating the anniversary of the Crucifixion, automobile riding and the like. Having no car but a good trusty No. 5 Underwood typewriter (all paid for but $25) I am at my office in a jubilant holiday mood. I have pronounced Miss Prichard's prize Australian novel, *Coonardoo*, very good, and Miss Claire Spencer's *Gallows Orchard* as not quite convincing.[1] You see, out of the 7 leading characters, 4 were killed outright, the heroine stoned to death for having a baby unorthodoxly, 2 lost their jobs and the last one became a fugitive from justice, having committed a perfectly unnecessary murder. And it's a gloriously sunny day, and I just couldn't believe all that gloom. But there, I mustn't reveal, much less joke about, the workings of my inner mind, or you will lose the awe and respect that every right-thinking novelist ought to have for every being who calls himself a critic.

You mustn't care about Canada's seeming indifference. We are an inarticulate people; and have a certain domestic grumpiness that we got from the damned Scotch. You have become a great author. You thereby bid for their dislike. (These new psychologists call it 'defence mechanism'). It's inverted admiration – soured pride in you. Last year – let me underline that – last year, Alexander Carlyle, lateral descendent of Thomas (the old crab) put up a monument to Thomas at the old family home. I got hold of the local paper telling all about it. And will you believe it, the editorial was actually trying, in 1929, to pour oil on the waters, and quell the bad feelings arising from a dispute that had arisen during Thomas's early years as an author, as to whether or not there were possibilities in the young man. It was resented that young Thomas should set himself up as somebody; and the fight still raging among the cottages of that Scottish village actually goes back to events prior to Thomas Carlyle's birth, but in some obscure way supposed to be connected with the dispute as to whether Thomas could write a book that was worth reading. They now decide, though not quite unanimously, that he has made good ... when the rest of the world has ceased reading him altogether. So don't you care, Mazo. Some day I'll be rotten egged for unveiling a statue to you in Queen's Park. Please think charitably of us. We mean well.

Thanks for the J.C. Squire[2] review of *Bad Verse*. Do you think he might like to see my *Four Jameses*? It's better than this truck he is writing about.

And will you please advise me? I want to place an article on Canadian literature or some phase thereof with the best literary publication in Britain. What should I send it to? *The Bookman*? or one of the Reviews, or what? You pick the paper or magazine. Then I'll shoot at it, with due regard to their style, length, &c.

I hope your visit to Clemence Dane doesn't mean you had to read *The Babyons*; which I didn't like – much too artificial, made to pattern.

The dog book and the third instalment of *Whiteoaks* sound good to me. The news about your health sounds better. Rheumatism is painful but not fatal. Naval officers are more dangerous.

There have been several good Canadian books this spring. Dent's *Show Me Death*[3] is first rate though he is a bumptious young ass. *Wheat* (non-fiction) by a couple of Saskatchewan University men,[4] is moving to any one with imagination; and Morley Callaghan's *It's Never Over* is an advance, in my view. What do you think? I enclose my review of that,[5] and would be grateful for your opinion, based either on the book if you have read it, or my discussion if you have no other guide. You know some of his work, I think.

Let me hear from you when you get back in July if you will. My regards to your cousin, who was probably only scared that time I met her, and to you my very best,

Sincerely,

Congratulations: You will be away. In June, Toronto will be the temporary home for five days of more than 300,000 shriners – should one capitalize?

1 Katharine Susannah Prichard (1884–1969) and Claire Spencer (b. 1899), the latter a Scottish-American novelist who moved to the United States in 1917. Their novels dealt respectively with aboriginal Australian and rural Scottish communities.

2 John C. Squire (1884–1958) was an English humorist and critic who edited *The London Mercury* from 1919 to 1934.

3 Walter Redvers Dent (b. 1900); the novel *Show Me Death*, published in 1930, was based on his experiences as a soldier in World War I.
4 Written, in fact, by one author, William Walker Swanson (1879–1950), *Wheat* (1930) was one of the first accounts of the grain industry in Canada.
5 'Morley Callaghan Climbs to Safer, More Solid Ground,' *The Mail and Empire*, 22 March 1930. Attacking adverse American reaction to Callaghan's novel, Deacon praised it as a success for its objective and direct narration, while remarking that Callaghan's content was not always commensurate with his technical skill.

---

## To Francis Dickie April 18, 1930

Dear Dickie,

On the anniversary of Our Lord's death I write you because, next to him, you are the least fortunate man I know.

On receipt of your letter of March 15th I sent Carrier's a request for return of *The Wilderness Passes*. I have had a reply from Alan Isles of New York that he has done so. I trust he has. He also asked me about *The Prairie Tamers* and I replied that there was no dodging the fact that they got the ms.[1]

The firm is now Louis Carrier and Alan Isles Inc, of 33 East 10th St, New York. Their Montreal office is all but closed. They have been on the verge of bankruptcy. Legate left them last fall to take over the book page of *The Montreal Star*.

Of course I never received your *Umingmuk of the Barrens* for review. No such luck. Not for us. When you publish one, you tell me what publisher is guilty and I'll go after my copy from this end. You really do have the damnedest luck.

Things are all right with me. Stock market crash last fall and non-sale of much western Canada wheat has made tight money and newspaper advertising has fallen off, which means smaller papers and many men fired. I've lost two small papers I contributed to, but still have the bigger ones. A battalion of reporters was let out of *The Toronto Star* in a bunch. Another six months and we'll be back to normal.

I never see any of your work and you never see any of mine; but that doesn't matter. One of these years I'll get to Paris and you can show me the Arc de Triumph [sic] – also Eiffel Tower. Meanwhile I'm so glad to know you are carrying on somehow and I still (being incurable optimist) believe that one day you will publish a book and I'll get a copy and be able to review it. I tell you right now it's going to be a prejudiced review. You deserve what I have never yet done for God nor man. I'm going to log-roll for the only time in my life. Count on me.

With very best regards, and remember that though I've little time for letters, there is one guy in Canada who does care what becomes of you, and who is very anxious for your success.

Ever cordially,

1 Dickie's two book-length manuscripts had been sent for consideration to Louis Carrier who had misplaced *The Prairie Tamers*. In his 15 March letter, Dickie had asked Deacon to request the return of the manuscript of *The Wilderness Passes*.

---

## From Francis Dickie

La Sarrazine
May 1, 1930

Dear Deacon: –

The opening lines of your letter of the 18th gave me the first good laugh I've had in days. It reminds of the time I terribly shocked an acquaintance of mine, a deacon in the methodist church, by arguing (quite logically it seemed to me) that Good Friday always came on the same date, for certainly no man, not even the Lord, could die on two different dates. Which will give you an idea of how little I know, and how little I kept track of that day.

Re the book manuscripts: I enclose two letters received.[1] Thanks to you, it seems they may reappear. As to you not having any of my books, I am frightfully ashamed. And, helas, at the moment, in keeping with most writers, I have not an extra copy of anything on hand, except a book of mine which has just been published in French, translated by my wife.[2] If you read French let me know and I will send you one. I am sorry you are not running across any of my stuff. I have had on an average of from one to two articles or stories a month in *The Star Weekly* for the past two years, and a couple stories in the *Saturday Night*. If you can possibly get a copy of *The Country Guide*,[3] published at Winnipeg, issue of April 1st, do so. It contains one of the few things written in the past two years of which I am really proud. I suppose in Toronto you don't see *The*

*Western Home Monthly*, I have done one travel article a month for them for the last 36 months. Some of them are pretty bad, but the one describing a bullfight I saw in Madrid, I am not ashamed of, in fact, I think it's better than Hemingway's.[4]

As for myself. The past few months have been bad. I came down to the land of eternal sunshine in January, and by God it's rained almost every day for four months. While in Paris, where winter is usually bad, they've had warmth and sunshine, it happens once in every 398 years. But it just happened that this particular year I left Paris and came here.

I think I told you in my last letter about going to visit Somerset Maugham. He is one of the few authors who have not proved a disappointment. I had tea the other day with Frank Harris. And I was the guest of Gracie Fields the big musical hall artist of London. She was here visiting a very good friend of mine, and we had several trips together, finishing up at Monte Carlo day before yesterday. As for writing I pour out quite a lot that sells to the newspapers and magazines, but [for] the two worth while books that I have written (done in Canada long ago) I as yet cannot find a publisher. They are really good pieces of work, things that I wanted to do. But when one sees the Niagara of books pouring out, it brings realization of how really little it matters. As Maugham says: 'most writers are so busy writing that they never have time to live,' and I don't want to be that way.

Life hasn't been very good to me. But recently I have developed a taste for good wines and food (I always had the taste for good food and cigars). Here one can get good wine, very fine vintages even, fairly cheap. And in this region, there are many little vineyards that put out small vintages peculiar to themselves. If one noses around sometimes they make marvellous discoveries. Just recently from near here I found a marvellous little wine. (It all depends on the lay of the vineyard to the sun, the soil etc. which gives the certain flavor). I have drunk up nearly the man's entire crop. He was selling it for 5 francs a bottle (20¢), so by raising the price an extra franc a bottle, I got it all. This may [seem] incredible to you. And this same wine, or its equivalent in flavor would cost in Paris about 30 francs a bottle. But why should I tell you all this? Simply because every man likes to talk of his latest hobby, I suppose.

Being in France (although I believe it is quite a good custom now even in Canada, or at least in the United States) I manage to find myself an agreeable mistress wherever I go, and keep her on one side of the town and my regular household on the other. One of these days I am going to write a scathing article called 'Why Girls Leave Home' symbolic of course of Canadian artists. The main point of the article will be to point out that while thousands of big companies have made fortunes out of Canada, and both native Canadians and Englishmen and Americans have become multimillionaires out of the Dominion not one company or individual has ever given an endowment to help Canadian writers, painters or musicians. While look at the United States. There is the Guggenheim for one, gives about fifty artists a year, 2500 each. etc. etc. However, I will send you a copy of it for reading when I get it done.

Thanks awfully for all the kind promises about the write up. Musson and Company published *Umingmuk of the Barrens*. If you know any of that gang I'm sure they'd give you a copy, that is if they have any left, which is probable, seeing as they never sent out any review copies.

Well, my boy, I must go to work. I am trying to master this damn French language. The first two years I was here, what with constant visits to the hospital trying to cure the tuberculosis, and make a living at the same time, I did not make much headway against rough conversation. And believe me, it is an incredible language, difficult no end. About your coming over here. It shouldn't be so difficult from Toronto.

I met last year (he came to me with a letter from Moore[5] of *Maclean's*) a fellow named Norman Reilly Raine (a poor fish it turned out) but he got a free trip through some American steamship company for doing a little writing for them. Don't the Canadian National touch London. There ought to be some way a man as well known as you can work it.

Incidentally, I take my hat off to you, a man who can put over a syndicate of book reviews etc., in the Canadian press. Once and awhile [sic] when in Paris I saw something by you in *The Vancouver Province*.

Very sincerely,
Francis Dickie

I don't know where I go from here, probably back to Paris in two weeks, or if I got an unexpected check, I think I would go to Italy.

1 On 1 April and 16 April, Paul Gouin of Carrier's Montreal office apologized for the delay due to the firm's reorganization and located the MS of *The Wilderness Passes* for Dickie, arranging to forward it from New York, where it resurfaced, to the author in Paris. *The Prairie Tamers* remained misplaced.
2 *Le Solitaire de la vallée*, translated by Suzanne Dickie, was published in 1929 in Paris by J. Tallandier. The book never appeared in English.
3 Originally known as *The Grain Growers' Guide* (from June 1908 to April 1928), it was first published under the auspices of the Manitoba Grain Growers' Association. The 1 April 1930 edition featured an autobiographical excerpt by Dickie entitled 'What Empty Pockets Taught Me.'
4 *The Western Home Monthly* was a homemaker's magazine published in Winnipeg, to which Dickie contributed travel articles and short stories. He is probably referring to his piece 'Bravo Toro!' in the November 1928 issue.
5 Henry Napier Moore (1893–1963), journalist; at this time an editor at *Maclean's*

---

## To W.T. Allison November 1, 1930

My dear Allison,

At the beginning of Canadian Book Week, may I, without impertinence, congratulate you, and as a Canadian author thank you, as critic and missionary, for the noble and unselfish work you have carried on for so many years through your various papers in the West? I appreciate your patience and kindliness to emergent authors; and perhaps as I am a critic myself I know better than others the labor and worry this has often cost you.

The burden and heat of the day has brought you, at last, to what I think is a bountiful harvest. Canadian literature is producing good ripe fruit now, with promise of better to follow. As these fine novels, poems, histories come in profusion (compared to earlier years) I would like you to know that I believe no man has done as much as you to produce these results. Empty honors are few and material rewards none at present for such as you, who have ever been ready for the Canadian author with the word of encouragement or caution. I can only hope you are satisfied at realizing how successful your literary life has been, and of what importance to Canada.

In admiration, friendship and gratitude,

Ever sincerely,

From Vernon Rhodenizer[1] Wolfville
November 17, 1930

Dear Deacon:

I was 'tickled pink' by my discovery of your review in *The Mail and Empire,* and completely bowled over when I learned that you had syndicated the review.[2]

Out of my gratitude I pass on to you a bit of my philosophy of criticism which you do not seem to read between the lines of my discussion of Mazo de la Roche and Grove (neither of whom I have ever met).

I certainly do not confuse realism with tragedy, and no more do I confuse it with comedy. I agree absolutely that one cannot say that tragedy is better than comedy or *vice versa*. But I do say that one can compare tragedy and comedy as to artistic merit, and 'realism' is *one* standard by which such comparison can be made. Modern taste demands of prose fiction (if not of other forms of literature) that it *seem* probable, plausible, true to life, realistic, call it what you will. This is because prose fiction *purports to represent life*. Now, other things being equal, prose fiction may be judged by this ascending scale: – (1) lacking in probability (producing *farcical* comic material or *melodramatic* serious material), (2) plausible or probable, (3) inevitable. In her humor it seems to me that Miss de la Roche frequently hovers around the lower end of the scale and rarely if ever gets to the upper end of the scale. Grove in his tragedy often approaches the inevitable, and seldom if ever descends below the middle ground of the probable to the melodramatic (getting serious situations by sacrificing truth to plot or character). And since in other things he is at least her equal, he is greater than she because his work *seems* more true to life than hers.

If there is anything wrong with this philosophy of criticism, what is wrong with it? If the philosophy is sound, am I mistaken in my impression that Grove on the whole creates a greater 'illusion of reality,' *seems* more true to life?

Sincerely yours,
V.B. Rhodenizer

1 Vernon Blair Rhodenizer (1886–1968) was a professor of English at Acadia University in Wolfville, Nova Scotia, remembered for *A Handbook of Canadian Litera-*

*ture*. In the 1920s he was one of the first to teach courses in Canadian literature through the medium of radio lectures and reading lists printed in *The Halifax Herald*.

2 Deacon's review of *A Handbook of Canadian Literature* (Graphic 1930) appeared 8 November 1930 and was very positive, although he criticized it for the omission of Duncan Campbell Scott and the berating of Mazo de la Roche.

---

## To Vernon Rhodenizer November 20, 1930

Dear Rhodenizer,

My own feeling is one of regret, and I apologize for not giving your most excellent history more adequate consideration. Actually it was a case of ditching Arnold Bennett's and John Galsworthy's latest books to find even this much space for yours; and I went on the notion that some mention was better than none, and a little promptly was worth more to get your book launched than a long, considered article, which is impossible now but might have been possible next January. (When will the Canadian publisher learn to avoid the Xmas rush? What object was there in issuing your thoughtful, trenchant critical history to compete with Christmas gift books?) Personally I would have liked to wait till I could do the job properly; but I thought it in your interests to shoot at once, and I only hope this is what you wanted.

I agree with principles laid down in your letter of the 17th.

On the Roche-Grove question I offer this suggestion: Truth is more than fact; and the truth we get from a novelist is inevitably strained through his temperament. Scandinavian and most north-European literature is tragic, gloomy, sordid – not that life is much different there from other countries, but the tense creative mind of [the] literary artist sees it so. Grove is a Swede. He would make a description of a wedding or a circus a grave and a sad business. That is truth for him and that is artistic truth as revealed through him. And, when I am reading him I accept that view of life – absolutely.

Mazo is an Anglo-Celt, with a Gallic streak. Life to her is much brighter. Her emotions are more resilient, more mobile. She reveals through her characters a variation of mood. Mazo is Canadian.

Now, my lad, this Canadian people about whom they both write is not perhaps an exuberant people; it may be a stolid people in some respects. But by God, old man, we are a damned happy lot compared to those turgid Scandinavians. Confirmed pessimists are in the hopeless minority: our eyes strain forward, hopefully. We laugh a good deal; we smile a good deal; we cry readily enough; but there is a warm, happy, comfortable feeling among us, and for one another; and most of us are damn sure that 'everything will turn out all right in the end.'

Therefore, I reason, regardless of which author may be the more accurate a reporter of physical fact – the hard fact of the materialist, not necessarily the psychological fact of the artist – Mazo feels us in mind and heart and this Swede cannot. In mood, regardless of what her characters do, in their moods and emotions they approximate nearer to the Canadian soul than Grove's human wrecks do. That lift of the heart that cannot be explained is in the Celtic peoples; through the Irish-Scotch, and the trace of Norman-French, the real Canadian has that cheerfulness. Grove can never be aware of it, Mazo instinctively is. Hence her truth of the mind and heart of the Canadian people is much more true than the essentially foreign Grove's. We critics must see more than geometrical facts; we must perceive this invisible thing and gauge the truths that cannot be grasped by finger and thumb.

Now let us turn to your ground of plausibility and probability of acts. It distresses me to see you commend the realism of *Possession*. For it is not at all in accordance with observed fact. It is mere 'realism,' an imitation of a Russian tragedy or something like that, and has no relation to the sort of people Mazo is writing about.

1. Derek, a successful architect of Halifax, sells his practice and goes to live on an Ontario farm he has never seen. I do not know a single Canadian male of 30, university graduate, and right-minded, who would ever do anything so silly.

2. The farming does not go well. Derek stays right there and sinks into the mud. Would he do that? Never. What distinguishes the young Canadian man is his mobility. When he does not 'get on' in one place or one job, he moves on. I have myself. My friends have. You know how we 'try Edmonton,' or 'take up teaching' or 'go in for law.' I've just been talking to Joe McDougall[1] who founded *The Goblin* 9½ years ago and has been its editor ever since. It has failed. Joe has meanwhile written two or three books, and some good poetry. He is today salesman for an advertising firm, to earn his living. (On the side he is just finishing his novel). Now what would Derek do in real life? He'd probably come to Toronto, less than

20 miles from that farm, and find a connection with some big architects here. He might do a hundred things. The one thing he would never do is stay on the farm and perish. A European, rooted to that sod for centuries, might be unable to break a family tradition. But what kept Derek chained to his failure? Nothing in the world but the author's mistake – her lack of plausibility, failure of observation, probably unconscious copying from some European model. (And because you are a student of literature, which is mostly European life as reflected by those novelists, you conclude that Mazo in *Possession* has reality, the probable, the plausible).

3. Fawny. This middle-aged virgin knows nothing of the sexual life of a squaw and the white man's normal relations with a squaw. All squaws hope white men will lie down with them; and often beg them to. As literal transcription from life, the notion of having to seduce an Indian woman is laughable. It is quite the reverse. Further, it never occurs to the squaw afterwards to expect the white man to marry her; much less would she dream of scheming for that end. Nor would the white man of Derek's stamp ever give the subject a thought. That part is an hilarious joke to any one knowing what the real life is like.

I object not to your principles but to your application. *Possession* is not real at all – in any part. It is all wrong. It is a composite plagiarism, unconscious of course, of a congeries of English and other north European masterpieces of tragic fiction. It bears no relation whatever to the life of Canadians along the shore of this lake within an hour's ride of here. In mood it is non-indigenous. It is all thoroughly bad.

Then you might consider mere writing. Grove attains a power which is partly the result of scriptorial fibre, and partly the reflection of sombre subject matter. Mazo is much more dexterous, flexible, and always more clever and graceful. Grove's style suits his work, Mazo's style suits hers. Their works of different genus, worlds apart in spirit, cannot be compared fairly to either, and to no advantage, because there is no common denominator. Each is properly approached along a separate path.

I have miles more to say on the subject, but have no time now. Forgive me for appearing to correct you; but you asked for it. I think I have said enough so you can follow my reasoning. And possibly yours and mine will never meet. For once you have laid down a critical *method*, my boy, you are sunk. Creative art is not built on methods. It arises out of conditions. The inspired critic intuitively salutes the art; then he examines the conditions to find out what produced the specimen of art; then he finds words to explain the phenomenon to his readers.

You have broken with much of the sterile academic tradition with its 'cramping rules.' Better forget the rest, the few tag ends of theory that stick to your back. Recognize that Canadian writing must be new in subject matter, in mood, in everything; and that therefore we must, by study of it itself, evolve new criteria by which to deal adequately with it.

Jehovah has spoken. Go, and the God of peace go with you. You have done a most excellent job of difficult work, and we are all in your debt exceedingly. We pioneers must hammer a way through. We can only arrive if we can squabble freely over our – each other's – real or supposed myopias.

With a very tender regard and great respect,

1 Joseph Easton McDougall (b. 1901), writer and advertising executive, manager of *Goblin*, a Canadian humour magazine, from 1921 to 1930. He was the author of humorous books, magazine articles, and radio scripts.

---

## To B.K. Sandwell

November 26, 1930

Dear Sandwell,

The book you mean is V.B. Rhodenizer's *A Handbook of Canadian Literature* (Graphic $2). It is brief and discriminating; and mingles history, criticism and propaganda in the way we need *now*. It answers the casual enquirer without killing any potential enthusiasm he may have for the subject. R is head of English dept at Acadia, Wolfville. He is a man my age; and is doing a lot for Can. Lit. by radio talks, extension lectures etc. If you like his book, drop him a line. He is so damned isolated that it is a positive disadvantage in this work he is doing. He is an awfully nice fellow; and level-headed – that is, he thinks as I do on most questions.

It was kind of you to speak of my page. I seldom hear that now, being a fixed institution and taken for granted. (Also, those who hate what I say have given up protesting).

I seldom see your work as I make it a point not to see *Saturday Night* so I shall not have any opinion on the work of my successors. But I did see and enjoyed your *Golden Dog* piece;[1] and I have a little more dynamite to stick under our revered classic, as soon as I have the time to write it out. I think I told you I have reserved your 'For Sale in Book and Seed Stores' for the anthology I shall someday compile of masterpieces of Canadian humor.

By the way, do you know my *The Four Jameses*? If not, I have some copies here and should like you to know the work. In it you will recognize the use I made of that quatrain from Lady Roddick[2] you recited in my office something over three years ago.

I saw by the papers you were lecturing up here on the Waterways (St. Lawrence) scheme. Next time up try to reserve a lunch hour for me. Call at my office for me, and I'll take you over to the Writers Club. I believe you'd like the atmosphere and I'm sure the boys would like *you*.

With best regards,

1 Refers to Sandwell's article 'Debunking *The Golden Dog*' (*Saturday Night*, 4 October 1930, p 5), which examined the historical evidence behind the novel's romantic myth

2 Lady Amy Redpath Roddick, English-born second wife of Sir Thomas George Roddick of Montreal, was a poet and dramatist whose play *The Romance of a Princess* (1922) supplied Deacon with this quatrain from a lullaby:

Little one, thou art sweeter far
Than any petal textured star,
Sweeter than a lover's gift,
Thou art joy that God hath whiffed!

---

## From W.T. Allison

600 Gertrude Avenue
Winnipeg
January 18, 1931

Dear Deacon, –

I have thought of you often during the last two months and every time I did so my nonconformist conscience creaked on its hinges like a rusty garden gate. I intended to answer your very generous letter a few days after it arrived. But, alas for good intentions, I didn't get round to the job just then. So I postponed it until Christmas. Then I was snowed under by exam papers. I intended to send you a Xmas card but thought it would be a scurvy reply to such a lovely letter. I said, 'No, I'll wait until after New Year's day and then write a good long letter.' So, once more I did the postponing act. Well, here I am at last, on Jan. 18 seizing a half hour on Sunday afternoon to say How are you?

Needless to say I appreciated your letter. It was just about the handsomest missive that I have ever received. I have tried to be decent to Canadian writers but I cannot agree with you that what I have written about them and their books has had one tenth of the effect you say it has. You have always been a good friend of mine and I think your personal feelings have prejudiced you in my favor. Just the same it is very cheering to receive a letter such as yours, for, from your own experience as a reviewer, you must realize that there is mighty little gratitude shown by these hounds who will snap all the publicity you give them and never say thank you, never even let on that you are alive.

One of the worst cases of ingratitude that I have experienced has been that of Frederick Philip Grove. I did much to boost his early volumes of essays; I gave a radio lecture on his *Settlers of the Marsh*, as well as a syndicated review; I did the same for his America book. When he published *Our Daily Bread* I read it and thought it was altogether too gloomy to give the world even a fair idea of farming life in Saskatchewan. Still I knew that Grove was very hard up and I made up my mind that the kind thing for me to do was to pass the book up, not to write a word about it. I told A.L. Phelps to let Grove know the reason for my silence. But what do you think Grove did? He copied out on a page of foolscap a long, fulsome review by Morgan Powell, put this into an envelope without attaching his name to it, and sent it to me, as if to say – 'Here is what a real critic thinks about my novel!' This was certainly an original way of rebuking me for my silence. I suppose I should have been relieved that he did not add some stinging comments of his own. But how does he expect me to come through with more publicity for F.P. Grove?

I suppose you will have heard that Prof. A.W. Crawford[1] has retired from our staff. Due to poor health, he retired on a pension and is at this moment enjoying the balmy airs of Florida. Professor A.J. Perry[2] and I were raised to the purple. We share the English throne in Manitoba University between us – a dual monarchy I call it.

We have both been here for a long time and it would have been embarrassing if one of us had been put over the other. We have two professors in the department of philosophy who are on an equal footing.

Did you know that my younger son Carlyle who is on the staff of *The Saskatoon Star* is the father of a bonnie boy 16 months old? I feel that I am in the ancient class now, although I do not worry about it. My grandson was here for Christmas. He can toddle around and say a few words. Naturally I think he is the best ever.

Next summer the C.A.A. is going to meet in Toronto and I expect to be there and one of the pleasures that I am looking forward to with the greatest anticipation is a good talk with the literary editor of the Toronto *Mail and Empire*.

Well I must close now by thanking you most heartily for your very kind letter and extending to you best wishes for a successful New Year.

Ever your friend,
W.T.A.

1 Alexander Wellington Crawford (1866–1933) was a Methodist minister, professor of English at the University of Manitoba, and the author of *The Genius of Keats* (1932).

2 Aaron Jenkins Perry (b. 1876) was also a professor of English at the University of Manitoba until his retirement in 1941.

---

## To W.T. Allison January 21, 1931

Dear Allison,

Thanks awfully for your letter. I was beginning to fear you had forgotten me. Congratulations on being grandfather and full professor. I don't know anything about the grandfather business yet from personal experience – my eldest child being only 7 1/2; but I am delighted Crawford is out. I have looked on him as an obstructive factor. Unenlightened. Injurious to the young.

I guess everybody has had similar experiences with Grove who is this minute, I suppose, the most personally unpopular writer in Canada – despite the open hand everywhere. Graphic had to get rid of him for reasons I can explain better when we meet. I am sorry for the poor cuss but you simply can't do anything with him.

I came into the story considerably after you. Having to review a good many other books each for good reason, it was too late when I got around to *Prairie Trails* to do it at all, to my regret. But Phelps kept at me, and when *The Turn of the Year* came 8 or 9 months later I did the brace at once, giving the whole of my first page to it (3 cols) putting his photo in center page, which I thought a handsome apology for previous neglect. Grove did not write me but Phelps sent on G's letter to him containing a blistering comment on my delay.

Next came *Search* [*A Search for America*]. It was 27 years finding a publisher. I found the publisher. Phelps brought me the ms. at Bobcaygeon and I said 'I'll attend to that' and I did. I handed it to Graphic with a strong piece of advice about taking it on. They were somewhat slow with the printing and Grove gave me unequivocal hell. However the book got out at a nice time in the fall, and as you may remember I made it the leading article on page l of the October 1927 issue of *Sat. Nite Lit. Section*, using a drawing of Grove which I paid my friend Comfort to do for a frontispiece. I heard nothing from it.

Oh yes, I had in the interim reviewed *Settlers of the Marsh* enthusiastically, and not being a professor with a board of education to think of, I could go further than you. I also used the controversy between you and Roberton to hang subsequent articles on, and had many personal notes about his health and all that.

He came East and landed in Toronto Mch 31 1928 – three days before I was fired from *Saturday Night* and being considerably worried knowing full well what was in the wind. In that crisis, I spent 24 hours with Grove and spent $30 of my precious dollars. I had him interviewed by the press, I paid his hotel bill, I introduced him to all sorts of useful people, I paid his taxi bills and he walked nowhere. I took him to my club. I did everything humanly possible. Never heard a word, not even casual thanks.

But I know authors too well to expect much, thank God; and when *Our Daily Bread* came I stood up to that. I thought it the weakest and poorest of his books and said so frankly, but not unkindly. Grove himself had told me in so many words that this was his own opinion. I just put it in to show I missed nothing.

I reviewed (briefly, of course) *Now It Must be Said,*[1] which contained nothing that needed to be said, and nothing which had not been said frequently before on many occasions. My review was loose, casual, reporting but neither approving nor condemning.

When *The Yoke of Life* came last fall I gave him my leader of 1½ cols, photo extra, and rated this book as a masterpiece. For the superlative praise – deserved I think on the merits – I got one single line of thanks. It might not have been grudging thanks but its brevity was suggestive.

What I have told you is about the gratitude that was lacking, the negative side. I have not told you, and shall not, the malice he has shown towards me, the contempt in which he habitually speaks of me, and the libellous untruths he tells of me. He seems to have the idea that I am his inveterate enemy, traducer, and that I am utterly incompetent because I have failed to appreciate his genius. How his brain works I don't know. But next to Phelps and yourself I have probably done more to 'put Grove over' than any other human being. – However, that's the way it stands. I will no longer associate with him, nor recognize his existence as a human being; but when his books come out they will be reviewed as faithfully and cheerfully as if he were my best friend. What I really believe is that he imagines I know nothing whatever of how he has been behaving towards me for the past three years. Well, I suppose it doesn't matter. The creative artist does not seem to develop the sympathy and understanding a critic must.

If we collaborated to make a joint article 'What Critics Think of Grove' we'd have so many aspiring collaborators that the resulting piece would be the size of the phone book. I wonder whether Phelps retains Grove's friendship. I have not seen nor heard from Phelps in several years. There's another odd personality. Perhaps they suit one another, the selfishness of the one balancing the other. But I fear this has grown into a rather malicious letter.

I am so glad to know all goes well with you; and I hope when you are here next summer that you will not only make a little time for me but that you will informally address The Writers Club, of which I have honor to be Vice Pres. – 100 men who make a living, or what passes for such, by professional writing. You may not have any idea how many Toronto freelances are keeping body and soul together. Arthur Irwin,[2] Associate editor of *Maclean's* is the Pres. I am chairman of the Speakers Committee, and should like you to gossip to us on 'Who is Writing in the West' – that is, unless you prefer

to make a set address on some topic like 'How Should a Native Writer Regard Canada.' It's just a lunch-hour job, very simple.
With best regards,

Sincerely,

1 *It Needs to be Said* (1929), a collection of essays on literary topics
2 William Arthur Irwin (b. 1898), editor of *MacLean's* from 1945 to 1950 and subsequently Canada's High Commissioner to Australia and Ambassador to Brazil. Together Irwin and Deacon anonymously wrote the club's *Canadian Writers' Market Survey* (1931).

---

## From Laura Goodman Salverson

96 High Street South
Port Arthur, Ontario
February 1, 1931

Dear Mr. Deacon:

Do not be unduly alarmed, I have not developed a sudden notion that it is your duty as scribe & critic to undertake my enlightenment!

No – I need a great deal of it I know – but I was reminded so forcibly of you a few weeks ago when on the train going West – Here I discover A. Deacon on the page I was about to flip past – & such a string of honors attached! I was bound for the good old West to jabber away at one city & another – women are that way as you may have discovered.

My sole defence lies in my Norse harshness of character. I do say things that are a little like Thor's thunderbolts. And the queer part is I get away with it in public. On paper, sincerity seems taboo.

That is where you come in – Tell me, if your good will can spare that much time, why, in times like these must we continue in these sickening hypocricies? [sic] Why must magazine Editors insist upon pointless idiocies, stupid & childish sophistries supposedly novel & new – is it because, like contented cows who give good milk, contented asses do the same for the powers that be? Surely, I've never read of, nor witnessed less results from greater opportunities! Yet our smart young men & *Free* young women prefer to eat, drink & be jazzy rather than *risk* a single foible for the betterment of life in general. I think what erks me most is the silly phrase about our *brave* young – fearless moderns! Lord bless us where does the courage come in? Every little 'high-bender' knows the ropes. Licence is safe. Nothing short of actual crime endangers either individual or social safety – where then is the greater courage?

And tell me honestly what is the use of paying critics to tie into the poor scribe who lives by writing for such a crew, when no one would touch a sincere bit of creation?

Perhaps I've grown bitter. I tried to do my best with this language against rather trying odds – constant illness in childhood & extreme poverty coupled up with greater sensibility because we were not fortunate enough to be *peasants*. But all my best work goes begging. I know it is the best – rough perhaps, because I need more time to wrestle with the pesky English preposition – my biggest enemy – but strength is natural to my pen and feeling. It should be. I've lived through enough hardships. And ever since I can remember I've been creating characters.

To me, plot-mechanical stunts are odious. Not the least true to life nor necessary to an intelligent reader. Providing of course the story has human interest & something to tell.

I suppose I've gotten away with as many plain tales of plain people as any ass in Canada but that is not the point. The point remains & always will so far as I'm concerned, that I'd go through seven hells to write beautifully! But who would read it? Who publish?

I've gone about a bit – I've questioned librarians – except for the older folk no one takes out the classics. They sit the shelves in solitary grandeur. Meanwhile the Crime Club & the He-She hunters go on from peak to peak.

My latest grievance lies in having had to write quickly a story I had collected material for over a period of 8 years. To write it while I was both sick, in the craziest situation & just after loosing [sic] all I had in the world – not much to be sure.

And then I have to sell it as a serial! Even if it lacked something from my point of view it was too *dignified* too strong for the paper – my heroine was the lefthand daughter of a *Bishop*. My lord, that would not do!

Without waiting for my reply to the request for a change in title, he is made into a duke! Now we never had Dukes in Iceland! And to get the story to space, it leaps along in that terrible modern fashion; when it should move *splendidly* in the *slow measured* way typical of the 17th century!

Dear Mr. Deacon forgive me. But I said once – you were the only real critic in Canada – I still think so. So I've risked writing thinking you might suggest some magic condiment to sooth my ruffled breast.

Since my dear friend Mr. Bothwell died I have no one to whom I dare look for any genuine advice. The pity is I dared ask so seldom. But at that I'll try to stay true to my own queer ideas.

L.G. Salverson

---

## To Laura Goodman Salverson

February 28, 1931

Dear Mrs. Salverson,

Work not indifference has prevented an earlier reply. I was glad to hear from you because I had wondered at times where you had disappeared to, and why.

Your problem is a major one confronting the Canadian author. If you will be good enough to consult *Yearbook of the Arts in Canada, 1929* (Ed. B. Brooker) you will find an article by me of some length dealing with the point.[1] My arguments, which are on your side of the case, have never been answered, and cannot be. They have just been ignored. (If your public library has not this book, try to get them to get one (Macmillan) because it is a reference work of some value; and I haven't time to repeat my argument here.)

As a matter of fact, conditions in this respect are improving but not nearly fast enough. The worst feature of all is that you are the first Canadian writer (except myself) whom I ever heard going so far as to complain about a ridiculous, and quite unfair handicap on the native author in this respect.

The worst of it is that the editors are right. They do lose circulation in great chunks if they publish anything carnal, though these same subscribers read the same and far worse in English or American magazines right along.

All I can suggest is that you ask other Canadian writers to join you in a sort of campaign, pleading for a more enlightened attitude on the part of subscribers to Canadian periodicals. Agitate. Educate people on the point. Write about it. Quote me in that book. Take it up for debate at the Canadian Authors Association. Don't rest till you have made some impression.

You are the only Canadian author who has ever raised a voice against what is manifestly absurd and obviously unfair. Go on complaining. I'll back you up. Make an effort to read first what I've already said in print about the situation. If you can get a newspaper in Port Arthur, Winnipeg, Calgary, to take an article from you about the matter, send me a clipping and I'll try to get it copied and discussed in papers down here. Get into print somehow with your grievance. Then send the clipping to me with particulars of where it appeared, and my friends in Toronto will take up the cry and that will bring it to the attention of the wider public for the first time.

Go on fighting.
With best regards –

1 'Literature in Canada – in Its Centenary Year' appeared in the collection edited by Bertram Brooker (1888–1955), author, artist, and advertising executive who also won the first Governor-General's Award for fiction with *Think of the Earth* (1936). Brooker edited the *Yearbook* again in 1936.

---

## To Emily Murphy June 26, 1931

Dear Janey,

I was sorry to hear from Mrs. Scouten and Mrs. McClung[1] that you are not as well as usual, and somewhat amazed to learn that you are thin. But to hear of you at all was something.

You are a great old politician aren't you? As soon as Nellie told me she had been reading *Pens and Pirates* (which I have almost forgotten) I thought I detected your hand, and recalled your former urgings of me to increase my admiration for Mrs. McClung. And here the poor soul was trying to bone up on my book so as to appear to be interested in me. It was pathetic but charming. Not to be defeated, she mentioned me and the essay 'Booze, Religion and Poetry'[2] on the Thursday afternoon during her talk in Simpson's store – quite a pretty gesture.

Now comes the odd thing. At the grand banquet that night I felt impelled to go and speak to her at the head table afterwards, and to introduce Sarah. And that was where and how she got the chance to tell me about mentioning me in her lecture. Otherwise I should not have heard of it. I suppose the sight of her made me think of you, and I concluded that any friend of yours must be half decent. I also thought it courteous to speak to delegates from afar. Unfortunately I couldn't profess to extended knowledge of her work & knew better than to bluff & pretend to admire what I didn't know.

Thanks for the clippings. I enjoy anything from you always. Thanks for sending Mrs. McClung to me. I see she is an able woman and I expect that in her better moods she is an amiable one also. I hope we have an opportunity to become friends. As for yourself, take as good care of the carcass as you can. For your soul's good I've only one admonition this time. When you get patriotic, remember that Canada is a signatory to the peace pact; and it is therefore the duty of every citizen to prevent our government from engaging in war, which would be a violation of our own treaty. I see they are using the schools for recruiting points, via the cadet system; and there is a lot of militaristic talk going about. Therefore we pacifists (and that includes you Janey) must make our final effort now. War is a passing institution; and if we can keep Canada out of such criminal folly for the next 20 years, it means that no Canadian will ever have to engage in legalized slaughter as a patriotic act from 1918 until this dead star of ours disintegrates.

May I in closing, ladies and gentlemen, call your attention without modesty to a book called *Open House*,[3] of which I am senior editor and which I hope will be published in the early fall. It is a compendium of opinion – the majority of it liberal and intelligent – by 22 Canadian men between the ages of 25 and 50. Each of us (myself excluded) has a message he burns to deliver to his countrymen – and I am giving them the chance to talk out in meeting. Later I hope to send you a set of page proofs with request that you read the book in advance of publication and say something short and strong that the publisher can quote you as saying in his advertising. In case you dislike the sentiments expressed, the words hell and damn are short and strong and are not barred.

With best wishes

1 Nellie Letitia Mooney McClung (1873–1951). Author, feminist, and political

activist who, with Emily Murphy, Irene Parlby, Henrietta Edwards, and Louise McKinney, fought and won the famous *Persons* case
2 One of the comic essays published in *Pens and Pirates* (1923)
3 A collection of purportedly radical essays on various topics by members of the Toronto Writers' Club, among them E.J. Pratt, Charles G.D. Roberts, Bertram Brooker, and Merrill Denison. Edited by Deacon and Wilfred Reeves, and published by Graphic Press in 1931, the book was meant to promote and challenge freedom of speech through its 'controversial' content. With a few exceptions, Deacon found the book tame and he was disappointed by its critical reception.

---

## From Emily Murphy

405 Sylvia Court
1154 Gilford Street, Vancouver
July 18, 1931

My dear William:

Your letter has followed me in a very circuitous route and has finally reached me here where I am spending a couple of months, having secured 'leave' in order to recuperate from an illness of this Spring. I am picking up wonderfully and will soon be alright again.

I am *much* interested in *Open House* (an extremely attractive title) and will look forward to seeing the proof pages and to write something about it for the publisher. The idea is a spendid one – Every person between 25 and 50 *does* burn to deliver their soul of a message, so the book is sure to be intensely vital ... Please address it to 11011 – 88th Ave., Edmonton. If I am not there it will be forwarded here. I shall be in Toronto with Mrs. Burke[1] in October.

I am glad you met with Mrs. McClung. She is the best scout ever, and *really* amiable although you seem to have an idea to the contrary. Of course, she stands to her guns when occasion requires: she would not be any good if she did not, and she is capable of a really fine volley when she goes to it. She and I differ on one or two subjects but we decided we would never discuss them – that we were too good friends to even *seem* to differ.

Last evening Evelyn[2] and I spent several hours with Mr. and Mrs. Price (our 'Bailey') at their cottage at Point Gray [sic]. The other guests were Mr. and Mrs. Napier Moore who are *en route* to Alaska. Napier told us how you took up arms anent the remark made about all the Canadian authors being unable to crowd a bathroom at the Royal York without anyone sitting in the tub.

Professor Pelham Edgar called on me yesterday morning & we

went together to a luncheon of ten held at Hotel Vancouver to discuss the Canadian Author's Foundation. A 'setting up' Committee was appointed and we seem well off to a start. I arranged for groups to meet him here at Vancouver and at Edmonton. I am to address the Canadian Club this week on the subject of 'Canada, Her Book' (Biblios). I am trying to keep quiet and relax but it is very difficult to escape people. I have an idea they think the folk in Alberta grow fur and so are curious.

I was much interested in what you said about Canada being a signatory to the peace pact and that therefore it was the duty of every citizen to prevent our government from engaging in war. I had a talk on the subject with Dr. Perkes Cadman[3] of New York who spoke of it last week in England. I also had a long talk with Mr. Moore about it last night. He has some rather startling revelations to make in the *Maclean's* now on the press. Look out for it.[4] I'd like to go to Geneva on that Committee which goes in February to discuss disarmament. I am conceited enough to think that I have written more on the subject in Canada than anyone else, and have completer files. I was also Convenor of Peace and Arbitration for the National Council of Women of Canada, and for a time a member of the General Committee of the League of Nations. There is no use in my even hinting it though, for no mere women would have any chance whatever. I realize that the situation is frightfully serious. I tell you William, no civilization has lasted much over 1,500 years – no nation has ever attained the goal although some have come near to it – and it looks to me just now, in this year 1931, that the worst is to be feared. At any rate, whoever is sent, I hope they won't look upon it merely as a trip at the expense of the government, but that they will realize something is expected of them in the future by the people of this Dominion in the way of *definite leadership ... The time has come for action* ... O Lord, I should say it has!!!

Good bye, Lad ... Give my love to dear Sarah.

Always your old pal,

Janey Canuck

I am sending you some snaps so that you may see I am not wasting away by any means.

1 Emily Murphy's sister

2 Emily Murphy's daughter
3 Samuel Parkes Cadman (1864–1936) was an American Congregationalist pastor, author, radio personality, and pacifist.
4 The 1 August 1931 issue of *Maclean's* published an article entitled 'Salesmen of Death: The Truth About War Makers,' a denunciation of the world armament industry by Lieutenant-Colonel George A. Drew. 'In the Editor's Confidence,' a regular feature, carried a commentary by Moore strongly commending Drew's article and concluding that at the impending 1932 international conference on disarmament, 'public opinion and the appointment by each nation of delegates who are proof against cunning' could reverse the habitual futility of such meetings.

---

## To Francis Dickie July 30, 1931

Dear Dickie,

Many thanks for sheets from *The Country Guide*. Your story makes me shudder. Not that I blame you for the depths of your pessimism but it makes me feel very sorry for you, through your hardships, and I feel like a pampered lapdog beside you. I haven't gone literally without food since 1914, though since 1912 I've always owed more than the total of my assets. Just as I nearly get crawled out of the infernal hole some other thing comes along to tack on a few extra hundred and I get down to pinching pennies and saving and paying off again. It's been going on so long now that I take it as a matter of course. God knows I shouldn't grumble; I've been able to feed and clothe a family of five, and I even own a six-rooms-and-bath house, subject to the interests of first and second mortgagee (and the further fact that my taxes are a year and half behind.) But it's this bloody year in year out of never having $100 that's mine; that I can consider, now what'll I do with it? My credit's first class. I always keep even. But I can *just* do it, son. For economy's sake I've smoked the cheapest brand of tobacco so many years that I can't endure any other. I've never owned a car. $250 for an operation or something means a year's slavery to get squared away. And I'm one of the successes of Canada, commercially speaking. I'm so hard up I had [to] rent a dress-suit to go to the C.A.A. dinner last month. Yet I don't know that I'd like any other life. I never regret having given up law – so much sawdust.

I have to thank you too for copy of *Le Solitaire de la Vallée* which you went to the trouble of having bound for me. This goes with a very special collection of works I'm saving – association copies, not for sale, books whose writers I know, and about whose production I know more or less too. I don't know what'll happen to them when I'm dead, but they mean something to me they can never mean to anybody else; and there are no words to say just what they do stand for to me – tears and sweat.

Congratulate your wife on the clarity of her translation. It almost enabled me to read the story. However many common words have left my memory and I didn't feel able to discuss it critically. I lost the thread too often. So I'm running a rather queer little review, which is partly news item, partly my impression of a Simon-pure Canadian story conceived in English and rendered in a foreign language, partly hot air, which is the stock-in-trade of critics. I find you only have to keep talking long enough to be believed, whether you're talking nonsense or not.

I hope your throat infection clears up with the sulphur treatment. I'm addressing Paris as usual, which is probably safe. I do enjoy your descriptions; and if I had a paper I'd employ you as regular correspondent.

There is nothing mysterious about your not getting a Graphic prize. The whole scheme was the product of F.P. Grove, who acted as chief judge.[1] He is a Swede, who lived for upwards of 40 years at Rapid City, Man. and came into prominence here as a novelist just after you left. He's quite the big noise in heavy fiction. Yes, it's very heavy. But it's also very good. Only he knows it too damn well; and is by all odds the most conceited ass we have in the game in Canada. As a business man he was a wash-out, and as he can never see anything beyond his own work, his own style and his own views, naturally he was a hell of an editor and a rotten judge. He was fired from Graphic for a rather special kind of malpractice; and says he is now going to live in Italy and earn his living translating current European books into *English*. His personal story is tragic; but personally [he is] most objectionable, which is why – and the only reason – as the most famous of living Can. writers he is getting out.

You are cut to different pattern from different stuff, and what is unlike himself is bad, in his eyes. Therefore no prize.

The publishing situation here is awful. We are absolutely without a single house in Canada that is entirely satisfactory to the native author. If Graphic wants your book let them have it. There are 100 things wrong with them, but 1000 wrong with most of their rivals.

Now the heat – it's been a terrible summer – has kind of knocked me out and I'll have to quit, for I've more work to do yet before I lay me down to sleep.

I'll send you clipping of my comment on your mastodon,[2] and do know that I appreciate your thoughtfulness. If I ever get a dictaphone you'll hear from me often and at length. Many things have changed in Canada; but on the glorious 12th the Orangemen walk in Toronto just as in Dauphin. The comedy is far from fini.

Best regards –

1 Deacon appears to have been under a misapprehension. When Grove joined Graphic Publishers as a reader in December 1929, its literary contest for the best Canadian novel submitted to it in 1930 had already been announced. There were three ranked prizes of $2500, $1500, and $1000, of which the first went to *My Star Predominant* by Raymond Knister, who only managed to collect $1500 of his prize money before Graphic went into receivership. Knister's novel was published posthumously in 1934 by Ryerson.

2 'Canada in France,' Deacon's brief review of *Le Solitaire de la vallée*, appeared in *The Mail and Empire* on 3 October 1931. He described the book as a 'good adventure story' with 'exotic appeal.'

---

## From Duncan Campbell Scott

108 Lisgar Street
Ottawa
August 2, 1931

Dear Deacon

Your 'Introduction'[1] gave me pleasure to read. It is one of the best things written about my poems. I have been so long out of the world of letters so far as current events are concerned that I felt you had re-discovered me, a lost island, in the vast ocean. Many of yr observations are acute & well stated & yr chosen quotations are excellent & show that you really know what good verse ought to be. I am glad you dwell on my essential Canadianism. I think that is true & I hope to make a few more such poems when I am released from my fifty years' imprisonment with the Savages.

Yours sincerely
Duncan C. Scott

1 'Introduction to the Poetry of Duncan Campbell Scott' (*The Mail and Empire*, 1 August 1931) claimed two-thirds of the book page in order to discuss Scott's work in some depth.

---

## To Duncan Campbell Scott August 5, 1931

Dear Dr. Scott,

It was considerate of you to say you liked my article. Space precluded anything adequate. What was needed was a good deal of exposition, the pointing out of things, the drawing of distinctions and revealing of meanings. And that was exactly what I cannot do in a newspaper. The editor of a daily has only one rule – make it shorter. Anyhow this is the longest thing I have published in three years, and I took every last inch I thought I could get away with.

For I am convinced that, not only will the native note ensure enduring and growing appreciation of your poems, but they would be popular now if known. You have been presented as a highbrow, instead of as a man and a prophet. I have no difficulty kindling enthusiasm where I have a chance to read your work and talk about it. The pity is that those best capable of understanding it and you, and most open to and in need of the inspiration you provide, are too often the persons who tell me either that they have never heard of you at all, or that you are just a name to them and they have never read any of your verse.

Unfortunately, Canadians have such a low opinion of themselves that it is impossible for a Canadian critic to publish a volume of appreciative and expository essays and pay costs. But times are changing, even in that respect; and whether or not I can get my ideas about you out in book form, I'll find other ways to do so. A quarter of a million people have had a chance to read this; and some of them have done so.

Hoping that this will help and that the next chance will come soon, sincerely –

## From Morley Callaghan

46 Avenue Road
Toronto
September 12, [1932]

Dear Bill;

Thanks a lot for the review of *A Broken Journey*.[1] It should help a good deal. I don't know how the book is being received elsewhere, though there was a fine review in the Sunday book section of *The New York Herald Tribune*.[2] But you have certainly done all that you could do for it.

With all good wishes,
Ever yours,
Morley Callaghan

1 'Morley Callaghan of Toronto Hangs Out a Red Bottle Rag,' in *The Mail and Empire* of 10 September 1932 discusses the author's 'gradual rise to genius' and considers him the 'representative Canadian novelist of his generation.' Deacon compares Callaghan to Dreiser as the 'authentic voice of the proletariat' and praises the realism of his characterization.
2 "Prison of the Emotions," by Margaret Cheney Dawson, appeared in the Sunday *Tribune* of 11 September 1932.

## To Morley Callaghan

September 14, 1932

Dear Morley,

Thanks for your note. You have a very forgiving spirit. My article was pretty lousy; but I like you and admire your work and gave you space and display – the gifts of most practical value to you at this time. As for the lack of intelligent appreciation, which both you and I see in my review, why I did my best to understand and believe I shall gradually learn what you have to teach me.

If you knew me better, you would realize (as you may not have) that – 1. I am writing for the public, not for the author, and – 2. that I hold very strong beliefs about the critic being taught about literary art by the creative writers and not vice-versa. Of course an experienced critic of sound inner judgement can tell a lot to a mere factory-hand in a fiction mill; but all we ever know of the real art comes directly or indirectly from watching the real creators, of whom I believe you are one. (My discourse to the Canadian Authors Association at Ottawa this June was mainly explanation of the true relations in which critic and creative writer stand to each other, as per above).[1]

Now there is just one other angle to this. I am of the last pre-war crop; you of the first post-war; and inevitably there is a gulf. On my part I am not willing to play only with the has-beens and it is much more important to me than to you that I should understand you. I am doing my damnedest and trust you will be patient in view of my limitations.

The hope of the future as far as the personal situation is concerned lies in the fact that gaps in outlook due to age close quickly after one is 30. Ten years ago men who were ten years older than I were my seniors, and I scorned 'em as nitwits. Now I am their contemporary and I have a good deal of sympathy for them and feel no gap, no youthful superiority. You and I are both very conscious now of the dozen years or so that lie between us. By the time you are 40, my boy, you will be my contemporary, though that is hard for you to credit now. Time fights for youth, at first; but later adults find a mental common-denominator in spite of everything some of them do to avoid just that.

I wish I could see more of you. I hate feeling I do not know well any writer as distinguished as you who is so close geographically. Maybe we can induce you back to the Writer's Club. We want you as a member. If you won't, then I'll have to invite you to lunch as my guest ...

Incidentally, let me have a good photograph of you now that we are in touch. I want it for my files and to run on the next suitable occasion. I've run that drawing three times in *The Mail* and in both our interests there ought to be a change.

I'm glad to have your address, and if I don't see or hear from you within a reasonable time I'll write you a bid to The Club.

Sincerely,

1 'The Practice of a Critic,' *The Author's Bulletin* x, 1 (September 1932) 30–3, a transcription of Deacon's speech, claims that the critic is a specialist in 'reasoned admiration' but nevertheless remains a subjective reader: 'there are no ultimate standards in literature because life is always changing.' The critic as 'ideally

understanding reader' must possess a strong personality, only to transcend it by full immersion in the text: 'understanding can only come in the fullest by an act of self-surrender to the author, as the creative writer surrenders himself to life ...'

---

## From E.J. Pratt

Victoria University
Toronto
Sunday p.m. [5 November 1933]

Dear Billy:

Your tribute to Emily Murphy[1] was a beautiful thing. I do not know when you wrote a more lovely article, as fine and as touching as anything that ever appeared in *The Mail*. It was read from beginning to end last night aloud and before a group of eight men. It hit us all right in the emotional ganglion. You must have loved her to write like that, and I realize that you write best when you feel deeply.

I will take any bet that thousands of *The Mail* readers appreciated it.

Affectionately,
Ned

1 Deacon's obituary in *The Mail and Empire* of 4 November praised Murphy as a pioneer feminist and nationalist, but above all stressed her writing and political action as a pacifist, in keeping with his own conviction that Canada as a nation should not be drawn into a European war.

---

## To E.J. Pratt

November 6, 1933

Dear Ned,

It was most kind of you to write me about the Murphy article. You have no idea with what mistrust I publish anything like this, and consequently how relieved and pleased I am when a person of discernment approves. I am an old story now, and few ever say any more whether they like a thing or don't. Of course, we are all so busy, each hoeing his own row and paying little or no attention to the others.

But I really think Canadian literature is going to be better off when all of us writers develop the habit of commenting on each other's work, especially where we see a fellow going up what we think is a right alley. We are rather undemonstrative. Like the Scotch wife who, after 30 married years, faced her dying husband and asked: –

'Have a made a good wife to you? Ye've never telt me.
He replied: 'Weel, I canna' think o' onything to complain aboot.'

The Scottish blood is strong in Canada, and I thank God for it. I think the Scotch are wonderful people. But in their caution, they are unconsciously, and passively cruel. We could well stand more expressed approbation. I know how it helps me by cheering me up, and removing doubts.

What I did with Janey's death is inexcusable as a mere matter of manners. I made her corpse dance as a piece of propaganda. But I knew she wouldn't care. Maybe her daughter will be hurt. I hope not. But, anyway, I saw here a chance to preach another sermon; and I knew Janey would heartily approve and, at the same time chuckle over turning a funeral into a political demonstration.

Right now, the peace issue calls for every atom of strength. We can't afford to be over-nice in what means we use to win our points. I had a letter from Beverley Nichols today.[1] He reports *Cry Havoc* outselling any novel in England, but regretting the cool reception in U.S.A. and Canada. I had the pleasure of telling him the demand here has grown to the point where they had to print separately in Toronto to supply the calls.

*My Vision*[2] seems to be starting on a brisker course. I am proud of the cards displayed in the stores. When it came to making up this little folder,[3] there were far more nice remarks in my scrap-book than could be used. Thanks again for your contribution. This will also appear, about a month hence, as the body of an advertisement printed in seven leading dailies from Montreal to Vancouver.

Some day I want to see you when we are not so rushed. Just now I have to go on with this peace campaign to everyone who will listen; and you don't need any instruction – dear, loyal man that you are.

Most cordially yours –

What I couldn't print was that Janey was telling me about trying a prostitute for stealing 24 pairs of orange and green pants from a department store.

1 Popular British author, b. 1899, remembered for his war novel *Cry Havoc* (1933)
2 Deacon's last and most ambitious book, published in 1933 by Wilbur B. Best, owner of the Ontario Publishing Company. A utopian and prophetic romance of Canada's promising future, the book was anti-imperialist, pacifist, and socialist, strongly coloured by Deacon's theosophical belief in the 'dharma' of national destiny.
3 Advertising flyers for *My Vision of Canada* incorporating laudatory remarks by prominent Canadians such as Pratt, Charles G.D. Roberts, Athol Murray, Carlton McNaught, and Emily Murphy were pasted into Deacon's scrapbook of clippings and reviews about the book and its reception.

---

## From Morley Callaghan

456 Brunswick
Toronto
February 5, [1934]

Dear Bill;

You asked me once for a photograph so you could have it in your file when my next book came out. That strange event is to take place almost at once so here you are, or rather, here I am.

With all good wishes,
Morley Callaghan

---

## To Morley Callaghan

February 20, 1934

Dear Morley,

Hearty congratulations on *Such Is My Beloved*.

I'm going to try to get to the luncheon; but if I should not, don't let any of those gossiping bastards make you believe my absence is from any lack of respect for you or your wife, whom I still have hopes of meeting.

I smile at wondering how Lady Willison will treat your whores in her review for Eaton-Macmillan advertising. I have walked warily myself for obvious reasons; but I long for the day when I can print whore frankly, and employ in criticism such telling semi-obscenities as half-assed. My work will be lightened when I can, also more illuminating to the reader thereof.

My review is done and will run Saturday with cut.[1] It had to be finished in advance of my possible meeting with you, because I never want to discuss a book with the author between publication and the writing down of my opinion. I am not afraid of being lobbied, but fear the review might be an argument with the author, arising out of conversation, instead of straight impression from the book on my unguided mind, as the thing strikes me.

Your work has already become a genuine job for a critic and I foresee where it is going soon to be so engrossing that I'll be unable to handle your books to my satisfaction in the maximum space editors think a mere novel is worth.

Greetings.

1 'Morley Callaghan Still Simple But Showing Increased Insight' appeared in *The Mail and Empire* on 24 February 1934, and praised his honesty, clarity, and sympathetic portrayal of suffering.

---

## From J.S. Woodsworth[1]

House of Commons
Ottawa
February 26, 1934

Dear Mr. Deacon, –

Last fall I had from you a proof page of your new book [*My Vision of Canada*] together with a note. This I put aside intending to write you as soon as I could read the book. Unfortunately my intentions were much better than my actual performance for, although I have had the book beside me, I really have as yet had only time to dip into it. The day-by-day detail of my job seems to leave me little time.

I can say, however, that I agree very heartily with your Canadianism. It has long seemed to me that we in Canada were laboring under the handicap of living beside a powerful neighbour which dominated us economically and socially, and being a member of a powerful empire which dominated our political thinking. You seem to have had imagination enough to turn this situation around a bit and, though you may have exaggerated our importance, you would at least teach us very necessary self-respect.

Just how far we are to travel along the road of economic nationalism remains to be seen. I find that now even my friend Henri Bourassa[2] is repudiating the current nationalism. How quickly words alter their connotation and the march of events alters our ideals.

Some time when we can get together we must have a chat over many of these things which we have in common.

Yours sincerely,
J.S. Woodsworth

I'm honored by your reference in your preface to my Massey Hall speech.[3]

J.S.W.

1 James Shaver Woodsworth (1874–1942) was a Methodist clergyman, politician, and author. He was an early proponent of the 'Social Gospel,' a transfer of dynamic Christian involvement to the sphere of social and political reform, often of a socialist orientation. He left the ministry in 1907 to run All People's Mission in Winnipeg, became involved in that city's General Strike of 1919, was elected to Parliament in 1921, and was instrumental in founding the Co-Operative Commonwealth Federation (CCF) party in 1932, serving as its first chairman. A pacifist and socialist, Woodsworth wrote about the plight of the immigrant in *Strangers Within Our Gates* (1909) and *My Neighbour* (1911).

2 Joseph-Napoléon-Henri-Bourassa (1868–1952), French-Canadian journalist, politician, and nationalist. He opposed French Canada's participation in the Boer War and World War I. Between 1910 and 1932, he founded and was editor-in-chief of *Le Devoir*.

3 Woodsworth's speech of 20 May 1933 had claimed that Canada was not making rational use of its resources.

---

## From Athol Murray[1]

Notre Dame
Wilcox, Saskatchewan
April 25, 1934

Dear William Arthur,

It is hard to say what may come of this Authors Association move. They appointed a Committee to devise ways and means of assembling service club executives and educational authorities at a dinner and have me address them on the *Vision* – with a view to rallying the young folk in Regina of matriculation age and presenting it to them. It'll be a *win* if it goes over.[2]

I do wish you'd left out the socialization chapter – it's so apt to let knockers rap it as CCF propaganda – and with political alarms and excursions right now in Saskatchewan, that's dynamite. Of course I've insisted on it being made clear that recognition of the book's high inspirational value does not mean endorsation of its full philosophy.

However you won't feel hurt. You may not note the 'tie-up' in the rather rambling report of the meeting. I presented Erasmus as the stormy petrel who gave vision to the XVI century just when Cartier was discovering Canada – And Wm Lyon Mackenzie who gave us vision through his little York paper at the start of the XIX – Neither Erasmus nor Mackenzie were altogether right – but they *gave vision* and – great things followed.

God bless you always –
Athol Murray

1 A priest and an educator, Athol Murray (1892–1975) came to Saskatchewan from Toronto in the 1920s. In 1927 he took over Notre Dame convent and parish in Wilcox, Saskatchewan, and there in 1933 founded Notre Dame College. A unique educational institution housed in clapboard buildings, it was officially non-sectarian but operated in affiliation with the University of Ottawa and under the auspices of the Roman Catholic Church. The college was a product of the depressed 1930s and embodied Murray's ideal of a place of learning for students from all walks of life, which combined academic study with athletics, especially the college's famous hockey team, the Hounds. Deacon was inspired by Murray's dedication and arranged to have Mary Weekes, a freelance writer living in Regina, write an article on him for inclusion in 'Open Minds,' the projected but never published sequel to *Open House* (1931).

2 *The Regina Leader-Post* of Friday, 20 April 1934, summarized Athol Murray's speech about *My Vision* on 19 April at a Saskatchewan branch CAA meeting. 'The branch decided to appoint a committee to consider the best method of bringing Father Murray's inspiring message to the youth of the community and their leaders.'

---

## To Athol Murray May 2, 1934

Dear Father Murray,

Thank you indeed for the kind attention, and clipping. I don't altogether grasp the nature of the proposed scheme, beyond some sort of effort to connect young people and *My Vision*. Of course I am very happy to have anything like that done.

Too bad if the socialism gets in the road. Repudiate it as much as you like. The socialists have endorsed the book, barring the fact that, according to them, I am *no socialist.* I know you also disagree elsewhere. Quite all right. The views of one man are not going to prevail; but in the end Canada is going to prevail, *after* there has been sufficient discussion and public disagreement between us all, so that we find the right road between us. My book is for use, where and how and by whom it can be used.

I owe you a long letter; but my secretary[1] took sick seriously about the time yours arrived, and many things have gone undone for many months. If I ever get straightened out again ... Meanwhile, best wishes to Notre Dame and your lusty self,

Sincerely,

1 Mrs May Sharples, fellow theosophist and close family friend, was employed by Deacon as a part-time personal secretary from January 1927 to January 1934, when she had a stroke. She died in January 1935.

---

## To J.S. Woodsworth June 30, 1934

Dear Mr. Woodsworth,

Congratulations on the respectable beating the CCF got in Ontario. To me, the fine, strong showing of your candidates was not only hopeful, but the most significant item in the news. I have just finished writing my regular 'despatch,' as they call it, for my Australian paper – *The Argus* of Melbourne[1] – and the thesis is that the Liberal victory means nothing but vague discontent, and will result in nothing constructive, but the election is notable as marking the first definite step of the CCF towards power in a few years. I suggest in my article that Conservatives and CCF must ultimately fight it out to a finish; but they will first eliminate the Liberal party, as a faction without principles of any sort.

A year ago, I celebrated Dominion Day by doing a preface for *My Vision of Canada.* This year I should like to mark the date by enlisting in your party, provided you are willing to take me on without committing myself to act blindly in party discipline.[2] That may be too much to ask of you, but I should like to be more than a sympathizer as in the past. I voted for the CCF candidate in the provincial election, as did McAree who is also of *The Mail and Empire*. Yet I got there by a process of elimination. I did not care much for my candidate; and you know when I say the CCF creed I have to change it just a little bit to fit my conscience. But as I considered all the men and platforms, it became clear that nobody else represented me at all, and your aims are about 90% my own; so I swallowed the uncongenial candidate and forgot slight differences in my viewpoint and your official party program.

So you will not be buying a pig in a poke, what I chiefly fear from your party is inculcation of a class-war spirit on English Labor lines. It worried me considerably at a municipal meeting some time back to see a loyal disciple of yours working hard for a cut in the reduction of the moderate salary of a water-works engineer, on the grounds that he was a white-collar man, and also complaining in the same way about the salaries we pay women teachers. I felt very uncomfortable. I believe you, like myself, wish to raise wages to an equality with those incomes now earned by the more fortunate among the educated. But, in this part of the world, many ardent CCF-ers can't understand that the real enemy is international finance; and the proletariat and salriat [sic] are natural allies, and must be allies if we would free ourselves. Inculcation of class hatred is dangerous in my eyes, as beclouding the real issues, and as heading straight for revolution, which is always an immediate calamity, whatever its ultimate results. I therefore wish to remain independent enough to criticize the party openly, where I feel I should. I make this request because I feel (1) nothing adequate in the way of reform can come out of the old-line parties, and (2) what we of the CCF accomplish will be determined almost wholly, I believe, by the type of leadership we develop within the party – as by debates that educate the members, and that will lead us to adopt the wisest policies, not election dodges, like our opponents. I believe in government by intelligence; and that the present situation offers a clear opportunity for men of the best intelligence to be put in power and held there by unthinking masses.

In view of the next test of strengths at the federal elections, I should like, with your permission, and subject to such reservations, to call myself a CCF-er. If you think discipline too important for personal variations, I shall happily go on being party-less, with all active support thrown your way, since your party is the only hope.

You know my strong national feelings; and, if I am with you, you must be prepared for whatever happens to me as an anti-imperialist. It may scare people. Behind my nationalism is (a) the desire to avoid being dragged into Britain's wars, (b) the belief that socialism will only work, at present, when confined to a country – that, to exercise control, as we wish, the sphere of control must be strictly limited geographically. I consider as impractical a common vague international socialist sentiment. I want firm and exclusive control of Canada to set up herein a workable and working socialistic economy.

I wish I could find to send you a copy of a short article of mine attacking the Central Bank as an instrument forged to enslave Canada to the Bank of England, and through it to international finance. This was published in *The O.B.U. [One Big Union] Bulletin* and perhaps you saw it there. Brownlee approved of it, and the chief financial writer in the Mail – Sabiston – alluded to it not unfavorably.[3] Here it is: I enclose it as a specimen of how I am liable to break out; and if you would be more comfortable with me outside the formal ranks, I shall continue independent. From my standpoint, I can't afford to be gagged; but I don't want to embarrass you, either. That is why I take up your valuable time to consider the wisdom of my open adherence.

Only one other item seems important enough to mention. In view of the coming federal election, shouldn't you have, or we have, a weekly news-and-opinion sheet started at once, say from here but to cover all Canada, to be received by all members and to be on sale on the stands? I think this ought to be done at once. I understand it was left to Graham Spry,[4] who has done nothing, and whom I would not choose for the job. It is a vital work of education and propaganda. It will not finance itself but must be partly paid for from outside. I think LeBourdais[5] is your man, though he does not want the job. He has to earn his living, having given a great deal of time to the party. If he were chosen, a small salary would have to be provided. I gather he is anxious to avoid clashing with Spry and others, and feels he has done enough in the general cause. Personalities are secondary, but neglect of this obvious instrument of communication strikes me as improvident. General-circulation newspapers have been generous but many matters of instruction should be conveyed to party members which the dailies cannot carry. Between the stump-speech and high-brow articles in the *Forum* by

Underhill,[6] there is quite a gap. And in that gap are the body of your potential supporters. A skilfully planned weekly during the next few months would win thousands of votes. It need not be an expensive printing job, but it must be well edited, so that the cartoons are hot stuff – cartoons, satire, solid argument etc.

Having made the inroads you have into the staff of *The Mail and Empire*, I think you should be encouraged; but the doctrines will have to be expounded without let-up. I am getting out a book this fall that is pretty frank propaganda.[7]

Barring accident, I suppose Mr. King will be the next prime minister;[8] but you should follow him.

With best wishes,

Sincerely,

1 *The Argus* was a Melbourne, Australia, newspaper for which Deacon wrote a series of articles on Canada between 1931 and 1935.

2 In fact, Deacon did not join the party.

3 Probably Thomas Stuart Brownlee (d. 1968), night editor at *The Toronto Star* and Colin Sabiston (1893–1961), on the editorial staff of *The Mail and Empire* and subsequently *The Globe and Mail*

4 Born in 1901, Spry was national secretary to the Association of Canadian Clubs (1926–32). He organized the Canadian Radio League in 1930 and became an authority on Canadian broadcasting policy. Active in the League for Social Reconstruction and one of the multiple authors of *Social Planning for Canada* (1935), he was at the time of Deacon's letter vice-president of the CCF's Ontario section.

5 Donat Marc LeBourdais (1887–1964), journalist, author, and for a time editor of *The Canadian Nation* (1919–21), in which several of Deacon's articles appeared. Defeated as the CCF candidate for High Park in the Ontario provincial election of 1934, he ran again without success in the general election of 1935 and was supported by Deacon, who wrote a biographical sketch on behalf of LeBourdais' candidature.

6 Frank Hawkins Underhill (1889–1971), member of the University of Toronto's Department of History (1927–55), nationalist, a founder and editor of *The Canadian Forum* (1920), charter member of the League for Social Reconstruction (1932), and responsible for the 'Regina Manifesto' (1932), the party platform of the fledgling CCF party. In the 1930s, Underhill spoke and wrote against Canada's British connection and for isolationism.

7 The projected 'Open Minds,' which never appeared

8 William Lyon Mackenzie King (1874–1950), Liberal Prime Minister for all but a few months from 1921 to 1930, was defeated by R.B. Bennett. However, as Deacon predicted, King decisively won the 1935 general election and remained in power until he retired from politics in 1948.

From J.S. Woodsworth

House of Commons
Ottawa
July 2, 1934

Dear Mr. Deacon, –

You surely have a sense of the dramatic. When I came down to my office this Dominion Day your very welcome letter was waiting to encourage me.

I am very glad indeed that as a journalist you think that the Ontario election was far from being disappointing. That is my own feeling. We have now had general elections in British Columbia, Saskatchewan and Ontario and in these three provinces have polled some 300,000 votes. It seems to me that even with the methods we have used in the past, it will not be impossible to make that 300,000 into a million.

Then I was even more delighted to know that you had practically decided on definitely coming into the CCF.

With regard to your anti-imperialistic ideas – I think that you are not more anti-imperialistic than some of the rest of us. You fear a vague international socialism. May I suggest that all of us, capitalists and socialists alike, are being forced away from a vague internationalism into a very definite national planning. But I would point out that this does not necessarily mean an isolationist point of view. International relations are so close and complex in the modern world that I doubt if it is possible any longer for any one nation to live to itself. The older capitalist internationalism was built up on the export of surplus commodities. With the extension of the capitalist system into even less developed nations, this type of export is steadily diminishing, and even the capitalist faces an entirely new situation. With this there is bound to be a revision of socialist tactics.

While we may recognize that capitalism is the same the world over, and that we cannot have a full measure of socialism until there is a socialized world, I think we must insist that our first job, as I tried to emphasize last year at Regina, is to set our own house in order, and that in doing so we must reckon with our distinctively Canadian situation and traditions. Here, of course, we come somewhat in conflict with the older socialists, most of whom have a European background. But our CCF is distinctively Canadian.

Then again with regard to the position of the 'white collar' section. As you are aware, up until recently there have been the two groups – Farmer and Labor, and these working almost in watertight compartments. The CCF sets out to effect cooperation between these two, and also to bring in the third group of business and professional people whom I would in the old phraseology characterize as the new proletariat, and who, if they can be won, will undoubtedly contribute very largely to the organization and policies of the new movement. In attempting to bring together these three groups we are undoubtedly up against a very great problem, but it is either a case of getting them together or heading right into chaos or fascism. The background and psychology of these groups have been very different. It will require a great deal of patience on the part of all, and further, a very steady effort to interpret the one class to the other. But I think that it may be done.

With regard to discipline – it is, of course, desirable that in so far as possible we may present a united front. No organization can tolerate those who are seeking to undermine it, as was the case with certain near-Communists in the Toronto affair.[1] But, on the other hand, it seems to me that any party is in danger of becoming stereotyped which does not permit of free discussion, and even considerable divergence of opinion. We have had to face that in our little caucus here in Ottawa, and I have always contended that while it is desirable to get a solid vote of our group, it is not right that this should be achieved by forcing men to vote against their conscience. There are questions of tactics in which one does not object to bowing to majority opinion, but there are matters of vital importance by which no man can surrender his own best judgment without stultifying himself.

Under these circumstances I see no reason why you should not be able to definitely join the CCF. Of course we are a democratic organization, and in joining you are apt to run up against some unreasonable individuals in certain local organizations. I am afraid that the wrangling that often goes on has sometimes disgusted those who would otherwise associate with us, but I fancy that you would be able to pick a group which you would find congenial. If this is impossible there is still the LSR,[2] through which you could do definite propaganda work. But as the CCF is a definitely political group, I would hope that you would find it possible to get right into the fray.

Thanks for sending me your article on the danger of Canada's

Central Bank becoming a bit of imperial machinery. I suggested this in my first speech on the Central Bank. The only remedy, it seems to me, is to make the bank directly responsible to Parliament.

With regard to the publication of a 'News and Opinion' sheet – this is undoubtedly important, but the question is one of finance. I do not know whether you realize that we have carried on now for nearly two years with practically no financial support. At the present time, even at headquarters, we are behind with our printing bills and our postage. The precipitation of election campaigns has prevented us from building up any reserves whatever. However, I think that as some of you men who are accustomed to organization work come into the movement we may succeed in tapping certain resources that hitherto have not been available to us.

Again let me say that it is tremendously encouraging to realize that a new Canadian movement, which I think really represents many of the old pioneer ideals is now gaining ground in our country.

If you receive an extra copy of *The Melbourne Argus* with your article you might let me have it.

Yours sincerely,
J.S. Woodsworth

1 In 1932 there had been a riot at the Kingston Penitentiary during which prison guards had fired shots into the cell of Tim Buck (1891–1973), the leader of the Communist Party of Canada. He had been jailed earlier that year for seditious conspiracy and was charged with having shouted encouragement from his cell during the rioting. A.E. Smith (1872–1947), head of the Canadian Labour Defence League and himself a Communist, claimed that Prime Minister R.B. Bennett, who had been determined to make an example of Buck, was morally responsible for the shots fired at Buck. Smith was subsequently charged with sedition for his statements. His free speech trial took place in the winter of 1934, at which he was acquitted by a jury of the charges. Frustrated in his attempts to form a united front with the fledgling CCF party, an amalgamation opposed by Woodsworth, Smith accused the CCF leader of instigating the charge of sedition against him. Some members of the party vehemently opposed Woodsworth over the amalgamation issue and one Ontario section was expelled from the party. As a result, the 1934 CCF provincial congress adopted constitutional measures to ensure that disciplinary action could be taken in the future. See Kenneth McNaught, *A Prophet in Politics: A Biography of J.S. Woodsworth* (1959).

2 The League for Social Reconstruction, formed in the fall and winter of 1931–2 by Frank Underhill, F.R. Scott, and others as a forum for social progress, intellectual debate, and public education. Woodsworth wrote the foreword to their manual, *Social Planning for Canada* (1935). Members of the LSR were involved in the

formation of the CCF, issuing from the *Regina Manifesto* (1932). For many who feared the repercussions of membership in a socialist political party, the League offered an alternative.

---

## From Athol Murray

Notre Dame
Wilcox, Saskatchewan
July 9, 1934

Dear William Arthur,

Just before pulling out for the East Mrs. Weekes[1] long-distanced me to be sure to write you a word about Notre Dame and the local Wilcox High-school and also about prospects of Carnegie Corporation helping us this coming year. With regard to the first – it might be well to soft-pedal it altogether as nothing definite has yet been done; though it is understood the High-school will suspend activities, due to hard times – which means the students will go to Notre Dame. Later I propose approaching their board for the use of their building. As to Carnegie – I have their assurance that they will give thought to helping us on our way when they hold their Fall meeting in September. They said they would be greatly influenced if we managed to 'get by' the first year satisfactorily. I have an idea your book will probably clinch it.

Things look pretty black for the West right now. The 'hopper menace is now a reality. From day to day they are developing into a tremendous plague. Reports from Stoughton and other points south indicate they are even taking the bark off the trees. In addition we were hit by a heavy frost last Thursday – July 6th! – and farmers rather fear it caught the wheat berry in the milky stage. Altogether prospects are about as dismal as they have ever been or could be. Which means Messrs R.B. Bennett and J.G. Gardiner[2] have plenty of grief ahead – with close to a million Saskatchewan folk looking to them for 'relief' through the coming winter. What then to do? Never more did Canada need men with the faith and courage and vision such as yours. That alone is what will bring us through. These are truly great days in our country's history provided we have the men to save the people from going 'hay-wire.' Possibly you were even more of a Prophet than you dreamed; certainly the course of events overseas are rapidly implementing your forecast.

I enclose a summary of O'Dwyer's campaign.[3]

Bien à vous,
Athol Murray

1 Mary Loretto Weekes (b. 1885) was a Regina freelance journalist, author of several books with romanticized Indian settings, and in 1934 president of the Saskatchewan CAA. Deacon had originally arranged for his and Murray's mutual friend Laura Lee Davidson to write the Notre Dame article for 'Open Minds.' Her wavering and Deacon's subsequent overtures to Mrs. Weekes resulted in confusion involving both Deacon and Murray. Within two months, Mrs Weekes had submitted 'A University College that Grew Out of Nothing,' a 3300-word article, never published but preserved in the Deacon Collection.

2 James Garfield Gardiner (1883–1962), Liberal Premier of Saskatchewan (1926–9), Leader of the Opposition (1929–34), re-elected Premier 19 July 1934. His letter to Murray listed the various library services instituted by the Liberal government for Saskatchewan's rural residents, and promised future co-operation between his party and benevolent organizations promoting the circulation of 'good publications.'

3 Pat O'Dwyer, a Notre Dame teacher, eventually published the first of a series of articles about the need for a national chair of libraries in *The Reginan* of 24 February 1935 under the title 'Canadian National Library: A Plea.' O'Dwyer cited *My Vision* and its call for resources in support of Canadian teachers and intellectuals.

---

## To Athol Murray July 12, 1934

Dear Father Murray,

Thanks for your good letter of the 9th, which crossed my note. I regret the pinch you are in, meaning both Notre Dame and your people at large. I'll be tickled to death if the Weekes article in *Open Minds*[1] assists in getting needed endowment for you. I hasten to say that I don't see any chance of publication before October 1st and it may be later. Schedules delayed by poverty of contributors, and inability of Wilfred Reeves[2] to do anything to help with the work. Not his fault; but it would take us all our time to be off the press by October 1st, and I don't see how I can possibly do it alone.

Mrs. Weekes was through here and I saw a draft of article, which is just about right. L.L.D.[3] corrected two details of fact. Mrs. W., in terror of your modesty, had flattened down her own enthusiasm for your glorious project. I have suggested she revamp very slightly, to let indicate her own real approval. Of course it would never do for you to see text during constructive stage; but I think you can trust these two women and me to do the decent thing, without making the sort of vulgar fuss that might embarrass you.

I'm passing on to her information about local high-school so that her wording can be adjusted to the situation.

Pat O'Dwyer's library plan strikes me as very important. Is there any reason why benefits should be confined to Saskatchewan? Would he make up an article for the book by (1) stating arguments to show that book circulation [is] vital (as I am sure he did in his speech) and (2) outline the plan itself, perhaps a little more fully than in this newspaper report? I presume the skeleton plan could be covered in 1,000 words or less; but the article ought to be readable, and reasons for comprehensive library service ought to be developed pretty fully, as preliminary; so I suppose the whole should run to around 2,500 words. Will you kindly speak to him, asking him to write me whether he would be willing to broadcast his plan by this means. It would add a note I should be glad to have in the book.

Of course one of the main reasons behind the Notre Dame article was and is favorable publicity to result somehow in practical support. I feel the move is a right one, but just who is to be moved I can't say. Probably for five years this book will be circulating; and even if there are not many copies in esse, still you ought to be hearing from it from one quarter or another. It is my business to broadcast the seed. Net results I can't control nor bother with. Higher Powers must direct the effects; but I hope you get a harvest. Experience makes me think that the fruits will be of various size, and some of unexpected nature.

The heat in this city is terrible this summer –

Good luck to you,

1 The projected sequel to *Open House* (1931), which was to include more general articles on pacifism, trade unionism, nationalism, birth control, and other progressive or controversial issues and causes, was never published due to lack of funds.

2 Wilfred Reeves (b. 1901), freelance journalist, member of the Writers' Club and, with Deacon, editor of *Open House* (1931) and of the projected 'Open Minds.' In 1934, he was the editor of *Confectionary, Biscuit, and Chocolate Journal*, which he founded in 1927.

3 Laura Lee Davidson (1871–1949), a Baltimore, Maryland, school teacher and author of *Winter of Content* (1922), the autobiographical record of her winter in

an Ontario cabin. She had sent the manuscript to Deacon, who reviewed it enthusiastically upon publication. Its sequel, *Isles of Eden* (1924), described a summer at Bobs Lake, where she met and befriended Athol Murray. Deacon had originally wanted her to write the chapter about Murray's college for 'Open Minds.'

---

## To Athol Murray November 11, 1934

Dear Father Murray,

My warmest thanks to you for the many addresses on *My Vision of Canada*, which you have delivered to Regina schools. I am proud of your interest and support, which I like to feel is because my book in some ways expresses your own ideas on the future of our country, to which you are making so signal a contribution. Mrs. Weekes sent me a clipping from a Regina paper mentioning your lectures. I presume an orator like you never uses typed material; so there is no convenient way of getting the benefit of your remarks. If this exists in print, I should be grateful for copy.

My life is one continuing apology for things that do not get done; and now I must add my tardiness in expressing appreciation for your generous efforts. Believe me, I should rather have this book discussed before young men and women than any other class. In Toronto, some teachers and principals have taken the book to their hearts and pressed it (privately) on the brighter students; but at no point in Canada, other than Regina, have educational officials of any rank taken public notice of the publication, as you have. I therefore feel my silence is the less excusable.

The fall is always a stressful time with me; during three months 60% of the year's important books are issued; and reading them, now that novels have grown from 300 pages to 500, 600 and 1,200 pages, is an Herculean task. Due to shortness of funds, I have had to move my office home.[1] No letters have been filed for a year, so I can't locate information. My correspondence is very heavy; and I don't dare drop it, though often I am writing letters till 2 a.m. It is five minutes to one now. Formerly I had some assistance but not in the past year, when 'the' book has caused people to write me from Australia, Peking, U.S., England, Ireland, and every part of Canada. People are most kind, most appreciative. The least I can do is say Thank you. During last fall, 1,400 copies got distributed. Since last Christmas, the total sales have averaged just under two copies a week. The trade takes no interest in a last year's book. I spent possibly $200 in cash, perhaps more; my royalties to date are $79.50. So you see, being an exclusively Canadian author hardly pays. Except in whatever good is done and *friends*. For the first time in my life I feel that, through the book, the people to whom I really belong are making themselves known and making overtures.

One further apology I have to make. Despite some magnificent stuff in ms for *Open Minds*, there is no publisher yet for it; nor have I been able (since Reeves can't help with routine) to complete my own editorial work. This has been a grief as far as my feelings for the contributors are concerned; but chiefly I have regretted that it was not out doing its bit for you and NOTRE DAME. It is not abandoned but I dare not yet name a date of publication. In a way I am glad it did not get launched this season, which has been fatal to Canadian books so far. Not one native book has had any sale among those bearing 1934 imprints. I trust 1935 will be different and that *Open Minds* can get away to a strong start before spring.

There is so much I have not time nor strength to tell you – all about the inside of the publishing business, the revolution needed in that branch; the growth of nationalism; the insuring of our peace if and when Europe next goes berserk. I regard that fight as won. I wish you could see, or I were able to make copy for you of 'A Canadian Catechism' drawn up by the Ewart Foundation.[2] It is a masterpiece of 12 foolscap pages and I expect it will form part of *Open Minds*.

Many plans are being discussed for a publishing house, for a weekly opinion sheet in which you and I and all the other articulate nationalists may swap ideas and information, and reach the public; for adequate lecture circuits for same purpose; etc. etc. So far we have no end of talent, lots of sympathizers but no money. However, I feel that all this talk and discussion is leading to something practical and that they will crystallize in definite action. Till then I'm tied up to a hard grind and pinching pennies.

All I wish to say is: Don't be discouraged. There is no need. The *spirit* is abroad and many feel it. It will be made manifest in deeds soon. The clearer we can each see our desired objectives, the more quickly we shall realize them as soon as the doors are open. I had lunch the other day with Harry Stevens and was much impressed by his simple sincerity.[3] He does not give a hoot what happens to his career so long as his reforms are accomplished. I suppose you have great faith in Mackenzie King, who now seems certain of election next year.

I *must* pass on. Don't measure my gratitude by my neglect. I am truly deeply touched by your interest, and value highly the work you have put in. I don't think it's lost or wasted. Incidentally, it heartens me very much; and I hope the day is not far off when I may be able to thank you personally.

With every good wish for you personally and your fine College,

Sincerely your friend,

1 Deacon had rented an office in the Wilson Building, 73 Adelaide Street West in the fall of 1928 when he was hired by *The Mail & Empire*. He gave it up in October 1934.

2 'A Canadian Catechism,' a list of approximately 200 questions and answers, was a nationalist document written by the Ewart Continuation Committee of the Ottawa assembly of the Native Sons of Canada. The committee had been named in honour of John Skirving Ewart (1849–1933), the Canadian nationalist, Ottawa lawyer, and author of *The Kingdom of Canada* (1908) and *Independence Papers* (1925, 1932).

3 Henry Herbert Stevens (1879–1973), at this time Minister of Trade and Commerce (1930–5) under R.B. Bennett, was heading a parliamentary committee which from February 1934 to February 1935 investigated price spreads, price-fixing and mass buying on the part of large corporations. As the result of what he felt was government inaction in the face of his committee's report, Stevens resigned his portfolio, left the Conservatives to form the Reconstruction party, and decisively weakened Bennett's shaky government, which lost to a Liberal landslide victory in 1935.

---

## To A.R.M. Lower[1] December 3, 1934

Dear Lower,

For God's sake, what have you been up to? Carey[2] sent me clippings and I have just written a letter of thanks and approval to Riddell, along lines of his nobility in protecting you;[3] that we must have freedom of speech for professors without King Gordon penalties,[4] in order that educated intelligence may supply political leadership in Canada.

I see my uncle[5] has been raising hell with you. He is a good old scout, but too old, too set. Had my father lived he would have been horrified at my views. Follow Robert Owen's[6] advice: Never argue; repeat your assertion.

See McNaught's article on professors in affairs current issue *U of T Monthly*.[7] The joke is he wrote it to support Underhill and C.H. Mitchell (who is a Babbitt and head of S.P.S.)[8] took it to himself and formally thanked Carl. Look that item up.

Newspaper report of your article very unsatisfactory and I'm too busy to write at length. If your paper is printed, send me a copy, please. Meanwhile I'll pass on word that you are in trouble and to be backed up – regardless what your thesis is.

Don't treat this lightly. I've always noticed that Wpg is a crucial point, where people get het up, and love to fight issues to a finish. The air is stimulating there and everybody knows everybody. Here controversies get lost; too many are indifferent to any one issue. The peace fight has been the big one with us. I consider it won. Concentrating on demand for plebiscite (due to misunderstanding of what Meighen said at Hamilton)[9] Canada is *not* going to support Britain in the coming war. Feeling in some sections will be almost as bitter as in civil war; no govt can now wage war without the plebiscite and that will mean a huge peace majority – no matter who the participants, what the cause.

Your position may be far more significant than either Underhill's or Gordon's. Everything depends with [sic] Riddell. If he backs you, you will not become a casualty. Whether you fall or not, the right of professors to speak will be won. The new forces coming into play as the younger men take over secure that result. I also firmly believe that no man who stands for a principle ever loses by it in the long run. Should you be martyred, the next turn of the wheel will exalt your horn – provided you have stuck to your view of truth through thick and thin.

I've no clear idea of what you've said and I don't give a damn. You fellows have got to be allowed to speak out in meeting. Otherwise our whole university system proves itself emasculate. You may be feeling uncomfortable under the punishment but it is the very best publicity you could have for your ideas or personally. This kind of trouble must never be sought – nor avoided. When it is a clear case of the truth as you see it, compromise would do something to you inside that you'd never recover from.

Best luck –

1 Arthur Reginald Marsden Lower (1889–1988), Canadian historian and nationalist, who from 1929 to 1947 taught at United College, Winnipeg. On 6 November 1934 he gave the College's public lecture on 'A Foreign Policy for Canada,' in which he eschewed the principle of Canada's loyalty to Britain in the event of war. Calls soon came for his dismissal, but they were ignored by J.H. Riddell, President of Wesley College. Lower and Deacon were united by broad democratic principles and, more specifically, by their mutual commitment to the cause of Canadian nationalism. For a period, they became interested in the 'Native Sons of Canada' movement, but soon decided that it lacked the substance necessary to the realization of their goals. Lower proposed a new nationalist group, prepared a draft charter, and sent it to Deacon. The group, however, never materialized. In 1947 Lower became Douglas Professor of History at Queen's University, where he remained until his retirement in 1959. His best-known works are *Colony to Nation: A History of Canada* (1946) and *Canadians in the Making: A Social History of Canada* (1958).
2 N.T.W. Carey, president of Winnipeg branch, Native Sons of Canada
3 John Henry Riddell (1863–1952), Methodist clergyman and President of Wesley College (1917–38), had written a letter in support of Lower which was published in *The Winnipeg Free Press* on 24 November under the title 'Colleges and Free Discussion.'
4 John King Gordon (b. 1900), the son of Charles William Gordon ('Ralph Connor'), was dismissed from United Theological College in 1934, ostensibly because of budget restraints. Deacon and Lower were convinced that his involvement with the League for Social Reconstruction and with the CCF party were the causes of his dismissal and that the censoring of such activities put at risk the issue of academic freedom.
5 Thomas Russell Deacon (1865–1957), owner of the Winnipeg Bridge and Iron Works and mayor of the city in 1913 and 1914, sponsored WAD for his law training in Manitoba. In a letter published in *The Winnipeg Evening Tribune* on 10 November 1934, T.R. Deacon took issue with Lower's lecture.
6 British reformer and socialist (1771–1858)
7 Carlton William McNaught (1883–1963), advertising executive and Canadian nationalist, who from 1936 to 1948 was associated with *The Canadian Forum* as its secretary-treasurer and editor. His article in the November 1934 issue of the *University of Toronto Monthly*, 'Twenty-Three Years After: A Graduate Reviews His Idea of University Education,' argued that 'professors should not be merely specialists in a particular department of study, but men of the world and men with opinions; and that they should have the fullest freedom to give these opinions the weight and backing of their own personalities.'
8 Charles Hamilton Mitchell (1872–1941), civil engineer, soldier, and Dean (1919–41) of the University of Toronto's Faculty of Applied Science and Engineering, which began as the School of Practical Science (SPS) in 1873 and was frequently

designated by these initials for years following its constitution as a faculty in 1900.

9 Nine years earlier in Hamilton on 16 November 1925, Arthur Meighen had given a speech in which he argued that immediately following a declaration of war by a Canadian government and before any troops were despatched, a general election should be called to pass judgment on the decision. Many Conservatives attacked Meighen as an ultra-nationalist who wished to sever Canada's connection with the British Empire. Others argued that a national election on such an issue was, in fact, a plebiscite and therefore inimical to a parliamentary democracy.

---

## From A.R.M. Lower

Wesley College
Winnipeg
December 12, 1934

Dear Mr. Deacon:

I am delighted to find out that here and there in Canada there are people who are ready to spring to arms in the cause of free speech. God knows we need them.

My own case is not particularly important, I suppose. I delivered a public lecture in Wesley College on the Foreign Policy of Canada in which I examined our relationships to the sacrosanct, and, touching the ark of the covenant, ought properly to have been struck dead. I would have been if MacTavish of *The Tribune* and his pack of unlettered wolves were to have their way. It seems as if it were treason in the eyes of one section of our people – not necessarily the old-country born – even to suggest that our own country, its future and its needs demand our attention before those of the Empire. It is hard to convince many Canadians of their duty to Canada: they are colonials.

That is the attitude against which you inveigh in your book, and very properly. I hope we may wish each other success in our mutual crusade.

I have seen your letter to Dr. Riddell and must thank you for your work in that quarter. You may have seen his really fine letter in *The Free Press*, pledging his unqualified support to the principle of academic freedom, a letter which gives a lead, I think, to all our college heads, timorous as many of them are.

Again thanking you, I am

Very truly yours
A.R.M. Lower

## To A.R.M. Lower December 20, 1934

Dear Lower,

I am delighted to have made contact with you over this. I send you copy of *The New Commonwealth* with my short article in it.[1] If I had not been terribly busy with Christmas literary supplement I should have had a bigger article in a more conspicuous medium; for the matter is important and Riddell's statement was masterly. Unfortunately we control no press as yet; but at the rate *The Mail and Empire* is opening up to radicalism of all sorts it may not be long till the chief Tory daily is our mouthpiece.

It is as well for us to know where to find each other as the Crisis may come suddenly. Difference of opinion is so sharp that I'm afraid we can't avoid bitterness and something very like civil war. However, I've not the faintest doubt about the result. Canada will go neutral by about 73% to 27%. The thing to concentrate on is demand for a plebiscite, as Mr. Meighen was misunderstood to say at Hamilton. Pamphlet with his Winnipeg speech explains he didn't say anything of the kind, still less did he mean to keep Canada out of war. But everybody thought he said that, and the idea (promulgated by me, among others) has caught on and no end of bodies have passed resolutions about it. I say let us stick to demand for plebiscite (not election) and we are safe, considering the French, Russians, pacifist veterans, women, clergy with guts, et al. We'll run up a nice decisive majority. I think Bennett's government has probably already committed us; but they simply dare not ignore the howl that will echo across Canada.

What Meighen did say was this: The cabinet will declare war as usual, and 'commit the country to the conflict.' Then call parliament together and vote confirmation of cabinet. This is sure as it has now become a disloyal act to oppose the government. Then 'while busily training and equipping the troops and pressing recruiting' (or words to that effect) but before said troops leave Canada, hold a general election, which is sure to return government because it will be disloyal to vote for opposition candidates. The people have had their say; a new government has a mandate to prosecute war, and five years without any need to consult the people.

That was what Meighen said. Did you ever hear of worse political chicanery? That's why it is God's mercy he was misunderstood to say plebiscite, when he actually said election. So the game is to stick to stubborn demand for plebiscite, which will set a world precedent and be the first step in abolishing war. We can get that plebiscite and win a big majority – truly democratic.

I suppose the Canadian people are about as stupid as others; I often think more so; we so lack initiative and moral courage; but it is an error to imagine them mindless or spineless, despite several colonial generations, who were taught not to think about foreign affairs.

When I published *My Vision*, I thought I was alone, and if there were converts, these would be children or shallow-pates who had fallen for the obvious emotional appeal I made consciously on the strategy that hardly anybody is convinced by logic: you must stir their feelings. Hitler and I are entirely at one on that technique. (By the way you should read *The Third German Empire* by Van Der Bruck, 1923 and now translated, Nelson, $3.25; it explains the Nazi principles; and I think you would heartily agree with the philosophy, esp. attack on laissez-faire liberalism.)

But I have found in the past year and a half that readers of *My Vision* are sound and sane and solid folk; and when you see all the different sorts of people who think with us, and are getting up courage to say so publicly, one's respect for Canadians goes up.

You might be interested in A.A. Milne's *Peace with Honour*. He is helping me to place my article 'Canada Won't Fight' in *The New Stateman and Nation*.[2] I'd be glad if you would get the December issue of *Gold*[3] with my article 'Canada's Conquest of Canada,' and also secure the pamphlet *The Sedition Bill Explained*, 6d, published by *The New Statesman*, 10 Great Turnstile, W.C.1. This has become law and is serious business re free speech despite amendments made as a result of this pamphlet, prefaced by J.B. Priestley.

I can't secure another copy of *The New Commonwealth*, so I wish you would show my little piece to Dr. Riddell. But keep the clipping yourself. God knows what may come up where you'll be glad of a little pulpy support. I suppose you know Harold Innis of U. of T. (Economic Geography) is strongly with us; and there are many thousands of equally bonny nationalists, apart altogether from the nationalist element in the CCF alloy. Among others Armitage,[4] my close friend, a native of Australia but considers himself Canadian though he is down there now. He has just sent me carbon of article he has mailed to *Free Press* on relations of Australia and Japan. Be on the look out for it.

As I see it, events are driving us daily to the independent position. The Statute of Westminster really ended the empire but a neutral Canada will finish it. Leacock's recent article deploring provincialism and calling for a stronger central power at Ottawa is very good.[5] He gets converted late but is coming along, still trailing his imperial umbilical cord. He says here that Brit. Govt paid the $1\frac{1}{2}$ million $ to Hudson Bay for the prairies and donated it to Canada. Is that a fact? I thought Dom. Govt put up its own money.

Plug away, and never get discouraged for we are going to win this campaign. Merry Christmas –

1 We have been unable to locate the journal or a copy of Deacon's article.
2 The essay was not published in this journal.
3 *Gold*, 'A Magazine of the North,' edited by Wallace J. Laut, began appearing in 1933. Deacon's article was written to combat 'the colonial hangover' in Canada's policy-making.
4 John Armitage (b. 1885), Australian journalist and labour union activist, who came to Toronto in 1925 from China where he had worked as an editor of the *Hong Kong Daily Press* (1922–5). He was a member of the Toronto Writers' Club, worked as a freelance writer, contributed an article to *Open House* (1931) on China as a future market for Canada, and in the early 1930s moved to Winnipeg to work with *The One Big Union Bulletin*. In the fall of 1933, the *Bulletin* office was raided by the police and Armitage found himself implicated in charges arising from a subscription competition. Discretion being the better part of valour, he returned to Australia in early 1934.
5 'Is Canada Breaking Up?' (*The Ottawa Journal*, 15 December 1934)

---

## To Archibald Belaney[1] January 19, 1935

Dear Grey Owl,

Knowing authors like to see what is said of their books, I send you my page from today's *Mail and Empire*.[2]

Also, I offer congratulations on a book which moved me considerably.

Permit me to say, as a critic, that I believe a reviewer has an important function in reporting and explaining books to the public; but I do not believe there is one chance in a thousand of a critic saying anything useful to the author. Go your own way; don't pay any attention to what any of us say in print about your work.

Privately, I will tell you that I enjoyed *Pilgrims* the more because it is a drama of the individual soul; I think men are most interested in the actual struggles, inner and outer, of some particular man. It was also better because it does not bear the same evidence of conscious care and high polish that *Men of the Last Frontier* does. Historically, your first book is the more important; but for general interest and as literature, *Pilgrims* has the advantage. I fancy both will be kept permanently, and believe your success is of a very solid kind.

With best regards,

Sincerely,

Beaver Lodge
Prince Albert National Park
Saskatchewan

1 Archibald Stansfeld Belaney (1888–1938) was born in Hastings, England, and emigrated to Canada in 1906. Attracted by the outdoors, he travelled to Temiskaming, Ontario, and immediately began the assimilation into bush life that gave him his new identity as Grey Owl, the self-styled Scottish-Indian conservationist and wilderness writer. The films made about him and his books made Belaney internationally famous in the 1930s and took him on two highly successful tours of England and the United States in 1935–6 and 1937–8. His works include *The Men of the Last Frontier* (1931), essays portraying the Ojibway culture as Belaney first knew it in 1907, *Pilgrims of the Wild* (1934), a memoir of his journey to save the beaver from extinction, his children's book *The Adventures of Sajo and Her Beaver People* (1935), and *Tales of an Empty Cabin* (1936), stories of humans and animals in the wilderness. The most complete biography is Lovat Dickson's *Wilderness Man: The Strange Story of Grey Owl* (1973).

2 'Grey Owl Feeds His Beavers' was written on the occasion of Belaney's appointment as honorary ranger to Prince Albert National Park, Saskatchewan. Deacon provided biographical information, mainly through a description of *Pilgrims of the Wild.*

## 159 January 1935

From A.R.M. Lower

Wesley College
Winnipeg
January 29, 1935

Dear Mr. Deacon:

I should have answered your very interesting letter sooner, but must plead the usual delays. I read the clipping from the *New Commonwealth* with interest as also the article in *Gold*: they are both of the right sort. I am sending you a copy of a radio address I made here some time ago under the auspices of the Canadian Institute of International Affairs.[1] It was very well received and I have had many approving comments on my position from quiet people here and there throughout the province. So that I think the nationalist movement is growing in Canada.

Your remarks on Mr. Meighen's famous speech and what he really said are completely novel to me and I would be very much indebted to you if you could either secure me an authenticated copy of the speech or inform me where I could get one. Personally, I doubt very much if we shall be put to the test in this issue of war, at least not for a long time. But I am also equally certain that the old Imperialist school in England is playing its game again and would like to have us all nicely tied up in advance. I am curious for example to know what Sir Maurice Hankey[2] was really doing over here. It happens that this winter we have a group of the Institute here studying Canadian Foreign Policy and as chairman, I have drafted the programme which I enclose.[3] The members are good fellows but even people of the calibre of Dafoe do not seem to realize the need for knowledge first and abstract theorizing afterward. My aim will be to make our position on the Pacific as clear as possible and then deduce from it the obvious conclusion: – that our policy there is as elsewhere, one of minding our own business. We had a set to in the Institute the other night, when men like MacWilliams and Prof. Osborne,[4] both of whom you probably know, attacked me, but got little support, indeed some men came quite enthusiastically to my defence. Both these men are colonials of a hopeless type.

Your friend Mr. Car[e]y wants to start some sort of nationalist group here, for study and propaganda, but so far he has not got any converts of sufficient calibre to make it worth while. I have one or two of the younger academics with me, but there are few people who are really 'sold' on the question, few who see that the sole condition of our continuance as a political entity is the development of a genuine national life. How far that can be hastened I do not know, but I do know that I for one feel the heavy weight of the culture of other and older lands upon me and would like to have a life of my own, not an imitation of life, as in so many respects it is the fate of a Canadian to have. For we cannot escape the fact that we are all colonials, more or less, simply because we are units in a colonial society. We need our own 'prophets,' our own movie stars, our own songs and all that sort of thing.

Is there any use talking in terms of an organization?

Yours very truly
A.R.M. Lower

1 Founded in 1928 by a group of private citizens to encourage Canadian research, discussion, and publication in the field of international affairs. Lower was very active in the Institute in the 1930s and 1940s.
2 Maurice Pascal Alers Hankey (1877–1963), British diplomat, cabinet minister, and imperialist. As early as 1932, he had attended an imperial economic conference in Ottawa at which Deacon was also present.
3 The draft of the program has been lost.
4 Roland Fairbairn McWilliams (1874–1957), Winnipeg lawyer who, under the pseudonym Oliver Stowell, wrote with his first wife Margaret *If I Were King of Canada* (1931), a portrayal of monarchist solutions to Canada's economic problems; McWilliams later became Lieutenant-Governor of Manitoba (1940–53). William Frederick Osborne (1873–1950), author of *America at War* (1917) and other books, was for many years a professor of French at the University of Manitoba.

---

## From Archibald Belaney

Beaver Lodge
Prince Albert National Park,
Saskatchewan
January 30, 1935

Dear Mr. Deacon:

When I went to Europe with the Canadian Expeditionary Force I thought, in my ignorance, that I was fighting for Canada. I thought Canada was an independent Nation. Under the yoke of Cockney Sgt. Majors, who would have still, many of them, been cleaning spitoons in the Palmer House only for the war, (& whose attempts at vituperation, by the way, I found very inept & unimaginative) – I found the difference.

I was born in the United States, which country I respect & admire (less the emasculate gigolo element we hear in the monkey band over the radio), but I have been in Canada since 1905, & am intensely loyal to this country. Aside from the fact that I have been made a Canadian citizen, my status as a native-born has been conceded by the Native Sons of Canada, who very courteously invited me to become a member. I am rather proud of my acceptance by them, & of my membership (Assembly 118).

But the formalities of my enrolment as a citizen affected me in a different way. How I was to be a *subject*, first, & a citizen afterward. Now I read, in the folder you so opportunely send me, that the representatives of the Canadian people have refused to consider having a flag of their own. Our (pardon me if I say 'our,' I feel that way about it) 'Maple Leaf,' or 'O! Canada!' is submerged beneath the funeral strains of that servilely sycophantic Imperial Anthem. If the real Canadians took more interest in their country, & did not leave the handling of affairs to outsiders, such things could not be done. Hence I look forward with pleasure to reading your book *My Vision of Canada*, which I have sent for.

I must thank you for your very kind & discerning criticism of my own poor work. Knowing authors as you do, it is not much use me telling you I thought it poor, but it is customary to say that, apparently. I am no writer & have no intention of becoming one, professionally, realizing my limitations. But for a man who is trying his unskilled best to paint a few word-pictures of one phase of Canadian life that will soon be a thing of the past, opinions such as yours are a great encouragement, invaluable indeed.

I cannot agree that expert criticism by a reviewer is irrelevant from the author's point of view, not at least, in my own case. Your statement to the effect that *Pilgrims* is better written than the *Vanishing Frontier* book, is a very valuable piece of information, to me. I had expected to be censured for having written too freely, supposedly with the carelessness of one who is just a little too sure of himself. The fact was, I made no attempt to dress the story in its Sunday best, but let it wear its own well-fitting, if simple attire. It is only by taking instant advantage of such hints that I have been able to evolve some kind of a method; they are my only guide posts, as I am quite alone here & have to do the best I can.

Therefore, again, I thank you.

With kind regards
Yours Sincerely
Grey Owl

---

## To Archibald Belaney

April 24, 1935

Dear Grey Owl,

Thought you might like to see enclosed review of *Pilgrims of the Wild* from Australia.

Met an acquaintance of yours[1] from the woods who says you are all Scotch without a drop of Indian blood in you; and suggests you assume the Red Brother for artistic effect. Do you want to deny the charge? What proofs of origin have you?

Sincerely,

1 Sandy MacDonald who, according to Deacon, was a bush pilot

---

## From Archibald Belaney

Beaver Lodge
Prince Albert National Park,
Saskatchewan

Dear Mr. Deacon:

May 10, 1935

Received your kind letter & the Australian review. Kind of reaching out eh? Have just sent away the M.S. of a book for children, 45,000 words, 18 sketches besides thumb-nail sketches for chapter headings.[1] Lots of Wild Life; nearly every animal in the woods depicted. Believe my sketching technique is improving.

Now about my friend who suggests I have no Indian blood, but am all Scotch. Firstly, the only people who have known me real well since I came to Canada 30 years ago, are bush people & Indians of the type who do not go to Toronto, nor speak of 'artistic effect.' No one living in this country knows anything of my antecedents except what I have chosen to tell them.

If I have not analysed my blood-mixture quite as minutely as some would wish, let me say here & now that here are the component parts.

Mother – 1/2 Scotch (American)
1/2 Indian
Father – Full White, American,
*reputed* Scotch descent.

Therefore I am a quarter Indian, a quarter Scotch & the rest reputed Scotch, tho unproven.

Now there it is. You may know that all persons of 1/2 breed 'nationality,' also all persons having less divisions of Indian blood, are known as half-breeds. I never even stopped to figure the thing out. My friend whom you met, has only my word for it that I have a drop of Scotch blood. Some people, you must know, object to having a 'native' accomplish anything. As my whole life-training, my mentality, methods, & whole attitude is undeniably Indian, I have given credit for anything I may have accomplished to the people whom I look on as my own. Unfortunately most men of my type, in whom the Indian, at first glance, is not so strikingly apparent, spend much time denying their Indian blood, & claiming to be French or smoked Irish or something. This I refuse to do. Give all credit for my small success to the white people, (no offence intended) & leave the Indians, who taught me what I know, holding the bag? No sir. It is the admixture of Indian blood that I carry, with some pride, that has enabled me to penetrate so deeply into the heart of Nature; yet undoubtedly the White part has enabled me to express it adequately.

There are thousands of mixed bloods like myself kicking around the North; some favour the Indian, some the white; those that favour the white deny their Indian blood which makės me mad as a wet hen. It is a strange anomaly that my wife who is nearly full-blood Indian, could not, when she married me, speak 10 words in any Indian language, even her own, & knew no more about bush life than a young miss from the sidewalk on Yonge Street. I, who was 3 parts white, was the better Indian. Civilization plays strange tricks on us. Right now, so quickly she picked things up, Anahareo[2] can shade many a practiced woodsman, both in skill & courage. This last attribute is her most outstanding characteristic.

When I first commenced to write a few articles, the Editor asked who & what I was & I said I was a bushwhacker, a man of Indian blood. What I meant was, I was tarred with the brush, & felt I was admitting something. I expected he would at once turn me down.

This has happened, socially, before, & often since. The artistic effect I never even thought of. I figured I would write a few articles till I got enough money to move the beaver to Ontario, & then quit, & follow my natural way. That the writing business would assume the proportions it since has, never even occurred to me. When the Government took me up, they used the word Indian in describing me, as they said 'breed' was derogatory, God knows why. I did not figure I should call myself a white man, because when it was found out, as it eventually might be, that I had Indian blood, down I go with a wollop. I feel as an Indian, think as an Indian, all my ways are Indian, my heart is Indian. They, more than the whites, are to me, my people.

So my good friend was astray even in his knowledge of my Scotch ancestry. I can only claim of a certainty 1/4 Scotch. His evidence is unreliable.

I do not intend to deny the 'charge' publicly. The Government is very strict on me avoiding any debate whatsoever. It is a queer paradoxical situation; the one thing that I was so particular to tell about, for fear it would be found out & so destroy me (apart from my sense of justice to these people), that same thing is now denied in the form of an accusation! Perhaps the gentleman is Scotch & would like to have me so also. I have never seen Scotland, cannot understand them when they are talking, & never thought very much about all these things one way or another until all this damnable publicity started ramming stuff down my throat. The wonderful reviews about my books, recognition for my work with the beaver, I welcome gladly. I never figured on all this racial stuff. I am a man, a kind of a one, who loves the woods, the waters, a good canoe, a good pair of snowshoes, my wife, my beaver, – and little children, I think, above them all. I am trying to do a little good in this old world of ours, so my life will not be entirely a reproach, & certainly don't want to get involved in any foolish racial quarrels with anybody. If I hadn't been part way successful, no one would care three hoots in hell what I was. Dogs will bark & snap at my heels, but I will, as you advised yourself, just keep on going, no matter who says what.

I wrote this Winter, what I feel is a beautiful little story of two Indian children & their beaver pets.[3] I put my heart & soul right into it & used as characters a young Indian boy & girl I knew away back in 1906. I have never seen them since I left that village, & to me they have never grown up, neither they nor the beavers (Chilawee

& Chikanee), & so I see them still as they were in those dear dead days of my youth, that are now far behind me. I hope by means of this book to become endeared to thousands of little children, while they learn, as they read, of the hopes & the fears, the struggles, the sorrows & the joys of others, both human & animal, who are not perhaps so well gifted as themselves; yet whose feelings are so very much like their own. This I consider to be much more important than bickering, or attempts to establish who or what I am. Who the devil cares.

A man can call him [sic] a Chinaman so long as he keeps on buying the drinks, but let him try to step out of the rut & do something, & see all the hands reaching to pull him back again. It would take very little, just a touch or two of discord & I will fold up my foolish pieces of paper & my piles of crazy notes & notions, & go back into the obscurity to which I belong, where I can at least be happy. Somehow all this public stuff has me buffaloed. Perhaps a fellow will get used to it. But the temptation comes very strongly at times to drop everything & hit for the North, where I don't have to wonder if some Smart-Alec hasn't twisted some of my statements to suit his fancy, & got me in wrong with somebody. It is only the beaver that hold me. I will be faithful to them, so long as either they or I shall live. My wife & daughter can follow me, but they cannot. And they are so utterly dependent on me for their safety. Always they *know* I am there; I am part of their lives. And they trust me. So I stick. Though I wouldn't give one acre of Northern Ontario for 5,000 square miles of this depressing Western Country. Homesickness has me down at times, & I sit for hours beside a fire, thinking of my few, but good friends at Bisco;[4] they seem to bé so far away & unattainable. You have heard the wind singing in the pine trees perhaps? There is no tree in this country can reproduce that sound. And then I hear that some one of my old acquaintances is taking what he considers, poor fellow, to be a rap at me. I wish some of them knew how I feel about *them*, counting the days till I see them again.

Though nothing has been decided, there is talk of me touring Great Britain on a lecture tour. If it materializes I intend to stop off in Toronto, & may call on you for a little advice.

Pardon this very long & very dull letter. Blame it on nostalgia; it is a hobby of mine. I suppose a man of any strength of character would push it out of his life, but I can't; too firmly rooted in the pine lands, & white water, & the smoky, balsam scented tents of the Ojibway Indians.

Hope you will like *The Adventures of Chilawee & Chikanee* when it comes to you. The reviews of the *Pilgrim* book, in Canada, U.S., & England, have somehow given me a new outlook, have aroused in me a desire to make good before all these men who have taken my faltering phrases & called them Art. I feel somehow in debt to you reviewers; you are showing me the road ahead, & by God I must step along right manfully & keep their, your, good opinion if I can.

Your book *My Vision of Canada* did not arrive yet, as nothing can come in save the lighter mail until the ice goes. Am looking forward very much to it.

With best wishes I am

Yours sincerely,
Grey Owl

1 *The Adventures of Sajo and Her Beaver People* (1935), written for his young daughter Dawn. There were, in fact, nineteen sketches.
2 The Iroquois woman who was Belaney's common-law wife and the mother of Dawn. *Devil in Deerskins* (1972) is Anahareo's memoir of her life with Grey Owl.
3 Belaney is still referring to *The Adventures of Sajo and Her Beaver People*.
4 The abbreviation of Biscotasing, a lake and hamlet, situated in the Mississauga Forest Reserve, eighty miles north of Sudbury, Ontario. Belaney lived in this area from 1912 to 1914 and from 1917 to 1925.

---

## To Morley Callaghan September 10, 1935

Dear Morley,

When your wife asked me how I liked *They Shall Inherit the Earth* I side-slipped, disappointing her I fear. The truth is that I was about to begin composing my review and find it disconcerting to talk with an author (still more so with his wife) about his work when I am trying to co-ordinate my impressions for discussion before a general audience. In such cases, my public remarks are apt to continue the conversation with the author, and the poor public does not get told What Every Public Should Know.

Allow me, now that the last paragraph of my piece is finished, to congratulate you most enthusiastically on this novel. I am not only particularly pleased with it per se, but rejoice over the tremendous progress you have made over the past two years. You must be conscious of and heartened by this increase in your powers.

In some ways I regret that I am not addressing a literary audience, because the nature of your book made it necessary for me to use much of my space for elementary instruction of unsophisticated readers. I want to anticipate objections to clear the ground for you; and I am not ashamed of doing pick-and-shovel work to let you get unimpeded into the consciousness of Ontario, because the capture of the home town is the hardest fight your popularity is every going to have. And when you win Toronto the rest of Canada will follow like sheep.

In admiration,

---

## From F.P. Grove

R.R. 4, Simcoe, Ont.
September 15, 1936

Dear Mr. Deacon,

I hope the enclosed[1] will fill the bill. It's the best I can do out of distant memories.

I was surprised to see that there still are people who bother about my books, after such a lapse of time which has made me an old man.

Yes, I have written a few more books; but publishers fight shy of them. I am just now, in the intervals of a desperate struggle for the daily bread, as a farmer, finishing the second draft of an Ontario novel.[2] Whether it will ever appear, I can't tell. And I don't suppose it matters.

Sincerely,
F.P. Grove[3]

1 See page 169 for a reproduction of the drawing which Grove sent in response to Deacon's queries as he prepared his *Literary Map of Canada*.

2 Grove is referring to *Two Generations: A Story of Present-Day Ontario* (1939).

3 Deacon wrote 'Answered September 22, 1936' on this letter but did not keep a copy of his reply. Frederick Philip Grove (1879–1948), the Canadian novelist, was living in Simcoe, Ontario, at the time of his correspondence with Deacon.

Deacon had championed his work in the 1920s, defending *Settlers of the Marsh* (1925) from charges of indecency and urging the publication by Graphic Publishers of Ottawa of *A Search for America* (1927). Grove's subsequent position as reader with the Graphic Press (1929–31) was disappointing to Deacon.

---

## From Marshall Saunders

62 Glengowan Road
Toronto 12
September 19, 1936

Dear Mr. Deacon,

You are quite right about *Beautiful Joe* – the scene was laid in Halifax, but Joe was an Ontario dog.

In 1892 I was visiting my brother Jack who had been put into the Finance Department by Sir Charles Tupper.

In our Ottawa boarding-house was a girl from Meaford, Ontario – Louise Moore by name. She was studying music, and soon became engaged to my brother.

I went to Meaford to visit her family and took a great liking to their dog Joe who had been cruelly treated by a tenant of Mr. Moore's and had been rescued from him.

Joe and I became great friends, and when I went home and found that the American Humane Education Society of Boston was offering a prize for the best story about domestic animals, I resolved to move Joe from Ontario, group our family pets about him, and try for the prize.

My first step was to start a number of scrap-books labelled dogs, cats, horses, cows, sheep, etc., and to get my parents and friends to tell me all the stories they knew about animals domestic and wild.

My Father dictated the wild animal chapter to me. We had Indians all about us and he had been much with them for hunting. They liked him because he did not swear as some of the other white men did.

I had a good deal of practice in writing stories, but none of them had interested me as much as this one of my own family and I wrote rapidly.

You know Nova Scotia and understand how much we are like our American cousins. It was no trouble to turn Halifax into Fairport, Maine, and Canadians into New Englanders, and it was a polite gesture toward the country offering the prize.

Mr. and Mrs. Morris are my parents – Jack, Ned and Willie my

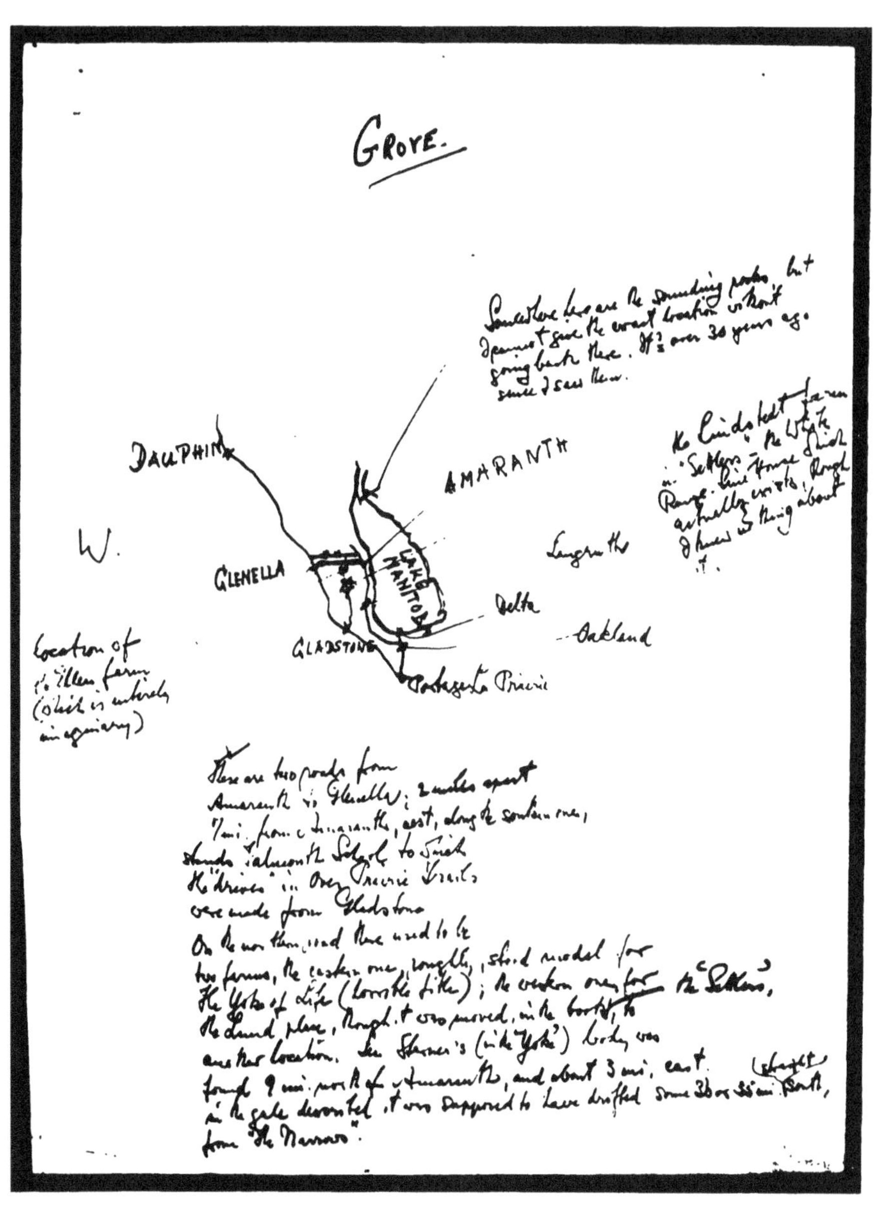


Grove's first sketch submitted to Deacon for the *Literary Map of Canada*. See letter of 15 September 1936.

brothers. Laura our lovely, saintly sister who died at seventeen – and the most of the other characters are taken from life.

Malta was our cat at the time, Jim and Billie our dogs, and we had 60 rabbits in the carriage-house loft beside other pets.

I was delighted when the prize was awarded me by Edward Everett Hale, Hezekiah Butterworth and Dr. Philip Moxom,[2] but not nearly as much surprised as I was sometime later when I took a second prize from this same American Humane Education Society.

The subject was 'Crime – Its Cause and Cure,' and Edward H. Clement of *The Boston Transcript*, Edward F. Sweeny editor of *The Boston Evening Traveler*, decided that my essay had won the prize.

My parents were born philanthropists and had taken me with them to the old gray penitentiary down in Point Pleasant Park, to the County Jail, the City Prison and the Poor-House where I played the organ for twenty years. So I knew something of criminals. However, this is another story – I assure you of my pleasure in hearing from you, for I chafe against not seeing my friends and the resting time of some months yet.

With best regards to your wife and love to the dear children.

Yours faithfully
Marshall Saunders[2]

The prize given for *Beautiful Joe* was $200 – the one for the crime essay $300.

1 Hale (1822–1909) was the Unitarian minister of the South Congregational Church of Boston, Chaplain of the US Senate (1903–9), and an author whose books include *Franklin in France* (1887) and the autobiographical *A New England Boyhood* (1893) and *Memories of a Hundred Years* (1902); Butterworth (1839–1905) was assistant editor of *Youth's Companion* (1870–94) and author of juvenile books such as *In the Boyhood of Lincoln* (1892) and *The Patriot Schoolmaster* (1894); Moxom (1848–1923) was a Baptist clergyman, University Preacher at Harvard (1894–7), and the author of, among others, *The Aim of Life* (1894) and *From Jerusalem to Nicaea: The Church in the First Three Centuries* (1895).

2 Margaret Marshall Saunders (1861–1947), remembered for her animal stories for children, of which *Beautiful Joe*, the best-selling 'autobiography' of a dog, is the most famous

From Arthur Stringer

75 Laurel Hill Road
Mountain Lakes, N.J.
September 20, 1936

Dear Bill:

Thanks for your kind note of the 13th, which should have been acknowledged before this ... As you may have seen by the public prints, I motored up to Western Ontario last month and tried to buy back my old home at Cedar Springs. But that Kresge millionairess of Detroit out-bid me and I'm not, after all, getting the old place back. (And on the way up, between you and me, I was pinched and fined for speeding, within fifty miles of the old homestead. How's that for dramatic irony: the expatriate hastening to the scenes of his lost youth, glowing with anxiety to reach once familiar fields, – and then a King's Highway motor-cop gathering him in!)

The locale of *The Prairie Wife*, though not definitely mentioned, is southern Alberta. The ranch which I still own out there is seventeen miles south-west of Calgary. In this connection the A.L. Burt Company are just re-issuing my prairie trilogy (*The Prairie Wife*, *The Prairie Mother*, and *The Prairie Child*) in one volume, under the title of 'The Prairie Stories.' (And in this connection again F.P.A.[1] once asked in his column why I didn't do 'The Prairie Dog' and then I'd have the whole damned family).

I *do* hope *The Canadian Poetry Magazine* can be kept going. Something like that is needed on our side of the Line. And I'm glad to see you're giving a helping hand. Good luck to you![2]

Yours in the Faith,
Arthur Stringer

1 Probably Franklin Pierce Adams (1881–1940), whose humorous column 'The Conning Tower' ran from 1914 to 1941 in four New York papers: *The Tribune*, *The World*, *The Herald-Tribune*, and *The Post*. *The Diary of Our Own Samuel Pepys* (2 vols, 1935) was culled from the column.

2 From January to July the first three numbers of *The Canadian Poetry Magazine* had appeared with losses of $1800 and there was talk of suspending publication. Its new business manager, Dr Jacob Markowitz, provided practical business sense and generous financial support, and helped re-establish the magazine, the fourth number of which appeared in March 1937.

## From F.P. Grove

R.R. 4
Simcoe, Ontario
September 24, 1936

Dear Mr. Deacon,

Enclosed please find an outline map with the line of travel roughly sketched in.[1] I have not read the *Search* since 1920; but I think the list of cities in the corner of that map roughly gives the picture as traced in the book. My *own* trek across America was vastly more complicated – and longer.

By the way, do you know any Canadian magazine that might print, as a serial, a short Ontario novel of mine (though whether I could call it a novel, I am not so sure), about 70,000 words, dealing with the *economic* situation and its consequences as it has developed during the last decade or so? Nothing very grim or dark-coloured, though in a way tragic: it sprang out of my profound admiration for the indomitable courage of the farmer; and it is very 'up-to-date,' ending with the end of 1935. I am most anxious to get a few pennies out of it to relieve my desperate financial situation.

Sincerely
F.P.G.

P.S. – I hope that map does not seem too grudging. It seems to be the best I can do at the moment.

1 See page 173, a reproduction of the map in question.

## From Adjutor Rivard[1]

Cour du Banc du Roi

Québec
25 septembre 1936

Dear Sir,

I beg to acknowledge receipt of your kind letter of september instant and I take much pleasure in giving you the very simple informations you are asking for. C'est de votre part une attention dont la bienveillance me flatte et dont je sais faire la plus haute en même temps que la plus juste appréciation.

Though giving you very willingly those informations, I know

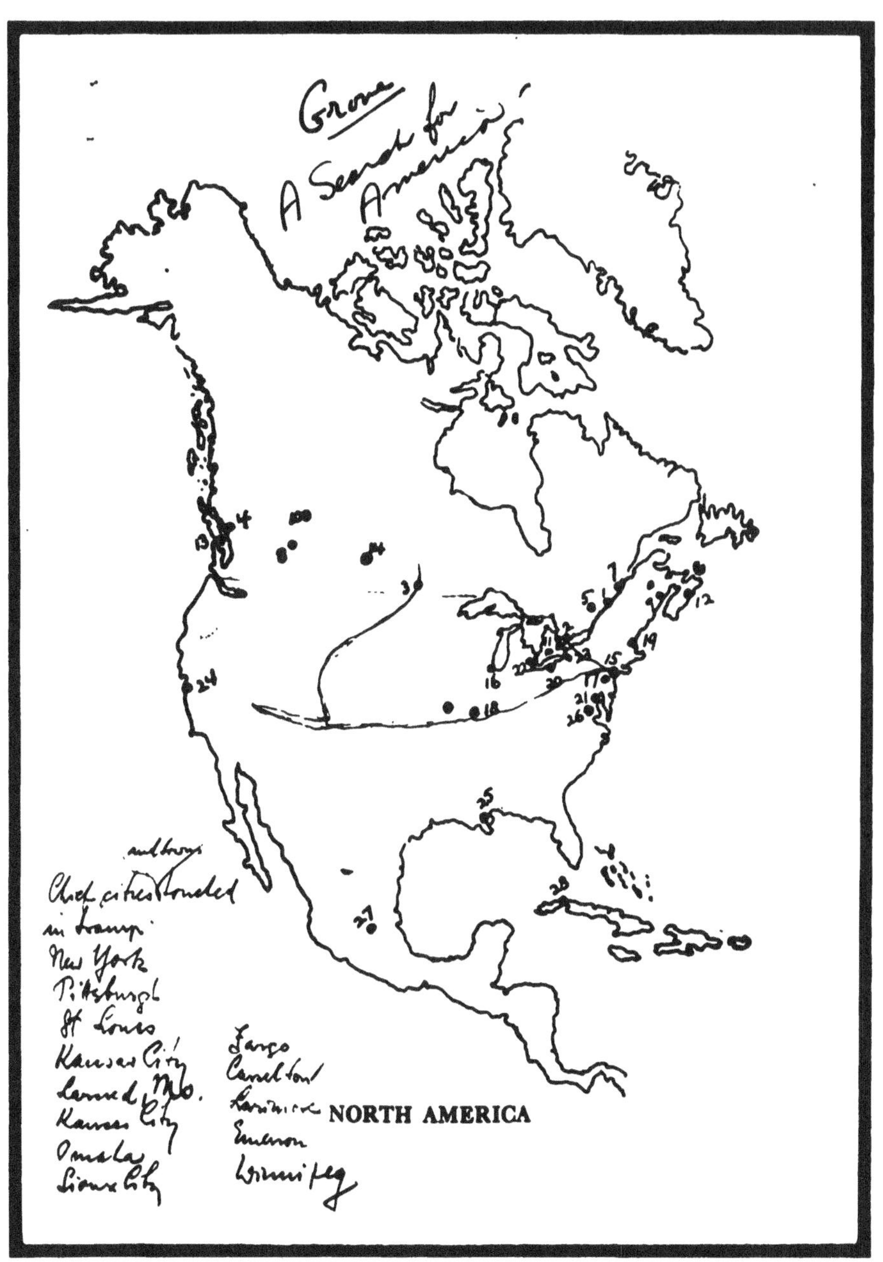


Grove's second sketch submitted to Deacon for the *Literary Map of Canada*. See letter of 24 September 1936.

perfectly that they are of no importance at all; you want to get them only, I am sure out of a kind sympathy for the author of *Chez nous*, and for that you may be assured that I am most thankful.

I was born in a little village in the county of Nicolet, on the south shore of the St-Lawrence opposite the city of Trois-Rivières. The village is called: La Rochelle, probably because it was, if not founded, at least mostly inhabited by french acadians whose ancestors had come in New France from the place so called in the province of Saint-Onge not far from Bordeaux, in France. Actually the name of La Rochelle is very seldom used and one rather say the parish of St-Grégoire, near the little town of Nicolet. It is there and in the adjoining parish of Bécancour that I have lived for many years and that after coming to Quebec, I have returned times after times and spent many happy days. Therefore the things and the people I have tried to describe are mainly of this part of the country.

Je pense que c'est là ce que vous voulez surtout savoir. Ces détails sont sans doute de peu d'importance, mais parce que j'y attache moi-même un certain prix, je vous suis reconnaissant de l'intérêt que vous voulez vous-même y porter. It is probably useless to mention it to you: but the life of our people is nearly the same all through our province, though many find here and there slight différences in the language, the traditions, etc.

I beg to remain

Yours truly,
Adjutor Rivard

1 Magistrate and writer (1868–1945), remembered primarily for the sketches in *Chez nous* (1914) and *Chez nos gens* (1918), which were combined as *Chez nous* (1919) and published in 1924 by Ryerson as *Chez Nous: Our Quebec Home*, in a translation by W.H. Blake

---

## From A.R.M. Lower

Wesley College
Winnipeg
September 28, 1936

Dear Mr. Deacon:

I should have written you long ago, in appreciation of your kindness and hospitality and also to do something about your suggestion for a group of some sort. However I am just getting squared away for the work of the term and am cleaning up these matters now.

I am enclosing a short document which would be my idea of what has to be attained before we get into a satisfactory position in this country.[1] This could be made into some sort of general statement representing the ideas of reasonably likeminded people, and circulated to them. This would give a certain degree of unity to our thinking. We could then by correspondence elaborate on points in it, clearing up our own ideas, and out of it I would expect some writing to come. We could also formulate our position with respect to current matters and perhaps get something done. Just now, for example, the talk is all of more immigration and I am very much afraid that we are in for another douche that will still further reduce any prospect of forming a national spirit and temperament. Perhaps between' us, if we were more or less organized, we could do something to meet that, by getting the counter-forces to work, in this case, labour and the French.

At any rate give me your ideas on what I enclose. If we could only start off with half a dozen people, we might accomplish something, especially if we had a centre and clearing house, such as you suggested Ewart[2] to be possibly willing to become.

Very truly yours.
A.R.M. Lower

I suggest beginning with the following: R.A. Mackay.[3] Mr. Ewart. Frank Underhill. Possibly Forsey[4] of McGill and the president of the Native Sons.[5] A Frenchman? E.K. Brown, U. of M., Wpg.

1 The document is appended to this letter.

2 Lower is referring to Thomas Seaton Ewart, whose father, J.S. Ewart, had died in 1933. T.S. Ewart was a lawyer and prominent member of the Ottawa assembly of the Native Sons of Canada. On 13 August he spoke at Couchiching about Canada's independence within the British Empire, a speech reported by Deacon in the *Mail & Empire*.

3 Robert Alexander MacKay (1894–1982), political scientist and diplomat, was at this time a member of the Department of Government and Political Science at Dalhousie University (1927–47). He was a member of the Powell Royal Commission on Dominion-Provincial Relations in 1938, and later in his career was Canada's ambassador to the United Nations (1955–8).

4 Eugene Alfred Forsey (b. 1904). His book *Towards the Christian Revolution* had appeared in 1936, and he had the previous year contributed to the LSR's *Social*

*Planning for Canada.* He had been a lecturer in economics and political science at McGill since 1929.

Programme (Prospectus, Manifesto? Statement? Creed?) of the
'SONS OF LIBERTY'?
"COMMITTEE OF CANADIAN CORRESPONDENCE?
NATIONALISTS?
CANADIAN INSTITUTE OF INTERNAL AFFAIRS?

The objective of this group would be to clarify from every possible angle the position and condition of this country and to exert what influence it could in the direction of guiding policy along the lines it had come to some agreement on.

In a broad way, the group believes that Canada can never solve its problems satisfactorily until its people come to look at them from a national point of view as contrasted with a provincial, colonial (or Imperial) or racial point of view. Its ultimate aim, therefore, is to establish Canada as a nation in the completest sense of the word. While the group deprecates the extreme expressions of nationalism manifest in such countries as Germany and Italy, it nevertheless is of the opinion that for a loose and scattered country such as Canada, with its lack of homogeneity in the fundamentals of race, religion and economic interest, the only common bond that will be found sufficiently strong to make our divergent elements into one society is the bond of a common country, in other words, nationalism. The group therefore would be prepared to make both a practical and a philosophic defence of the principle of nationalism in the case of Canada and believes that one of the most necessary tasks for the well-being of all our citizens is the heightening of the spirit of Canadian nationalism. This is virtually synonymous with strengthening the sense of social responsibility, for it implies the creation of a spirit which will put the public good before private interest, which will put the whole (the country) before the part (the province or section) and which by centring all our loyalties here rather than abroad will go a long way to heal the gap between the races.

The group conceives that its objective would require

A. In general terms:

1 A change in loyalties. The old 'loyalty' to Great Britain must disappear (there is no reason why the old cordial relations should: 'affection' for the mother land must be distinguished from loyalty to it) from English-speaking Canada, to be replaced by loyalty to Canada.
2 Making war on colonialism in every sphere. An effective counter-sentiment in English-speaking Canadians must be engendered to set off against their inherited Imperial sentiment.
3 Racial and religious toleration as between English and French.
4 Frank acceptance of the fact that the Canada of the future must be one of many racial strains, no longer merely a British country.
5 Strengthening of the Federal government, diminution of the powers of the provinces.
6 Attempts to weaken provincial loyalties, which sap national loyalties.

B. In particular terms:

1 An enunciation of the principles governing our foreign policy which would preclude any possibility of taking it for granted that we would be in the next British war.

2 A campaign against further immigration, except of the most limited and self-propelling nature. No national life in any real sense is possible as long as the personnel of the population continues to be renewed from foreign countries generation by generation. This to include immigration from Great Britain.

3 Some policy on the revision of the B.N.A. Act.

4 Termination of appeals to the Privy Council.

5 Limitation of the right of the defence forces to correspond with their opposite numbers in G.B.

6 A policy of national defence, without reference to our 'obligations' to the Empire.

7 A cultural programme of an active nature.

Advocacy of agencies along the lines of the Dominion Drama festival.

Consideration of a national theatre and national encouragement to the literary arts. National encouragement to the visual arts is already extended through the National Gallery. National encouragement to scientific research is common. Recognition that the arts play an even more important role in national life than the sciences, must be sought.

Multiplication as energetically as possible of every device for heightening national consciousness and giving it an adequate content. Examples: national festivals, as above, art galleries, museums, marking historic sites, etc. An open air museum has recently been suggested, along the lines of the 'Skansen' at Stockholm. Note the recently established Quebec Provincial Zoological Park, a collection of Canadian animals and birds.

8 An educational policy: The old drum and trumpet history should disappear from the schools and the history of the Canadian people take its place. Lamentable deficiencies of the average teacher of history to be attacked, as also minor place of Canadian history in the curriculum.

Since little agreement on economic policy can be expected, it is purposely omitted. But the point is that until we become a self-conscious national unit, which implies a sense of individual responsibility to the country as a whole, economic problems will never be satisfactorily solved. As long as 'Canada' remains a term, a geographical expression or a hazy intellectual concept, there cannot be expected much within its legal framework but the self-interested strife of warring interests and groups.

A healthy society lives not so much upon economic well-being, though that is necessary, as upon certain moral or spiritual concepts. These inner matters are the real things that keep mankind going. They are social dynamics. In Canada where the traditional dynamics of race, religion, language, etc., divide rather than unite, what common dynamic can be found? There would appear to be no other but nationalism – a common system of law and government and a common allegiance to a common country.

5 This point was subsequently the subject of a 'Brief Submitted to Royal Commission on Dominion-Provincial Relations by The Native Sons of Canada,' dated Winnipeg, 8 December 1937 and written by Lower, R.O. MacFarlane, and J.B. Coyne.

---

## To Adjutor Rivard September 28, 1936

Dear Sir,

Please accept my thanks for the important information about *Chez Nous*. Of course I understand these genre sketches are generic; but for map purposes they must be localized, and your book is so widely known that many will wish to trace your essays to their source.

Since writing you, Macmillans have accepted the map for publication; and my leisurely ways must be mended. It is the intention of the publisher to exhibit first at the Book Fair here in November 7–14; and then to try to place copies with the schools right across Canada. I have about a week to complete data for the artist. You will understand that this is a pictorial venture. Items must be related to places, and suit the purpose best when they can be illustrated by tiny drawings.

While I have always been deeply interested in Canadian literature, I suffer from the usual handicap of my race over languages. Hence my knowledge of Nelligan, Cremazie, Frechette[1] and other big men of French-Canadian literature is not intimate enough to serve me for the hurried research that is now necessary.

In the name of Canadian literature and culture, may I call on so busy a man as yourself to suggest a list of novels, poems and essays in the French language to go on that map? I require to know location, title of the work, whether novel, poem or as the case may be, and author. The well-known, 'obvious' names are to be preferred. Your list might run from 25 to 50 nominations, with as much geographical spread as possible. If convenient, it would be better to divide them into essential and possible – that is, first and second importance.

The idea of this is that a whole mass in one spot will ruin the graphic harmony, and that where literary works are too thick, we shall have to select rigidly, whereas greater hospitality can be shown in districts otherwise blank.

The location should be that of the setting of the literary work rather than the home of the author. Par example, *Maria Chapdelaine* is entered for Peribonka, north of Lake St. John. In the anthologies, I see many possible items, such as 'La Cloche de Tadoussac' by Charles Gill,[2] but I simply do not know the relative popularity and importance of these compositions among the French people themselves.

I am one who believes in a Canadian culture that will be, ultimately, Canadien. It is therefore a matter of personal pleasure to see that Quebec and the French writers are adequately represented on this map. But it is also a matter of national pride and practical importance. The boards of education in the various provinces will demand mention of the most eminent French-Canadian men of letters (not historians or critics, but creative writers only).

With time, I should have completed my own researches. Since speed has been forced upon me, I can only appeal to fellow-craftsmen of the sister race to supply me with pre-digested material.

My apologies for venturing to trouble you further; but it seems to me we have in this project a splendid opportunity for education about the native literature, and in the name of our common national and cultural interests, I trust you can spare an hour or two to dictate a memorandum for my guidance.

With sincere appreciation,

1 Emile Nelligan (1879–1941), French-Canadian symbolist poet; Joseph-Octave Crémazie (1827–79), romantic author of patriotic verse, guiding spirit of the 'Mouvement Littéraire du Québec,' often called the father of French-Canadian poetry; Louis-Honoré Fréchette (1839–1908), poet, lawyer, journalist, politician. As 'Le Lauréat,' he was the best-known French-Canadian poet of the nineteenth century.

2 Charles-Ignace Adélard Gill (1871–1918), French-Canadian romantic poet linked with the 'Ecole Littéraire de Montréal'

---

## From Robert Choquette[1]

Emissions Radiophoniques
Chambre 1029, University Tower
Montreal
October 2, 1936

Dear Bill,

Here's a list of poets, novelists and what might be termed essayists, in reality columnists in our papers, magazines, etc ... In most cases, unhappily, nothing more interesting than the birthplace could be found. I have, whenever possible, in the case of novelists, attached to the name of the writer that of a region covered by one or some of his books (Ex. *Les Habits Rouges*, by Robert de Roquebrune).[2] As many of the poets have written some of their works, at least their first books, in the town or village where they were born, all is pretty well taken care of. You'll have trouble about Montreal writers, probably; have a few swim in the St. Lawrence. I am sure you never had to deal with so many 'Saints,' Saint So-and-so, etc. ... DeMontigny,[3] of Ottawa, once spoke of Quebec's 'geographical martyrology!'

How's everything? I have spent my summer down around the Gulf of Mexico. Big fishing, sailing and keeping on with my sea poem, which has reached three thousand lines by now. But I am taking my time; I want the thing to fall from the tree of its own accord, round and mellow.

Hope to see you again sometime. I am resuming my radio work for the coming winter. I have a daily broadcast, the story of a French-Canadian village, for the National Breweries.

Cordially yours,
Choquette

Don't be impressed; this flashy stationery was a birthday present.[4]

1 Robert Choquette (b. 1905), Canadian poet whose works include *Metropolitan Museum* (1931), which won the Prix David, and *Suite Marine* (1953)
2 Robert de Roquebrune was the pseudonym of Robert Laroque (1889–1978), whose historical romance *Les Habits rouges* was published in 1923.
3 Louvigny de Montigny (1876–1955), journalist, writer, chief translator to the Senate, and author of *Antoine Gérin Lajoie* (1925) and *La Revanche de Maria Chapdelaine* (1937). He was instrumental in the establishment of the Canadian Authors' Association and La Société des Ecrivains Canadiens.
4 Referring to a printed drawing of a radio microphone on the personalized letterhead

---

## To A.R.M. Lower October 11, 1936

Dear Lower and Ewart,

Excuse me for writing you jointly but I am at the peak of my year's literary activity and writing at all is a problem. That is why I proposed a loose skeleton organization of sound Canadian nationalists to exchange ideas and clarify philosophy and program, pooling correspondence for convenience and looking forward to spreading out as soon as we understand each other well enough to be sure we are agreed on the fundamentals. I am impressed with the need of flexibility (we shall have to embrace pacifists and militarists, capitalists and socialists, etc.) and nobody must tie up others doing nationalist work just because of these differences of view on the incidentals.

Subject to foregoing, I approve Lower's document and nominate him for the position of philosopher. He will decide, after listening to others, on the verbiage of the basic vows. He thus becomes, as thinker the virtual head of our party; whether he chooses to be known outwardly as head is wholly for him to say. He is the one to admit or reject adherents; but I warn you both it must not be a narrow platform. I must be at liberty to take a more optimistic view of Canada's material future and to say I wish our bloody navy were sunk. I vote for the name Canadian Nationalists, but want to leave final vote with Lower as to the essentials of our doctrine.

Ewart, if he will, should act as secretary, disseminating news among us, as by mimeographing. Does Ewart want us to pay in the odd dollar for mailing costs or shall we leave that until we see how much work and then assess members?

My own special function is that of publicist, and when we get around to printing some kind of magazine, I can act as editor to take that much off Ewart, who may by then be mailing stuff in all directions.

I nominate Professor Jean Bruchesi,[1] 850 est Boul St. Joseph, Montreal, as our first link with our French co-nationalists but hope he will be encouraged to bring forward others of his race, as soon as possible. We simply must have the French.

Having read Ewart's document,[2] I approve of it and would like to see this got going right away. There is no time to lose.

Do either of you fellows want your documents back???

My general criticism in both cases is that the movement is likely to swing along faster than Ewart with his legal precisions and Lower with his academic cautiousness. King's speech did more in an hour than we could do in a year. The subject is alive. King said nothing new but he said it in the spotlight, and that encourages others to line up.[3]

In view of awakened interest, I should very much like to have our documents passing immediately through the hands of some of my friends, who might under Lower's and my original scheme have been secondary men to be brought in with the second wave. Young Bruce Morris, eg. who was at the Conference. I should also like to see us take in early Frank G.J. MacDonagh, former secretary of Native Sons, who is re-organizing that body on nationalist lines. He is a lawyer, a Catholic and keen. Would there be any objection, Lower, to having from the start two kinds of members – Grade A, who would contribute directly to discussions and others who would be merely observers, though interested, sympathetic observers. ??? This is important. If we do not let in the second rank now, I should move that we plan to admit 20 or 30 within six months, because the need is here to spread what light we have, when it may do more good than more accurate statements later.

I enclose (1) MacAree's column from yesterday's *Mail and Empire*, showing the kind of talk found in Tory papers.[4]

(2) I am addressing Masons here on the 20th on Canada's Foreign Policy (30 minutes) and enclose text of speech, one version slightly altered to serve as a magazine article. I am offering it first to *The Canadian*. Editor Rutledge consented by phone to consider it.[5] If rejected there, I shall go on to *Macleans* and others of that group. If used, it will be answered, opening the way for one of the other nationalists to reply.

I think R.A. MacKay should be admitted at once in any case. His knowledge is valuable and his diplomacy is valuable. By all means take in Frank Underhill. I think Lower has the coolest head and ought to be IT, with Ewart as legal expert and for matters bearing on history of the independence movement. Underhill and I are about equal as voices – mouthpieces – he for logical statement, invective and hard-hitting, while I can be more persuasive because my evangelical tone is congenial to the Canadian people. They are used to preaching, and I don't mind putting a quaver in my voice to win recruits. Decisive movements have, perhaps must have, logic at bottom, but they win by emotional appeal.

I move that we eschew foreign or pedantic words, or those with any connotation – such as manifesto – and speak of creed or statement of faith. By sticking to the simplest English, plain words, we shall avoid not only the hackneyed in phrase but the hackneyed in thought, which is a vital matter. We are going a new way and must never use the old catch phrases if there is a common-place synonym.

Lower's Statement of Faith should have a passage in it about independence. We wish to establish Canada's independence in every sense of the word.

It's 2 a.m. and I must go to bed. Apologies for hasty writing and for sending uncorrected carbons of my speech-article.

MacKay made a good job of the Report of Conference called 'Canada's Responsibility for World Peace.' Buy copies and spread it. I had the luck to write a digest of Lord Snell's oration on British Policy.[6]

Regards to you both –

1 Jean Bruchési (b. 1901), scholar, historian, public servant. He was active in the Canadian Authors' Association and La Société des Ecrivains Canadiens. His *Le Canada* (1952) was originally published in Paris by Fernand Nathan, reprinted in Canada by Ryerson.

2 Ewart had prepared, in the form of a petition, a document entitled 'Recommendations by the People of Canada to the Prime Minister of Canada. In Question of Peace and War: Should the decision be made by Canadians or Should it be made elsewhere for us?' The document asked that the Prime Minister present, at the 1937 London Imperial Conference, a series of resolutions that affirmed the right of each Dominion within the British Empire to declare war, remain neutral, or make peace for itself without acting on behalf of any other country within the Empire.

3 In a speech to the League of Nations in September 1936, Prime Minister Mackenzie King had rejected the principle of collective security and said that Canada would decide for itself whether it would participate in a war. In his speech he did not suggest the British Commonwealth as an alternative to the League.

4 McAree's column for that day contained incidental items along with a letter from Archdeacon Wallace of Hamilton, who commended McAree's recent columns on the Spanish Civil War which had been sympathetic to the Republicans and critical of the insurgent Nationalists.

5 Joseph Lister Rutledge (1885–1957), journalist and variously editor of *Maclean's*, *Canadian Magazine*, *Liberty*, and *The Canadian Author and Bookman*

6 The proceedings of the 1936 Couchiching Conference on 'Canada's Responsibility for World Peace' were published as *Canada: The Empire and the League* (1936) and introduced by R.A. MacKay, who had given papers on 'Canada and the Empire,' 'Canada and the League of Nations,' and 'Canada's Defence Policy.' In a footnote to his introduction, MacKay acknowledged Lower, Ewart, and Deacon. Deacon's summary pertained to 'British Foreign Policy,' a speech delivered by Lord Snell (d. 1944), economist, leader of the Labour opposition in the House of

Lords, Chairman of the London County Council (1934–8), who advocated naval power, alliances with European nations, and support for the League of Nations as avenues towards peace.

---

## From Archibald Belaney

Beaver Lodge
Prince Albert National Park,
Saskatchewan
May 13, 1937

Dear Bill:

We expect the ice to go out in a couple of days, so am dropping you a line ready to send as soon as transportation is open again.

I regret very much that you missed the picture owing to the tardiness of our arrangements with the operator, but when we come to Toronto with the Mississauga, to finish it, which should be around middle of July, you will get a birdseye view of the whole Canadian wilderness scene that you yourself know and love so well – both pictures.

Say, Bill, I hope you will forgive the lapse from grace. There had been rather a difficult time in many ways, & the constant travelling was beginning to get my goat. But there will be no repetition of this on my next expedition to Toronto or elsewhere; & as I do not tolerate the darned stuff in the bush there are very few days in a year that I ever even smell it.

There is, mixed into our happiness, one piece of bad news. Our poor old moose lays dead not a mile from this camp & is now buried. Causes unknown, but he was all skin & bone like all the moose in this area this spring. We are all at a loss to account for it.

Do you feel like taking in the Mississauga trip? Let me know how you feel about this, will you?

A separate booklet is being made by Lovat Dickson of 'The Tree' (one of the *Tales of an Empty Cabin*) & I am soon to get busy on the sketches I am to provide for illustrations, as in *Sajo*.[1]

Dawn is growing up tall & lanky & her conversation consists principally of knives, tomahawks, scalps, guns & the expert killing of bears. Going tough on me.

I cannot write very much Bill, as my correspondence is quite heavy, for me, so will write again later when there is something of more interest to discuss.

Please give my love to those three grand youngsters of yours, & tell them we will have a get together next time we come to Toronto during our free time, of which we had very little this last visit.

Please give Mrs. Deacon our very kindest regards, & ask her to please accept my apologies for my stupid remark at the studio that day. I was not myself, & a great deal of social stuff had been going on & I get sometimes pretty well confused even at my best. Ask her to please try to understand, to remember the vast gulf that exists between my normal life & the everyday life of a big city. I am sometimes rather at a loss.

With warmest regards from us both.

Very sincerely your friend
Grey Owl

1 *The Tree* (1937), published in London by Lovat Dickson and in Toronto by Macmillan, included six sketches by Belaney.

---

## From Frederick Philip Grove

R.R. 4
Simcoe, Ontario
November 24, 1939

My dear Deacon,

Thanks for sending me the script.[1]

I am sorry to say that in spite of everything the confounded book is not moving. I don't know who's to blame.

I have been debating with myself for some time whether to write you a few facts regarding my life and my circumstances with regard to which there is the wildest legend afloat. My hesitancy arises from a profound aversion to have such things mentioned in the public press. At the same time, knowledge, on your part, of the facts of the case might stop the legend from growing and errors from gaining currency. Would you promise not to use the facts directly if I give them to you?

Sincerely,
F.P.G.

P.S. – I am sending you, under separate covers a copy of the Limited Edition.

1 Deacon had sent Grove a copy of his review of *Two Generations* (5 August 1939) in which he called the novel Grove's best book and 'one of the best novels ever written in Canada,' whose 'chief literary merit is a rigorous simplicity.' The review was followed by a résumé of Grove's 'official' biography.

---

## From Laura Goodman Salverson

608 Stradbrooke
Winnipeg
August 9, 1941

Dear Bill:

It seems ages since I wrote to vex your uneasy life! And perhaps we have all lived ages of experience in these horrid months of madness. But I shall not bore you with silly comments upon a confusion of human ills.

Since last writing all sorts of things have colored and clouded the Salverson ego, the only one of which of much importance is a violent setback in my eyes. Really serious – and so I doubt that I shall do much more mischief in print. But I shall try for I mean to die with my boots on if possible. And who would not be inspired to this noble resolution after receiving a check for three dollars and twenty six cents from Ryerson Press for *Confessions*![1]

But what I am writing about is not my purse nor yet to borrow carfare, but to ask you to write me a letter of reference – even house maids get them – for I am thinking about trying for a scholarship and have to have three such letters. Mr. Cranston[2] has given me one. I must prove that I am white and free and have some ability as a scribe. I know I am white, dear boy, NOT free but you must pretend to believe that I have a way with words.

Nothing may come of it and your stamp be wasted. To begin with I can only work a very little each week and, therefore, may be too late with my manuscript, and besides American subjects are preferred. But the Knopf people also publish mss. of merit and that is all I want. I cant quite face doing another novel for absolutely nothing. I have to work too hard and, after twenty years of the most dismal discouragement I am getting fed up. Fed up but still the itch is in my system.

Must be the blood. My poor old cousin in Iceland after nine years as premier and I dont know how long as supreme court judge, now retired and nearing 70 has broken out in a rash of books. What can you do with fools like that? But I wish to God my people had never left Iceland!

I wanted to go to the convention this year and for the first time in all these years I was actually asked to come, but hell broke loose in our household this summer and we have never been so broke, so I shall not see any of the glorious company, nor yet the sea – which is what I really wanted to see!

I hope things are better than good with you folks and that you were able to escape from the furious heat; it was horrible here. But today in true Manitoba style it is so cold my hands are blue. Lord what a province I picked to be born in.

Last week, having nothing better to do on a dark day while the rain pounded on the roof like seventeen devils, I got the fancy notion to paste up the clippings of my two last books.[3] I got a kick out of reading them and comparing the ones from England Ireland Scotland Australia etc. to the ones from here. Amusing as hell. For where, say, the London *Times*, which gave me a very long review, judged the book simply as a book most of the Canadian critics held it up by the tail to get the Canadian whiff, so to speak. This does not apply to yourself of whom I have always said that, being creative yourself, you had the requisites of a critic – but it does apply to so many so-called critics and also even more to professors who damn all things Canadian with ridiculous judgement.

What I mean of course is that any book should be reviewed without regard to its birthplace. My faults and weaknesses were not caused by anything peculiar to Canada. I should still have had them no matter where I was born if fate had fixed upon me the same obstacles and given me the same energies to contend with them. Canada has nothing whatever to do with it.

One review in substance said this: unfortunately the *Weaver* is cast in a romantic mould but this seems to be an inescapable fault of Canadian literature, but need not detract from the interest of this fine book. What wisdom! Heaven knows I dont object to the romantic mould but I do object to foolishness passing for logic. I seem to recollect that other countries have produced romanticists!

I never met any other people than the Canadian who apologize for living. I am getting so tired of it that I wish to God I could fly to the Solomon Islands where human animals just ARE. It would be such a comfort after suffering so many fools ungladly.

Give my regards to Mrs Deacon and, if you will be so kind as to write the letter for me, I shall be grateful, but you need not rush about it. I dont need it until October.

Sincerely yours
Laura S.

1 *Confessions of an Immigrant's Daughter* (1939), her autobiography
2 James Herbert Cranston (1880–1952), journalist and author, on the staff of the *Toronto Star* for many years and from 1935 to 1947 editor/publisher of the *Midland (Ontario) Free Press*
3 *The Dark Weaver* (1937), winner of the Governor-General's Award for fiction, and *Confessions of an Immigrant's Daughter* (1939), which won the non-fiction award

---

## To Cecil Goldbeck[1] November 8, 1942

Dear Cecil,

I owe you something and now I pay you.

Freeze onto this guy[2] – quick. His poetry will go in the States, greased. Some of it grand traditional stuff like this, some of it smartly moderne. Both the arty Americans and the plain Americans will go for it. They'll love it because it's so damned honestly Canadian.

He's at home at present – 40 Hazelton Ave., Toronto. Wire him to hold U.S. rights for you and to mail you printed copy.

Silly Ryerson Press printed 500 copies [of *David and Other Poems*] in a year when Canada is book mad and crazy for their own authors. I'll bet it goes 5,000 here.

My advice is: Make separate contract with Birney unless the poor Boob has signed away his soul, in which case you'll have to deal with Ryerson, who will take 50% of his American royalties.

It is a book of 40 pages and you will do well to purchase plates from Ryerson, who have employed the artist-typographer, Thoreau MacDonald, as designer; and he has made the swellest possible job of it.[3] With plates, you can slap her through this month and catch a Christmas sale at $1.25. I pride myself on knowing when a book is going over and *David* is.

Enclosed is my review and all the advance Ryerson gave me. I had no particular hopes of it till the completed book reached me last week. Then I jumped. Now you jump. You couldn't possibly lose much on a 40–page book. It is my belief it would move right smartly in the States; and if you don't grab this bugger somebody else will because he's going to be the most famous war-poet in Canada inside 30 days. He is no friend of mine – nodding acquaintance only.

I don't send you completed book because I fear if I part with mine – review copy – I'll never get another first edition *David*. I am not too stingy to buy one; but (confidentially) I have a government war job and am keeping my *Globe* connection as best I may with my wife doing a large part of the work. I haven't time to go out and buy a copy. You wire Birney and his wife will jump.

If you can stand a long-winded title and keep your mouth shut, I am Executive Assistant to the Administrator of Publishing, Printing and Allied Industries, in the Wartime Prices and Trade Board. I have been at work a week, but my civil service appointment may not come for a month yet. The Administrator is an intimate friend of mine and gently conscripted me. The red tape will take longer; but I'm on the job. My intimate friend John Atkins[4] is a sort of Czar of magazines, books and newspapers for the duration. He's a dying man and wanted me to sort-of bear the torch.

Yours ever –

1 Cecil Goldbeck (1897–1958), American literary agent and vice-president of the New York publishing firm Coward-McCann

2 Alfred Earle Birney (b. 1904) is one of Canada's most highly regarded poets, whose works in the 1940s included *David and Other Poems* (1942) and *Now Is Time* (1945), both recipients of the Governor-General's Award. He had been literary editor of *The Canadian Forum* from 1936 to 1940. After his years in the Canadian Army (1942–6) he became, for a brief period, supervisor of the International Service of the CBC in Montreal before leaving to join the Department of English at the University of British Columbia in the summer of 1946. Deacon was largely responsible for Birney's appointment as editor of *The Canadian Poetry Magazine* from September 1946 to June 1948.

3 Born in 1901, Thoreau MacDonald is the son of James Edward Hervey MacDonald (1874–1932), one of the original members of the Group of Seven. A largely self-taught painter and illustrator, he became known for woodcuts commissioned by Lorne Pierce for many Ryerson Press books. MacDonald is probably best remembered, however, for his woodcuts in W.H. Blake's translation of *Maria Chapdelaine* (1921), published by Macmillan.

4 Atkins, who suffered from chronic ill health, had first met Deacon at the Toronto Writers' Club in the 1930s.

From Earle Birney

45 Isabella Street
Toronto
December 6, 1942

Dear Mr. Deacon,

Just a note to tell you that your continued support of *David* has given me a great deal of pleasure. I have followed your comments with pride and am glad that the sales have, so far, justified your predictions – if indeed they are not partly the result of your predictions!

I have just had a pleasant note from Ralph Gustafson,[1] together with his new *Lyrics Unromantic*, limited to 100 copies. Have you seen it? I have heard, also, from A.J.M. Smith,[2] whose anthology is still hovering on the brink of publication, and swelling in size while it hovers. Gustafson, by the way, writes that he is to guest-edit the Spring issue of *Voices* which will be a Canadian number. His anthology, as you probably know, has gone into a 2nd ed., with stiff covers for text-book purposes.

Do you follow the Vancouver quarterly, *Contemporary Verse*, edited by Alan Crawley?[3] The current issue leads off with a poem by Dorothy Livesay[4] on the emotions and delirium of childbirth. Considering the difficulty of the subject, I think she does remarkably well. At any rate it is greatly improved over its form when I first saw it this summer in MS.

Cecil Goldbeck wrote me this week: 'I enjoyed & admired the poems but to save my life I don't see how we could get a successful sale of the book here in the U.S. Times being what they are I think it would be best for me to let it go ...' He wants to see anything else I do, etc.

The army seems to be taking to the 'On Going to the Wars' verses.[5] The *Blitz*, monthly organ of the Officers' Training Centre, Brockville, is reviewing the volume in its January number, re-printing 'On Going to the Wars,' and adding a pen & ink sketch of me by Capt. Elmer Sager, their official portraitist.

Larry Fisher, who reads short story classics over the radio weekly on a western Canadian hook-up, is substituting 'David' for one of his stories on his schedule, next week I think. This, together with John Coulter's review & Claire Wallace's remarks,[6] has given me some publicity in the west but I'm unable to cash in on it because booksellers won't stock a single copy without a previous order. This is rather exasperating when the poems nearly all have western Canadian backgrounds, and I myself lived most of my life west of the prairies.

Excuse the length of this. Thought some of the details might interest you, in view of your own very large share in making *David* known.

Sincerely,
Earle Birney

1 Ralph Barker Gustafson (b. 1909); *Epithalamium in Time of War* (1941) and *Lyrics Unromantic* (1942) inaugurated his second phase of poetry, marked by its ironic voice. He had moved to New York after some years in Britain and Canada, and in 1942 was employed in the Manhattan Wartime Bureau of British Information Services.

2 Arthur James Marshall Smith (1902–80), one of the 'Montreal Group' affiliated with *The McGill Fortnightly Review*; his *Book of Canadian Poetry: A Critical and Historical Anthology* (1943), a college textbook, appeared the same year that he won the Governor-General's Award for *News of the Phoenix and Other Poems*.

3 Lawyer and bibliophile (1887–1967) who moved from Ontario to British Columbia in 1934. After blindness forced him to give up his practice, he edited his own poetry magazine, *Contemporary Verse*, from 1940 to 1952. Crawley published poets such as Birney, Dorothy Livesay, P.K. Page, James Reaney, Jay MacPherson, Anne Marriott, and A.J.M. Smith.

4 Poet and social activist, b. 1909, whose poems in *Signpost* (1932) had explored feminine sexuality using imagist techniques; in the 1940s she generally published more explicitly political poems in *The Canadian Forum* and *The Canadian Poetry Magazine*.

5 One of the poems in *David and Other Poems*

6 Coulter was an Irish-born playwright (1888–1980) who emigrated to Canada in 1936. His best-known Canadian works are his plays *Riel* (1962) and *The Trial of Louis Riel* (1968); he was presumably the anonymous reviewer of *David and Other Poems* in the December 1942 number of the *Canadian Review of Music and Other Arts*. In the same issue Coulter's signed article, 'Canadian Poetry,' also made reference in a postscript to Birney and his new book of poetry. Claire Wallace was the pseudonym of Mrs. James E. Stutt (1900–68), Toronto radio personality and author of several books on Canadian etiquette. Her weekly CBC radio program 'They Tell Me' was broadcast nationally from 1936 to 1954.

## From Thomas Raddall[1]

Liverpool, Nova Scotia
December 2, 1944

Dear Mr. Deacon,

A word of thanks for your ripsnorting review of my *Roger Sudden* in last Saturday's issue.[2] I have a rosy picture of all the sixteen-year-olds in Toronto rushing to buy the book, and – who knows? – I may become the Frank Sinatra of Canadian literature despite the news-photo at the head of your page, which makes me as bald as any victim of Roger's scalping knife.

Yet I must quarrel with your notion that *Roger Sudden* is a 'frankly escapist' yarn. My dear sir, it is an historical tract, written in what I hope is a palatable coating of fiction. I have long wanted to do a story showing what really happened in the first ten years of English settlement in Canada. A multitude of escapists from the truth, beginning with Longfellow, have so obscured the period that no historian would recognise it. Indeed, one of the most recent novelists (no names!) went so far as to house the Micmac Indians in 'tepees' made of 'buffalo hides' (although 'tepee' is a Western Indian word, and the buffalo were never seen east of the Great Lakes), to dress them in 'deer hides' (although there were no deer in Nova Scotia at the time), and to provide them with 'peace paint,' 'proud headdresses,' 'sleds with dog teams,' and a number of other things they never used. I may add that the same novelist's description of a ship in a North Atlantic storm still makes our salty Bluenoses split their sides.

This is not to claim infallibility for myself. But at least I have kept my eye on the documents. 'Roger Sudden' is a fictitious character, of course; but his adventures and business methods are well in accord with certain affairs recorded by the historians. Actually it was Joshua Mauger who sold the Acadian cattle to His Majesty's navy, and he engaged in other practices which I have described. Eventually he retired to England, where he died in 1770, leaving a fortune of 300,000 – which makes Roger's haul seem very small indeed. I have drawn 'Roger' to a considerable extent also from the career of Michael Francklin, a young English gentleman who came to Halifax in the early days with his pride (and little else) in his pocket, amassed a fortune and eventually became lieutenant-governor of the province.

Le Loutre, Gautier, Father Maillard, Gorham, Jean Baptiste Koap are actual historical characters, faithfully described. Madame Ducudrai really did keep a cabaret at Louisbourg, and her husband really was the chief French spy at New York. Captain James Johnstone, the Scottish Jacobite exile at Louisbourg, was a real person, and all the details of his extraordinary career were taken from his own memoirs – there is a translation of them (they were published in Paris) in the museum library at Louisbourg. I provided him with a beautiful sister; I'm sure his shade won't quarrel with me for that.

You speak of the stretched arm of coincidence and mention 'the meeting of Mary, Roger, Wapke and Wolfe' in the Cape Breton stronghold. I know what you mean, of course; but there is an obvious implication here which is not according to the book. Mary never met Wapke or Wolfe anywhere. Roger never met Wolfe again after the brief interview in Halifax, although he caught a glimpse of him in the fight at Coromandiere. And Wapke never saw Louisbourg.

But your mention of coincidence reminds me of an interesting point in the construction of my plot. Wolfe commanded the 20th Foot in the Highlands. His predecessor in the command was none other than Cornwallis! And since Wolfe was a 'man of Kent' himself there is no valid reason why he and Cornwallis could not have been travelling on leave together in the Rochester coach when Roger robbed it. Certainly Cornwallis was in the vicinity of London at that time. As you can see, this opened all sorts of possibilities for my plot, but after consideration I rejected it and made the colonel of the 20th Foot a purely fictitious 'Colonel Belcher.' Truth may be stranger than fiction but a fiction writer must be tender of his plausibilities.

All of which, as the lawyers say, 'without prejudice.'

Sincerely,
Thomas H. Raddall

1 Thomas Head Raddall (b. 1903) is the author of historical novels and short stories that often have Nova Scotia as their setting. His first work, *His Majesty's Yankees* (1942), a story of the American Revolution as viewed by a Nova Scotian, established his reputation, but he is also known for *Pride's Fancy* (1946), the story of West Indies privateering; for *The Nymph and the Lamp* (1950), his romantic novel which takes place on Sable Island; and for his collections of short

stories, *Tambour* (1945), *The Wedding Gift and Other Stories* (1947), and *The Pied Piper of Dipper Creek* (1943). The last collection, which won the Governor-General's Award for fiction, contains in its title story a warm and vivid evocation of James D. Gillis, one of the four Jameses discussed in Deacon's famous celebration of Canada's worst poets. Raddall won two other Governor-General's awards for non-fiction with *Halifax: Warden of the North* (1948) and *The Path of Destiny* (1957).

2 In 'Ripsnorting Adventure Tale Features Fall of Louisbourg' (*Globe and Mail*, 25 November 1944) Deacon had described *Roger Sudden* as 'a wellhandled, frankly escapist story of great variety, fast-moving and robust.'

---

## To Thomas Raddall December 10, 1944

Dear Mr. Raddall,

Your letter gives me a welcome opportunity to congratulate you on the fine work you are doing in fiction. I have enjoyed your three books and was glad you received the Governor-General's Award last year.[1] In *His Majesty's Yankees*, especially, you opened the eyes of Canadians generally to a chapter almost unknown to them. *Roger Sudden* is another valuable step, though the English-French conflict in Nova Scotia has been better known than the situation of Nova Scotia during the U.S. war of independence. I particularly liked your short stories in *The Pied Piper*.

You letter was so valuable, and I so busy (being deputy administrator of publishing and printing and at present only literary editor emeritus) that I did not have time to consult you about the use I made of your letter. As you will see, I abstracted relevant parts and used them as an article, which is most timely and interesting.[2] Our readers are buying the book in spectacular quantities and the information you kindly supplied should reach as many persons as possible. Accept my thanks for the contribution.

Put to that use, it was effective publicity. As an admonition to me, I regret your use of the word quarrel. If you have contracted the Nova Scotian touchiness and wish to quarrel with any reference to you in Ontario, I fear it will be a one-sided engagement. I have no wish to do battle with any author, let alone one as competent as yourself.

If I may speak both kindly and candidly to one who is my junior in years and in the craft of authorship, please consider the futility of trying to correct the misapprehensions of your readers. Having published a book, let the public, or any particular reader or reviewer, interpret it as he pleases. It is his right, and you can never catch up with what people say about your books. The business of an author is to write, to publish if possible and, having published, to leave his work to the consumers and go on with fresh work. You cannot make people think of your work what you believe they should think; it is a waste of your time to try. Stop reading reviews as soon as you can. They are not addressed to the author and seldom please him. This is a part of the operation in which you should be inactive and indifferent.

It was a great disappointment not to see you at Hamilton last September to receive your medal. We, your fellow writers in Canada, established these awards some years ago to assist authors of worthy books. We spend a good deal of time and some cash on the award system. Your friend, Lord Tweedsmuir,[3] refused to spend a nickel on the project. It would have been gracious to appear.

You might even have enjoyed it. May I say that I think you should be prepared to assume your natural place in the Canadian Authors Association, and that I think you might even be helped by making friends among your kind from other provinces. A creative writer is apt to see himself as a unique being, wholly independent of his contemporaries. This is an illusion. The problems we face are similar. Knowing each other by sight is generally pleasant and often of practical help.

If Canada were compact, there might be a reason for avoiding herds and cliques. But we are dreadfully separated by geography and we lack means of frequent meeting. When you find it convenient to explore the central provinces, you may be surprised at the number of potential friends you have here. It is my hope that [you will] take occasion to establish contacts with the large number of gifted people in Quebec and Ontario who, like yourself, are contributing to the advance of the Canadian novel in this decade. Rest assured that a hearty welcome awaits you. Your success is a source of gratification to us all.

Of course, when a man is writing, he does it alone; but we have common interests to be served; and meeting others of one's kind often is most fruitful in ideas. Anyway, we need you even if you don't need us.

Accept my apologies for giving unsolicited advice. I have found how foolish it generally turns out to be. However, I shall continue to hope to meet you in the flesh. Otherwise this will be the end of our association because correspondence is impossible during these war years.

Being a lawyer myself, I might have written a diplomatic letter without cause of offence. Since I have not, I shall not conclude 'without prejudice.' You will have to take my goodwill on trust, but it is genuine.

Canadian subject matter does not bar a book from readership in other countries as you know, but inevitably it means that most interest will be displayed by your Canadian readers. I suggest this market is of primary importance to you and its importance will increase. That is another argument in favor of a postwar trip to Canada.

As journalist I was grateful for a timely word from you on my page and, if you were injured by what I said (which I doubt) your remarks were the best antidote. Thank you most cordially and good luck for the next novel.

Sincerely,

1 For *The Pied Piper of Dipper Creek*

2 ' "Historical Basis of Roger Sudden" by Thomas H. Raddall' (*Globe and Mail*, 9 December 1944)

3 John Buchan, Lord Tweedsmuir (1875–1940), was a popular British author of adventure stories, among them *Prester John* (1910) and *The Thirty-Nine Steps* (1915). As Governor-General of Canada (1935–40), he agreed to let the name of his office be associated in perpetuity with the national literary awards established by the CAA in late 1935, but refused to make provision for money to accompany the awards.

---

## From Frederick Philip Grove

R.R. 4
Simcoe, Ontario
February 11, 1945

Dear Mr. Deacon,

I wish to thank you for the very fair and kind review of my book.[1]

I should like to be permitted to make a few remarks. You know, of course, that I had a severe stroke on April 14 last and cannot move anything but one finger of the left hand; or I should write more fully.

It is not quite correct to call THE MASTER my valedictory; that valedictory consists of 3 books of which this is only the first. Of course, I did not mean to prophecy the fate of mankind; but merely to point out one possible development, in my own way, in the form of fiction. Before writing the book (1930) I had pondered it for thirty years or longer. It was only in 1934 that I adopted the present technique, fully aware of the fact that it would repel the public and most of the reviewers. You are quite right in assuming that considerations of length guided me. The first completed Ms. would have made 1200 pages in print. Dr. Alexander[2] put me on the present way by saying, 'This should be retrospect'; unfortunately he died before he saw what a monster grew out of that casual remark.

May I add a word as to the last sentence of your last but one paragraph? I was trying to make clear two strains in the old man's revisualisations.

In one he thinks and remembers; in the other, he relives the past. In the latter he is the young man; and he is absolutely accurate, though he slips out of this rebirth of himself every now and then.

Friends of mine wrote and phoned me in numbers to call my attention to your review. They had already called the reviewer in *Saturday Night* and other papers 'a cad and a dunce,' and the reviews 'extremely puerile.'[3] You may not know, and this is confidential, that Pacey, of the U. of N.B., will bring out a biography of mine within the year.[4] I hope he'll make the most of the fact. Of course, he thinks OUR DAILY BREAD and FRUITS OF THE EARTH my two best books. He is just now reading the 2nd volume of my 'valedictory' as you so felicitously call it.

Thanks and best wishes,

your
F.P.G.

(I cannot write even my signature. This took me 3 hours to hammer out).

1 In 'Grove's Machine-Age Novel His Most Ambitious Effort' (*Globe and Mail*, 10 February 1945), Deacon stated that *The Master of the Mill* was Grove's 'most thoughtful and technically most complicated work' in which 'flaws are trivial, merits substantial.'

2 Probably William John Alexander (1855–1944), Professor of English, University of Toronto (1889–1926)

3 In his review of 20 January 1945, Jesse Edgar Middleton (1873–1970) had criticized the implausibility of character and action imposed on Grove's novel by his 'distorted and unreal' theme.

4 Desmond Pacey (1917–75), Canadian critic, whose *Frederick Philip Grove* appeared in 1945, and who edited *The Letters of Frederick Philip Grove* (Toronto: University of Toronto Press 1976)

---

## To Frederick Philip Grove February 13, 1945

Dear Mr. Grove,

Please know how deeply I am touched and how greatly pleased by your note, though I am contrite over the labor it cost you. It has been a matter of sincere regret to me to know you were laid up. I have so often thought of you and hoped you were comfortable and recovering. Long ago I should have expressed sympathy but was prevented by conviction that, for some reason, you disliked me. This was surprising because my admiration for your work has been constant. I recognized your genius and have honestly proclaimed it in various wordings throughout the more than 20 years during which I have reviewed each of your works to the best of my ability. I am very partial to the austere virtues of correct form and firm expression. There is no other writer, who has published an equal number of books, whom I have followed so carefully from volume to volume. Generally, after reading one author through 3 to 6 books, I feel I have got everything he has to say and that I have nothing more to learn from him in style or method. Your work has been not only consistently good but varied enough in its merits to hold my attention. As a journalist, I note the best-sellers that are of ephemeral interest only; but I have a great respect for literary art and I have admired your artistic integrity. You have never adopted a romantic formula or any other formula to sell your books. You just made them good, in a sober workmanlike way. The net result is that you have not sold half a million copies but you have put out a series of novels and essays of enduring worth. Your contribution is permanent and your example of sound craftsmanship will be an inspiration to writers for a long future. I had hoped something of the respect in which I hold you was apparent in my earlier articles but evidently I lacked the skill to convey my precise sentiments. It is therefore doubly welcome to me now to have you realize something of my profound satisfaction in your work over the years. Errors in interpretation there may well have been, since I know from long experience how fallacious the conclusions of critics can be. I brought to my remarks the best intelligence I had because I knew your work was important. If the present article shows me more understanding than that of other reviews, it is not because I have more ability but because I do not pretend to clairvoyance. I have to read the work to know what the author has said. Many of our contemporaries do not hold this to be a necessary labor. They sample, guess and comment. I always read the books, and yours most carefully. Be assured that I shall look forward with keenest anticipation to the other two novels of this series.

Thank you for telling me of the biography. I do not know the man but hope he has the requisite ability to interpret as well as merely to record. From what you have revealed about the iron discipline of your life, I confess regret that you are not doing a self-story. I trust that Professor Pacey has before him enough of your own memoirs so that he can quote your own words liberally.

Please do not tax your strength by attempting any reply. I just wanted to thank you for the opportunity you have created for me to tell you personally of the high regard in which I have always held your work. I trust you take merited satisfaction in the esteem in which you are held. Possibly only a few thousand yet appreciate your stature as a writer but the number constantly grows, and will continue to grow. Further, it is the best judges who think most highly of your accomplishment.

Remembering your delight in snow,[1] I hope you have been able to watch this winter's storms from a window and that by spring you will be on your feet again.

Most sincerely yours,

1 Deacon is referring to *Over Prairie Trails* (1922), a collection of essays in which Grove describes his trips through rural Manitoba, several of which take place by horse and sleigh in the winter.

From Hugh MacLennan[1]

1178 Mountain Street
Montreal
April 8, 1945

My Dear Deacon:

Thanks for the grand review of TWO SOLITUDES in yesterday's GLOBE & MAIL.[2] I know any writer is pleased by a good review, and delighted by the kind you gave me. But quite apart from my own personal pleasure, I think you deserve congratulations on your handling of a book which must have been nearly as difficult to review as it was to write. A sensational handling of it – as it got in many American reviews – would have been the last thing desirable, from many points of view; for, as you rightly said, it was not so much the Quebec problem, as a Canadian novel.

From my standpoint, I had to write that book to orientate myself toward any future work I might do. It is my complete conviction that no writer can function in a vacuum. As his point of view, his method of regarding phenomena, derives from his childhood environment, he can't help writing out of the society in which he was produced. It gradually dawned on me – very gradually, I'm afraid – that so far as I was concerned my own society was obscure, not clear-cut, a queer congeries of various subtle inner and outer relationships which in my own time were gradually coming into focus. Unless it were possible for me somehow to effect something of a fusion of this Canadian dichotomy, I felt myself stymied. TWO SOLITUDES was the result of that, and now that it is finished, I feel greatly released. Whatever the book may have done for others, for me it has put something like solid ground under my feet.

You are certainly correct in assuming that the book will cause a lot of controversy. I knew it, I suppose, while I was writing it. But for me personally there was no sense of controversy at all; merely a prolonged and often mind-breaking effort to bring the various pieces into focus. So far among the French, and even among some of the clergy here, the reception has been much better than I had feared. There is no doubt that some aspects of French-Canadian life will loathe the book, for you know what a proud people they are. Yet if anyone is capable of understanding what he reads, he can hardly fail to detect a deep respect and affection for French-Canada within the book.

Undoubtedly, the treatment of English-Canada is less inclusive. It couldn't be, for the artistic theme rendered it impossible. I was forced to deal with those English elements which, by working so much harm among the French, are in many cases cynically responsible for much of the trouble we have here. And while writing so largely of the situation which is at the core of Canada, I kept in mind that I was writing for English-Canadians, who so constantly make the error of regarding Quebec as a monolith, and not a society in rapid transition under the impact of modern industrialism.

This letter has run on far too long, and certainly has told you nothing you did not know anyway. I'm awfully sorry I missed seeing you when you were in Montreal, but Dorothy[3] greatly enjoyed talking with you. Next time you come to town we may be able to have a drink together.

Sincerely,
Hugh MacLennan

1 'French-Canadian Problem in Daring and Timely Novel' (7 April 1945)
2 Dorothy Duncan (1903–57) married Hugh MacLennan in 1936. She published three books: *Here's to Canada* (1941), *Bluenose: A Portrait of Nova Scotia* (1942), and *Partner in Three Worlds* (1944), the last of which won the Governor-General's Award for non-fiction.
3 Hugh MacLennan (b. 1907) and Dorothy Duncan became two of Deacon's most cherished literary friends, their correspondence arising from Deacon's review of *Two Solitudes* (1945) and continuing for the next two decades. His meeting with them on a CAA visit to Montreal in January 1946 was a prelude to Deacon's discovery of contemporary French-Canadian fiction, which he came to know through MacLennan's glowing recommendation of Gabrielle Roy's *Bonheur d'occasion* (1945).

---

## From Hugh MacLennan

North Hatley, P.Q.
September 9, 1945

Dear Bill:

Many thanks for your note, and particularly for being so good as to advise Violet King.[1] I hadn't expected you to do more than to pass her on to the C.A.A., but I do appreciate your good-will in this. I hope she's written a good book.

Thanks also for your good advice about not hurrying the next book.[2] I hope I don't, but I also hope it won't swell into anything as long and difficult as TWO SOLITUDES. At present it seems simpler, which may well not be the case later on. *T.S.* would have been better had I been able to cast it off when I had finished it, and taken a complete vacation for about six weeks, then spent another three months work on it. But if I had done that I would not have been able to finish it until next Christmas owing to school work, and would still be back at school this fall. And I certainly did a colossal amount of re-writing – used about 7000 typewriter pages in all. In retrospect, the trouble seems to me to have been mainly this: I had not realized the full weight of Athanase Tallard, and the effect his death would have on the subsequent chapters.

However, I musn't prolong this note, which is merely intended to thank you and give you our best wishes.

Sincerely,
Hugh MacLennan

1 Violet King was a Toronto clerk who contacted Deacon about contract advice for her novel *Better Harvest* (1945), a story for juveniles about pioneering life in Upper Canada in the early 1800s. The copy of Deacon's note is missing in the Deacon Collection.

2 *The Precipice* (1948)

---

## To Gabrielle Roy[1] February 16, 1946

Dear Miss Roy,

My friend Hugh MacLennan has told me about his high regard for your novel, *Bonheur d'Occasion*, and of its great success. I had the pleasure of quoting him to this effect last month in this newspaper.[2]

It is my intention to visit Montreal in March. I should like to go to Rawdon and talk with you about the novel and your work as a writer, if you would be good enough to receive me. Having other business, I cannot yet set a date.

I have asked Mme Germaine Guevremont[3] to order a copy of your novel for me. I do not yet know the name or address of the publisher.

Is there to be an English translation? If so, who is doing the translating and who will publish the book in English?

While in Montreal or Rawdon, I should like to obtain a photo of the author suitable for a newspaper reproduction. This is a detail that your publisher can probably arrange for me.

I must apologize for inability to speak or understand French. It is unusual for a person speaking only English to take an interest in novelists, who write in French. But I believe it is time we tried to know each other across the language barrier. Anyway, I am sure the readers of this paper would like to hear about you; and I hope soon to be able to say when I shall be in your Province.

Will it be convenient for you to receive me some day between the 15 and 30 of March? An interview would be greatly appreciated.

Sincerely

1 Deacon first heard of Gabrielle Roy (1909–83) through Hugh MacLennan and arranged for a review of *Bonheur d'occasion* as soon as it appeared. He subsequently provided Roy with advice concerning translation and other contracts. Although she soon made it clear to all that her uncertain health and her commitment to her work precluded any public appearances, Roy cherished her early visits with the Deacons in Toronto, and remained a life-long friend of Bill Deacon in his capacity as fatherly adviser.

2 'Wood Fires of Montreal Warmed Authors' Chats' (*Globe and Mail*, 26 January 1946)

3 Quebec novelist (1900–68) remembered for *Le Survenant* (1945) and *Marie-Didace* (1947) which, translated as one book, *The Outlander* (1950), won the Governor-General's Award

---

## From Gabrielle Roy

Encinitas, California
February 27, 1946

Dear Mr. Deacon,

I very much regret this long delay in answering your letter of Feb. 16th, which took considerable time to reach me as I have been travelling quite a lot in the last few weeks. It is a lovely letter and I greatly appreciate the spirit that prompted it. 'To know each other across the language barrier,' as you put it, has always been my aim and I am truly delighted to see more and more signs of better understanding between Canadians of French and of English expression.

Needless to say I would very much enjoy a long talk with you. However, I do not know when I'll be back in Canada; possibly by the end of March, but it may be later. I am enjoying the sunshine of California so very much.

At any rate, I am sending you to-day a photograph of myself. And, although this is not as satisfactory as a personal interview, I shall be glad to answer by letter any questions you may wish to ask me, if I am not back in time for your visit to Montreal.

I appreciate the fact that it was through Mr. MacLennan that you first heard of me, as I have the greatest admiration for the integrity of his writing.

If you have not secured a copy of *Bonheur d'Occasion* through Mme Guèvremont, please drop me a card, and I shall see that you receive one from the copies I have left in Rawdon. It may be that the second edition is sold out. Better still, I'll ask my business agent to send you one copy directly.

I hope very sincerely that, if I can't meet you next month, it shall be some other time not too far away.

Gabrielle Roy

General Delivery
Encinitas
San Diego County
California
U.S.A.

---

## To Hugh MacLennan March 5, 1946

Dear Hugh,

In view of your remarks about what the academic critics did to you, I submit my article on Pacey's *Grove*[1] as evidence of my fight of decades against the critical dicta of Canadian professors on Canadian literature.

I request that you put it among your archives in case you ever wish to illustrate the two points of view.

Importation of Englishmen was originally responsible for our universities' contempt of Canadian writing. When its popularity began to be substantial, they had to say something and uttered fallacies. I have fought in print with E.K. Brown, A.J.M. Smith et al.

My speech next week in Montreal[2] sets forth my fundamental principles of criticism for better or for worse. At least they are founded on 25 years of daily experience.

They do and say such silly things. E.G. they list and quote any magazine, no matter how obscure or cock-eyed; but never a daily paper. Thus *U of T Quarterly* solemnly quoted *Canadian Bookman* at its worst in the late 1920's, but systematically ignored me because my carefully prepared articles were in a newspaper. Artificial distinctions like this, without any sense in them – merely mechanical – would of course have excluded Ste. Beuve's 'Causeries de Lundi' – Paris *Temps*.

Regards,

1 In his review of *Frederick Philip Grove* (12 January 1946) Deacon praised Pacey's 'meticulous' analysis of Grove's books, but objected to the young professor's condescending attitude to Canadian criticism and his magisterial but fallacious implication that Grove lacked imaginative power. Deacon also pointed out that as an academic, Pacey was characteristically unable to see his own views as subjective and in the tradition of 'opinion writing.'

2 The Montreal branch of the CAA hosted the meeting of the national executive at the Windsor Hotel on 16 March. Deacon also gave a speech at the branch meeting, probably 'Reasoned Admiration: A Craft Talk on Criticism.' This popular speech was repeated on subsequent occasions.

---

## From Hugh MacLennan

1178 Mountain Street
Montreal
March 7, 1946

My Dear Bill:

By all means when you come to Montreal, come straight to our apartment. Here you can shave and wash to your heart's content, and also have a drink. We can all go to the Club Canadien together by taxi. It's quite a distance east.[1]

Thanks for the article on Pacey's book on Grove. I had read it, in the language of the clergy, 'with great acceptance' when it appeared in *The Globe & Mail*. Also, I had previously read Mr. Pacey himself. An academic friend had given it to me with his blessing. How utterly right you are about those guys! That book was not only poor; it was downright incompetent. I thought you were pretty kind to him. Since then he has written an article of unbelievable incompetence in the Fall issue of the *Queen's Quarterly*.[2] One of the things he finds fault with Canadian writers for (especially Hutchison, Gwen and myself)[3] is that we have no 'philosophy.' Later it appears that we also fail to approximate to the combined spirits of Gide, Proust and Joyce, and also fail to improve on their techniques!

I can truly say that I know the academic grove in my sleep, and on the humanities' side, in all its aspects. The dankest corner of it all is labelled 'English literature.' English literature should never be studied in a separate compartment. Personally, I had two courses in it only, and both were compulsory. The result of such academicism is the production, not of a man who can appreciate books, not of a man who has learned either philosophy or history, much less economics and science, but a specialist operating in a vacuum. Their complaint about affairs in Canada is so naive it is pitiful. They feel a grievance we have no writers who can produce sufficiently abstruse books to warrant endless academic articles written by them!

E.K. Brown seemed to be a little better than most, but he said nothing right that you hadn't said twenty years ago, and he said a good deal wrong you never said at all. The truth is that professors, for all their boasts to independent thought, are conventional through and through. The political type of professor is as conventional, seemingly, as an Ontario old maid. The rebellious one is conventional in reverse; i.e., they are automatically against anything which happens to be popular. I know that nineteen books out of twenty that are excessively popular are tripe. Any newspaperman knows far more about the gadgetry that makes a popular best-seller than they do. But ever since Q.R. Leavis, back in 1932, wrote THE NOVEL AND THE READING PUBLIC,[4] they have automatically assumed that if a novel sells more than 10,000 copies it is *ipso facto* bad. I think Canadian literature has been done harm by the indiscriminate praise bestowed in the past on costume novels and third rate stuff. That is beside the point. The whole issue, to my mind, rests now on whether it will be possible for us to join the mainstream of world literature or whether we are doomed to be considered regional. This is highly complex, and requires a knowledge these professors not only lack, but don't want to obtain. Fundamentally, we must somehow jog the minds of American critics to make them see exactly *what* the position is here, vis-a-vis the literature of the U.S.A. A deplorable article, stupid, arrogant and dull, appeared in the NATION a short while ago by a Professor Weaver, who must at least have lived in Canada to have been familiar with the names he used. And that wretched paper, the NATION, has a wide critical influence. He dismissed the current French writing in about four lines, saying it was virtually impossible for anything to be produced here under the censorship of the Catholic Church.[5] At the moment I am in the middle of *Bonheur d'Occasion*. Beyond any shade of doubt, it's the best novel of any large city ever done by a Canadian. Provided the reader has a frame of reference – and possibly the American reader hasn't got it, and there's the rub – this book is every bit as good and valid as Dickens at his best, written with terrific verve and a command of Saint-Henry dialect which is literally magnificent. Granted the frame of reference, there [is] no American book except Farrell's *Studs Lonigan*[6] [which] has the merit of this, in its own class. And her French-Canadians, poor as dirt and ignorant though they are, have a certain spice and richness the Chicago Irish never had. The Church, judging by the way *Le Devoir* reviewed Gabrielle Roy,[7] were highly indignant about the book, but they could do nothing against it. Nor did the book duck out on anything. So far, and I'm half way through, she simply doesn't mention it at all. She doesn't have to. The people in that district are almost uninterested in the Church.

Just in case I wasn't clear – my article was merely submitted to the *Atlantic*, and only a week ago. I've had no word from them. Very possibly they will refuse it. If they do, I'll try *Harper's* and then *The Yale Review*. I want it to appear in the States if possible.

All the best,
Hugh

1 On the evening of 15 March Deacon was to introduce MacLennan as a speaker in the lecture series entitled 'Your Favourite Author,' sponsored by the Montreal Municipal Library; MacLennan's subject was the contemporary Canadian novel.

2 'The Novel in Canada' (*Queen's Quarterly*, Autumn 1945, pp 322–31) was written in response to the popular and critical success of MacLennan's new novel. Pacey argued that, except for Grove, there were no great Canadian writers; Callaghan had betrayed his talent, and everyone else wrote second-rate historical romances. The rest of Pacey's article was an attempt to rationalize the failure of the Canadian novel in the twentieth century.

3 Bruce Hutchison (b. 1901), then assistant editor of the *Winnipeg Free Press*; he won the Governor-General's Award (non-fiction) for *The Unknown Country: Canada and Her People* (1943), and published a satirical war novel, *The Hollow Men*, in 1944. Gwethalyn (Gwen) Graham (1913–65), author of two novels, *Swiss*

*Sonata* (1938) and *Earth and High Heaven* (1944), both of which won Governor-General's Awards.

4 Q.D. Leavis's *Fiction and the Reading Public* was published in 1932. MacLennan is confusing her initials with those of her husband, also a well-known critic.

5 The 16 February 1946 number of *The Nation* published in its 'Books and the Arts' section an article entitled 'Notes on Canadian Literature' by Robert Leigh Weaver (b. 1921), subsequently editor of *The Tamarack Review* and of CBC's 'Anthology,' whom MacLennan obviously did not know. MacLennan had misread the article, for rather than talking about church censorship, Weaver remarked that 'two factors are dominant in the literature of French Canada – Roman Catholicism and a passionate desire for continuance as a living cultural entity' (p 200). Weaver spoke of Canadian literature as 'still struggling to establish itself' (p 198).

6 James Thomas Farrell (1904–79), American author of the naturalistic *Studs Lonigan: A Trilogy* (1935), which criticized American society and attacked capitalism

7 Albert Alain, 'Bonheur d'occasion,' *Le Devoir*, 15 September 1945

---

## From Gabrielle Roy

Encinitas
March 11, 1946

Dear Mr. Deacon,

It is quite unlikely that I'll be back before April and perhaps even later. I regret it very much for I discovered through your letters that we have several things in common and, no doubt, we will unearth many more when we do get together.

I too was born in Manitoba, in the very catholic little French town of St. Boniface. I went to convent there, and learned that although English and protestant people might go to heaven by some indirect route, it wasn't right for us to mix with them. I was a good little girl, very studious, the youngest of a family of eight. I went to Normal school in Winnipeg and, following in my sisters' tracks, I became a school teacher. My mother thought that it was a profession noble, lady-like and highly respectable. I taught school in a small village the first year and then in St. Boniface.[1] Throughout those dreary, empty years I found escape in theatricals playing with amateur groups such as Le Cercle Molière who won the French trophy twice in the drama festival and also with the Winnipeg Little Theatre.[2] I had some success as a small town actress and I fancied myself gifted with great histrionic possibilities. I saved as much as I could of my small salary and eventually I had enough to start on a trip to Europe. I studied dramatics in London,[3] but I found myself attracted to writing so much more than to the stage. Before leaving Canada, I had had a few stories published in English and a few in French.[4] A trip to France, a brief stay in Paris finally convinced me that the French language was my proper medium. I used up the last bit of my money, by the way, on a walking tour of the south of France with a girl friend. After nearly two years in Europe, I returned to Canada six months before the war and settled in Montreal as a free-lance writer. It was tremendously difficult and tremendously exhilarating. I sometimes think those were the most wonderful years of my life. I wrote short stories, reportages, feature articles for several French-Canadian periodicals.[5] I laid aside two or three months each year to write my novel. It seems that it is quite a success and this surprises me greatly for I wrote a simple story about people and a way of living evident to all.

I am now in California trying to forget that I ever wrote *Bonheur d'Occasion*. As you must have experienced yourself many times, joy springs not from what is done but from what is to be done. I really came here to find solitude, a condition which I have dreaded all my life and which I have found impossible to elude. For more than a month now I have lived in a cottage by the sea. The only people I know around here are some distant relatives whom I hadn't seen since I was a child. To say the truth, in spite of the sea and abundant sunshine, I am very lonesome.

I too love Canada dearly. My folks, originally from Quebec, led a pioneer life in Manitoba, and I feel as they must have the thrill of adventuring along fresh trails. No, I don't think that I would care to live in any other country although, of course, I should be glad to visit France again some day.

I don't know if these details will help you much. Our life cannot be told in facts, don't you think, but in inner strivings and conflicts, very difficult to record.

I cannot tell you what my next book will be for it isn't clear in my mind yet. Perhaps it is that I do not choose a subject matter, but that a certain subject chooses me. I know this is poorly expressed; I haven't written in English for a long time and I'm full of misgivings concerning the propositions.

I still think that it is very kind of you to show so much interest in my work. When I return to Canada, I shall read your books with I feel, much profit and pleasure.

Yours sincerely,
Gabrielle Roy

G. Delivery
Encinitas
California
U.S.A.

1 During one month in the summer of 1929, she was assigned to a school in Marchand and in September began a year as teacher at Cardinal. Between 1930 and 1937 she taught at the Institut Provencher in St Boniface, and in the summer of 1937 at an isolated posting in the Water Hen district.
2 Le Cercle Molière, St Boniface's theatrical company established in 1925 by Arthur Boutal and his wife, is Canada's oldest continuing theatre group. The troupe twice participated in the Dominion Drama Festival in the early 1940s, winning the Bessborough Trophy on both occasions.
3 In the late fall of 1937, she enrolled as a student at the Guildhall School of Music and Drama.
4 Roy left for Europe in the fall of 1937. Two short stories were published in the Montreal weekly *Le Samedi* in 1936: 'La grotte de la mort' (23 May) and 'Cent pour cent d'amour' (31 October). We have been unable to locate any other French stories or any stories in English published before 1937.
5 Among them: *La Revue moderne*, *Le Bulletin des agriculteurs*, and *Le Jour*, all published in Montreal

---

## To Gabrielle Roy March 24, 1946

Dear Gabrielle Roy,

As a critic, I cannot commend you too highly for waiting to get *Bonheur d'Occasion* out of your system before tackling the next book. All your instincts are RIGHT!

This letter is to tell you that all your worries are over. I have the great honor, evidently, to be the first to assure you that you stand on the brink of a great career. You are FREE. There will be money, honors – all the freedom an artist needs to create. And I hope you will be happy because you will be a very famous, privileged person, too important, perhaps, to write long, informative letters to critics who are inquisitive. When you come into the kingdom that is preparing to receive you, please remember that I am a literary parasite, who depends for a living on knowing people like you.

I am just returned from Montreal, where I spent the most exciting week of my life. French writers and publishers received me. I introduced Hugh McLennan when he made his Bibliotheque address for Votre Auteur Prefere. I interviewed Dr. Panneton,[1] Germaine Guevremont and many others. I have enough live copy for a month's writing. The page I enclose is merely the beginning of the fruits of this trip.[2] Our Canadian literature is just at the beginning of a rich interchange between French and English. (I will tell you a great deal when I see you. This is the first great harvest, like the bumper crop of wheat in 1916 on the prairies – 400 million bushels.)

Then I come home and here, waiting for me, is your wonderful letter. It tells me exactly what I need to know. We have formed an acquaintance at a perfect hour for me; and I even hope to be of use to you. Though, to speak truly, you do not need any help. Nothing can stop you now.

Your success with Pascal amounts to sale of 7,000 copies at $3, with the steady demand of 1,000 copies a month in Quebec.[3] That is big for Quebec.

Your succes d'estime lies in the fact that, wherever I went, French and English told me that Gabrielle Roy is the biggest writer we have. Dr. Panneton said that. Hugh McLennan said *Bonheur d'Occasion* is the greatest novel ever produced by a Canadian. Some only say that you are first rate. Nobody said one adverse word. Tastes differ and all do not put you absolutely first. But those, in whose judgment I have confidence, say you are Canada's greatest novelist of all time or in any language.

My respectful homage! (Eh bein [sic], we must keep up the honor of Manitoba – n'est-ce pas?)

I am so happy for you. This loneliness will pass. It is the last calm moment you will have for many years. Fame is yours and if you wish solitude in future, you will have to hire guards to keep the people out.

I was lucky about getting a copy of the novel. I found one in Canada Book Co., on St. Catherine St., near my hotel – La Salle. (I won't go to the big English hotels any more to be pushed around.) A girl in Pascal's told me they had none and no store had any; but I found it.

I had a long talk with your publisher and like him very much.

He will do well. He was very nice to me.

Most important thing is that *Bonheur d'Occasion* is in the hands of Reynal and Hitchcock of New York for English translation. He is at present the greatest and finest publisher of English books in the world. He will deal fairly with you and will succeed with the book.[4]

There was only one point. I could not make out whether there will be a separate contract and edition for English Canada. There should be in your interests. I fear it may be too late. Probably Mr. Reynal included English Canada in the contract. If that has not been done; or if Mr. Reynal is willing now to give up Canada, I can talk over with you, when I see you, what arrangements you might make here in Toronto. I suggest you find out whether it is still possible for you to arrange a separate contract for English Canada – using the same translation, of course. It would mean double royalties to you and this territory will give you a very large sale. It is worth looking into.

Please do not bring my name into it. Critics should not be interested in money matters; but this means a lot to you in dollars; and I want you to get the best possible deal.

It doesn't matter when you come back. I have the book which will be reviewed in my newspaper by one who understands French well.[5] I shall supplement this review with a personal article based on your letter. We have the photo. Mr. Dagenais amazed me by saying you are a small person. From picture, I should have thought you a good size. But it is the head that counts in a writer.

Now, two personal things. The Little Theatre end brings us still closer. Perhaps you were busy with the stage in Winnipeg when Marguerite Syme was also playing in Marjorie Pickthall's 'Woodcarver's Wife,' Shakespeare etc. Margot is my wife's daughter. She married Robert Christie[6] of the Holden Players – a stock company in Winnipeg. They went to England before the war and played with success at Old Vic and both toured. Margot played in *The Women*. Bob was making a name for himself when war broke out and they went through it. Last fall they came back with their little daughter and he is now doing radio work in Toronto. Margot is expecting another baby.

No. Don't read my books when you come home. They are all long out of print; and I have grown beyond them. I am ashamed now to have been once so young, so naive. I can't write again till I retire, which I am planning for 1950, when I shall be 60. I have nothing to retire on but cannot stand the pace forever; besides, I wish to write a few books myself. Not fiction. I am not creative. If I ever had that sort of talent, which I doubt, it disappeared in 25 years as a professional critic. My real mettier [sic] is the light essay – whimsical.

(Oh, let me tell you quick. One person in Montreal told me in Montreal I could not talk to you because you had no English! It is to laugh.)

I went to Manitoba in 1911 when I was 21. Born at Pembroke, Ontario, on the Ottawa river. My father died when I was 9 months. So I was brought up at Stanstead Quebec. I was 24 when I went to Dauphin as a law student, in 1914, and learned law under the little rat Frank Simpson, now a judge. He taught me well, though it was painful for me and perhaps for him too. In 1917 I changed to Pitblado's office in Winnipeg.[7] I got LL.B. from University of Manitoba in 1918 and stayed with Pitblado until I gave up law for writing in 1922. I then came to Toronto and became literary editor of *Saturday Night*. In 1928 I went to *The Mail and Empire*, which was merged with *The Globe* in 1936.

I am the father of an Air Force son, [Billy] 23, who is studying music in Paris for three years; and I have two daughters. The younger [Mary] is a student nurse in hospital here. The elder [Dierdre] will be a writer, we both hope.

During the war I was Deputy Administrator of Publishing and Printing for the Wartime Prices and Trade Board (rationing paper to newspapers and magazines; books were not rationed.) My wife took my place with the newspaper as literary editor for those three years. She is a much better speaker than I am; but I am the better writer.

I give you all that because you must know the kind of man who is so deeply interested in your career. I am chairman of the Governor General's Awards Board and have been nominated as next president of the Canadian Authors Association. Now you know everything, except what I had for breakfast this morning; and I'll tell you that, also, if you wish.

As prospective C.A.A. president, I was delighted to meet Mme Guevremont, who feels as you and I do about bringing writers together in Canada. It is splendid to know you will be an ally in this cause.

Of course I want to see you. Perhaps you will return via Chicago, Detroit, Toronto. If so, could you stay over a day? If we know in time, accommodation can be secured.

Or I am quite willing to go to see you in Montreal. Or in Rawdon, or anyplace. I had talks with Mrs. B.D. Simpson,[8] who told me you live at the Ford Hotel, when you are in Montreal. You see, I heard of you from everybody in Montreal. They all say: 'Ah, monsieur, but you should see Gabrielle Roy. Have you read *Bonheur d'Occasion*?'

Certainly, you must write in French. (They told me in Montreal that a reader of your novel could *smell* St. Henri.) But you are a writer of the world, not just Quebec; and it is most important of all that your novels shall be known and read in English Canada. The translation route is correct.

If you were not coming back, I should start for California to see you. But it is better, je pense, that you go on thinking about the new novel until you feel like returning. Then please tell me well in advance. I can meet you where you say.

Finally, my thanks to you for the great kindness you have done me in sending this beautiful letter, with everything in it. I can now write and give English Canada its first real news about Gabrielle Roy, celebrated author. And when we meet, we need not waste time with preliminary discussions. We can get right down to business as quite old friends. At least, I hope your letter means that.

Later, when *Bonheur d'Occasion* appears in English, all my friends will wish to meet you; and we will have to arrange a Toronto reception for you. Do not make any mistake. The United States is a big, rich country; but English Canada is going to love and honor you because you are one of us. To those Americans you will be just another novelist. Comprenez? But we, Mam's'elle, we shall take you to our hearts as one of our own. We shall be proud of you, more glad of your success than if you wrote originally in English. And making the French-Canadian mind known to English-speakers will be the most important work you ever do in your life.

In all that, I shall help you as best I can.

After the review in my paper by a competent person, I shall get out my dictionary and try to read the novel for myself. Once – 40 years ago, I could read French fairly well. But I never spoke it and have had no use for it; and now it is all gone. But perhaps a little will come back. Meanwhile, you are charitable to write English to me.

So the next letter I get is not be from an unknown young woman but from a famous novelist. Remember! I know my trade pretty well. When I pick a literary celebrity, I am generally right. So you must hold your head high, and glance proudly about, and think of all the things you are going to do with all the money you are going to make. (We'll have to see about translating those short stories, too, for sale to magazines using English. You will have quite a bit of revenue from that. Don't forget.)[9]

You will need a manager, one day, perhaps, and can afford to pay him more than you have ever yet made in a year.

It is a very good thing that you should realize what success is going to mean; and that this knowledge should come to you while you are alone and can think calmly.

No more loneliness! You will return not yet great but on the threshold of fame. One year from now you will be really famous.

There, by the sea, adjust your mind to these changes in your fortunes. Come back to conquer. Come back *knowing* the teacher and free lance writer, quite poor in money, is now a novelist of superior class. You may not be really Canada's best novelist – peutetre [sic] only No. 2. But you will be very high; and with American sales and soon translations into other languages. We shall be able to buy books by Gabrielle in Madrid, Buenos Aires, Cape Town. The France you love will read your books and think of you as a great writer.

I would not deceive you. It would be too cruel. All this will happen. Be careful of the money. So many writers throw it away foolishly. Ask me to talk to you about that. You must save most of what you take in. There may be stretches in the future with no income or very little. Prepare for these now out of the winnings of this novel. A Government annuity is the best thing – Canadian Government bonds next.

You will be tired of reading all this. Thank you again and congratulations on a great achievement.

BON CHANCE!! [sic]

1 Dr Philippe Panneton (1895–1960) who, under the pseudonym Ringuet, was best known for his naturalistic novel *Trente arpents* (*Thirty Acres*), published in 1938

2 On the book page of 23 March 1946 appeared the feature article 'Will the World Know Canada by Her Novels?' in which Deacon described and quoted from

MacLennan's address to the Montreal Municipal Library for their series 'Your Favourite Author.' Other articles followed in subsequent book pages: an interview with Panneton (30 March); a feature article on Canadian publishing in French (6 April); and an interview with Germaine Guèvremont (13 April).

3 Editions Pascal in Montreal, under the direction of journalist-publisher Gérard Dagenais (b. 1913), published the first edition of *Bonheur d'occasion* in two volumes in August 1945. Pascal operated from Dagenais' Dorchester Street office until 1950, when he went out of business.

4 Eugene Reynal (1902–68) and Curtice Hitchcock (1892–1946) founded Reynal and Hitchcock in 1934. Shortly after Hitchcock's death, it merged with Harcourt Brace in 1948. Reynal subsequently formed Reynal and Company in 1955 and was its president until his death.

5 Edith Ardagh reviewed *Bonheur d'occasion* in *The Globe and Mail* on 28 April.

6 Robert Wallace Christie (b. 1913) worked with the John Holden Players from 1934 to 1936, performing in Toronto and Winnipeg; Margot Christie, (b. 1909), subsequently became well known as a Canadian actress, as did her daughter Dinah.

7 Isaac Pitblado (1867–1964) was the co-founder and senior partner of the Winnipeg law firm Pitblado, Hoskin & Co., which employed Deacon from 1917 to 1922. Frank H. Simpson (b. 1880) of Minnedosa, Manitoba, under whom Deacon articled in Dauphin

8 Montreal publisher-bookseller who issued twenty-four French titles during her first fifteen months in business (1946–7). She used her living quarters in the Ford Hotel as a business address and planned to publish her own translations in both languages.

9 In May 1948, *Mademoiselle* published 'The Vagabond' – a translation of 'Un Vagabond frappe à notre porte.' The short story had been first published in *Amérique française* in January 1946.

---

## To Sinclair Ross[1] April 4, 1946

Dear Sinclair Ross,

Where in hell are you? Your friends and admirers want to know, and that includes me. Please come clean.

Are you going back to the bank or what?[2] Have you written another novel? If so, is it placed yet? (If not, I strongly urge upon you advisability of a separate Canadian contract. Publishing conditions have changed out of recognition since you left and you ought to look into the business end of writing before signing any new contract. See me or one of the more commercially successful of the new novelists).

Did you get married?

You were kind enough to send me a couple of cards while you

were in the army. I appreciated them but I took on a difficult and arduous war job and could not keep up with anybody. I reverted to civil life Jan. 1. Records tells me you were discharged March 22 but that it is against the rules for them to tell me where you are.[3] I therefore send this letter in their care to forward, hoping you will materialize from somewhere.

Pardon me not writing you in wartime, and do now, please, give me an address and basic information, such as 'Were you wounded or incapacitated? What are your plans – 1. literary; 2. occupational?'

If you happen to be in these parts, my phone number is MOhawk 7068 at home and WAverley 7851 at *The Globe and Mail*, where you once called.

Hoping all is well with you and that another novel is completed or well on the way,

Sincerely,

1 The prairie novelist Sinclair Ross (b. 1908) had published *As for Me and My House* in 1941; from 1942 to 1946 he was stationed with the Canadian Army in England.
2 Ross worked as a clerk for the Royal Bank in a series of Saskatchewan towns upon completing high school; he remained with the bank until 1968, when he retired to the Mediterranean and eventually to Vancouver.
3 On 3 April the Department of National Defence responded to Deacon's inquiry of 28 March, informing him that Staff-Sergeant Ross was 'struck off strength the Canadian Army' on 22 March, that it was against the rules to reveal his civilian address, but that mail would be forwarded to him if directed to the Department of Records.

---

## From Sinclair Ross

7 Lancaster Apartments
Winnipeg
April 15, 1946

Dear Mr. Deacon:

My sincere thanks for your letter, which found its way to me just this morning. It's awfully nice – and encouraging – to learn that someone remembers and takes an interest in me. I deserve neglect, for apart from family letters I didn't write half a dozen during my three and a half years overseas.

No, I didn't get married. Afraid I'm destined to be a grumpy, solitary old batchelor [sic]. The ones I want don't want me – though I will say I don't work very hard on it.

No, I wasn't wounded or – at least to my knowledge – incapacitated. Stayed in England – London, most of the time – experienced nothing more dramatic than the flying bombs. Enjoyed London thoroughly.

No, I haven't a novel completed, but am hard at work on one.[1] A long one – perhaps too long. I find myself with an abundance of material, and am going straight ahead with it. About 100,000 words done – first draft -and at least that many more to go. I will do some whittling and tightening, of course, when I get to the revision.

Yes, so far as I know now I am going back to the Bank, but not till about July 1 – I'm taking as much time off as I may and working on the novel. I write slowly, though, and won't have the first draft done in that time, but should have its back pretty well broken.

I don't look forward to going back, but I don't see how I can better myself. I think I would take the plunge if I were alone,, but my mother is 70, nearly blind and dependent upon me. We live comfortably now, and naturally I don't want to expose her to the hazards of a free-lance's income. Besides, being practical about it, I'm not at all sure that my commercial possibilities as a writer amount to much. I hope this novel will give me an answer.

I appreciate your suggestion of looking into the possibility of a Canadian publisher. Reynal & Hitchcock have the option on this one, of course, but as you say a separate Canadian contract might be arranged. Especially as what I am doing this time is all-out Canadian – Americans might not be interested. Incidentally I have just had a letter from Bernard McEvoy of Longmans Green, and an invitation to submit a novel to them for consideration if and when I have it completed.

I'm afraid it will be the end of the year anyway before I get East; when I do arrive, though, I shall certainly drop in and say hello. Thanks again for your letter and interest.

As ever,
Sinclair Ross

1 Ross's next novel, *The Well*, did not appear until 1958.

From Germaine Guèvremont

Jeudi saint [18 April] 1946

Cher monsieur,

Le premier que je dois remercier c'est vous qui êtes un tel ami du *Survenant*, quoi que j'ai bien aimé aussi l'article de Mlle E. Ardagh.[1] Elle a bien compris *mes* personnages. Je lui écris aujourd'hui même.

Votre page m'intéresse beaucoup. Chaque lundi maintenant je me rends à la bibliothèque pour la lire. Seulement, je crois que Ringuet[2] a fait une légère erreur quand il dit: 'We have exhausted rural areas' – il voulait dire 'Rural areas have exhausted me ...' Je crois que les sujets de la terre, les romans de la terre sont comme la terre elle-même: éternels. Même si j'écris un livre où l'action se passe dans une ville, mon opinion sera la même.

Vous avez raison quand vous écrivez, au sujet du poète Bruce, qu'il faut soumettre sa plume à une discipline.[3] Louis Bromfield[4] s'oblige à écrire deux heures par jour.

Quant à la traduction, je crois qu'il faudra passer par Plon,[5] tout de même, je comprends qu'il sera plus avantageux pour moi si la proposition m'est présentée d'abord et que je l'envoie ensuite à Plon – on m'a fait des conditions fort avantageuses, que j'ai acceptées. Le contrat final devrait me parvenir à la fin de mai, car j'ai retourné le premier accepté le 12 avril. Seulement tout ceci est confidentiel. La publicité à outrance qu'on a faite autour de mauvaises oeuvres m'a souvent donné la nausée et me rend méfiante envers elle.

Joyeuses Pâques et toute ma reconnaissance.

Germaine G. Guèvremont

1 Edith Ardagh was one of Deacon's reviewers at *The Globe and Mail*; he counted upon her to review books published in French. The letter refers to her 13 April 1946 review of *Le Survenant*.

2 The pseudonym of novelist Philippe Panneton (1895–1960)

3 In 'New Bruce Poems,' Deacon had reviewed Charles Bruce's *Grey Ship Moving* (13 April 1946). While praising Bruce's collection, Deacon said that he had not yet attained first rank because he lacked the 'discipline in steady production denied to those who write sporadically and publish infrequently.' Bruce (1906–71) is remembered for the poems in *The Mulgrave Road* (1951), which won the Governor-General's Award, and for his novel *The Channel Shore* (1954).

4 American novelist (1896–1956) and Pulitzer Prize winner whose books dealt with his country's agrarian middle west
5 The Paris publisher of *Le Survenant* and *Marie-Didace*

---

## To Sinclair Ross April 24, 1946

Dear Sinclair Ross;

Congratulations on getting safely through the war and being so far along with your next novel. I'm indeed glad to know where to lay hands on you in emergency.

On the whole I believe in the principle of professionalism. A man working all his time and living by it may master his craft more fully. But the artist has advantages in amateur status. He can write what he likes, not just what will sell. The success d'estime of your first novel indicates that earnings may be moderate for some time. Only time will tell. Public taste is unaccountable.

Reynal and Hitchcock are the No. 1 publishers in English at present. They are decent and honest men, even generous. They may permit you to make a separate Canadian contract and it is highly desirable from your standpoint.

Longmans here are first rate and anxious to build a Canadian list. They are acquiring some excellent native talent. Theodore Pike,[1] Canadian manager and also sales manager for U.S., is my oldest friend in the trade. Extremely shrewd and ditto honorable. He won't look at you unless you have obtained a release of your Canadian rights. He will not negotiate with R & H. You'll have to do that; and I should do it – when you send ms just say you desire a separate contract for Canada. No point in concealment of your plans. They may say yes or no. Or, as you hint, your novel may be too Canadian and they will reject, in which case Longmans here are in splendid position to place it with one of their related firms – say Coward-McCann. I'm glad you have no disabilities nor awkward problems. It is good to see a Canadian novelist who can just go ahead and write without complications.

Confidentially, anticipating my presidency of Canadian Authors, I hope you will join that outfit. They are weak out there and need you. We have become very practical with the new success for Canadian books. We are at work on copyright, income tax, standard contracts, and are already of real help to our members, if they are authors. You should be in touch via membership, get our literature and throw in your own weight and prestige. A lot is going to happen at the Toronto Convention June 27–29.

Give me notice when you make plans to come East and some arrangements can be made to introduce you. December is my peak but there is a let-up after 25th.

Regards and good luck –

1 Theodore Fay Pike (1886–1953) emigrated from Atlantic City in 1915 to work for Macmillan before going on the road for the British firm Longmans, Green & Co. He opened up Longman's new Toronto branch in 1922, serving as its president until his death.

---

## From Hugh MacLennan

1178 Mountain Street
Montreal
April 28, 1946

My Dear Bill:

Just a note that requires and expects no answer.

I thought the page on Gabrielle Roy splendid, and believe me a grand thing for inter-provincial relations.[1] She is becoming, in a mild way, adored in Quebec.

We finally made her acquaintance, and she spent three hours over tea with us. Her personality confirms, and more than confirms, the opinion I had formed of her from her book. She's a first-class human being, and probably the best natural novelist this country has ever had. I think she'll go on beyond *Bonheur d'Occasion* and keep on developing.

She said, by the way, she was much touched by the grand reception you gave her in Toronto. She's so warm-hearted those things mean a lot to her.

Both of us continue much as ever and hope to get back to Hatley in another ten days, if the weather is merciful. Violet King called up about ten days ago, but fortunately I was out. So Dorothy took the call. Somehow she had heard about the GG Award before it was announced.[2] She certainly didn't hear from me. I don't dare write her anything any more, and haven't sent her but a card since New Year's. She sent Dorothy a long letter telling her she might have an operation; also that she was thinking of writing short stories. One of the oddest cases I've seen. I doubt if she herself knows clearly where the fact stops and the imagination begins.

Too bad the paper turned thumbs down on Stockholm.[3] But I dare say, on reflection, you may well have felt as Dorothy did on reflection: that the world is grim enough anywhere without having to face Europe too soon on top of it all.

All the best,
Hugh

1 'Magnificent Canadian Novel from Pitiful Montreal Slum' (*The Globe and Mail*, 27 April 1946) contained a photograph of Roy and E.J. Pratt; Edith Ardagh's review of *Bonheur d'occasion*; and Deacon's biographical sketch of Roy, along with his statement that 'Miss Roy's gift to Canadian literature is a firm, sharp realism of observation.'

2 MacLennan had won the Governor-General's Award for *Two Solitudes* (1945).

3 Deacon had been increasingly involved in PEN as local secretary-treasurer in the 1940s, but gradually drifted away from the organization after *The Globe and Mail* refused to subsidize a trip to the Stockholm convention of 1946.

---

## From Gabrielle Roy

Rawdon
May 30, 1946

Dear Bill,

Thank you so very much for your lovely long letter of May 29th. I had received your two previous letters and was on the point of answering them when this one came along.[1]

And now I shall try to answer your questions before we get down to anything else. I have rented a small log cabin, just outside Rawdon and it isn't bad, although I'm still lonesome, very lonesome. The new novel is coming along, although slowly. I will tell you more about this later on. The death of Mr. Hitchcock may delay the publication of *Bonheur* in English, although the firm, of course, is still going on and is promising me a quick translation. Hannah Josephson,[2] reputed as a very sensitive and skillfull translator is now working full speed on it. Shortly after his very sudden death, which occurred as you probably know, a few weeks ago, Mr. [Reynal][3] wrote me a fine letter in which he expressed all the difficulties he had met in securing a good translator. But, at last, he was overjoyed, as he said, to have Hannah Josephson on the job.

About the association, I am sending a cheque to-night to Mrs. MacLeod at the address you give me.[4] I would have done so before, but didn't quite know how to proceed about it.

And now I'd like to say that my memories of our Easter week-end are just as pleasant as ever, tinged perhaps with a sense of melancholy, for I have withdrawn for the time being from all contacts.[5] It has taken me so long to capture that complete possession of character & subject matter which I find essential before I start working at all, that I dread the smallest distraction. I would like to accept your invitation more than any other, and perhaps I shall, but it is very small 'perhaps.' I understand perfectly all the good reasons you give me for attending this wonderful meeting of writers from all parts of Canada. Certainly this is a great step in the history of Canadian literature. I agree wholeheartedly with you that I should go, but my work is at the stage where it is perilous to leave it even for a few days. It is not quite enough advanced and in a way too much so. My characters are so elusive yet, and at the same time so exacting. A great deal of suffering has come to me already from such conflicts as I now find myself in. I cannot, however, in the matter consider my interests. Certainly, for the sake of my interests I should attend this convention. However my small person, whether I become rich or not, all this is of the least importance. Only what I can create, throughout some force mostly superior to myself, has any importance. Dear friend, I wish you could know how really painful it is to me to temporarily renounce friendship when my very soul cries for it. I am considering however that, to a small extent, I might contribute to the realization of your plans by attending this meeting. And this is the great temptation. So the only promise I can now make is that, if my work[6] has sufficiently progressed from now to the end of June, I may go. Will you be satisfied with that. I think you will for I have felt in you uncommon understanding.

I shall be happy later, when I will feel that I have earned at last the admiration and love of my friends. Then I will come again to your charming house and I will invite you here in Rawdon.

My best regards to Sally, to the girls, and a special pat shake to Winky.[7]

Yours sincerely,
Gabrielle

Box 307
Rawdon
P.Q.

1 Deacon had written Roy urging her to attend the twenty-fifth anniversary convention of the CAA.
2 Hannah Geffen Josephson (1900–76), American journalist, author, and translator
3 Gabrielle Roy had mistakenly substituted 'Hitchcock' for 'Reynal.'
4 Mrs G.R. MacLeod, President of the Montreal branch of the CAA
5 Roy had spent the previous Easter with the Deacons on her way back to Montreal from California.
6 Her next published novel was *La Petite Poule d'eau* (1950), translated as *Where Nests The Water Hen.*
7 The Deacons' cat

---

## To Catherine Grove    June 6, 1946

Dear Mrs. Grove,

We have been saddened to hear that Philip is not improving. I have asked Watson Kirkconnell[1] to visit you to learn whether there is any hope of bringing you and Philip to Toronto for a ceremony at the [CAA] Convention June 27th. From what rumors have reached me, I fear this may be impossible.

Thank you for the editorial from *The Brantford Expositor.*[2] Of course I knew of the degree from Rod Kennedy; but I was not publishing the fact in hopes that the ceremony at Toronto would offer the best chance of publicity, with photos etc.

In view of the uncertain state of your husband's health, I am putting in a brief mention of the honor on Saturday morning. This will not interfere with a more extended notice if you two come to Toronto on the 27th.

Please explain to Philip the great anxiety and distress which his condition is causing his fellow-writers throughout Canada. All I have talked to resent the implications of Pacey's book[3] and we are looking forward eagerly to the publication of the autobiography. In my presidential address on the 29th,[4] I name the emergence of Philip as the real birth of the Canadian novel; and he may rest assured that the solid worth of his books will cause them far to outlive the misguided notions of young Dr. Pacey. .

I regret that, between my newspaper duties and the urgent affairs of the Authors Association, I am unable to visit you at present; and I still hope Philip may improve sufficiently to be driven to Hart House on the 27th.

With most cordial regards to you both,

Sincerely,

1 Kirkconnell (1895–1977), the Milton scholar, linguist, and translator who was at this time head of English at McMaster
2 The editorial of 26 May – 'F.P. Grove Honored' – dealt with Grove's honorary Doctor of Letters degree from the University of Manitoba. In the fall of the same year, he was awarded an LLD by Mount Allison University.
3 See note 1, letter from Hugh MacLennan, 5 March 1946.
4 Deacon was national president of the Canada Authors' Association from June 1946 to June 1948.

---

## From Vernon Rhodenizer

Wolfville
June 13, 1946

Dear Bill,

The broken leg I mentioned in a P.S. more than a year ago did not heal, and on June 26th last I had an amputation above the knee. I went on crutches for the academic year 1945–46 and taught appreciation to 212 Sophomores and journalism to 18 upper classmen. Now I have the artificial limb, but am not ready for travel yet. Besides, the Convention comes too near our Summer School, so unfortunately we cannot be there.[1]

I like your report on Awards.[2] Since you are recommending awards in new categories, I suggest one in journalism. That would avoid such a critical travesty as that perpetrated in 'academic non-fiction' this year. How in God's name or any other name can the work of Ross Munro or Mrs. Tranter be called 'academic?'[3] And if *Gauntlet to Overlord* is 'academic,' then why is Heaps's *Escape from Arnhem* 'creative' instead of 'academic?'[4] I am glad that Ross Munro got an award, but I am not critically satisfied to have him get it in a field in which his work does not belong, especially when there was genuine 'academic' work in that field deserving of the award. University Presidents may not be good judges of literary categories, but the people who put the books in their categories should be. In fact, that is just about as important as picking the best book within a category.

I could very easily have broken the tie if the matter had been referred back to me on the discovery that the University Presidents had both chosen journalistic books and neither had mentioned one of my books.[5] The tie could only have come because they had them in the reverse order, and my vote would have been most emphatically for Munro as between him and Mrs. Tranter. In spite of my presidential colleagues, I should not want people of critical acumen to think either that I voted for the tied books or that I could not have decided which of the two was better.

Best of luck.

Vern

1 The annual convention of the CAA was held in Toronto in late June 1946 and marked the inauguration of Deacon's term as national president (1946–8).

2 Deacon served as first chairman of the Governor-General's Awards Board from 1944 to 1949 and worked to revise and codify the criteria and procedures associated with the awards. Rhodenizer was a member of the adjudicating committee for the authors of books published in 1945.

3 Robert Ross Munro (b. 1913). Journalist who won the Governor-General's non-fiction award for *Gauntlet to Overlord: The Story of the Canadian Army* (1945). Gladdis Joy Tranter (b. 1902), Winnipeg author and CBC personality, had just published *Ploughing the Arctic*.

4 Leo Heaps, author of *Escape from Arnhem: A Canadian among the Lost Paratroopers* (1945)

5 Munro won the academic non-fiction award; the creative non-fiction prize went to Evelyn Richardson (b. 1902), the wife of a Nova Scotia lighthouse operator, for her autobiographical *We Keep a Light*. N.A.M. MacKenzie, president of the University of British Columbia and A.W. Trueman, president of the University of Manitoba, put Munro's book and Joy Tranter's *Plowing the Arctic* at the top of their academic non-fiction lists. Rhodenizer voted for Burpee's *The Discovery of Canada*. The entire Awards Board was brought in at the recommendation of Deacon to break the tie between Munro and Tranter.

## To E.J. Pratt

July 6, 1946

Dear Ned,

First let me tell you how much the Association feels honoured by the honour which has properly come to you as the ranking Canadian poet.[1] I was immensely pleased with your speech at the convention and with your presence at several sessions.[2] I think you see that the men and women who have now taken national offices are thoroughly representative of Canadian writing and that a new day has dawned for us all.

In this achievement, there has been probably no single factor of greater importance than the fact that, in a period that has stressed the emergence of a commercially successful prose group, poetry has risen to new heights through your efforts. You are exerting an enormous influence on your juniors. I notice in the work of Birney, Bruce and others that you are setting a pattern for that generation as surely as Roberts did for the Confederation group.

The enclosed letter to Birney indicates the action we have taken.[3] It is frankly based upon the idea that we had better risk the ship and endure disaster if necessary, rather than go on with a policy so conservative that we do not carry the younger element with us. I, personally, feel sure that Birney is the key man for these younger people of talent such as Dorothy Livesay, Charles Bruce, Anne Marriott, et al.

I do not intend to put pressure on you by demands for frequent services,[4] but I would request that you write Earle a letter of advice. As the first editor of the magazine, you can doubtless teach him much and I assure you that his War experience and his year in radio have made him much more receptive to the opinions of others.

Above all, we must remember that from this [time] out we play as a team and not as individuals. Each must place his experience and capacities at the disposal of the others in a common cause.

I hope that you have a pleasant summer and that when your retirement comes, you will welcome it as an opportunity to further your writing interests without the handicap of teaching. I, personally, feel that it has been a very great privilege to have been your classmate, your friend and your vocal admirer during all these years and I am perfectly satisfied that your present fame, honestly won, now puts you in an ideally independent position for outstanding work in your crowning years.

With kind personal regards,

1 Pratt had recently been named a Companion of St Michael and St George.
2 The CAA had just held its annual convention in Toronto in June, at which Deacon had become national president.
3 The letter to Birney, who was being urged to become the new editor of the *Canadian Poetry Magazine*, has been lost.
4 Pratt was then teaching at Queen's University summer school.

---

## From E.J. Pratt

Summer Session
Queen's University
Kingston, Ontario
[July 1946]

My dear Bill:

Your letter is characteristic in your generosity and warmth of friendship. The two men in Canada who have meant most to me in literary stimulation are (academically) Pelham Edgar and (in the broad public field) your esteemed self. Whatever the Canadian Authors' Foundation may develop into, I trust that, whenever your retirement comes, the Foundation will regard you as its foremost beneficiary. I have consistently preached the debt Canadian writers owe to you and I feel sure the debt will be honoured in due time.

I am writing Birney along the lines suggested in your letter. I had a chat with him before he left and I emphasized the importance of preserving the golden mean of letters and avoiding the rasping edges of intolerant extremes. I think his year in Montreal showed him that the local coterie there were interested only in themselves and that their screaming abuse at everything and everybody gone before them was only a bit of inflated exhibitionism. They pretty well sickened him – I mean the Anderson-Layton-Souster gang. They may grow out of it in time. In the meanwhile the new *Canadian P.M.* may reap the sincere poetic labours of *all* the 'groups.' I think he appreciates the fact that the history of literature in its permanent form is a combination of tradition and experiment and that between the two there should be mutual respect. As you say, team play counts as much here as it does in the field of sport competition.

I believe in Birney. He has exceptional intellectual talents.
He is maturing and mellowing and his editorship, if he accepts it, will cover the young as well as the more established writers. I shall give him every help by way of advice and friendly practical cooperation. We have great days ahead of us Bill and nothing gives me more unalloyed delight than your Presidency of the C.A.A. You are worthy of the highest honours and I say this not merely out of a profound love and loyalty to you but out of an objective appreciation of your gifts.
I wish also to pay a tribute to good old Sal who so well sustained your book-page when you were heavily involved in patriotic duties during the last six years.
We shall have a reunion in the Fall.

Very affectionately
Ned

---

## To Earle Birney July 8, 1946

*Re: Canadian Poetry Magazine*

Dear Earle,

This is the first opportunity that I have had since convention to acquaint you with the fact that the National Executive meeting on June 30th agreed unanimously to appoint you editor of *The Canadian Poetry Magazine* at an honorarium of $50.00 per quarterly issue, subject to our reaching a mutual understanding on the various points raised in your letter to me of June 14th.[1]
Let us first have a very clear understanding on the attitude of the Association toward you as editor. It is quite true that a few members of the Association who are directly interested in poetry felt that your literary creed was too far to the left. On the other hand, Pratt, Cox[2] and myself all spoke very definitely along the lines that you are the logical man for the job and we hope you will take it. The new executive met on the Sunday following the convention. Sixteen of us were present, representing all parts of the country and, I would say, all shades of opinion. These people also felt that you are the very man for the job and Miss Anne Marriott[3] said that your influence with the younger poets would be of inestimable value. She saw

now the one chance of uniting the poetic interest in Canada. We were very glad to hear from Miss Marriott because some of the rest of us are not younger poets, as she is, and we could not gauge their feelings towards you.

The essence of official feeling on this appointment was that, while we have no capital to invest in the magazine, while its Board of Management has had to beg money for years to make up deficits, and while we are very comfortable now in the knowledge that the magazine is standing on its own feet financially, we yet reminded ourselves that the CAA is not in the publishing business for gain. This magazine was founded about 10 years ago in order to perform a literary service for the country and for our own members. We are conscious of the fact that the starting up of several rivals by groups of younger poets at different points indicates very clearly that there is some lack in the service that the magazine is now performing. To put it shortly, we feel that the sale of advertising to balance the budget ought not to be the first consideration in publishing policy. We look forward with keen anticipation to having you take this publication over and edit it in such a manner that the greatest number of poets and the greatest number of poetry lovers will take a lively interest in it.

We would wish to continue to print it here (you could use air mail for sending the proofs back and forth) and you will find Mr. A.H. O'Brien,[4] Barrister, 320 Bay Street, a very competent business manager. He was in youth a great athlete and an original member of the Argonaut Rowing Club and a paddling partner of Pauline Johnston in regattas. You will have to work out with Mr. O'Brien a technique for sending down copy and getting proofs. I would suggest that all the printing business be left with him and his committee.

As to amalgamations with other publications, I cannot see any difficulty in this unless you plan to change the name, which I hope may not be necessary. Any deals that you make with other periodicals or groups should come before the National Executive for consideration. Our next meeting will be in Toronto on Sunday August 25th. I would suggest that you go ahead with your editorial plans on the assumption that you will be the editor and in the meantime lay before us in the form of a memorandum any pending deals you have with outside interests, which we hope under your editorship will become inside your partner interests. We have not the capital to finance the purchase of other magazines, but you intimated that the suggestion might be the reverse, namely, that Mr. Alan Crawley is now financing *Contemporary Verse* at a loss and now might be willing to contribute to the costs of *The Canadian Poetry Magazine.*

I am personally with you in your desire to pay contributors. I think that we are standing on bad ground when we urge our members to insist on payment from editors and we, ourselves, as publishers, do not pay them except by this prize system.

Before we can adopt a schedule of rates, we shall have to see what commitment this involves. Kindly suggest what you think would be a fair basic rate per line or per page, and put in a memorandum an estimate of the total outlays per annum on this basis, offsetting what is now being paid out by the prize system. For your guidance, we originally began by paying contributors at a basic rate of $5.00 per printed page. This means about 10 a line. When I was buying poetry for *Saturday Night*, I paid 50 a line and the richest American magazines that used poetry all paid $1.50 a line for their most valued material. I would suggest that you consider very carefully whether the 10 a line rate would be adequate for a start. It is always possible that you may make this magazine so popular that we could afford to give more to contributors.

I do not know whether you were present during the convention when we discussed the difficulty of *Canadian Poetry Magazine* arising out of local chap-books put out by CAA Branches in Edmonton, Ottawa, Montreal and elsewhere, but excluding Toronto. Though Toronto has probably never supported the magazine any better than anybody else, at least we did not go into competition with it.

I had quite a debate on the floor with George Hardy[5] your regional vice president of the University of Alberta. I expressed myself as feeling that these local efforts, often connected with contests, represented distinct disloyalty to our own publication. The recent book put out by Ottawa Branch was, I thought, very creditable, but undoubtedly it contained a certain amount of material for which there would not have been space in a National publication. The local people have always felt that they needed the stimulus of their own publications and, unfortunately the members on average have not been too ready to pay an extra dollar a year for a subscription. (Non-members are charged a $2.00 a year.)*

I suggest that you see Mr. Crawley, write George Hardy and Mr. O'Brien and get all the information for the preparation of a memorandum covering everything. In the meantime, Dr. Watson Kirkconnell, 31 Mount Royal Avenue, Hamilton can hand over to you whatever should be passed on to the new editor and, as he has been one of our most loyal and self-sacrificing officers, I have no doubt he can give you valuable advice, as well as Ned Pratt, who is teaching summer school at Queen's. I suggest that your appointment be accepted subject to understandings on these details. In making this proposal, I know that I am carrying out the sense of a very representative executive committee. We want you to do the job. We are confident that you can do the job. On the other hand, we ask you to have as much regard as you can for both our Association's budget and for the opinions of the people you call the traditionalists. We feel that there is some risk in a departure in policy but we wish to take that risk because there is no point in continuing to publish a magazine which is unsatisfactory to the average producing body in Canada. You must remember, however, that if the ship goes down the chances are extremely remote that the Association will renew its attempt to provide a poetry medium.

Yours sincerely,

* George Hardy suggested at Convention that there be a national section and a local section. He will explain his ideas to you.

1 This letter is missing from the Deacon Collection.
2 Leonard ('Leo') Cox (1898–1978), poet and advertising executive. He was President of the Montreal branch in 1932–3 and 1935–6, and at this time was the new national treasurer of the CAA.
3 Writer and poet (b. 1913) whose *Calling Adventurers* (1941) won the Governor-General's Award for poetry; *The Wind Our Enemy* (1939) is her best-known collection.
4 Author Henry O'Brien (1865–1957), Toronto lawyer, biographer of Thomas Chandler Haliburton, and business manager of *The Canadian Poetry Magazine* under Pratt and Birney
5 William George Hardy (1896–1979), writer and professor of classics at the University of Alberta. Among his historical novels are *All the Trumpets Sounded* (1942) and *The City of Libertines* (1957).

---

## To Vernon Rhodenizer July 27, 1946

Dear Vern,

We improvised the Convention at such a speed that it is only now I am able to express regret that we did not see you and Mrs. Rhodenizer. This regret is much deeper because of the tragic circumstances that caused your absence. If it is any comfort to you to know it, I have always felt that if I had to part with a portion of my carcass before disgarding the whole of it, I could do without a leg far better than anything else. I hope that you will soon master the technique of walking on your ersatz limb and that we shall see you both at Vancouver in mid-July, 1947. A great many members, I find, are already planning to spend their summer vacation in this way. It is a good thing for the Association to have a large representation from Eastern and Central Canada and the people on the Pacific Coast tell me that they are expecting large numbers of Americans from Seattle and San Francisco, and even Los Angeles. I want the Canadians to hold up their end by appearing in substantial numbers. I do not know whether you are personally acquainted with our new western Vice President, George Hardy, but he is a first-rate fellow, both as a writer and as an executive. The next convention will be largely his show.

I hope you are working in close harmony with Bird,[1] Raddall and Andy Merkel. Bird thinks that there are a good many people in the Maritimes who should be in the Association but are not. He is going to do a good deal of travelling among the branches.

I would ask you to read most carefully the September *Author and Bookman* and 'Votes and Proceedings' which will accompany it. These will give you, almost verbatim a report of the convention which was by far the most important in our history. The Association is now getting practical results. Between the income tax victory and the work of the Contracts Committee, we feel we have added many thousands of dollars to the revenue of Canadian writers within the past few months. The executive is exceptionally strong and keen. The National office is being moved to Toronto. The term of office is astonishingly short and writers of such distinction and ability have undertaken the executive posts that we feel there is need for haste in enlarging the work of the C.A.A. and its usefulness to all writers. The territorial representation is by no means an empty gesture. The movement has reached a point at which we can only go on under thoroughly democratic principles. Every officer and every member must be active and we shall have to attain a craft solidarity quite unknown in the past.

I know that we can count on you and I hope for a friendly chat with you when I visit Nova Scotia which, I think, should be in the spring of 1947.

Thanks again for all your helpful advice.

Yours sincerely,

1 William Richard Bird (1891–1983), Maritime writer and author of regional historical romances, would succeed Deacon in 1948 as national president of the CAA.

---

## From Frederick Philip Grove

R.R. 4
Simcoe, Ontario
November 11, 1946

Dear Mr. Deacon, –

I am seventy-five years old, and I have done what I have done. And still my wife has to make the greater part of my living. The pension is not enough.

If that is not failure, I wish to know what is. What do all the university degrees matter? When I have these worries on my head?

Sincerely yours
F.P. Grove
Per Leonard Grove

---

## From W.O. Mitchell[1]

High River, Alberta
March 3, [1947][2]

Dear Mr. Deacon:

I have just read your review of my book, and I imagine I feel a lot like Brian when he finally got his tube skates. I have had those from *The New York Times* and from *The Chicago Tribune*, but my wife and I feel that you have come closer than either of these to an appreciation of what I was trying to do in WHO HAS SEEN THE WIND.

If it is any satisfaction to you, the two descriptive passages you quoted are ones that I had to fight for with Little-Brown editors. I am very fond of them myself.

Mr. Gray of MacMillans[3] has just left us. In conversations with him I learned that you could give me information I need in regard to the new ruling on income tax for writers. I am not clear on this, and I would appreciate very much any information that will help me at the end of the month. I damn near starved to death until royalty advances and serial rights payment came in on *Who Has Seen the Wind*; I want to make certain that I salvage as much as possible.

I have just received a letter from Dr. Hardy with an enclosed application form for membership in the Canadian Authors' Association. My wife and I are hoping to get out to the July convention.

We look forward to seeing you then.

Sincerely,
W.O. Mitchell

1 William Ormond Mitchell (b. 1914) had just come into prominence with his novel *Who Has Seen The Wind* (1947).
2 Mitchell had misdated his letter 1946.
3 John [Jack] Gray (1907–78) was with Macmillan of Canada from 1930 to 1973 and became its president in 1955. From the beginning of his directorship of the Canadian company, he supported Canadian writers.

---

## To W.O. Mitchell March 5, 1947

Dear Mr. Mitchell,

Thanks for your nice note. I'm having lunch with Jack Gray tomorrow so your ears will burn.

Glad to hear that you expect to be with us at Vancouver. A good crowd are coming from Ontario and Quebec.

In general, the concession we got from the Income Tax Dept. last year says that an author may spread his royalties and book earnings over the period it took him to write the book, and three years is not an unreasonable period. That means, if you get a flock of money in 1947, 1/3 of it will be 1945 income for tax purposes, 1/3 1946 and remaining third 1947. That prevents putting you in the upper brackets for 1947 and draining most of it off in taxes.

Of course you are now only reporting on 1946 earnings and these will only be whatever advance royalty you received.

Whatever they nick you in U.S. (I believe 15%) is credited to you by Can. Govt. just as if they had been paid that much tax by you. So you don't pay double.

Before you know what your 'taxable income' is, you must deduct your expenses as a writer. These include travelling to gather material or on business, paper, stamps, typing, rent of a room to write in, and almost anything you can think of. The Government looks with calm eye on the expense account. Put in everything you can think of and then let them object to items.

Then after you have made these deductions for expenses, you spread the revenue over the three years, and see how much tax for each year. Then you deduct the U.S. 15%.

You will normally file your tax return in Calgary, I suppose. The Inspector of Income Tax there may not be familiar with all the special things that apply to authors. But go there first and see how good a deal you can make. Sometimes they favor the local boy in these matters.

If your local tax-gatherer takes a dim view of the whole business or bears down too hard, give all the facts and figures to us in a sealed envelope. We shall send it unopened to Robert J.C. Stead at Ottawa, former president of this Association, a Westerner novelist like you, and just retired from the civil service. Bob will go to town on your behalf with the head lads at the capital.

You don't need to worry in 1949 about 1947 intake – that comes up in March, 1948. But, when you know how much money you are really dealing with, there is no harm in having a preliminary talk with your local tax man. As a married man, of course, you get the usual $1,500 exemption – that is zero tax on the first $1,500 you earn net after expenses; and then you get a lump off for each child. Unless you are going to take in away up in the thousands, there isn't much to worry about.

However, we'll hope, for your sake, it's an awful lot of money. In that case, work out with your local man how much he wants for 1945 and 1946. You need not actually pay anything beyond the U.S. 15% (deducted at source) until Bob Stead has looked over the figures, if you would feel safer.

The money is 'earned' when it's in your jeans, not when somebody just owes it to you. And there is no damn rush about this sort of adjustment. Better put your mind to work on the 'costs' – the expenses. If you have a car, charge up the depreciation, gas. If you have had to go to New York or Toronto, put it all in – hotels and everything.

The report you file this month is for what you actually took in during 1946. I think I'd save the expenses to plaster against the book royalties, though. It all depends on which is the big end. Expenses can go against any writing income, but of course not the same expenses twice.

Talking about expenses, you have created some for me. I'm buying four copies of *Who has Seen the Wind* to give to friends. Gave one to my managing editor. At my request he sent my review as a gift from *The Globe and Mail* to *Winnipeg Tribune, Calgary Herald, Regina Leader-Post* and *Saskatoon Phoenix-Star*, – in case they wished to use it. We don't know whether any of them did.

What you say about fighting your editors to get these passages in prompts me to remind you that you can't help being a Canadian and, ultimately, you will find Canada a much bigger market that U.S. You talk Canadian to your own people and we understand you and like it. I thought my wife (Elm Creek, Carman, Winnipeg) would weep over some of your prairie descriptions as I woke her up in the night to listen to them.

Hugh MacLennan, Bruce Hutchison and those boys are all finding their per copy sale greater in Canada. Naturally, what the hell do the Yanks care about us? but we are getting to care about ourselves.

Look at it this way. I take the N.Y. papers. I saw the lousy 7 inches of patronizing comment *The Times* printed. What were you worth to *The Globe and Mail* (in the middle of a newsprint shortage, too)? – 26 inches of type 5 1/2 of picture (even a poor picture). *Who Has Seen the Wind* will sell in Canada, slower at the start than *Two Solitudes* but a darn sight longer. This will just go on and on, like *Sunshine Sketches of a Little Town*. How fast it starts to snowball here depends mainly on how much advertising your publisher does and neither you nor I can control that.

I can't guess what distribution you expect. Every new book is a gamble. But you are safe for a decent sale here and it may be a very big one. A second edition was ordered here the day the first was published. That doesn't mean they had sold out, but advance sales indicated that the first 5,000 would hardly last during the weeks it will take to print and bind the second. (This is *confidential*, friend;

they were not decided whether to order a second 5,000 or make a second run of 10,000). So you will be eating for the next year and if you can't draw an advance from either of your publishers (as you probably can), a modest bank loan is indicated.

Napier Moore was telling me he is very proud of you as a graduate of Maclean's where, he says, you got your start.

Well it's 12:30 a.m. and I must go home. Excuse rambling letter but it gives me a thrill to see a Canadian novelist come up like a rocket. Doubly so when it's a story that I like and which moves me as yours did. I'm really delighted with *Who Has Seen the Wind.* 'I goddam am.'

Oh I see you have got royalty advances. Well, it's only income in the year received. If what [you] got was in 1946, and if it was substantial, you better speak to your local tax gatherer. Idea of the spread is to prevent peak income, which is unfair to the author. Perhaps the Inspector would just as soon have you wait to see what comes in 1947 so he can do his sums all at one time. But an interim return filed and a nominal down payment will hold them all right. Idea of speaking to him about the problem is to avoid penalty for failure to report. In some cases it is months and months before they know what a man should pay. If the returns straddle over two years, they should be added together and then split over three years.

Best of luck! I'll make sure our readers are well informed as the new editions come along. Meanwhile, I hope you are at work on something new, though a crop of one book every two years preserves the market – not every year.

Sincerely,

---

## From Margaret Coulby[1]

16 St. Joseph Street
Apartment 49
Toronto
April 17, 1947

Dear Sir:

May I please seek your advice?
I am just graduating from the University of Toronto in Honor English and like most such students am seeking the usual career in writing. Ryerson Press is publishing my first small volume of poetry[2] in September and my poetry appears in *The Canadian Poetry Magazine*

on occasion. It has also doubtfully graced the pages of the university periodicals and I have been a drama critic and feature writer on *The Varsity* of exceedingly active nature. I even went through the customary stage of editing a high school magazine, working in an office for over a year, and working in two research labs for several years.

Thus armed with a B.A. in English and various amounts of assorted experience I began to fish for a job. Oh there are jobs in Toronto all right ... all kinds of them, but did you as an amateur ever try to crack a press or newspaper, if you are a woman? It seems completely impossible. I have been offered jobs ranging from librarian to research biologist in a government lab or private secretary to a director of research of a large local industry but not one nibble in the field to which my talents fit me ... writing. Well, only half a job. *The East Toronto Weekly* wants me to write special features for them, a movie column, drama criticism, book reviews; which is very fine but hardly enough to keep me alive in this striving, competitive metropolis. I really *can* write given a single thimbleful of encouragement. Undoubtedly I have become a cynic for life. The imprinted idea that a garbageman with four years public school can earn twice as much as a university graduate who is an intelligent human being, ready to work fingers to the bone, full of young ambition and some varied experience, is enough to make one a corrupted neurotic. By now I am convinced that women cannot obtain reporting jobs on newspapers regardless of ability, education, or even enthusiasm. Are there any openings at all for women on *The Globe and Mail*? What do women do in this writing game?

I am sorely tempted to take a small-paying job as librarian, do the feature writing for *The Weekly* in my spare time. Together I could survive until I finish a second and third book. (The Oxford Press promises to publish my next book of verse if it is as good as the first one ... which it most certainly will be given another year to grow on!) (And did you ever try to live on books of poetry?). Would there be any opportunity for a striving, brilliant young graduate to write the occasional book review for *The Globe and Mail* ... or even recipes?

I now realize why my devoted father suggested, even urged that I embark on a career in Biochemistry rather than writing or English (especially since I absolutely refused to ever teach!), why he used to mutter in his beard when I remarked loudly and cheerfully that I wanted to be a writer, 'Writing is no field for a woman. It's a *tough* sport!' At the time I youthfully and egotistically thought that he just didn't acknowledge my talents. I could, of course, accept my family's kind offer to loaf at home this summer at the cottage and then return to University in the fall for an M.A. in English but where in heavens would an M.A. get me if a B.A. isn't doing any good? I'd be two years older and still trying to start from scratch. I absolutely refuse to accept the inevitable. I am still going to be a successful writer in ten years, even if I do have to discard my well-heeled but resentful family (who are all reared in the traditions of science!) and live on one meal a day. That undoubtedly would cure the evils of my rather over-plump, but none the less attractive, figure and I might then be enabled to make a much lusher living with a lot less work, having sacrificed by too-idealistic philosophy of life.

I would be truly grateful for any advice or suggestions you could offer me, barring only the one, 'Go home to the family and science.' Are there any openings for women on your paper?

Thank you for listening to this very indiscreet and (naturally) unconventional tirade. I would appreciate your help or advice.

Yours very sincerely,
Margaret Coulby

1 Margaret Evelyn Coulby Whitridge (b. 1924) is the editor of *Lampman's Kate: Late Love Poems of Archibald Lampman, 1887–1897* (1975), and *Lampman's Sonnets 1884–1899* (1976). Although she set aside early hopes of becoming a journalist for a career in the civil service, she eventually realized in the domain of literary scholarship and editing the ambitions which Deacon early encouraged in her.

2 *The Bitter Fruit and Other Poems* was published in the Ryerson poetry chap-book series in 1948.

---

## To Margaret Coulby April 18, 1947

Dear Miss Coulby,

I am leaving for Halifax in a few hours and reply now only because you are graduating and time is vital to you.

You will get over the cynicism if you are as good as you think you are; and you are right in thinking it will take you ten years to become anything much as an author or free lance. You can become a newspaper hack reporter in less. If you want that kind of job, you should call in the late afternoon on Mr. Douglas McFarlane, our City Editor.

I buy a certain amount of book reviews, have about 30 people contributing. There is no livelihood in this yet. I am the only Canadian who can support a family on it and it has taken me 25 years, after eight years in law.

Poetry is unlikely to support you. It is only an established big-name poet who can make as much as $500 on a book of verse. That is not just in Canada.

All you tell me about yourself is encouraging. Of course you can be a professional writer, if you care enough about it to undergo a long, hard apprenticeship – teaching yourself how to write, getting experience – living. You must accept the fact that nobody at 22 has anything of great value to give the world. The B.A. is fine, but you start from there, as a child. By 32 you are still young enough to take the first real steps in a writing career. Meanwhile, keep your eye on the ball, write, write, write, publish as and when you can, getting as much for your stuff as you can coax out of editors.

With graduation, start to read. That is your real literary education. The B.A. is just an entrance exam. If you can get going at 32, you can arrive at 45, will have 15 years on top of the world and thereafter coast on your reputation.

Your letter again reminds me I've never written that essay of advice to young, aspiring writers. It would save me so much time.

Practically, and in haste, the sensible idea is to go through any open door. If you can combine library work and critical work for *The Weekly*, grab it. When you can better yourself, you can leave, but meanwhile you are actually at writing; only your toe is in the door but it is a toe-hold however humble.

One thing I shall someday say in that essay is what I often tell junior audiences: More writers fail because they have nothing to say than because they can't write. We all use words, many with ease and effect. But, as it says in *Hamlet*, 'but the matter, my lord?' You are still an ignorant girl. Time, willpower and practice will cure that. Meanwhile, learn something definite to write about. Master a specialty. You have to fill the tank before you can pump it out.

As a sample of just how raw you are, I notice you request me to give you an hour of my time and you don't even take the trouble to learn my name and address me by it. You need lessons in public relations. Go to the trouble of finding out who people are and address them properly. It pays.

You will note, please, that I am not speaking as literary editor. In that capacity, I'd have thrown your letter away. This is a personal, private communication; and I take this time I can't afford because I was young like you, ignorant like you, aspiring like you; and there wasn't a damn soul to tell me even as much as I can get into this unconsidered note. My child, we've all been through it, all come up the same road. It's a wider highway now, much easier than 35 years ago. You're not crazy for wanting to write. It is a good life, the best I could imagine for myself. But it is tough in the early stages.

If you want journalism, then forget the poetry and try to get yourself accepted as a student in that course at the U of Western Ontario.

But I think it is the other thing you want. It's harder but pays off far better in every way – if you can stand the waiting, the disappointments and so on. It's a long-range program. If you are going to devote your life to it, you will get somewhere; but if you just want to play for a couple of years till you marry, then writing effort is wasted. Better sell lingerie.

You really must think more, plan carefully. Many men would hold against you that, in asking for advice to help you (not them) you omit the common courtesy of enclosing a stamped self-addressed envelope. I don't need the 3 cents; but if you are going to spread your personality around like this, you might as well observe the amenities of civilized behavior.

I'm not going to have any particular time to give you till I get back from Vancouver the end of July. And I really need a rest in August. But if you care to tell me your troubles in September, I shall be happy to have a talk with you then. From the age of 30, I began to discover authors and learned a lot from them. Especially because, by that age, I had acquired a certain humility. I was starting to listen. You will find your seniors in the craft sympathetic, kindly; but you must remember they are busy people with livings to earn and all they have to sell is their writing time.

The times were never more favorable for young folks like you to take the initial steps. Writing becomes more profitable every day. But you have everything to learn and unless you are patient you will not learn; unless you are conscious of your present ignorance, you cannot learn. With all the help everybody can give you it is hard enough so that you need to be a strong and courageous person or you will not last.

I hope for the best. Ultimately, the opportunities are rich.

Excuse haste and forgive my abrupt remarks.

Sincerely,

---

## To Gabrielle Roy

April 29, 1947

Dear Gabrielle,

How sweet of you to write me from New York with all the fuss going on![1] Your letter of the 21st was here when I got back from the Maritimes yesterday. I spent from 7:15 to 9:15 a.m. Monday in the CNR station but called nobody because it was too early.

I noted the newsstand had a whole glass case of your book – 35 well displayed copies in English, 15 in French. Looked good to me.

When speaking to three quite large audiences in Halifax on the 21st and Saint John on the 25th, I had the pleasure of telling them all about the greatest Canadian novel. They were all pleased to get the news slightly in advance of publication. Newall,[2] McClelland's Maritime salesman, landed there on Saturday and I told him I'd done his selling for him – it was in all the papers – and that he had nothing to do except deliver the books.

Meanwhile, Sally was putting to bed my *Globe and Mail* pages. I send you these, respectfully.[3] Note that I have restrained myself. As we had published 4 articles on you in a year, our readers were prepared and (more important) I've still got to have something to say on future. Occasions.[4] I fear that I shall not be able to drop *The Tin Flute* for years to come. So I have often said from platforms that it is the best Canadian novel so far published; but I've not printed that remark. I'm saving it.

Whenever anything new happens, tell me that, because my people will be avid for anything at all about you.

This is the largest advertisement for a single book ever printed in Canada – any kind of book. The half page makes a noise.

My friend Frank McDowell, whom you met at my house, tells me a girl by the name of Roy from St. Boniface tied for second place in the Stars of Tomorrow program of York Knitting Mills. Miss Roy received $500. It was her first appearance as a singer. Frank thought she might be a relative of yours. If so, tell me and I'll print the fact. This seems to be very good weather for the Roys.

Well, my dear, you are now on top of the world, as last year I told you that you would be. I'm happy for you, as always. You have now got freedom and leisure. You can have anything in reason, work or loaf as you feel inclined. Your sales will certainly be greater in Canada than any previous Canadian book. There is time to catch your breath before settling down to finishing the second novel. It should not be published till late 1948 or early 1949. You can fill in time with short stories.

As my life is devoted to Canadian literature, and as *The Tin Flute* is the finest specimen of it in the 26 years of my labors, there is simply nothing I can say to express my satisfaction adequately. I'm prouder of you all, you writers, than of anything I do myself; and when your book is really the best, artistically, as well as a success, my feelings are beyond words. I know words – not tongue-tied a bit. But I don't know how to tell you the great exaltation I feel because a Canadian has written as wonderfully as Flaubert. I'm very excited. Just as a writer, you mean more to me than I can say.

Then, on top of all that, you are a fellow Manitoban, and let me be your personal friend. So I am all lit up like a Christmas tree, inside; probably it shines out through the skin also. I am very fond of you. The day will come when you are used to great fame, perhaps even bored with it. But I want our personal relations to go right on. You are the best piece of copy I ever ran across; and I'm grateful to you for letting me write about you for the past year. But, happily, we have a great deal else in common, and I hope as the years pass we may be united in firmer bonds. Life is funny – I mean strange; and nobody can tell what will happen to us in the next ten years, but I have no doubt at all that our friendship will have ripened by 1957. Then, some distant day, when all these present events are ancient history, we can visit comfortably and enjoy ourselves.

When you are 60 and easing off, a very dignified woman, I'll be

82, a rather stiff, pitiful old man with a cane. Meanwhile, my girl – on with the work. May the honours and money roll in to you in ever increasing streams. But right now you have brought me great happiness.

I hope you will get and read W.O. Mitchell's *Who Has Seen The Wind* – the Saskatchewan novel. Think you will like it. This is the great year of Canadian fiction, you know.

Well, me, now, back to work.

I think Bobby Reade's review in *The Star* is very good – in some ways better than mine.[5] He has a French wife and reads French.

Wishing you all good things at this dramatic moment in your distinguished career, and with love from Sally and the girls –

1 *The Tin Flute*, Hannah Josephson's translation of *Bonheur d'occasion*, was published in late April. Roy had sent Deacon a friendly note from New York, where she had gone for the book-launching given by Reynal and Hitchcock.
2 Probably Desmond Newell, later sales representative for University of Toronto Press
3 Deacon's review, 'Superb French-Canadian Novel Is About Montreal's Poor Folk' (26 April 1947), praised *The Tin Flute* for its understanding, simplicity, and 'sharp reality,' described it as a story 'told with deep pity and without sentimentality,' and commended the translation. In Roy's attention to detail and in her understanding of her commonplace characters, Deacon saw affinities with Flaubert. Half the book page was taken up by McClelland and Stewart's advertisement of the novel.
4 A pun on the French title of Roy's novel
5 'Gabrielle Roy's *Tin Flute* Novel of Montreal's Poor' appeared in the Toronto *Star* on 26 April 1947. Acknowledging the translator's difficult task, Reade also compared Roy's work as a great writer to Flaubert's.

## To Constance Beresford-Howe[1]

May 6, 1947

Dear Constance,

*Of This Day's Journey* gave me quite a jolt. I've just finished my review for the 10th, so it is alright to say you passed with high honors. When I began reading the book, I was sorry for you because your novel follows so closely on *The Tin Flute*. This is a real handicap commercially in Canada, where everybody and his dog wants to read Gabrielle Roy after a perfect build-up of 18 months.

But when I was through with the luckless lovers, I had nothing but admiration for you and utter confidence in your future. Any author who can write as you do – based on straight thinking first and verbal facility second – has no need of anybody's sympathy. Accept my congratulations and best wishes.

What I think in detail will appear in my printed article, on which I spent careful thought.[2] This is not the sort of judgment one knocks off glibly.

Again I wish you would come to Vancouver for July 7–12th. Among others you would meet there are Malcolm Lowry, author of *Under The Volcano*, who has become a Canadian citizen, and Lionel Stevenson[3] of Berkeley, whose recent book on Thackeray, following his interesting life of Charles Lever, ought to interest you as a teacher of English.

Further, to talk to you parentally, you should not pump yourself out like this annually. It's no good for long-range policy. The tank has to be re-filled. Few writers who arrive in their twenties amount to much in their middle forties, when powers should be at their ripest. Certainly you are clever, probably intense; but do take care of the machinery. Your study plus creative work is a strain. Besides, there is this practical point that very few readers return every 12 months even to a favorite author. At this rate of production, your books will compete with each other.

However, you are an extraordinarily gifted young woman.

Salutations –

1 Constance Beresford-Howe (b. 1922) was twenty-four when her first novel, *The Unreasoning Heart*, a winner of the $1200 Dodd-Mead Intercollegiate Literary Fellowship Prize, was published in 1946. Deacon took an early, paternal interest in her and her work, and wrote her at length about the shape and pace of her precocious writing career. A Montrealer by birth, she studied at McGill and Brown universities, and from 1949 taught at McGill, where she became a close friend of Dorothy and Hugh MacLennan. She eventually moved to Toronto in 1970, where she is currently a member of the Department of English of Ryerson Polytechnical Institute. Her career as a writer has continued to flourish; her latest novel, *Night Studies*, was published in 1985.

2 'Canadian Girl's Love Story New Note in Native Fiction' (*The Globe and Mail*, 10 May 1947) praised the writer for the genuine passion of her story, her original use of three different points of view, and her lack of sentimental compromise in the portrayal of unhappy love.

3 Lowry (1909–57) had just published *Under the Volcano* (1947); Stevenson, expatriate Canadian critic (1902–73) and author of *Appraisals of Canadian Literature* (1926), built his reputation not on his theosophical poems, but on his scholarly work in the Victorian period, which includes *Dr. Quicksilver: The Life of Charles Lever* (1939) and *The Showman of Vanity Fair* (1947).

---

## From Constance Beresford-Howe

364 Lloyd Avenue
Providence, R.I.
May 12, 1947

Dear Mr. Deacon,

Your review of my new story arrived this morning and I herewith send you a low bow of gratitude. It was the first outside criticism of any consequence I've had since publication day – and therefore doubly welcome.

I think you stated the case very fairly and generously; above all you paid me the compliment of a thoughtful estimate. When one puts a year of work and genuine heart's blood into a book, it's heartbreaking to be dismissed with a shrug or a few words copied off the book-jacket. I write because I *must*; but also because I want to share something with the reader. And when someone responds as you did, the satisfaction is enormous. I tried very hard to make *Of This Day's Journey* a better book than my first novel; I think without undue conceit that it is a better book, if only for the fact that it is better disciplined. It's my sincere and firm ambition to keep on learning and trying until someday – even if twenty years off – I turn out a really fine book.

Don't worry about my being too productive; I haven't written a word since last summer, and don't think the rest has done me any harm at all. Even if I begin something this June, it could not possibly be ready for publication until the next year, nor offered to the public before 1949.

I'm rather tired right now, with the academic year grinding to its close, and look forward to a quiet summer on the cool St. Lawrence. The possibility of my getting out to Vancouver is pretty remote, I'm afraid, for financial and other reasons. But I hope you enjoy it and will tell me all that transpires there.

Again thanks for your perceptive and sympathetic review. I shall put it in a special place in my clipping-book, and value it as I value your faith in my writing future.

Sincerely and affectionately
yours,
Connie Beresford-Howe

P.S. I've been much impressed by *The Tin Flute, Continental Review,*[1] *Who Has Seen the Wind,* etc. Aren't we Canadians booming, though!

1 Published in 1946, Winnifred Bambrick's novel is a romance about a travelling troupe of entertainers in Europe during the late 1930s. It won the Governor-General's Award for fiction.

---

## To Constance Beresford-Howe

May 14, 1947

Dear Connie,

Thanks for your sweet and respectful note.

It is an error to pay any serious attention to reviewers, including me. My business is information and interpretation addressed to book readers. I do not lecture creative writers, since all that the critic learns of craft comes from watching their performances and then guessing why they did this and that. We are often wrong. Somerset Maugham in *The Summing Up* says he never learned one thing from any reviewer. Mordell's *Notorious Literary Attacks*[1] illustrates how famous critics were 100% wrong when confronted with the literary masterpieces, which were then new books.

I have worked out a philosophy of the important function of the critic for the public, based on what I've learned by experience. It is an error for a writer to be influenced by anything outside. Even in criticism, I am convinced that, objectively, there is no such thing as a good or bad book, per se, but only the degree of favor with which one particular reader receives the book at a given moment in social history – the whole experiment conditioned by the temperament of that reader (who may be the critic). This is academic heresy, with which to be corrupting a young English teacher; but I'm sure I'm right. Art appeals primarily to the emotions, which are variable; hence there can be no scale of values true at all times and in all societies. The opinion of an expert remains just an opinion. Critical opinion is as perishable as humor.

Take it easy, don't hurry. You most certainly have the qualities that will make you both a good and a popular fiction writer. But it is the 4th or 5th novel that clicks, on average. You are two down and three to go. Somewhere around 32 seems the right age for the first smash hit. That yields about 25 years of mature production, and then one coasts. There is no way of shutting a Galsworthy off from his last three ridiculous novels; they even sold fairly well. One can go on at writing indefinitely, despite lower physical powers and even mental capacity. What I'm going to inflict on the public after 65 will be pre-meditated crime.

You come in during the revolution, when Canadians suddenly want Canadian books. There are 9 Canadian novels to June, in 1947.[2] You never will know the uphill struggle when Canadians didn't want their own books, no matter how 'good.' One practical thing you must watch is separate Canadian contracts from the moment your original Dodd Mead option expires. Canadian novels are going abroad rapidly but the home market must always be the most important, here and everywhere, because it is the natural testing ground. Further, *Two Solitudes, The Unknown Country* and ever so many more actually sell more in Canada than in the U.S., and there is no sense giving half or two-thirds Canadian royalties to a N.Y. publisher, especially as the Canadian distributor has not enough margin on an imported book to do a good promotion job. *Remember Me* by Edward F. Meade is the latest sad case. He placed it with Faber & Faber, London, where it sold 10,000 in no time; but F & F would only ship 1,000 to Canada and refused Ryerson the right to manufacture here or to import copies from the United States. So this Canadian war tale lost its Canadian market almost altogether.

Have a good summer and keep me in touch, please.

Sincerely,

1 Edited with an introduction by Albert Mordell, it is a compendium of indictments by prominent critics and writers. Like Deacon, Mordell was a lawyer turned journalist and critic, who had anthologized, among others, John Greenleaf Whittier, Lafcadio Hearn, and James Russell Lowell.

2 These had been listed on the book page in *The Globe and Mail* on 31 May: *Who Has Seen the Wind* by W.O. Mitchell, *The Tin Flute* by Gabrielle Roy, *Of This Day's Journey*, *Hetty Dorval* by Ethel Wilson, *Consider Her Ways* by Frederick Philip Grove, *Under the Volcano* by Malcolm Lowry, *Fresh Wind Blowing* by Grace Campbell, *All This to Keep* by Maida Parlow French, and *Open Windows* by Clara Bernhardt.

---

## From Hugh MacLennan

North Hatley, P.Q.
May 29, 1947

My dear Bill:

Thanks for your note on the VOGUE article.[1] I'm glad you liked it and on the whole agreed with it.

As you doubtless guessed, it was a solicited job. They knew nothing of Canada, but were apparently led by the report of my *Maclean's* article, which was cut down in TIME,[2] to want a piece on the country. In limited space it was impossible to do any other than a personalized approach, and I'd never have written a piece like that for a Canadian audience.

I think, so far as I am concerned, I can call it a day on these articles on Canadian writing. After the publication of BAROMETER RISING it seemed to me necessary, in view of the confused attitude of American, and even of some Canadian critics, to my work, that it was necessary to do some defining. It was necessary even for myself, I suppose. I never much enjoyed those articles, but I think they've helped, particularly in the States. Apart from my last *Maclean's* article,[3] the other two and this VOGUE piece all blossomed out of the paper I read last June at the CAA Convention, which was published almost intact in the SRL [*Saturday Review of Literature*].[4] Irwin then wanted two pieces based on it, and VOGUE wanted one piece based on one I sent to Irwin.

After a very bad winter, in which we were seriously concerned for a time with her survival, Dorothy is a great deal better. Her heart makes it essential for her to avoid any great strains or heavy physical work, and next winter she or the both of us will have to escape the cold somewhere. She is much more like herself now, and is in the last lap of her first novel. I wouldn't be surprised if she finishes it before I finish mine.[5] I hope to finish by November, but it's much the most ambitious and difficult book I've written and so far much the best, at least in my opinion. About its popularity I know nothing, but *qua* novel, it's so far a 'purer' job than *TS* by a good deal in the sense that there is nothing in it external to the novel form, as there was in the other two books.

It's grand news about Gabrielle's success, but in retrospect I'm disappointed in the translation.[6] I saw Gabrielle while I was half through the English galleys and told her then I thought she needn't worry about it, but by the end I had changed my opinion. The prose went dead to me at the end. It's true that BONHEUR was weaker at the end than the beginning, but this seemed to me purely a matter of prose. The translator seemed tired. But then, no translator could have preserved the peculiar savour of Gabrielle's St. Henry dialect.

All the best,
Hugh

P.S. You know, of course, that none of these latter two paragraphs on Gabrielle[7]
– Excuse the scratch out. I was going to say that the paragraph on *Bonheur's* translation must not appear in 'The Flyleaf,' but then, it wouldn't in any case. H.

1 'Canada for Canadians' appeared in the issue of 15 May 1947.

2 'Do We Gag Our Writers?,' in *Maclean's* of 1 March 1947, was a scathing indictment of Canadian Victorianism, in answer to the question, 'Why is there no great Canadian novel?' MacLennan accused Canadian readers of being 'placid, puritanical and behind the times,' and blamed book-banning as a major source of spiritual despair and impotence among Canadian novelists.

3 'The Face of Power,' in the 1 May issue, is a long review of Yousuf Karsh's *Faces of Destiny*, a collection of seventy-five photographs of famous statesmen.

4 'Canada between Covers' appeared in *The Saturday Review of Literature* for 7

September 1946. MacLennan welcomed Canadian writers' 'serious attempt to interpret their cultural, economic, social and moral life,' criticized the narrowness of sectarian elements in Canadian society, and argued for the presentation of universal themes in a recognizably Canadian setting.

5 Dorothy Duncan's novel-in-progress was never published. MacLennan's next book was *The Precipice* (1948).

6 *The Tin Flute*, Hannah Josephson's translation of *Bonheur d'occasion*, was published in 1947 by the New York firm of Reynal and Hitchcock.

7 MacLennan had struck out this postscript.

---

## From Catherine Grove

Simcoe, Ontario
June 30, 1947

Dear Mr. Deacon,–

On behalf of my husband I wish to send greetings to the Authors' Association assembled at Vancouver. I am extremely sorry that he is not able to be with you to receive the honour bestowed upon him in the Governor-General's award.[1]

It would also be a pleasure to him to see how much the Association has grown since it met in Vancouver in 1926, and to meet the many new novelists and poets who are carrying on where the older ones paved the way.

May you have a pleasurable and an inspiring convention.

Very sincerely yours,
Catherine Grove.

P.S. Phil expresses the wish that you receive the G-G's award on his behalf. Thank you for all your thoughtfulness. C.G.

1 For *In Search of Myself* (1946)

---

## From Earle Birney

Canadian Poetry Magazine
University of British Columbia
July 22, 1947

Dear Bill,

This is a set of casual notes, in confidence – mainly things I didn't have time to talk over personally with you when I was here:

(1) THE CONVENTION – I think that, despite hard work and pa-

tience on the part of the Natl Exec., and particularly on your part, the convention was badly run, badly organized, not anything like as good as last year's. I suspect the reason was the incompetency of the local branch here. No doubt there were other factors. Perhaps the University didn't cooperate enough in making its facilities pleasant. If you or anybody has any definite complaints on that score I hope very much you will make them either directly or through me. I am anxious for the University's name in such matters, and to prevent discomfort to other conventions coming here. There was certainly a lot of legitimate complaining about conditions at Acadia – but it is difficult for me to know offhand how much of that was Acadia Camp's fault, how much was a lack of coordination between the Camp and the convention committee. For example, I know for a fact that the Camp dietician didn't know until an hour before lunch, the first day, whether there were 40 people coming or 400 or none.

Apart from the University's responsibility, the local committee has much to answer for. The programming did not utilize several prominent and available authors who would have come and spoken if approached in the right way. I am thinking of Dorothy Livesay, A.J.M. Smith (who spoke the previous week here at the Canadian Library Convention), Eric Nicol the humourist (whose book is coming out from Ryersons this fall), Roy Daniells, L.A. MacKay, Roderick Haig-Brown,[1] Alan Crawley the editor, etc. Perhaps some of these were approached; I wouldn't know. The only opportunity that was given me to advise or help was by a telephone call, after preliminary arrangements had been made, inviting me to an exec. meeting the same evening (I had an engagement I couldn't break). If I had had a chance, I would certainly have opposed such stupidities as the printing of R.A. Hood's doggerel on the program cover or the selection of old man Wilson as the chief speaker of the convention.[2]

I think the lesson to be drawn from all this (and more, if there were time to enumerate) is that national conventions, if you *must* have them, should be *nationally* arranged. Don't let a weak isolated branch exploit a national convention into a holiday for crackpots and for the eternally local celebrity. No amount of good chairmanship on your part can offset an Amateur Night convention.

(2) GG-AWARD-GIVING. Can't something be done to tighten up the way in which these awards are presented. It was sloppily done this year. I have on my desk a letter from Robert Finch,[3] thanking me for posting on his medal to him, with my explanation of how I

chanced to have it. He says in part: 'Thank you for ... sending off to me what must be the world's most mysteriously presented decoration. I say mysteriously because, apart from what has appeared in the papers, I have never received a communication from any one on the matter, until your present letter. Indeed, your letter contains a mystery too. I refer to [John Murray] Gibbon's announcement that I am going on the staff at Queen's. You say you were startled. So am I ...'

It is evident from this that, whereas someone got in touch with Lower and arranged a proxy for him,[4] no one did the same for Finch. I have not told Finch, and I hope no one does, of the fatuous and somewhat malicious presentation remarks of Gibbon about his *Poems*. It was bad enough to have to listen to them and then, without warning, to receive the medal in proxy from such hands. Don't mistake me; I'm not blaming you; it was evident at the time that you were caught by surprise too and had to think quickly to get the medal presented at all. But I hope that Gibbon will not be allowed to perpetrate his senilities at future conventions and that someone will organize the affair properly beforehand. I tried to say something, when I got a chance, which would soften the insult to Finch without starting a public brawl with Gibbon, but it was difficult to do and I probably would have said nothing at all if a note had [not] been passed up to me from one of the tables, signed by four fairly prominent local authors, asking if I could do something to offset what they felt to be an insult to Finch.

(3) Competitions in *The Canadian Poetry Magazine*. I have written O'Brien about this. Experience of 3 competitions has shown me, what I suspected all along, that verse competitions are not helpful to the mag. or to Canadian poetry. The money could be used much more effectively in the ordinary work of building up the magazine. The results are that poor poems get prizes, because the good writers don't compete. The poems which won the awards I presented at this convention were so mediocre that the judges recommended I do not publish them in *CPM* – and I agree with their recommendation. Moreover, running such a competition takes a great deal of work which I could better employ in other aspects of the magazine. Competitions should be left to local branches or to the CAA itself. Now we have this wretched EIRE prize.[5] See Sandwell's remarks (in an otherwise laudatory review of *CPM* in July 5th SATURDAY NIGHT) on the Eire Prize. I would suggest therefore that in

future, when anyone comes to you with money for a poetry prize you sick them on to me to see if I can't persuade them simply to donate the money for our general purposes. We can, of course, always memorialize the dead in the acknowledgement of the gift, without using the dead as an excuse to reward indifferent verse. What do you think?

This has been a letter of criticism but it is not intended to be directed at you. I admire the way you carried on and chaired firmly and patiently in the midst of much tribulation. You have a hard job and I don't envy you what you have to do. But I thought I should get these things off my chest before the details were lost in our memories. I'm sorry you could not have stayed longer and taken a rest. I hope you will be out west again.

By the way, is it possible to wangle an exchange of *CPM* with the Saturday *G&M*? I can't afford to subscribe but I need your bookpages in my function of a poetry editor, and the *G&M* is not accessible to me out here.

Sincerely,
Earle Birney

1 Eric Nicol (b. 1919), Leacock medalist and author of *Sense and Nonsense by E.P. Nicol (Jabez)* (1947); Roy Daniells (1902–79), professor of English at the University of British Columbia; Louis Alexander MacKay (b. 1901), professor of classics at the University of British Columbia, poet and critic, author of *Viper's Bugloss* (1938), a chap-book of lyrics, and associate editor of *The Canadian Forum* (1930–8); Roderick Haig-Brown (1908–76), British Columbia environmentalist and writer whose sketches and novels most often have a west coast setting

2 A Vancouver writer and insurance broker, Hood (1880–1958) was known for his books of Arthurian romance, his legends of Vancouver, and his melodramas about the wild west; Richard Albert Wilson (1874–1949), professor of English at the University of Saskatchewan until 1940 and author of *The Miraculous Birth of Language* (1938, 1942), whose second edition included a preface by George Bernard Shaw. He spoke about 'Vagabond Poetry' on the last evening of the CAA convention in July 1947. The address's romantic overtones were no doubt offensive to Birney.

3 Robert Duer Claydon Finch (b. 1900), poet and professor of French at the University of Toronto, who had just received the Governor-General's Award for *Poems* (1946)

4 *From Colony to Nation* had won the Governor-General's Non-Fiction Award.

5 The June 1947 issue of *The Canadian Poetry Magazine* announced that 'through the generosity of an anonymous friend,' the magazine was offering 'two prizes of twenty-five and fifteen dollars respectively, for the best lyrical poem written

to the tune of "The Last Rose of Summer" ... The tune to be followed is the familiar one, originally known as "The Groves of Blarney".' On 5 July 1947 in 'The Front Page,' the editorial section of *Saturday Night*, Sandwell commented that 'the immense improvement' in *The Canadian Poetry Magazine* under Birney's editorship made an 'oddity' of the 'Eire' prizes. He concluded: 'We can hardly wait until June of next year to learn the result.' In the June 1948 number of CPM, it was announced that the judges – L.A. MacKay, Roy Daniells, and John Goss, singer and teacher of music – had unanimously decided that none of the entries was 'of sufficient merit to receive an award.'

---

## To Earle Birney August 6, 1947

Dear Earle,

We are still thinking with pleasure of our short visit to Esther and you and your pleasant little home.

In reply to your kind letter of July 22, perhaps I view the recent convention with a perspective impossible for you as a relatively new member. It was the largest gathering in history and achieved its objective of a cross-section event. If you could have traded our first day in Victoria for the last day in Vancouver, you would have had a better impression. It is true that the local working committee was not as large nor as well drilled as at Toronto. We'd hoped that you would have been active in the branch and appointed to the working force. Experience shows that we have to start members in the branches. Otherwise they remain blind to many of the real problems. Effective national officers are always graduates of branch organizations. I am glad you met many of the visitors and different people from last year. That is one of the desirables.

As to the award giving, we can't do much when the recipients don't bother to turn out. Last year you all did except Ross Munro who was on duty in Europe. There [in Vancouver] I had to cancel the Governor-General's anticipated presence; it would have been rude to bring him out to present medals to substitutes. I am surprised that Finch should profess ignorance of the event or its details, since nothing was ever so widely publicized. He admits reading it in the papers, where it was set out, and he is not able to read but suggests he did read it there. Further, I met him at an Oxford Press tea and congratulated him and asked him whether he would come to Vancouver and gathered that he would not. Later, I tried repeatedly to reach him by telephone and in person but could get no response in any way. I concluded from his manner in talking to me and from his failure to answer my calls that he was indifferent to the whole business. Lower, who is my old friend, after getting $500 with his medal told me by letter that he would not come unless we paid his way. We could not afford the luxury, much as we should have enjoyed his presence. He has joined the Association, which is the first step. I was glad to see you, as a judge, come forward as Finch's substitute and reply to Gibbon.[1] Unknown to you, he had suffered a breakdown that day but felt he could go on. Nobody had any idea what he was going to say, and the man who has done most for the Ass'n for 25 years is a rather privileged person. It was my own error not to call on you, and I'm heartily glad you drew the omission to my attention. Next year at Ottawa we shall have His Excellency, provided the winners turn out.

I am glad to see you are against poetry competitions. The Association has always refused to conduct them, but many of the branches do. If *The Poetry Magazine* has fixed its policy against the holding of competitions, I presume you will announce this, with reasons, in an editorial. The National Executive will not wish any more such jobs on you.

No, it isn't possible to get *The Globe and Mail* exchanged with CPM for simple reason that we have no exchanges with anybody. We purchase *The N.Y. Times*, and a great many other newspapers, magazines, etc., as we feel we need them. They buy our sheet at full price, if they want it. There are no exceptions. Sometimes small periodicals feel offended at this policy, think we high-hat them and don't believe we have no free-exchange list. But it is the fact. Actually, I pay very little attention to poetry and you lose nothing. My reasons are (1) we reach a 1/4 million readers and in mere terms of newsprint our costs are terrific per column of space. Books of poems come out in small editions; I don't review any small edition book, prose or verse, for the reason that, if only 200 persons are interested, we can't afford space for considered review. We list it in small type. A review of poetry takes inordinate space because quotes are necessary and various aspects of the poet's style must be displayed. I can do an A.1. novel in a third of a column (it is a unit) but need more than half a column for a 50–page booklet of verse. Consequently, you, Pratt, and half a dozen others are the only poets we ever review, and no non-Canadians at all. (2) I am unfit to pass judgment on the new poetry as I do not understand it. I have a good knowledge of poetry from Chaucer to, say 1930, but I lack the brains to comprehend many of the newer poets.

Of course your letter was taken in good part. But I should make a general statement, between ourselves. The Association is the instrument of the literary movement in Canada; it has no other. We are a craft struggling in pioneer conditions for status, for recognition, for adequate pay etc. We have made tremendous strides in 25 years. We have proved our worth. But we have far to go. That does not mean any of us can sit down and say 'let George do it'; it means we must all go on and do our utmost, each in his niche. And none of us can get one foot further without patience. We have to work within our terms of reference, with the people and talents we have. It took 100 years to make this part of Ontario into an economically prosperous and fairly civilized society. I think it will take another 25 years to bring authorship into line with our agriculture and manufacturing. That is a long time, and men like you and me are not naturally patient. I have acquired a little bit of this virtue; not nearly enough for demands. I shall be dropping out in 11 months. A lot of you younger men must go the second 25 years. When things annoy you, try to be philosophic. You are going to be surprised that most of the people are nicer, abler and more reasonable than might be supposed; the level of merit in production is greater, the efforts – however weak or misdirected – are invariably rewarded with better results than could logically be expected. Let this cheer you. You are in a rich pocket; be friends with those people (who tend to be afraid of you); you not only have a considerable future in the organization but the work is worth doing – and your university will think so too.

The main thing about the convention is that it is over and the publicity throughout Canada was far more favorable and wide-spread than last year. You cannot know the big impression that was made nationally.

Warm regards –

1 John Murray Gibbon (1875–1952) was born in Ceylon and educated at Oxford. He was a businessman and writer, a founder and the first national president of the Canadian Authors' Association. Among his works is *Canadian Mosaic: The Making of a Northern Nation* (1938), which won a Governor-General's Award.

As publicity agent in Montreal for the CPR (1913–45), he provided free railway passes for many touring writers.

---

## To Catherine Grove[1]

Wilson's Point
R.R. 3, Orillia
August 6, 1947

Dear Mrs. Grove,

You and Philip received us most graciously and Sally and I enjoyed our visit very much. We are glad to know of the modest comforts you enjoy but I fear you work very hard. You need the car and it really ought to have had more service in the way of replacements and repairs. Not changing oil causes unnecessary wear from accumulation of dirt. It pays to treat machinery with respect; a safety factor also. On thinking it over, I feel sure Leonard[2] has the right idea, though you need a *reliable* mechanic to advise you; many garage men just run up bills.

I was very happy to get a photo for *The Globe and Mail.* Mr. Pierce gave one of Philip to *The Author and Bookman* – receiving medal.

We are snatching a little sort-of holiday at our cottage. I have to do my work just the same and spend part of every week in Toronto; but there are some periods when I can cut wood and do chores, which I find fun and relaxation from constant reading, writing, speaking and travel. We'll be glad when the term of my office is over. It is practically a full time job and involves big and little expenses that, in total, are far beyond what we can afford. I think I told you that I have been in every province except P.E.I. in the past year and away from my desk a total of 32 days in the 12 months. This means more than one month out of my working year (but a whole year's work to turn in). Even when in Toronto about 40% of my time goes to the Authors, leaving me less than half my time to do the work by which I live. Consequently, it has been 14 years since I had a book myself, and while I did get three magazine articles ripped off at top speed this year, all were hastily written, unrevised – one I did not even read over for mistakes in typing. That is not very satisfactory to a man who left a good position in law because he wanted to write in an ambitious way. However, I'll be through 11 months from now and then we'll see if I have anything to say worth paper and printers' ink.

This situation is explained in detail because I have been conscious of neglect of Philip – should have gone out years ago. Wished you to know the only reason I did not do so was because a constant round of duty has claimed *all* my time. I get done what I can and, to preserve my sanity, let the rest go. It is not a nice thing to be continuously aware, every day, of all the things that should be done and are simply not being done.

The trouble is, of course, a pioneering situation. For 25 years our craft has struggled for status, recognition, minimum returns permitting a writer to go on with his work. Progress has been clearly made between 1921 and 1946. But I fear it will take a second quarter-century to finish the job. None of us who worked through the first 25–year period will last to the end of the second.

Our regards to you both. Tell Philip we are all very proud of him[3] and happy that he is as well as he is. I deeply regret his inability to travel.

1 Deacon's friendship with Catherine Grove continued until the early 1960s when he advised her on the sale of the Grove Papers to the University of Manitoba.
2 The Groves' son
3 Like many other people, Deacon found Grove difficult to work with, but nevertheless he was the one who travelled to Simcoe in the summer of 1947, shortly before Grove's death, to present him with the Governor-General's medal (non-fiction) for *In Search of Myself* (1946).

---

## From Hugh MacLennan

Box 547
South Laguna, California
December 5, 1948 [1947][1]

My Dear Bill:

Although your missive of December 17 was addressed to the members generally, I hope you won't mind my writing privately to congratulate you on having achieved recognition of the CAA as a non-profit organization under the Companies Act of Canada. The practical advantages are, obviously, very great, and it always seemed to me that the Association was grievously handicapped in the past by the fact that it could not exist as a legal entity. The members, and Canadian writing in general, are greatly in your debt. There is no doubt that under the presidency of Rod[2] and of yourself the Association has advanced tremendously. We're grateful to you, Bill.

Dorothy and I are here, I'm afraid, for the rest of the winter.

The move was ordered by her doctor after the debacle of last winter, when she was in bed from New Year's until late March, and for several days was in grave danger. So, we were given a ration of U.S. dollars and released. We left the day after I finished correction of the new book (THE PRECIPICE, in case Collins hasn't told you) and set out with winter nipping at our heels all the way to the Gulf of Mexico. After two years and a month of almost constant work on this book, with six months pondering it before that, I feel like an empty pail. A writer should be able to hibernate for at least three months after finishing a long job. I've always been astounded by the stories about Balzac beginning his next book the day after he'd finished the previous one.

When the new book will appear I don't know. In the States probably not until September, but there's a good chance of a Canadian publication in May or June.

After travelling across the United States this time – the last time was before the war – I've been more than ever struck by the potential richness of Canadian society for a novelist as compared to the scene here. Superficially the United States offers a much easier environment, but this apparent ease is deceptive. More than ever before, Americans seem to be growing outward rather than inward. What they do is infinitely more important than what they think, feel or are; and what they do which is interesting is more conditioned by scientific and engineering techniques than by the characters of the doers. Also I feel that they are much more committed to history than we are. Their course has been to a large extent determined. This seems the reason why their non-fiction, at present and for the past half dozen years, is both more interesting and more important than their fiction. I don't believe any serious American writer today can feel the same kinship with the public, or get the same response from the public, that a writer can experience in Canada. As you yourself said in one of your recent lectures, the growth of writing in Canada has to a great extent been determined by the kind of response Canadians have given their writers.[3]

Dorothy joins me in sending all best wishes to Mrs. Deacon and to yourself,

Sincerely,
Hugh (MacLennan)

1 MacLennan misdated the letter.
2 Roderick Stuart Kennedy (1889–1953), journalist and author, was advertising manager of *The Montreal Star* (1922–39) and subsequently editor-in-chief of *The Family Herald and Weekly Star* (1939–53).
3 'Canada's Literary Revolution' was the title of Deacon's address inaugurating Canada Book Week which he gave at Windsor, Ontario, on 1 November 1947. It was printed in *The Canadian Author and Bookman*, XXIII (December 1947) 21–5.

---

## From Hugh MacLennan

North Hatley, P.Q.
July 7, 1948

My dear Bill:

I intend to keep your last letter, for it both heartened and touched me.

When I finished *The Precipice* and mailed it to Toronto and New York, I had a vague presentiment, which grew over the months, that the hopes I had once had that the book would mean a good deal financially were going to be dashed. The presentiment grew in spite of the fact that Duell, Sloan & Pearce felt it was the best book they had ever received and were confident of a BOMC [Book of the Month Club] selection. What happened with the BOMC I don't know beyond the fact that it was an 'A' book in March and was again sent up to the judges by Amy Loveman's committee[1] for re-reading in April, in which month the judges made no choice but merely assigned books on reserve up to and including October.

I now am in complete agreement with you that the book will be a long-term asset, if it is an asset at all. It is, of course, too early to predict an American reaction. So far as general reviewers are concerned, it may be better received there than it was here. You are certainly right in your assumption that it is the most 'Canadian' book I have ever written, and I'm afraid you are also right that in the first printings it will be far too close to home for Canadian readers to see it. Aside from your review, which I treasure,[2] the others indicate that Canadian reviewers simply don't know what I was trying to do.

About my next book I'm not yet sure. There are several subjects I want to tackle, and I seem unable to decide which until THE PRECIPICE has been read a little more widely and I get a more accurate feeling of how I stand with the public. Do you feel as I do, that a book has three separate existences – first with the author the moment it is finished, then with the public in the first weeks of its life, and finally with the public after the public's mind has been made up about it?

Now for your questions about myself: Born in Glace Bay, N.S., in 1907, went with my parents to Halifax in 1914 and lived in Halifax until I was 21, when I went to Oxford. Graduated Dalhousie 1928, went down from Oxford 1932, and left Princeton with a Ph.D. (which has been completely useless to me in its union card aspect) in 1935. Taught at Lower Canada College 1935–1945 with a year off in 1943 on a Guggenheim. Married Dorothy in 1936. *Barometer Rising* published 1941, *TS* 1945. *TS* has gone, by the way, into Swedish, Dutch, Czech, Spanish, German, Japanese and Korean and anyone who wants a Swedish or Czech copy can have one. The U.S. Army signed me up on the last three. It is not in French, owing to the fact that the French-Canadian publisher with whom I signed a contract in 1945 failed, and took about two years in the process.[3]

I'm sorry about the Income Tax trouble. Governmental departments scare me to death. I think there's no doubt that Rod Kennedy will be a much better man than Stead when it comes to handling the Income Tax people. Stead was a civil servant, I believe; a poor preparation for dealing with a governmental dept., for men like that never approach them with the right attitude. I remember that when Rod and I went to Ottawa, Steichman believed we had no chance whatever. We believed that if they didn't come through we could raise sufficient hell to make it worth their while to come through, and the idea percolated.[4] One must always approach a governmental dept. with this attitude; make it clear to them that it will be more trouble if they refuse than if they consent, for their sole purpose in handling anything whatever is to avoid personal trouble. But of course, you know all this.

Your picture of Lake Couchiching sounds marvellous. I'm sure it's free of hayfever, which this summer in our area has got me for the first time.

Things with us are better than they were so far as Dorothy's health is concerned, mainly because we finally managed to get a capable woman to come in and do the work. But these past two years have been at times such a heavy weight I've found it quite impossible to relax. Dorothy is getting better slowly week by week, but she was terribly ill and I'm afraid she will never be even near strong again. Her own novel needs a re-write. It will be at least a year before she will be fit to attempt it, if ever. However, her spirits are good and her mind is as keen as it ever was, and probably wiser.

Last two days I've been re-reading Roberts in Mrs. Bennett's *13 Bears*.[5] No doubt of it, Roberts is very, very good. I loved his work when I was a boy and wondered how it would stand up. It stands up wonderfully well. So long as he keeps people out of it, he's an artist and no mean one.

Dorothy joins me in sending affection to Sally and to yourself. Thanks for everything, Bill.

Sincerely,
Hugh

1 New York editor (1881–1955), head of the Editorial Department, Book-of-the-Month Club (1938–51)

2 'MacLennan Performs Smoothly in a Canadian-American Story,' in the book page of Saturday, 26 June, praised MacLennan's polished handling of the novel structure and of characterization, and concluded that as a love story 'the difficult feat of using human beings in a fiction to demonstrate a thesis and still remain natural is achieved.'

3 MacLennan's contract had been with Pariseau et Compagnie. Ultimately, *Deux solitudes*, translated by Louise Gareau-Desbois, was published in 1963 by the Parisian firm of Les Editions Spès.

4 In 1945–6 MacLennan had served on the CAA Income Tax Committee which was chaired by Kennedy. They submitted a brief to the Minister of Finance and in the June 1946 federal budget provisions were made allowing writers to spread over a three-year period income tax declarations associated with the sale of a single book.

5 Published posthumously by Ryerson in 1947, Charles G.D. Roberts's *Thirteen Bears* contained short stories that had been chosen and edited by Ethel Hume Bennett (b. 1881), popular author of juvenile fiction.

---

## To Hugh MacLennan July 11, 1948

Dear Hugh,

Thanks for data. Exactly what I needed.

Don't make any mistake about the permanent value of what you have done in *The Precipice*. It is far your best book – in the words of *The Toronto Star* (presumably Mr. McGeary, though they are all anonymous in that shop) 'as much an advance over *Two Solitudes* as *Two Solitudes* was over *Barometer Rising*.' It is something to go upstairs 1, 2, 3 like that. In fact, it is everything if you are a creative artist, which you are.

You have now discipline and experience. Whatever objections could be raised technically to the former books simply do not apply to *The Precipice*. This stands as is, and will be of interest as long as the social contrast continues and, I suspect, any changes on either side of the line will merely emphasize what you have said – not reverse the contrast into uniformity. So you have a book that will last and it is superb, with not only every page holding up but every line – not a wasted word, and every word *tells*. Hugh MacLennan the writer is made. Writing of this grade means terribly hard work; but, if you don't get lazy, you can plow right ahead. When I say you are 'established,' I mean exactly that; you have rubbed out all the question marks.

My theory has always been that the man who proves his ability by 40 is exactly on the beam. Your best 25 years as a writer are immediately ahead of you. In them, you will do increasingly good work; and Canada has reached the point at which a top flight novelist can be assured of a living. After 65, you'll be an institution – acceptance is automatic, no matter how lousy your performance. By 80, you'll be the Grand Old Man with whatever honors go with it. When you get absolutely punk at 90, the young lads will be writing biographies of you, and the nation will celebrate your birthday with a special issue postage stamp. Don't imagine that the literary Canada of the end of this century will be a small thing to be king of. You were just in luck to grow up between the wars and, if you work *hard* and maintain your artistic integrity, the remainder of your life will be smooth.

Now I have to repeat for your private comfort what I have proclaimed publicly and more generally. There is no particular causal relation between literary merit and the popularity, which means, finally, money.

Popularity is a matter of sheer chance – luck if you like. Popularity means that at the moment of publication the writer just happens to catch the public ear because it chimes with public mood at that minute. Public mood is a resultant of forces too complicated to guess at 2, 3, 4 years previously when the book is being written. Irene Baird's *John* was a best-seller. Her *Waste Heritage* flopped as a war casualty.[1] In the fall of 1939 nobody wanted to read about the late depression – any youth could have a job in uniform. Reasons in her case are easy to deduce. In other cases, God himself does not know why the public suddenly reaches for a particular type of book or, just as often, suddenly ceases to read a once-popular author. Look over 10-year-old magazines at any date and you wish to experiment [sic] and you will be amazed to find 90% of the sure-fire writers of a decade past have vanished from the table of contents. Joseph Hergesheimer[2] wrote steadily for 14 years and every single item he sent out was rejected – for 14 years. Then for 10 years he was read by all and sold lots and lots of unborn stories of all lengths for big prices. He collected all right but most of those stories were never printed because – for no known reason – Hergesheimer's decade of prosperity ended public interest in him.

You can't shoot at public taste because it is an unknown, unpredictable quantity. Your artistic integrity won't let you become a literary prostitute. Don't write what you conceive the public wants any more than you would write like a fake American to catch a market. You have accepted your nationality, with all its drawbacks and all its advantages. Now you must also accept the fact that you are a literary artist, a creative novelist; and, through the life, this will pay off better than production of saleable crap. Being honest as a writer – doing your best – may mean less pay per item, but not necessarily so (Maugham is really good and very rich). But in any case the way of the sincere craftsman is yours, and the pay is steadier. If you are like the majority of good writers, you will strike oil somewhere along the route. I expect to see you make a lot of money – in gushers. Don't imagine that will continue forever; it is exceptional experience when a writer is on easy street all the time.

I feel that it is a writer's business to write as well as he can, to publish to the best advantage, and then go on to the next job. No Canadian novelist of your ability in the middle of this century need fear the future. I think a writer handicaps himself if he expects to get rich. The world owes him a living; and you will get it – varied with the occasional flop commercially and jack pots from time to time. It will average up a damn sight better than the fellows who suddenly make a killing and then fade right out. The steadiness of Canadian character involves steady patronage for writers they respect. We're not as volatile as the Yanks – crown you one year and forget you the next.

A writer is entitled to a living, with reasonable comfort. The three novels, especially *The Precipice,* ensure this if you are the industrious lad and [have the] will to plug along. You won't be like Morley [Callaghan], the boy wonder who now can't [get] a novel accepted in either country. You will get your novels out. Each will bring its returns; more and more you will be living on your reprints. In about 10 years, you ought to have an omnibus volume or a numbered, autographed set, or whatever is the current fancy way of cashing in on general fame.

The Canadians will stand by you, Hugh, just as long as they feel in your work seriousness and sincerity. Their patronage is a growing factor; it will grow all your lifetime. Meanwhile, of course, more and more of your books will go out into other countries. That's the whole trend of the Canadian literary movement. Some of these books will happen to catch on and bring in a lot of money. You can't guess which. Sinclair Lewis was amazed that *Main Street* made his fortune.

You are in the peculiar position that this public (home public is always the most important) first loved you for your faults, just as we love our friends for their human failings, not often for their virtues. The explosion was magnificent reporting but, structurally, it blew up your story as well as the city. You lugged in the adultery of Mme. Tallard, which got you a lot of readers – and lost you a lot, too. But now, by God, you have given a demonstration of fiction so honest, so able, so effective; and it is on the surface less spectacular. Discerning readers will thrill to your sheer power; they will admire your restraints – no crude sex for one thing. Nothing crude or pyrotechnic at all. Just the goods. It was a hellish hard book to write to keep emphasis true at all points and you never slipped once.

Just wait and see where this takes you. In ten days you climbed to 9th position out of 12 in the Toronto Library list. Watch that list. *The Precipice* will climb steadily. No use guessing how high it will go nor how long it takes to reach maximum altitude. It would go faster if Collins put advertising weight behind it as Frank Appleton would have done. Even so, it will be fall before the big demand comes and it will go on selling.

You are very fortunate in your dates. Grove, Salverson and company in the 1920's were pioneers. Canadian public had been too well taught to expect its good stuff from outside. Not even *Jalna* (1927) broke that down – her Canadian sales were never proportionately as good as in U.S. But you came along when there is far greater internal interest, when Canadians realize their writers are standing up to foreign competition. And you are one of the leaders; you will ride the crest of this wave, which is going to augment as long as we both shall live.

*Barometer* was a one-bagger; *Two Solitudes* a brilliant two base hit; *The Precipice* is a home run. It's got the sure-enough stuff and it takes you handily over the plate. You give fellows like me something to write about.

Just don't ever let down on quality. I doubt whether you ever dare be frivolous; it would just upset your public. They expect you to be serious, not funny; and humor is perishable goods.

You will be successful – always enough for reasonable living standards, and when the big sums come in, invest them safely because it might happen only once or twice in a lifetime. And for God's sake don't worry. You can always sell out if you have to – take a job on a magazine or radio – but you don't have to, ever. You are a creator and a free lance and your own boss and doing what you like. The author of *The Precipice* is the last man in Canada to be discouraged. The equation is: 'Ten years ago I was nowhere as a writer; today I'm tops; ten years from now much higher and very secure.'

All luck to you and my great respect–

1 Baird (1901–81) was a writer and journalist who joined the National Film Board in 1942 and later became chief of information for the Department of Indian Affairs and Northern Development.

2 Joseph Hergesheimer (1880–1954) was a prolific American author whose best-selling historical romances were very popular in the 1920s and whose work frequently appeared in *The Saturday Evening Post.*

---

## To Germaine Guèvremont March 15, 1950

Chere Madame Guevremont,

It must make you very happy to have your novel published in both French and English and to be winning so much acclaim. I am glad that Eric Sutton consulted you about the translation. It reads well in English. Whittlesey House [New York] has made you a handsome book. The picture on the jacket is attractive. It will help the sale because it is so different from American novels in appearance.

Please accept my warm thanks for copy of *Marie-Didace,* which you so kindly signed and sent me some time ago. I postponed thanks because I find it embarrassing to correspond with an author from the time of receipt of the book until my review is in type. That was a long time because I was waiting for the translation.

Now my remarks are in the hands of the printer for publication this Saturday. But I wish also to express congratulations direct to you. In my opinion, *The Outlander* is a Canadian classic – beautifully done. Tres distingue!! No finer novel has been written by any Canadian.

It is a very quiet story and will appeal more to the discerning than to the reader who wants sensation. But McGraw-Hill has a great world organization and I feel sure that your total sales will be encouraging. What are you working on now?

I hope to see you at the Canadian Authors Convention, June 27–30.

You are a great artist.

Sincerely,

---

## From Germaine Guèvremont

1010 Sherbrooke Street East
Montréal
March 22, 1950

Dear Mr. Deacon,

Miss Byam[1] has perhaps told you how happy I was to hear that you were to write a review of *The Outlander.* Now that I have read it and received your enthusiastic letter, how am I to express my gratitude to you?

Often, during dark hours, I have wondered if writing was worth while. Now, I know it is. But as you say so well, with this book we shall 'take the pulse' of the reader in Canada. To my great surprise I learned that the first edition in New York was exhausted on the 10th of March. The subject, serene as it is, may appear a new one to Americans. But to Canadians?

Please accept my most sincere thanks for the generosity and the sympathy you bestowed upon my book.

I look forward to the pleasure of meeting you again at the CAA Convention in June.

Yours truly
Germaine Guèvremont

1 Barbara Byam, editorial assistant in the Toronto office of McGraw-Hill

---

## From Gabrielle Roy

5, rue Alpin
Ville Lasalle
October 22, 1950

Dear Sally, dear Bill,

Thank you both for the book and your sweet letters which I treasure. How I wish I could fly to Toronto to kiss you two lovely people! I'm not as ill as rumour would have me. Still, I'll have to follow a treatment for some time and rest, I suppose. I have a small toxic goiter, not very bad yet and I think it can be treated without an operation. So don't worry over me. I have a good doctor in Montreal and Marcel too looks after me with devotion.[1]

We have been wonderfully happy to-gether in France. Yes, dear Sally, our hearts ache for Paris. You ask me how it is that Paris captivates people so. I suppose it is through many qualities sweet in themselves, but mostly by their perfect blend, just as perfect, aged wine. Life in France is incredibly sweet and free and thoroughly humane. One breathes freedom in the very air. There is respect for love, for man and for whatever comes to his mind. There, I think, lies the charm of Paris and of France. Beauty too, of course. There is beauty for the eye, satisfaction in almost every street in Paris – La Place de la Concorde has perfect dimensions. It is really vast. And how wonderful to come across large, open spaces in a city of men! To see so many trees, water, statues, lovely vases! in other words, so much that is unnecessary, gratuitous. We reproach their impractical nature to the French, but in a way that is how they created beauty. Their motive is seldom practical; it tends to please the eye, the mind. And even nowadays, buildings and homes go up slowly compared to our standard, but what houses compared to our own! In the first months of our stay in Paris, I witnessed, for example, a curious thing. There were entire cities to reconstruct, bridges, ports, roads to rebuild; yet, along le boulevard Raspail where we lived, I saw a whole gang of men at work, derricks, a truck, all employed in planting a full-grown tree to match the others along the boulevard. There was work far more urgent. Yet who knows! Perhaps this tree is just as important as an office building. For weeks, I watched it, afraid to see it die. Men came to water it every day, and finally, in the Spring, I saw it come out into buds, as large, as beautiful as the other trees in the street. In the midst of strikes, of uneasiness and devastation, we also saw expert workers setting up the stained windows of Chartres, the reconstruction of Rouen's cathedral and of Orleans, of Lisieux, of Caen – Dear Saint-Malo, however, I'm afraid, is beyond repairs – Marcel has quite a collection of postcards: someday, I hope, we will show them to you.

It is very kind of you, Sally, to invite us to your home. I wish I could accept such a sweet invitation. But we are barely established in our new life. We have many things to buy yet. Then I hope to find a maid. I'm eager to settle down to work, as soon as I feel well enough. I've just completed *La Petite Poule d'Eau* which will be published in about a month's time in Montreal, a little later in Paris and, very likely, in New York, somewhere about next fall. The scene, this time, is north Manitoba, in the lake region – I do hope you will like it.

Mr. Reynal went with Harcourt, Brace and Co., and my financial arrangement, such as I submitted it to you, Bill, has been concluded with them. They will probably publish *La Petite Poule d'Eau*. I would like to please you, Bill, by sending a photo of Marcel and I for the press, but Marcel is not very fond of the idea – neither am I for that matter.

You know, by taste and necessity I am led to live a quiet and retired life – I have just enough health left for my work. I cannot afford to spend energy elsewhere. Therefore, I'm afraid I won't be able to be of much help to the Authors' Association, ever.

Jean-Marie Nadeau is supposed to have received my medal.[2] I must ask him about it.

Marcel sends his love to you all, children and grown-ups. Mine also flies to you.

Yours affectionately
Gabrielle

1 Roy had married Dr Marcel Carbotte in August 1947 and they had lived in and

near Paris from 1947 to 1950 while Carbotte undertook further medical studies in gynecology. They returned to Montreal in 1950 and then settled permanently in Quebec in 1952.

2 Author, journalist, professor of law (1906–60) who in the 1940s conducted with René Lévesque a political commentary column for Radio-Canada. Roy was under the mistaken impression that he had been sent the medal for the Governor-General's Award, which she had received *in absentia* for *The Tin Flute*.

---

## To Thomas Raddall October 23, 1950

Dear Tom,

I bow low to you.

You have far exceeded anything you have done in fiction in the past. What you have done is so fine and powerful that you will have difficulty beating your own record.

My review of *The Nymph and the Lamp* is now going down the chute to the lino-typers and will be my leading review for Canadian Book Week issue, Oct. 28th.

Frankly, Tom, I don't know how good your book is. It is in the top rank of Canadian novels, of course; but I'll not know till I've cooled off, weeks hence, whether it is slightly above or below A, B or C. Things like this need time to digest; but I'm a disciple of POWER, and this is strong.

I'm particularly pleased because I have always wanted a living picture of Sable Island and now I've got it – complete with a cast of characters.

Please keep me informed about developments, such as what the English think of it, whether you sell movie rights, etc. A stage play would restrict the action, too much, I think; and some of the erotic scenes could not be filmed either.

Of course, as literature, it's miles ahead of most novels published anywhere. Follow your own course, man; you know how to write them.

My humblest and heartiest congratulations –

From Thomas Raddall

Liverpool, Nova Scotia
Wednesday Night
November 1, 1950

My dear Bill –

I'm not writing to thank you for that heart-warming review, for that would be impertinent, but I do want to tell you it did just that – it warmed my heart. I've just been looking at my diary. Typical entry, last Feb. 14th – 'Working 8 to 10 hours a day on my novel but it still goes slowly, every sentence literally wrenched from my mind, & then mulled over carefully.' Again, four days later, 'Working on the novel 9 hours, & thinking about the next chapter as I took my afternoon walk to Milton. I am seldom to bed before midnight, sometimes at it till 1:30.'

Finally, on April 1st (an odd day to finish so long & serious a labor) there is this: –

'Saturday. I worked all day & towards five in the afternoon wrote the last word of my novel, which I began in November '48. Think I shall call it "Castaways" or "One Fair Spirit." It will take about a month to type clean copy for the publishers, & do the last-minute polishing. There won't be much of the latter, for my work is all edited & much rewritten at the close of each day. Now that the novel is finished the plot seems simple, even trite, & the characters in no way distinguished, yet it is the product of the longest & most arduous labor I have yet performed – deliberately refusing to "dash off" so much as a paragraph, & spending an hour sometimes over a single phrase. It is a romance of course but I think I have sketched faithfully life in an isolated wireless station as I knew it 30 years ago, & a glimpse of Halifax & the Annapolis Valley in the hectic post-war days of '20 & '21.'

There you see my state of mind at the finish – exhausted & despondent but clinging to my faith in the tale as something worth doing well. And perhaps you will see what such a review as yours can mean when the last step has been taken & the book is irrevocably out. Notice that I later changed my mind about the title. 'Castaways' sounded too much like an adventure tale for juveniles. 'One Fair Spirit' is of course taken from the lines of 'Solitude' that Carney recites on p. 159. But the practice of lifting titles from lines of verse – often by the crudest of Caesarian operations & dismally contrived – has become so banal that nowadays I'm suspicious of any book bearing such a label, & so I chucked it out. When after much thought I hit upon *The Nymph & the Lamp*, which said everything & was fresh & clean, I wrote it down & knew at once that nothing else would do.

The movies are enquiring – four of the leading companies have asked for copies of the book – but of course that means nothing. The British publishers will probably be Hurst & Blackett, but I'll let you know.[1] Little, Brown are releasing the book on Nov. 23rd, & we'll see what the Americans have to say.

All things good to Mrs. Deacon & you from Edith & me.

Sincerely,
Tom

1 The British edition of *The Nymph and the Lamp* was published in 1951 by Hutchinson and Company; in 1952 it was published again as a book-of-the-month selection by the Universal Book Club, London, an affiliate of Hutchinson and Company.

---

## From Hugh MacLennan

North Hatley, P.Q.
July 3, 1951

My dear Bill:

Thanks for your letter and good wishes. The news of McGill is true but not yet official, so perhaps you'd better not print it yet. The job is part-time and will help pay the bills. Also this summer I'm working in a consulting capacity with the National Film Board, and spend alternate weeks here and in Ottawa. Next month HOLIDAY at last prints my article on Montreal,[1] and I have sent them another, on order, on Nova Scotia, concerning which I have received no official reaction yet.

At least EACH MAN'S SON settled one question – nobody can live by writing novels in Canada at the present time. Indeed hardly anyone can do it in the States, either. The position of fiction is desperately bad. EACH MAN'S SON may sell 10,000 here by Christmas, leaving out whatever distribution the Lit. Guild makes – it probably will be less than 5,000 extra copies. In the States I don't think the retailers will dispose of the 12,000 advance sale, although reviews could hardly have been better and Little, Brown did a superb job of handling.

The reasons behind the state of the fiction market, as you doubtless know, are basic and serious. One is the high cost of living – that is perhaps the chief one. Another is the competition with pocket books – that has killed the lending libraries so that 90% of such libraries in the U.S.A. have folded within the past three years. Also, the pocket books are issuing titles so soon after the books first appear that the public is waiting for them. Pocket books must be faced and handled properly, since at present rates they operate in a closed and almost captive market and pay so little they can't support either writers or initial publishers. For this situation the publishers themselves are to blame. Finally there is the state of mind brought about by the hurricane of propaganda which is rapidly stunning the sensibilities out of the reading public. That is probably the most serious thing of all and the writers can't be held responsible for it. Television seems to be a minor factor. People who stare at a television set wouldn't read books anyway.

What the future of fiction will be I don't profess to know. I believe there will be a return to it soon. Perhaps – indeed probably – a new departure on the part of novelists is required. Maybe a genius is needed. Certainly the trend that began in the 1920s has petered out into insignificance, and I have been intensely hostile to books like Mailer's and Jones'[2] because they seemed to me only to drag the art of fiction backward into the swamp of materialism from which there is no escape or hope – and here I speak artistically, not morally.

Anyway, I shall go on writing, but I am thankful enough to have other work at the moment. It is an absolute necessity to have it, of course, which simplifies choices. More emphatically than ever I believe that we in Canada must paddle our own canoe. We can't learn anything from the Americans for the simple reason that at the moment they have nothing to teach anybody. What we must resign ourselves to is the fact that the best we can do is to write good books and forget about making sales in the United States. Only by the sheerest accident is a Canadian writer likely to crack the American market today. From this it follows that a Canadian novelist might as well realize that he will have to do other work and carry on his writing simultaneously as best he can. My own career would seem to be as conclusive proof of this as one could wish to find. I'm grateful I was able to be free to do nothing but write for as long as six years. They were crucial years for me, but they are over now, and perhaps it's just as well. Our society is too atomized anyway, and a writer living alone in time begins to lose touch.

Dorothy joins me in sending best wishes to Sally and to yourself.

Sincerely,
Hugh

1 'City of Two Souls,' *Holiday* XII (August 1951) 48–55

2 James Earl Jones (1921–77), popular American author whose *From Here to Eternity* (1951) was criticized by MacLennan over the CBC for its 'pessimistic materialism.'

---

## From Gabrielle Roy

Ville Lasalle
December 7, 1951

Dear Bill,

Thank you for the good hint and another proof of your kind interest in myself and in my work. How can I ever thank you sufficiently for such kindness!

I've written to Jack McClelland, sending him your fly-leaf concerning the suggestion offered from Ottawa that *Where Nests the Water Hen* could be used as a text book. Jack McClelland is quite willing to approach the various departments of Education. So, let's keep our fingers crossed and hope for the best. The whole thing seems too beautiful to be possible.[1]

I will write again soon. Most of our trials are on their departure. The greatest was the difficulty Marcel experienced in entering a hospital service. However, he's is now working at Misericordia Hospital. It is rather small, but it is a beginning anyhow and I am greatly relieved to see him at work at last and so much happier.

Affectionately yours
Gabrielle

P.S. About my medal from the Governor General: Mr. Nadeau thought he had received it. Then we discovered it was my Royal Society medal that he had in his keeping. Germaine Guèvremont whom I met lately claims Roderick Kennedy told her he had my medal. Do you think you might get to the bottom of this story? After all, somebody must be keeping [it] for me until he or they know about my address.[2]

Gabrielle

1 *La Petite Poule d'eau* was adopted as a textbook by the Ontario Department of Education in 1955.
2 Kennedy was, in fact, keeping the Governor-General's Award medal, which he quickly forwarded to Roy.

---

## From Sherwood Fox

270 Regent Street
London, Ontario
December 15, 1952

Dear Bill:

Ungrateful & insensitive would I be if I failed to acknowledge with alacrity the fine compliment you paid me in 'The Fly Leaf' on Saturday last.[1] When I say that, if I merit in any respect your good word on the quality of my effort in *The Bruce Beckons*, I owe a measure of it to you. When you reminded me in '46 that *'T Ain't Runnin' No More* was just a miniature (you wrote that in a personal letter), you drove into my mind a sharp goad: – that if I attempted to produce something on a larger scale the continuous maintenance of the effort would be difficult. In other words – you 'dast' me & I took your *dare*. I tender you my warmest thanks.

Sincerely
Bill

1 On 13 December Deacon had noted the appearance of the third printing of *The Bruce Beckons* and attributed its success to the knowledge and writing ability of its author.

---

## To Sherwood Fox

December 17, 1952
11:45 [P.M.]

Dear Bill,

Your good letter – the second[1] – comes when I have 15 minutes to wind up my work for the year 1952; and how better could I spend the time than with you.

I am very anxious that you understand the extent of your triumph. In my 32 years of reviewing, there has never been a season to compare with this for the numbers of big, fine books with all the elements of popularity. You are up against Hemingway and 100 others of that class. Evidently the trade publishers didn't want your book, so you took it to a University press, which knows nothing about campaigning. For subject you choose a tiny region in the Ontario backwoods.

My dear friend, the logical fate of your book – especially published in the *fall* – would have been 90% indifference and neglect. Instead of which you come up with a sales' record, which is 33% of the fastest moving book in Canada. You had something more than two strikes against you to start with ... but you knocked a home run!! It was just as though one of my six-year-old grandsons managed by some fluke to get onto the ice during a hockey game between the Maple Leafs and the Red Wings; and, before anybody realized he was participating, he had shot the puck into the net past Lumley. I do not exaggerate – much.

Well, from boyhood – let's say for 50 years – I've been training myself to be a critic; and this miracle you have pulled off needs explaining. Especially as my friend John Fisher[2] had intimated on the air that the subject was the key. On the contrary, your subject was a handicap. Who the hell cares about the Bruce? Certainly not I, till you got me excited through your book. That is *writing*. What if the subject had had immense inherent appeal? This life is full of material for writers – wonder and glory and power everywhere – and the writers louse it up because they are not skilful as writers.

Everything was against you – subject unappealing to 99.9% of people. Your professorial habits of thought were a handicap. With all the confidence I have in you, I should never have dared publish that book in a fall – any fall, let alone this particular season.

You achieved all this because of your writing ability and nothing else. It is one of those triumphs of genius over a rational world that I like so much.

It's a funny thing for me to say; but I congratulate you on taking my previous advice seriously. I am trained to distinguish between new writing of classical quality and verbal rubbish. I saw quite clearly that *'Tain't Runnin' No More* was a work of exceptionally outstanding merit. All it lacked was body; there wasn't enough of it.

So I suggested that you write a bigger work which would contain the same qualities. And you did. *The Bruce Beckons* is no better but it is more effective because it creates a greater mass impact.

I was excited. Your other readers were excited. We all yammered. 'Here is a man who delivers the stuff!' Of course you loved that bleak blob of land or you could never have got the emotion into the narrative. You took something out of your mind and made it a living reality to us. That is ART. That is the kind of miracle that silences people in the presence of great music or painting. You have stamped an image on the consciousness of men. In time, people will only see the peninsula through your eyes – your vision, your love. You have added to the world something intangible but stronger than anything material. Incidentally, you have established yourself as a writer, far beyond anything in your writing past. You have supplied the Bruce for all time with an eidolon – a soul.

My dear sir, I stand for values. I have to teach people what is immaterially great. There it delights me that the thing has clicked. And I had to come back to emphasize that it is you, who have triumphed – not because of your subject but in spite of it – and you triumphed when your chances of failure were very high. Finally, you have given us all an object lesson in courage as well as in skill.

My part was slight enough, but I am proud of the small impulse I sent your way. I have to thank you for a degree of trust in my judgment which others often have not. But there are 12 to 15 books of some importance which I told specific men to write – Wrong's *The Canadians*[3] is one (I have his inscription to that effect) and McDowell's *Champlain Road* is another. I couldn't have written those books; but I sometimes do know who should write what. I shall put your last letter proudly in my copy of *The Bruce Beckons*, and put it away in the locked bookcase, as evidence that my life has not been wholly wasted.

And believe me, William, it's a lot less labor to get other men to write books than to write them myself.

Best Christmas greetings to you.

No. I have no further suggestions. You are on your own now. But remember, the doors are open before you. You can do whatever you please. Possibly your judgment will be sounder as to the next venture if you wait until the present noise has died down. I want your intuition to be working in a calm when you make a decision.

1 Fox's first note of appreciation, written on 2 December, had good-humouredly characterized Deacon as 'supreme in praising with faint damns.'
2 John Wiggins Fisher (b. 1913), CBC commentator and Canadian nationalist, popularly known as 'Mr Canada'
3 George MacKinnon Wrong (1860–1948), eminent teacher and writer of Canadian history at the University of Toronto, best known for *The Rise and Fall of New France* (1928). *The Canadians: The Story of a People* was published in 1938.

---

## To Thomas Raddall January 6, 1953

Dear Tom,

Thank you for encouragement. For better or for worse I am now tied to a schedule for production of new volumes in 1954 and 1956 – the first an exposition and interpretation of Canadian literature from 1920 to the present. This work of what I hope is constructive theory will be followed by a book of personal anecdotes about authors, publishers and editors I have known – light and casual. Word portraits, humorous incidents, character sketches. Something to preserve the memory of our generation of writers as human beings.[1]

But, before I get to either of these big chores, *The Four Jameses* will reappear in 1953, after an eclipse of a quarter of a century.[2]

It can go just as is; but I believe two brief additions to the story of James D. Gillis[3] would improve it.

Henry Munro, Supt. of Education for Nova Scotia, told me an exquisitely funny story about Jas. D. when he was attending Normal School.[4]

Would that be in Truro? Such is my memory but I don't want to say he attended Normal School in Truro if it was Halifax. The *first* of several definite requests I have to make of you tonight is to check on Truro as the locale.

My *second* query is about the propriety of Munro's tale. It will at that point definitely break down the illusion that I am praising Gillis. If he is dead, it will not matter; nobody will be hurt and my book will be improved. If Gillis still lives, he must be in his 90's, and possibly disintegrating to the point where he will not care and will not be aware, perhaps, of the new edition of my book.

I presume there is somebody up where he lives or lived up in Cape Breton, who can supply the information as to whether Gillis lives; if so, what condition? Some postmaster, perhaps, can report on the present survival of the author of *The Cape Breton Giant*; or that bookstore proprietor in Halifax who published *The Cape Breton Giant*.[5]

I could, of course, go to Nova Scotia to do my own research; but I hope you are closely enough in touch with the situation to save me the trip. Especially as my publisher is putting *The Four Jameses* on his spring list May publication – and that means type-setting will start very darn soon. I am, as it were, just catching the train as it pulls out. There is no time to spare.

*Third* and most important. A few years ago in Halifax I remember having a meal with you, during which you delighted me by a recital of the week Gillis spent in Halifax, when you took him to Howe's grave and to deliver speeches at various places. I made no notes. I do recall that you will [sic] valuable work in recording certain music – tunes – which Gillis either played or sang. There were, you said, some broadcasts. Yourself and Gillis.

Now my problem is this: Have you printed any of this stuff? You are a very craftsmanlike and methodical fellow (which I admire). Have you plans to use the episode of the week in any future writing – such as essay, memoirs or magazine article?[5]

If you have published a record, where can I get it to quote from?

Should you not have published anything, but plan to do so, then I haven't any third problem at all. The stuff is yours; and you would certainly deliver it better than I could, and I shall leave it alone (as I guess I shall have to anyway if Gillis is still alive).

The humor of situation is so delightful that I covet the episode to round out *The Four Jameses*. I should also wish to include, in serious vein, mention of the broadcasts during which you performed the valuable service of collecting these tunes.

As you told the story to me, I was enraptured; and of course you can tell it better than I can. You would certainly tell it in greater detail than I wish to. Just what do we do? You are my only source of information. The relatively brief and general mention of The Week, which I should like to make, need not preclude you from working up your own full version for separate publication later.

If any of this material is available to me, can you write out the facts in time to let me get this book on the press?

My apologies for bothering you when you are engaged in the final work on *Tidefall*, which I think a marvellous title. You must be aware of my conviction of the great forward step you took in *The*

*Nymph and the Lamp*; and I am looking forward eagerly to reading it. I wish it could have appeared last fall, when the several Canadian novels were reasonably good but not exciting. Sally Creighton sneered over the air from Vancouver that they were 'competent.' For myself, I use the word competent as a compliment and not a reproof but I realize what she was trying to convey. Your *Tidefall* would have shone like a star among them. What else is coming in fiction in 1953 I cannot say. Certainly the biographies were far ahead of the novels in 1952.

Please be very frank about how you feel on these several points, especially this matter of my alluding to The Week.

Were you on the expedition to visit Gillis in Cape Breton when they held the poetry contest? Do you remember what year it was?

Andy Merkel sent me an elaborate report at the time; and it is barely possible that I can locate it among my papers. I used it in *The Mail and Empire*; but there must be a sentence or so about that in my book; but the date eludes me. Would it be about 1931? Was Robt. Norwood of the party?[6]

Well that's the story and you have my very humble request for assistance. *The Four Jameses* is going anyway; but it will be a much better book if I can round out Gillis with a page or two about (a) Normal School in Truro; (b) the poetic excursion to Cape Breton; and (c) highlights of The Week in Halifax.

I am, Sir, your very humble and
most obedient servant

P.S. The Toronto convention starting June 24 will be a much bigger affair than the one you attended here seven years ago – and YOU, me lad, will be a bigger personality there than you were in 1946, even though many Big Names coming. Isabel LeBourdais is holding a prominent spot on the program for a set address by Thomas H. Raddall on any subject he cares to discuss.

1 Neither of these was ever completed or published.

2 Issued originally in 1927 by Graphic Publishers, *The Four Jameses* was published in a revised edition by Ryerson Press in 1953.

3 A Nova Scotia school teacher, author of *The Cape Breton Giant: A Truthful Memoir* (1898), *Modern English: 'Leave the Old to Old'* (1904), and *The Great Election* (1915), James D. Gillis (1870–1974) also published the *Four-Pole Map of the World*, 'Blue Prints to be had from the author, South West Margaree, Nova

Scotia' (nd). His life and work are celebrated in Deacon's *The Four Jameses* (1927), which Gillis read for the first time in 1956, almost three decades after its publication, prompting a belated correspondence.

4 In late November 1934, Henry Fraser Munro (1878–1949), professor of political science at Columbia (1914–21) and Dalhousie (1921–6), and Superintendent of Education for Nova Scotia (1926–47), had written to Deacon for a copy of *The Four Jameses*. In his letters of thanks upon receipt of his copy Munro told Deacon that, for reasons unknown, Gillis had been granted a first-class teaching licence which, on his retirement, was yielding an annual pension of $630. Gillis was hale and hearty in 1953, and Deacon did not use the Munro anecdote.

5 T.C. Allen of Halifax issued reprints of *The Cape Breton Giant*, which originally had been published in 1898 by John Lovell and Son, Montreal. Raddall eventually made use of material from the report of his week with Gillis – 'Halifax Revisited' – in his autobiography *In My Time* (1976).

6 Merkel's report, entitled 'The Poets,' described the formation of the group of Nova Scotian poets called 'The Song Fishermen' under the unofficial leadership of Robert Norwood, their monthly song sheet of voluntary contributions, and the famous poetry contest adjudicated by Gillis which culminated in 3 September 1929 with a boat trip on the schooner *Drama* to McGrath's Cove near East Dover, where a picnic was held. There Gillis played both bagpipes and fiddle, while Norwood crowned with dulse Stuart MacCawley of Glace Bay for his prize-winning poem 'Taking a Stance in the Kelp.'

---

## From Lorne Pierce

York Mills, Ontario
January 14, 1953

Dear Bill:

I have been through your lectures,[1] once fairly slow, and once or twice on the run. Now I am taking a chance, and talking out loud. One ought perhaps say thinking out loud, but I shall not brag! When I have finished this letter, if it makes sense, I'll send it on to you as it is, without polishing, and no carbon.

You have more than one book in you on this theme, and we must plan for that. First a commentary upon modern Canadian letters, and then that leisurely personal book of memories, anecdotes, and casual criticism – your testament. I have tried for several days to work out a formula that might look respectable to you.

Let us say, in the first place, that I take it you do not want an academic type of book. You do not want a book coming grandly down, packed with research of the foot-note, appendix, and quotation type, and all beginning with the Garden of Eden or whenever it was. Pacey and others like that do that. They have graduate students eager at their bidding to research, read vastly in perios and dredge up the bottom of the sea. There will be a book by Rhodenizer much after the fashion of his first book, maybe in a year or two. Then someday there will be a revision by a team of my *Outline*, an encyclopaedia thing. Maybe five years from now, and I'll not have any part in it.

I have tried to visualize your book as good talk, like your *Four Jameses*. It would really be a series of rather long essays in the best coffee-house tradition, wise, mellow and pleasantly convincing. How can that be done, rather how can we organize the business? You would deal in the large view, pouncing upon particulars when they were worth a pounce and when they illustrated your main point. The book would be based upon your thesis so well stated; 'A national literature comes into being in response to the deeply felt need of every civilized society to understand itself.' Well, then, that is the book, a series of discoveries of these moments of creation, moments in which writers most clearly and persuasively put down their understanding of Canada. I try not to let Van Wyck Brooks[2] twitch my elbow here, but the root of the idea may be in him. We do not sweep to a grand climax in one long flight like a homing swallow; we zig-zag, dip and climb, wiggle and waver. And we do this as individuals and nations, or cultures.

Suppose we begin with that idea, and talk it over.

Well, then there would have to be a starting point, and I think you propose to begin with 1880, and the publication of Roberts' *Orion*. In that case I would have a brief sparkling opener on 'Our Fathers that Begat Us.' Boil it all down into a few pages, the writers breathless over the immensity of the new land, fearful of its untamed wilderness; the imitative rhythms and idioms so feeble in the face of the new immensity; the first break in *ideas*, the new wine dimly felt, but at work. It is true that many currents of world ideas, shaking the daylights out of society abroad and in the USA never reached us until my boyhood, but there were others, many others. And there was the need to unite in the face of the deep-shadowed vastness, a need that later appeared in Confederation and in a series of church and other unions unparalleled in any nation.

I am not sure whether this IS it, but we will find a proper springboard, that will land you into the middle of the thing.

While our best interpretation has come from the poets I wonder if we might take up the early novelists first? 'The Search for a Country,' a chapter in which you start with Major Richardson, and Kirby, and show how these great writers on down to Raddall really opened up the country, the national historians in fiction. McDowell would come in perhaps and others of course. These writers did more perhaps to make Canada an entity than any other group, at any rate they reached more people. 'This Fair Land ...'

Then you might go back to the Confederation poets, 'Songs of the New Nation.' These were the writers who kindled the artists later, and in the Toronto Art Students League and in the Group of Seven got the world by the ears. You ought to refer casually to parallel movements that add new meaning to the growth of Canadian letters, for as you hint in your definition, it was a total cultural venture. In this chapter you might use most of your Roberts lecture. However, in the book we see from here, you would not emphasize one writer too heavily, and to the exclusion of others. You sum up a period rather, as seen through the eyes of this group.

I thought we might then go on with the novelists, and confine this group to the regional writers, those who explored fully certain areas. There will always be a need for this kind of writer, since our country is so vast few will ever see all of it. Regional writers are as essential as good travel book writers. But they both paint on large canvases. Here you deal with a fascinating group, and all quite modern. This provided a rather nice balance between poetry and prose, the more intensive and the more extensive.

The next might be humour; it began early and has been with us always, but the more it changes, the more it is the same thing – a certain love of extravagance, the love of a whopper, the mouthful-word, the preposterous. Even when we are more sophisticated the extravagant breaks through, the tall tale, did-you-ever thing. Well, from Sam Slick to Robertson Davies, and Sarah Binks and your fathering of that school of clever fooling.

Perhaps we might then turn to the community, the cult of the back concession and so on. First the epic novel, then the regional and then the community thing. You have them listed in your outline.

The final refinement of the writer's search for Canada would come with the new spate of books of biography, in which at long last the Canadian no longer refuses to look at individuals. It emerges among the poets too.

Juveniles might come in, and Essayists must. But where to put them I leave to you. Likewise the French writers. I think I would do as you have done and simply crack it in as Four French Novelists, and the logic of it be hanged. This is on English Can. Lit. But who cares for a vagary, providing it is a nice one!

What has bothered me most is how to retain your notion about these landmarks, the Polar People. Suppose you did that, and made them the theme song. Roberts, Grove, Pratt, MacLennan, spreading them out through the book. Here are the Matterhorns. You will have to make peace with your own soul about Mazo [de la Roche] and Laura [Goodman Salverson] and Raddall or Will Bird. But it has to be done. You are doing it all through the book, the big names. There is no point in a catalogue, and in the few pages where you attempt lists you yourself have no heart in the business.

Well, Bill, my head is uncovered. Shoot, man!

L.P.

1 'Contemporary Canadian Literature,' a series of twenty lectures, was offered as an evening course at the Ryerson Institute of Technology during the academic year 1951–2. A general survey of Canadian literature from its origins to the present, the course occasionally provided a detailed analysis of work by major figures. Lorne Pierce expressed interest in publishing these lectures as a book, but agreed with Deacon that they lacked unity beyond the theme of literary nationalism.

2 American literary critic and cultural historian (1886–1963), best known for *The Life of Emerson* (1932) and *The Flowering of New England: 1815–1865* (1936)

---

## From Thomas Raddall

Liverpool, Nova Scotia
January 17, 1953

Dear Bill,

Sorry to have been so long in replying to your request of the sixth. Communications between here and Jimmie D's retreat in Cape Breton are poor at this time of year, and I am still awaiting word from friends in those parts regarding the present state of Jimmie's health. He was definitely alive and kicking last autumn and if he had died in the meantime I feel sure I would have heard of it. I expect definite word any day now but as you said time was pressing I thought I'd better let you have the other information you wanted. In reply to your questions: –

*One.* The Normal College is in Truro.

*Two.* I don't know what Munro's tale was, so I can't offer an opinion regarding its propriety. All I can say is, deal gently with the old boy. He is by no means an idiot and he could be hurt. The handling of him in *The Four Jameses* was all right. He is to some extent a figure of fun, of course, but one shouldn't forget the quality of mercy.

*Three.* I wrote an account of The Week in a little sketch called 'Halifax Revisited,' which I enclose, together with a copy of Jimmie D's own account.[1] Note that I wrote of Gillis in the past tense; I intend to publish it some day when he is dead, hence the terms in which it is couched. You are at liberty to use as much of it as you like; I know that I can rely on your good sense, and as you will see there are certain references (e.g., to D.C. Harvey and to Sir Joe Chisholm[2]) that I would not publish until a good many years have passed. I set down these notes as a matter of record at the time, planning to eliminate what was injudicious when the time came for publication. I was not present when the Song Fishermen made their famous voyage to East Dover (*not* to Cape Breton) in the schooner Drama; but I have had good accounts of it from Merkel and others, and have seen Merkel's movies several times. A few years ago, when Merkel was still in his right mind (he's gone quite potty now, a lamentable case) I went with him to East Dover and visited the spot, calling on the fisherman in whose field the picnic was held. Merkel called in a number of other fishing folk who saw that memorable feast and showed them the movies. Their comments were good, and they confirmed the accounts I had heard. The Song Fishermen were a high-spirited lot. Bob Norwood was their guiding genius and when he died their activities came to an end. The Drama voyage took place about 1930. I joined the circle at 55 South Park Street much later on.

Well, there you are. Choose wisely, and let me have these papers back again, for they are the only copies I have.

All the best,
Tom

1 Gillis's account, unlike Raddall's, has yet to see publication in any form, and follows this letter.

2 Joseph Andrew Chisholm (1863–1950) was Chief Justice of the Supreme Court of Nova Scotia (1931–50) and author of *Joseph Howe: A Sketch* (1909) and *The Speeches and Public Letters of Joseph Howe* (1909).

## MY VISIT TO HALIFAX IN MARCH 1945

By

James D. Gillis, author of The Cape Breton Giant, etc., (Certified a True Copy by T.H.R. [Thomas Head Raddall], April 13, 1945)

Melrose Hill, Inv. Co., N.S.
April 5, 1945

A.D. Merkel, Esq., Hfx., N.S.
D. Sir:

I beg leave to enclose the Sketch of my recent visit.
I read your recent enclosures – and I thank you and all donors.

Yours, etc.,
Jas. D. Gillis

After a recent sojourn in Halifax, I think it appropriate to submit a brief commentary thereof.

Halifax is still going strong – and stronger than ever. Truly I am surprised, nay amazed at the rapid expansion of the city in ground area, in building altitude and population. The ceaseless activity which one might term a good-natured harmonious jostle is part cause of the change. As a certain person aptly puts it, an occasional visitor 'feels lost' along the streets.

Providentially Halifax like other places in Nova Scotia has not been perturbed nor victimized by hostile warplanes. However we owe gratitude to our Artillery, and to our sentinel and scouting airship combined.

The Archives Bldg. in charge of Professor D.C. Harvey[1] has the necessary Divisions, Departments and Compartments with – 'a place for everything and everything in its proper place.' Students of History, Science, Mementos, and national development and Involution will profit by a call.

Dr. Martell[2] is the assistant of Professor Harvey, who ably succeeds the lamented Mr. Harry Oiers. Mrs. Dr. Martell performs her parts with suave grace.

This suggests further high spots and spotlights that I visited or met.

The Ca. Press Bldg., Granville St., is imposing within and without. With the third floor range I became well acquainted. Here officiates Mr. A.D. Merkel, Atlantic Supt. of the Can. Press. His affability and generosity seek no bounds. With his car he conveyed me to the very places I wished to see, and introduced me to the notables of the city, and opened acquaintance for me with persons resident in other parts of the province. He and others sponsored my address to the N.S. Authors Association – the Poets Branch; also my address on Music before the students of Pine Hill College.

Withal in the Academy Bldg., (Q.[ueen] E.[lizabeth] High School) I was happy to meet Mr. Colin B. Faulkner of Noel, Hants County. He is a teacher and writer of note. For some time he was Principal of Inverness High School. On the present occasion he took in the Poets Meet aforementioned.

On March 18th in company with Mr. Merkel and other Maritime notables, I visited the grave of the Patriot Joseph Howe. A sod cutting, bearing live and blooming Mayflowers was reverently inserted on his grave.

It is patently certain that the Hon. Mr. Howe was pioneer of practical Democracy in Nova Scotia. Furthermore he was a statesman of tact, an orator, and a gifted poet. His career tended to dispel the theory that our right was only the right to obey.

Along the week we interviewed Dr. Henry Munro, Supt. of Education. He has proved himself an intrepid reformer; and if his lieutenants exercise equal honesty and actual Democracy his keen eye and firm hand will accomplish perfection.

In touring the city I was pleased to meet a former resident of Marble Mountain, C. Breton. Of Central African origin, of fine physique, set off by a fine uniform, at home in Gaelic as well as English, to me the meeting was a recreation.

In my time I have not seen many premiers. In my earlier days Sir John A. MacDonald and the Hon. Mr. Holmes[3] were Foci. I have seen the Hon. Mr. Fielding[4] when he was Min. of Finance, and the Rt. Hon. Sir Wilfred Laurier. I was with the Rt. Hon. R.B. Bennett when he was campaigning in 1930. Now I have a handshake with the Hon. A.S. MacMillan.[5]

In some sense the aforesaid celebrities were somewhat alike, plain, straight and bluff as farmers in Spring.

I enjoyed a sumptuous supper in the palatial home of Hon. F.B. McCurdy.[6] The courtesy of Mr. and Mrs. McCurdy, family and entire household are unforgettable. His kinsmen of Baddeck, Vo. Co., were progressive merchants and statesmen: and one, David McCurdy,[7] performed his part in airship invention. He and a partner flew over one dimension of Baddeck Town, and some distance further.

Wren Ruth Whittaker, H.M.S. Stadacona, deserves notice. As a writer, etc., she will probably be heard from and heard of, when her duties as marine relax.

I have had the honor and pleasure of interviews with Miss Dorothea Cox of the Canadian Broadcasting Corporation. Should television be added, no house should be without radio. The gentlemen managers of CBH and CJCH are of ideal caste; and their exhibition and explanations of how things are done make an agreeable impression.

Miss Pauline Barrett, traveller, linguist, author and wife of a famous Naval commander, is a new personal acquaintance. Mrs. Barrett entertained as well as invited us to her apartments in the Lord Nelson Hotel.

I have had talks with Thomas H. Raddall of Liverpool, N.S. Three of these were broadcast. He has composed expensively [sic] and received the Governor General's First Prize for fiction published in 1943. He is quite approachable and a consummate story teller.

I have renewed acquaintance with Mr. Roy Lawrence, Barrister of Annapolis Royal. He is Asst. Clerk of Govt. Headquarters. He bids fair to be an honor to Inverness, his native county. He is a nephew of J. Maurice Maclean, the venerable retired pastor of Strathlorne and for decades a minister beyond the Province. Mr. Lawrence is an accomplished raconteur, and never fails to thrill.

I interviewed Mr. C.F. Fraser[8] of the Chronicle and Star publications. He is I believe Editor in Chief or Manager. He shows depth of thought without absent-mindedness, and perspicacity without oversmart loquacity.

Miss Laura P. Carten[9] (Farmer Smith) of the Herald and Mail, my faithful abettor and friend, as well as friend of juvenile readers, amuses, guides and educates in her columns. I meant to see her at the Herald Bldg., but incidentally I met her at the Academy and elsewhere. She does what she can for authors, poets, etc., of the Maritimes.

By the way, our Govt. Centres from the Municipal to the Federal inclusive have ably supported the Miners, Fishermen, Farmers and School Teachers. We have uncalled for branches of outside undertakings in our midst. Is it not time to recognize and subsidize and in case prescribe the production of our own girls, boys, women and men? It is not natural for us to be thinking with the minds of others?

This brief outline of my Halifax Trip would be incomplete without a tribute to the Hon. Harold Connolly,[10] Minister of Industry and Publicity. His attractive and intensive travelogue of Nova Scotia has few equals of the kind. His cordial welcome seems to brush dull care aside.

Did I see John A. Walker?[11] Certainly. Yes. He's still going strong and practising law. I regret my short acquaintance with this gentleman precludes long comment; but I knew his father and a brother John J., to be worthy citizens and poets of undisputed capacity.

I have had the honor of meeting three professors of Dalhousie University. The Mathematics Professor Mr. J.G. Adshead[12] interested me agreeably and I judge he is no stickler for orthodox hypothetic perfections, which change with the years.

Mr. Geo. Wilson[13] is Prof. of History. That's a hard subject too. From the rush and din of everyday life it is difficult to envision the past. And again it must be remembered that history exists not for sating curiosity but for making us older by hundreds of thousands of years – or at least that experience. However I believe Mr. Wilson is qualified for the job.

I spent a happy hour or more in the company of Education Prof. A. Mowat,[14] and others including this time again the genial and versatile author Thomas H. Raddall. Mr. Mowat, a sprig of the Edinburgh heather is witty and apt too. Indeed I opine the personnel of Dalhousie today is or are far superior to that or those of former years. I fancy there's a rational harmony, no indiscreet instigation, no useless gorging of memories – no pets.

My address on music at Pine Hill College was appreciated with rapt attention and politeness. This student audience handed me a present or gratuity with a Gaelic inscription of thanks. I wish as well as forecast them all a successful and honorable course and career.

In closing this short account I hope that if anything was left unsaid, others will fill the gap in due course. To end, I repeat that

Halifax has improved and expanded, which will be shown by census and other reliable results and statistics by 1951.

(signed)
J.D. Gillis

1 Daniel Cobb Harvey (1886–1966), historian and from 1931 to 1956 Nova Scotia Archivist
2 James Stuart Martell (1911–46), historian who began working in the Public Archives of Nova Scotia in 1935 and was Assistant Archivist from 1944 until his death
3 Simon Hugh Holmes (1831–1919), Prime Minister of Nova Scotia (1878–82)
4 William Stevens Fielding (1848–1929), newspaperman, Prime Minister of Nova Scotia (1884–96), and Canada's finance minister under Wilfrid Laurier (1896–1911) and William Lyon Mackenzie King (1921–5).
5 Alexander Stirling MacMillan (1871–1955), Prime Minister of Nova Scotia (1940–45)
6 Fleming Blanchard McCurdy (1875–1952), publisher of *The Halifax Chronicle* and Member of Parliament from 1911 to 1921
7 John Alexander Douglas McCurdy (1886–1961), who made the first airplane flight in the British Empire at Baddeck, NS in 1909
8 Charles Frederick Fraser (1911–61), at this time managing editor of *The Halifax Chronicle*
9 Laura Paty Carten (1882–1960), journalist and children's editor with the Halifax newspapers *The Herald* and *The Mail* from 1916. Her reviews of Canadian literature appeared under the by-line 'Farmer Smith.' She was one of Deacon's Maritime correspondents.
10 The Honourable Harold Connolly (1901–80), a former newspaperman with *The Halifax Chronicle* and former editor of *The Daily Star*. He was elected Liberal MLA for Halifax in 1936 and was provincial premier from April to September 1954.
11 John Archibald Walker, KC (1890–1977), barrister and Halifax MLA from 1925 to 1928. He was a member of the firm of Walker, Wickwire and Dunlop.
12 John Geoffrey Adshead (1904–79), who taught at the University of King's College, Halifax (1927–47) and at Dalhousie (1947–69)
13 George Earl Wilson (1891–1973), Head of the Department of History at Dalhousie and author of *The Life of Robert Baldwin* (1933)
14 Alexander Sutherland Mowat (1905–84), professor of Education at Dalhousie and author of *City and Rural Schools* (1938). Born in Bonnybridge, Scotland, he had been educated at the University of Edinburgh.

From Thomas Raddall

Liverpool, Nova Scotia
March 24, 1953

Dear Bill,

Forgive me for bothering you again so soon, but you are one of the few who know what really goes on in the Canadian publishing business, and the only one I can approach on a confidential basis to find out what is what.

What is the opinion in the trade regarding McClelland & Stewart? M & S have been my Canadian publishers from the start, simply because they were then tied in with Doubleday, who published my first novel in the USA. M & S made a big fuss over me when I went to Toronto in '46, but I soon perceived from old John's[1] conversation that it was all due to the impending rupture with Doubleday and the fear that I might switch my Canadian publishing to Doubleday's new Toronto branch. He (and one after another of his staff) informed me in solemn accents that Doubleday was a cold materialistic firm who thought of nothing but the dollar, that I was only a second-string author with them, and that I would be much better off with another American firm, preferably Little Brown, with whom M & S were making their new tie. I was non-committal but I had my own chilly impression of Doubleday and eventually I switched to Little Brown. I like Little Brown, not least because I like Salmen,[2] who goes to the trouble to come up here and see me from time to time, a thing that never occurred to any of Doubleday's people. Also I like the way he does business – a quick intelligence, a straight opinion, a mind combining culture with business acumen – something rare amongst publishers.

But I've begun to wonder about M & S. They fell down badly on the sales of *The Nymph* in Canada, although Little Brown made a best seller out of it in the USA and it has sold well in half a dozen other countries. (It has sold, in hardback and softback editions, over 430,000 copies to date, of which M & S sold about 7,000). Compare this with Canadian sales of 11,500 for *Roger Sudden* and over 15,000 for *Pride's Fancy*. It looks to me as if the firm was slipping. When I was in Toronto in '46 Bob Nelson was their top office man, indeed old John was training Bob to take his place, for at that time young Jack showed no signs of wanting to step into his father's shoes. All that has changed, and now Nelson, together with Foster and Scott (the two best salesmen M & S had) have quit and formed a publishing company of their own.[3]

All this makes me wonder about the future prospects of M & S. I have the distinct impression of an old firm gone to seed – perhaps I'm quite wrong. Old John always seemed to me far too interested in the immediate dollar to see much beyond. There has [sic] been various small things that irritated me. For example, whenever someone printed an anthology or a schoolbook containing something of mine previously published by M & S, old John saw to it that M & S retained 50% of the fee. This was quite legal, according to their contract with me; but these sums are always small and it seemed to me a niggardly procedure. Again, M & S tried to cut themselves in for 10% ('agents' fee') of Reader's Digest Book Club royalties on Canadian sales, although the arrangement had been made by Little Brown and M & S had not lifted a finger. I objected strongly and the matter was dropped, but this kind of cheese-paring annoys when I reflect on the feeble effort M & S put behind their own edition of *The Nymph*. It's so easy for them to put out a cautious first edition of a book and then sit back waiting hopefully to see the book become a best-seller on the reflected glamor of the American advertising – and to cut themselves in for a fat half of the subsidiary rights. Lately however young Jack has been sending me various schoolbook, anthology and other subsidiary fees (e.g. for the Canadian TV rights in *Roger Sudden*) paid to M & S for settlement with me, and without deducting the usual pound of flesh. Perhaps he's seen the light.

Here's an amusing sidelight on my visits to Toronto in '46. I was there twice, that summer and autumn, as you know. On both occasions I was entertained several times at George Stewart's[4] home. He is, or was, the hearty hail-fellow-well-met, the back-slapper of the firm. I dislike that type as a rule but I enjoyed old George. The only conversations I had with old John were in the office, where he invariably launched into a diatribe against Doubleday. I was not invited to his home. Foster explained to me diffidently that Mr. M. did not approve of liquor and that Stewart was left to do the personal entertaining *because I drank*. Well, so I do, but I can spend a happy evening without the stuff – I go for weeks without it and never care a damn – and I'd have been quite satisfied to sit down with a glass of milk in old John's home if he had anything interesting to say. My impression was that he'd never had much contact with authors and thought they all wore horns and a tail. Even Foster said to me, at the close of that strenuous speaking tour, 'You know, you're not what we expected. You seem quite normal – for an author.'

Yours, quite normally,
Tom

P.S. If for any reason you don't wish to comment on my query let it go. If I don't hear from you I'll understand.

1 John McClelland (1877–1968) began as an employee of the Methodist Book Room in 1890, opened up a book shop on King Street in 1906, and set up the firm of McClelland and Goodchild later that year.
2 Stanley Salmen (b. 1914) was the American editor with Little, Brown, which published *The Nymph and the Lamp* in New York in 1950 to coincide with McClelland & Stewart's Toronto edition.
3 Nelson, Foster and Scott Ltd was formed in late 1952 and was the representative of the World Publishing Company of Guelph and Isaac Pitman (Canada), and Canadian representative of Abelard Press and Bartholomew House of New York.
4 George Stewart (1876–1955). He came to McClelland and Goodchild in 1914 and replaced Frederick Goodchild when McClelland & Stewart was formed in 1919. Responsible for sales and public relations, Stewart also handled the marketing of Bibles.

---

## To Thomas H. Raddall March 28, 1953

*Confidential*

Dear Tom,

Oddly, I feel far more confident about advising you on the N.Y. end. Between L-B & D, I am sure you are far better off as you are.

It is a case of a class publisher vs a book factory. I had always felt this was the case but I knew it absolutely when D flew six of their top executives up here to consult me about publishing Canadian books. In assessing this market, I told them that Canadian readers 'are only interested in quality writing from their own authors. For the crap and trash, we are quite happy to import it.'

What I said was the truth but their interest in Canada died that second. They politely listened to what else I had to say, asked a few questions; but they have never attempted to attract Canadians as writers. Their big branch here is an outlet for their own American books and it is nothing else. It is a case of mass merchandising and mass selling. They might just as well be selling cordwood or shoes.

The real head here[1] is also a real Canadian and wants to set up a Canadian policy. His second man is dead against it; and I don't think any fight will be put up. Some of the firms here originally moved in as outlets for their parents in other countries and gradually became Canadian in spite of themselves. I think it will happen to all who stay here long enough; but, at 50, you haven't got 20 years to wait.

You, as a quality writer, belong with L-B. No argument.

As to Toronto, no such clear definition is possible. Policies change yearly or even daily. Whether a given firm depends wholly or partly on imports or has a really independent line (is really a publisher) has always depended on whether the head man cared about Canada.

Eayrs[2] did in the 20's and 30's. After his death his firm has shown real interest in its own educational line but now just imports completely made the books of the authors they originally published; and in my opinion they are not aggressive. Similarly Appleton, at a later period made his firm notable for Canadian books, which were pushed and succeeded. But, on his death, the Canadian authors were got rid of.

Now the basic thing here is that a firm that lives as a jobber on the small margins between import costs and wholesale prices (a few cents a copy) creates small men who are not courageous. They are thinking in terms of nickels, want to buy in quantities below what they think they can sell (so as not to be stuck with leftovers) and on that basis they cannot afford promotion work.

I can't give you figures because these birds are secretive. But if their gross profit is running at 10 cents a copy, they cannot afford to use more than 1 cent a copy for advertising. That would buy half a column of space in my paper for a 7,000-copy edition. And my paper is the No. 1 seller of books in Canada. So it's a bad lookout.

I think your last novel got one ad in my paper, not more than two.

The shrewdest operator in Canada at present is Pike of Longmans. He is my biggest advertiser and if he has faith in a book, he manufactures it. Several of his books have won U.S. markets only because he made them successful here first. He made Lower's *Colony to Nation* a best seller. Over 7 or 8 years he has brought a modest living to Jack Hambleton[3] with one boys' book a year – the older ones keep on selling as well as the new ones. Last year he took up an unknown radio woman's *A Mike for Marion*[4] (girls' stuff) and though it wasn't too good, in my opinion, it sold 3,200 in its first three months. Compare that with the 7,000 figure for a wonderful book by an established man. The only snag is (and he would be delighted to have you and would jerk up your sales) is that he is nearing 70 and not well. When he dies, his successors might not have the knowledge, the courage, etc., to carry on his policy. He is himself a great power internationally in his own firm. Afterwards? – God knows, I don't.

Of course Ryerson is now the largest producer of Canadian books; and they are good advertisers. They are wholly Canadian owned and are 124 years old. The *bulk* of their business is Canadian. They have some agencies but those are side-lines. I'm publishing with them myself because of their stability; because they are real Canadians; because they gave me my first chance 30 years ago. Lorne Pierce, the publishing head, is my age – 63 – and he, too, has no successor in sight. However, they will continue in business; and the big end of their business will always continue to be Canadian. I am satisfied with their general record. Financially, they are in an enviable position.

Now, if you want to change, Pierce would snap at you. I have no doubt you could make terms. For example, you might get a clause in the contract that they would spend $1,000 advertising your book within one year of its publication; and if they did I have an idea the book would move smartly in the stores. But you would also require a clear understanding that their investment would be substantial – not a case of importing 500 to 1,000 copies from New York after they got orders.

At the present time, few Canadian novels sell more than 7,000 in Canada; but, with more aggressive methods I think yours should.

I know almost nothing about the new firm. I know the two top lads casually. They are just importers. Since they are set up, they have never advertised anything with me – not once. What I should want to know about them is how long their purse is. That is the snag in publishing. As you go forward, the capital soon gets tied up in inventory. Doran[5] had the best instinct for books of any man of my day. He acquired a startling percentage of the very best British and U.S. authors – but he couldn't finance the tremendous business he mushroomed. D bought him out. These new fellows may do all right, in time; but all they are is travelling salesmen. But nobody should attempt to publish without a tremendous amount of capital. It is no game to start with a few hundred or even a few thousand dollars. I would not dream of starting myself, even in the most modest way imaginable, with less than $100,000. But one to five million would be better.

Old John has been the victim of the evils inherent in the agency business. He began before the first war when conditions were very different, and he has had quite a time adjusting himself. We are not the same type – as you might guess – and locked horns at the very beginning. Of recent years, more cordial relations have existed. We can talk over some of these things some day.

Without knowing any of the figures, I don't think there is the slightest chance of disaster. In 40 years they have accumulated assets. They have weathered bad times and at certain periods have been conspicuously prosperous.

Off-hand, I'd guess young Jack is shrewder than his father, better equipped to be a publisher; and I shouldn't wonder that he will pull things together nicely.

Nobody in the past decade ought to have imagined that the D agency was permanent, because they had dealt through several houses – each for five and never more than six years. Like all other agency people, they tended to be order-takers rather than salesmen; and only original publishers in a restricted sense.

Now that they have forsaken downtown and moved miles east into the sticks, where they have adequate room at what they can well afford to pay, they can rebuild on sounder lines. They certainly do not spend money advertising their books, that's a cinch. In 1951, for the whole year, they advertised on my page 12 times and stood ninth out of 22 publishers in bulk of advertising in my paper. But in 1952, they did better – 16 ads of a total value of $1,400. While this was less than half what Longmans or Ryerson would spend, it was an improvement. In the first three months of this year, I noticed they have cut their spending by half.

There is at least this – whereas Old John is reputed never to have read a book in his life, Jack does. He is reading mss and has ideas about them – right or wrong, he's trying to be a publisher. He is, further, a believer in Canadian books. What kind of internal nonsense he's up against I don't know. Certainly those old agencies never learned much about promotion – regarded advertising as waste. But today it is quite necessary. It should be budgeted for at about 10 cents a copy sold. If $700, even, had been poured into your novel, the score would have been higher.

If you did get a clause about $1,000 to be spent advertising your next book written into any contract, you could only check by providing that copies of the ads were sent you with dates and rates. And you wouldn't really know unless you put in an auditor. I have been told, but do not know it for a fact that $15,000 was spent to force one of Costain's[6] novels up to 15,000 copies in Canada. Between $2,500 and $3,000 was spent in my paper. Of course it was rather wasteful as the spaces used were obviously uneconomic – one full page for example.

What most of these birds have never learned is to be persistent in modest spaces. It is the cumulative effect that counts. $2,500 should be laid out in 33 consecutive weekly ads about 5 inches by two columns wide. That would do considerable business.

Many years ago I met Charlie Jenkins[7] on the street. He said he had just switched from McClelland to Ryerson. I asked: 'Do you think you will be any better off?' He replied: 'No; but my troubles will be different ones and I can't stand the old ones any longer.'

In general, it is not good to switch; but sometimes it is necessary. I can pick you a firm on the basis of today's situation; but it is liable to switch overnight. Right now I would not pick the new firm without knowing much more than I do about their finances. Yet, for all I know, they may be the big shots 10 years hence.

Right now, my choice would be Ryerson or Longmans. In both cases appoints [sic] of new heads is only a matter of a short time. Both firms will go on solidly; but nobody can know who these new men will be. Pike's successor might not be so keen on Canadian books; and, if he were, he might not be as shrewd and adroit as Pike. Ryerson will continue permanently to make Canadian books its chief business; but perhaps the new publishing head may have very different ideas about what kinds of Canadian books he ought to publish and to push.

It would surprise me greatly if Old John is headed for the doghouse. They have more than 40 years behind them. In their early days, so I've heard, they plunged and sometimes lost heavily. It has left them with a high degree of caution. They have done a sensible thing in moving – 20 years too late. They have some good agencies; they have some good Canadian authors. Of all the publishers who spoke in London last June, Jack was the only one to say emphatically that he could publish Canadian books profitably.

Ryerson and Copp Clark are Canadian firms, Canadian owned and making Canadian books their chief business. It makes a difference. Copp Clark is mainly educational – one Canadian novel that I remember. It may be that the new editor, Claude Lewis, will be braver than Jeanneret[8] in going after Canadian trade books. I don't know. Both of these firms are more than sound financially. They are rich.

But the niggardliness of Canadian publishers in general about advertising and other matters rises out of the fact that, for 50 years, publishing has been a starvling trade in Canada, owing to a limited market. Remove the French, the children under 16, the insane, the criminals, the poverty-stricken, etc., and the number of potential buyers is still small. That aggregate is growing; but so are the titles offered annually in the English langage. Canadians are asked to buy all the British books, all the American and all the Canadian. That is not true of any other country on earth. English and Americans only read a minority of each other's books.

Nobody has ever made a fortune out of Canadian publishing.

Only in recent years have Canadian books really been in demand; and still there is a limit. Bruce Hutchison's *The Incredible Canadian* ($5) was planned by Pike to sell 10,000 between October and Christmas. It was generously advertised with the result that it sold 13,000 copies in Canada by the end of the year. On the strength of the Canadian success, New York brought it out in February from Canadian plates. Pike goes forward independently here and estimates his sale in the first 12 months at anywhere from 25,000 to 40,000 copies.

Interest, of course, is predominantly Canadian. I cite this case to indicate that it is not necessarily overflow American publicity that sells Canadian books in Canada. All Callaghan's and Mazo's early books were published originally in Canada.

I don't know your contractual position – whether you have an independent Canadian contract binding you to anybody, nor whether you are under option for future books. You will know that.

If you are free to switch, you certainly have bargaining power; and my suggestion would be that you use it to ensure more money spent on promotion rather than higher royalties. The promotion has been the weak point. There are only 25 good bookstores in all Canada; and these are the targets of the travelling salesmen. But everywhere there exist readers and potential readers, who can be reached by newspapers.

We are in a happy position with a 250,000 circulation covering Ontario, since this province has 75% of all libraries in Canada, and a still greater proportion of volumes on library shelves. This means Toronto metropolitan area of 1,200,000 and a tributary population of around 4,000,000 in the province; and this is the area in which people read books. All these free libraries buy great quantities of books and in those places are the people who like to read books and can afford to buy them. We estimate 50,000 readers of the book page every Saturday morning – penetrating all these towns. Last summer an author friend of mine, driving around on holiday, enquired in several small places how the local library chose its books and how what passed for a book-store selected its stock. In every case the answer was *The Globe and Mail* was the only source of information since it did not pay travellers to visit those little towns.

Consequently we get the bulk of book advertising; but our revenues from this source amount to 50% of our costs of running this department. The trade has never yielded enough support to enable us to meet expenses on operations at their present scale, let alone enough to warrant us into expanding the department to the size necessary to give readers a reasonably comprehensive service.

Now, if you wish to do me a kindness, just destroy this letter; and don't pass on any of this information to anybody. It might be very bad for me to be on the record.

I haven't answered your questions. Nobody can; but between knowing and guessing, I've tried to make the situation clearer.

Yours –

1 George Nelson remained in charge of Doubleday Canada until his retirement in the late 1970s; his anthology of Canadian writing, *Cavalcade of the North* (1958), was published by that firm. Nelson was Vice-President of Doubleday Canada at this time.

2 Hugh Smithurst Eayrs (1894–1940) was born in England and sent to Toronto in 1912 by the Macmillan Company. He became President of Macmillan Canada in 1921 and from then until his death, he was, with Pierce, one of the two most powerful and well-known figures in Canadian publishing.

3 Jack Hambleton (1900–60), Toronto journalist and author of juvenile adventure

stories, many of them set in the Canadian North, such as *Forest Ranger* (1948), *Young Bush Pilot* (1949), and *Fire in the Valley* (1960).

4 The CBC commentator June Dennis was the author of this story for juveniles about broadcasting, which was published by Longmans in 1952.

5 George Henry Doran (1869–1956), famous Canadian-born publisher who became Vice-President of the Chicago-based religious publishing house Fleming H. Revell, which published, among others, the early bestselling novels of Ralph Connor. In 1908, Doran founded Doran and Company, which published Connor and others, and in 1927 merged with Doubleday and Page to become Doubleday Doran. His autobiography, *Chronicles of Barrabas*, was published in 1934.

6 Thomas Bertram Costain (1885–1965), best-selling, Canadian-born novelist whose books of popular history and historical fiction brought him financial success in the United States. He began his writing career as a journalist-editor with *The Saturday Evening Post* and eventually worked as an editor for Doubleday.

7 Charles Christopher Jenkins (1882–1943), Toronto journalist and author who joined *The Globe* in 1922, stayed on with the amalgamated *Globe and Mail* in 1936, variously serving in both as day editor, literary editor, and editor of the 'Bystander' column. His romantic novels are *The Timber Pirate* (1922), which deals with the pulp and paper industry in northwestern Ontario, and *The Reign of Brass: A Romance of Two Epochs* (1927), a story of love before and after World War I.

8 Deacon would get to know Claude E. Lewis (d. 1965) as president, Toronto branch CAA (1955–7). Marsh Jeanneret (b. 1917) had just resigned as Director of Copp Clark to become Director of the University of Toronto Press, a position he held until 1977.

---

## To Gabrielle Roy March 3, 1954

Ma chere Gabrielle (comme ca?) [sic]

The thrill of the day and many days is receipt of your new novel, *Alexandre Chenevert*. It is not lost on me that this is No. 23 of the limited de luxe edition. Your insciption is treasured, not only because you are a dear friend but so famous a writer. Germaine Guevremont is all taken up with her radio serial;[1] and thank God she is making real money out of it – because she needs it. MacLennan has got weary of being an artist in words and is teaching at McGill and busy with radio and journalism.

That leaves you and Tom Raddall (don't miss his *Tidefall* and *The Nymph and the Lamp*) as the two ranking Canadian novelists. I admire Tom's strength of conception and performance; but I think you are the subtle and artistic [one]. This is partly because your medium is French, and partly because you are a woman. Your deep understanding and sympathy always touches the hearts of your readers.

It is no small thing to be the leading Canadian writer of your generation. You will look back, 25 or 30 years hence, with great pride on your achievement. Because Canadian books are finding their way around the world and your appreciative circle of readers will widen all the days of your life. Congratulations.

This new novel cements your position perfectly. Therefore I wish to take care with it. I am sampling your lucid French; but shall really read the English translation because my audience consists of English readers.[2] Comprenez? No use giving them my reactions to a French version, which they will not even see.

Now when is the English translation coming? As *Alexandre Chenevert* is not mentioned in the McClelland & Stewart spring catalogue, I presume the New York version will be published this autumn? Vrai?

Next. What am I to do for a picture? I have now used up all the shots taken in this house, depuis huit ans. I want something that is worth two columns. It can be a studio portrait. If anybody has painted your portrait yet, perhaps a photograph (glossy) of that would be suitable. Contact prints of snap-shots are unsatisfactory for coarse screen engravings for our high-speed presses. So, if there is a specially good snap-shot you would like to use – peutetre avec action – please have it enlarged to a glossy print 8 x 10 inches. By that means details lost in the contact print come out and can be seen when our engravers reduce it again on the plate.

Quelquefois, je pense of your contract by which you were to receive $13,000 a year for 10 years. I have always been glad that this covered the period of your illness, also life in France and the post-graduate work of Marcel in Paris, and his establishment in the Quebec hospital. Now you are starting to earn again. I think you will always have plenty of money for the rest of your life. That comforts me.

*Maclean's Magazine*, 481 University Ave., Toronto (Editor, Ralph Allen)[3] is now paying $5,000 for serial rights for a Canadian novel, if they have first publication. Of course it would be condensed to about one-third of full size; and you might not like that. This would be equivalent to 40 a copy on 12,500 copies of the book sold in Canada. It would certainly reduce the book circulation here by the number of magazine readers; but it would gain readers, also –

people who heard about the book through the magazine.

I have no advice for you, whether you should do it. I think Ralph Allen would be glad to have it, though of course I have not spoken to him. One serious aspect is that *Maclean's* would probably wish to begin this fall, and that would delay New York publication of the book until the spring of 1955.

There is no harm in asking Allen over what period he would run the story, if he accepted it. I don't know what he has ahead.

Pour moi, Madame, a pension scheme was adopted by my paper Jan. 1. I am to retire May 1, 1960, when I shall be 70. The allowance is not large; but enough for us to live in careful comfort. Besides, I shall be *free* at last to write my own books. They will make hardly any money but I shall have a lot of fun writing them. Meanwhile – this is the *joke* – in preparation for retirement, I have to pay into the fund, pay off the last of the mortgage on this house, etc. etc. So, right now, more than half my salary is being invested in preparations for retirement. I tell Sally: 'We must be voluntarily poor for the next six years so that we can be poor for the rest of our lives after that.' Actually, we are not suffering now and shall suffer less after retirement because, of course, how much I then earn depends only on how lazy I am. (Et, vraiment, mon ami, I get lazier every day.)

With warm, tender regards to Marcel and you, whom we hold in firm affection,

Ever –

P.S. Don't take the economic plight seriously. When we began we were poor, naturally, because Canada didn't know it needed book reviews. The children came – 1, 2, 3 – followed almost at once by the depression. It seemed like quite a struggle at the time. As in your *Bonheur d'occasion*, the war helped us. My salary has been comfortable for some years. Besides (a secret pour vous) when I lately suggested to one of my bosses that my pension would only be one-third of my present salary, he said not to worry. From here, I shall be looked after – as in sickness – and if the pension is too small the paper will add to it. Really, I don't want that. I want to be free, not under obligations.

Do you remember my daughter Mary, who was just finishing her training as a nurse when you were here? In 1949 she went to Berkeley, California, where Sally's sister lives and her son, a doctor. Mary nursed in a hospital, latterly attending University of California in the daytime, nursing at night. Then she won a valuable scholarship. She gets her bachelor of science this June, and will enter public health nursing for the State of California at quite a handsome salary for a single girl of 28. She likes her independence, is so pretty she has many admirers and doesn't marry.

Sally calls out to be *sure* to say she sends her love and hopes you are quite *well* now. I do, too, of course –

1 From 1952 to 1954 Germaine Guèvremont adapted for radio her two novels, *Le Survenant* (1945) and *Marie Didace* (1947); the series then was serialized for television and lasted until 1960.
2 *The Cashier,* the translation by Henry Binsse (b. 1905) of *Alexandre Chenevert,* was published in 1955 by McClelland & Stewart and by Harcourt, Brace. Binsse translated three other books by Roy: *Where Nests the Water Hen* (1951), *Street of Riches* (1957), and *The Hidden Mountain* (1962).
3 Allen (1913–66) had been a staff member of *The Globe and Mail* who became managing editor of *Maclean's* and subsequently of *The Toronto Star.*

---

## From Gabrielle Roy March 16, 1954

Dear Bill,

Your letter made me very happy, and specially that you should explain so naturally, with such friendly truthfulness how you are setting about to retire and write as you please. With all my heart, I hope for the realization of your modest, so wise desires!

I think that you are absolutely right in waiting, to write about *Alexandre Chenevert* in your paper, that this book comes out in English. But when will that be! I begin to foresee endless delays as my translator, Mr. Binsse, is I'm afraid, a terrible procrastinator. Harcourt, Brace are worried, I think. They had hoped to bring out the book this coming April, but it certainly won't be ready. However, let's hope for the best!

The first write-ups about *Alexandre* have come out in the French press and it is just as I expected: they understand nothing. My dear Bill, I begin to see that this chord I'm always trying to touch – this theme of human love regardless of nationality, of religion, of tongue, this essential truth doesn't mean much to my people and although I know the necessity of patience, I'm a little sick at heart, sometimes. How can people be so blind to the one truth we should learn as we live, the one truth that matters!

Marcel and I send our love to dear Sally, to yourself and all your family. Good luck indeed in all your projects.

Gabrielle

Appt. 708
305 Grande Allée
Québec, P.Q.

---

## From Constance Beresford-Howe

4137 Oxford Avenue
Montreal
May 30, 1955

Dear Mr. Deacon,

When my new novel, *My Lady Greensleeves*, was published last month, I looked forward with special interest to the reviews, because it was something of an experiment – an escape from the tired old formula of the historical novel – and because it took me so many painful years of research to complete the work. I was especially eager to see *your* opinion, because you've been more perceptive and penetrating by far than any other Canadian critic, in your reviews of my other books.

I have no clipping service, and so have not seen any review yet from *The Globe and Mail*. I wonder if you could tell me whether any has yet appeared, and if so, if you'd do me the favour of sending me a clipping of it? The book was published April 19th, and has by now been reviewed in most, if not all, of the other major papers of eastern Canada. (*The Toronto Telegram* for instance delighted me by calling the book 'torrid'!)

Ballantine Books, the publishers in New York, report that the first edition is sold out, and plan to issue a paperback edition in September – earlier than first scheduled, to take advantage of the favourable review reaction here and in the U.S.

If you've read the book, I'd be keenly interested to hear your reactions to it, whether officially in print, or privately. It seems ages since I saw you. Are you ever in Montreal? Or are you planning by any chance to attend the Canadian Authors' convention in Kingston next month?

Hoping to hear from you soon, and with thanks in advance for your trouble.

Cordially,
Connie Beresford-Howe

---

## To Constance Beresford-Howe

June 22, 1955

Dear Miss Beresford-Howe,

For 30 years I read every newly published Canadian book of general literature, and was the only person on the planet to do so; but Canadian literary productivity has finally defeated me. In 1922 there were 5 or 6 Canadian novels a year, including 1 or 2 good or interesting ones. The number has risen steadily till, in 1954, there were 28 novels, of which I was able to read 18. A still more numerous division is the juvenile book, which rose from zero in 1945 till it greatly outnumbered the adult novel. History, which used to be sparse, is now frequent. Biography and personal narratives, once almost non-existent, have become quite important. Verse alone has declined in published bulk, thanks to the growing contempt of poets for readers. It used to be most popular. Till the 1930's, popular demand for Pauline Johnson's *Flint and Feather* exhausted a 2,500 edition annually. For many years it has been unobtainable.

There are now 30,000 new titles in the English language yearly. In our space, which has not increased in 20 years, we are able to review one in 200. And that is only by tight writing which increased the number of reviews by 50% of titles. Beyond this space economy we cannot go without damage to the adequacy of our comments.

As matters stand, one-quarter of the titles, one-third of our space is devoted to books by Canadians, which shows national bias beyond theoretical defence. Beyond this I cannot go. The result is that, increasingly, I must ignore an increasing proportion of Canadian books. Similarly, established British and American authors. My failure to read your current novel puts you in the class of Mazo de la Roche (the most successful writer of all time and my personal friend), J.B. Priestly, Compton MacKenzie, John Steinbeck, William Faulkner. *My Lady Greensleeves* is to be reviewed, not by me but by a contributing reviewer on request.

Personally, I wish you had remained Canadian in subject matter. I am still moved by your Montreal backgrounds. I was a child in Chambly, grew up in Stanstead. Increasingly, Canadian readers like the native scenes. Of course, writers must write about what they prefer and what they think will gain widest circulation.

Congratulations on the popularity of *Greensleeves*. Too bad the pay for paperbacks is so low.

Our production costs run to 10¢ a word; and sale of the copies at 5 leaves a gap that must be met by advertising revenues. The book trade is a starvling industry – 3% for a successful publisher, 1/2 of 1% for a good bookseller. Hence book advertising is relatively light and my department runs at about 50% loss. That's why we cannot command more space to review more books. We are able to review one book out of every 200 published in the English language – of Canadian books possibly half. I devote one-third of my annual space to comment on Canadian books – 25% of the titles we discuss are Canadian. That is generous representation for Canada as things stand.

There is no author on earth whose every book we can review. By no means every Steinbeck, Compton MacKenzie, Thomas Mann, Mazo de la Roche. We didn't review the last W.H. Auden. Why then do you think you have a right to expect us to review every Beresford-Howe? We have to be selective – even at the cost of leaving out some first rates. Doris Hedges[1] complained to the editor-in-chief that I had reviewed her first four books but had ignored her fifth. I replied that if she had scored 80% she had got more than her share. Even *The N.Y. Times*, in which I began, and which is the most comprehensive book medium on earth, is by no means able to [review] every new book in the U.S. – far from it, and they sometimes run to 96 pages in the book section.

The Canadian writer has a far better chance than anybody else in my dept; but not 100%. It's impossible.

Sincerely,

1 Author's agent and writer (b. 1900) published by Ryerson. The first four books reviewed by Deacon would have been her poetry *The Flower in the Dusk* (1946)

and *Words on a Page* (1948), and her two novels *Dumb Spirit* (1952) and *Elixir* (1953). The fifth book, which Deacon did not review, presumably was *The Dream Is Certain* (1954), another collection of poems.

---

## From Gabrielle Roy

Quebec
October 30, 1955

Dear Bill,

Although, I can't see how I remind you so much of Flaubert who was a very determined novelist leading his characters by the hand and just where he wished them to go – whereas I like to follow them wherever they decide to go and try to wait for them to reveal themselves to me – in spite of this comparison, my dear Bill, I do like your study of *The Cashier* very much, and I thank you for it most sincerely.[1]

I specially thank you for this sentence: ... 'which finally show the reader that Chenevert invariably did the best he could in his cruelly limiting circumstances.'

If we understood others fully, completely, we would seldom judge or condemn, would we not? Such is the vocation of the novelist, it seems to me; to plead for better and better understanding. In any case you have well understood the strange little man. And about myself you write lovely things which I would like to deserve, indeed.

How is Sally? The children and grand-children? I would dearly love to see you all again.

As you probably know *La Petite Poule d'Eau* has been accepted as a text book by the Board of Education of Ontario.

What a lovely triumph! I think that, in the beginning, you labored and worked towards this achievement, and I'm happy to express my gratitude to you for those efforts which maybe started the ball rolling.

Yours sincerely
Gabrielle

135, ouest, Grande Allée
Appt. 708
Quebec, P.Q.

1 'The Art of Gabrielle Roy' (*The Globe and Mail*, 29 October 1955) stated that 'as

implied social criticism, *The Cashier* is devastating; as literature, it is a beautiful work of art.' Deacon, like other reviewers, once again compared Roy to Flaubert, 'because of the delicate accuracy of presentation,' her precise language, and her deep understanding of her characters.

---

## To Gabrielle Roy    November 2, 1955

Very dear Gabrielle,

I have been wanting to write to you because I heard Marcel was seriously ill – pneumonia. Since you don't mention him I assume he is out of danger. Give him our sympathy and regards.

The heavy pre-Christmas season is on us; we're old now and it is impossible to write to you at length as I should like to do. Thanks for news of *The Little Water Hen*.

We won't argue about Flaubert. Let's say that you are both great, conscious literary artists. As such, every word counts and the scenes are so well etched that they remain clear in the mind for *years* – both of you.

As artist, you are my choice as the ranking Canadian novelist but I hope you will read Charles Bruce's *The Channel Shore*.

Comparison is difficult because each of you is trying to do something entirely different. Mazo at her best is wonderful. Raddall, especially in *The Nymph and the Lamp* and in *Tidefall*, gives us the sea as a sailor who knows it and this is strong stuff. Then there is Germaine. Together with two or three others, you people are establishing the novel in Canada not only as an art form but as a real force.

You have heart qualities above all the others. This is very important because, finally and inescapably, every writer records his or her own portrait on the printed page, no matter how objective a story is.

The current *Maclean's* has a feature article on St. Boniface that I hope you will like. Scott Young mentions you – briefly but in obvious respect amounting, I think, to awe.[1]

If I hadn't known you so well and liked you so much it would have been easier to review *Chenevert*.

We are anxious to know whether you fully recovered your health. That is important.

Love from Sally & me to you both (wish so much for a visit).

1 'St Boniface Is Nobody's Suburb' by Scott Young (b. 1918), journalist, sports commentator, and short story writer, appeared in the 12 November 1955 issue of *Maclean's Magazine*. A history and local colour sketch, it mentions famous Canadians associated with the town, such as Louis Riel and Gabrielle Roy.

---

## From Gabrielle Roy

Quebec
November 4, 1955

Dear Bill,

I should have told you that Marcel is now quite well, much better. This summer he was quite ill, suddenly. I had to come back from Paris in a hurry. He took two months' rest, and now he has resumed his activities, and all he needs is not to overdo things. Thanks for your concern. Thank you for your dear letter.

I know how you feel: it is difficult, is it not, to speak about one we know quite well and like? How I love to think that you like me that well.

My best to you all.

Gabrielle

---

## From James Gillis

Alderwood House
Beddeck, Victoria Co.
N. Scotia
September 7, 1956

Wm. A. Deacon Esq.
Writer & Pub'r.
*Globe & Mail*
Toronto.

D. Sir: –

Mr. Bert McLeod of Sydney has made me a Present of a copy of *The Four Jameses*, which I do read with pleasure. Kenneth Leslie,[1] (at least at one time) a resident of Granville, N.S. told me of this BK., years ago. But for the fact that I knew Ken & his brother Robert

I wouldn't believe his news or remember it. Later, once in a while I'd hear of the Book and had a mind to buy one but the time slipped – until this week.

I wonder at how you penetrated my mind when writing the Sketch of Angus McAskill's Life.[2] Such visualizing is very difficult & subtile – & many attempt this without success or results. I congratulate you on your power of *Concentration* – & shall be ever grateful to you for condescending to recognize me, & we, 4. Indeed Mr. Gay[3] I judge to have been a Poet by Nature.

Yours *&* c.,
James D. Gillis

*Inter nos*

I was thinking of writing up a comparison between the present & 60 or 70 years ago. One little story, I thought I'd include was the following which illustrates there were then some able sch. Teachers & bluff assertive farmers. ——————————

A Mr ____ remitted £3.d to Halifax for a Grant of 200 Acres of Land *to the Engineer* at Halifax. But the applicant waited & waited & wrote & wrote but no Grant. He spoke to the Teacher, Malcolm MacLellan, a Graduate of Kirkcudbright Academy, Scotland. (This Academy was backed by the Masonic Society) 'Malcolm' said I have no *idea* of Statute Law but my brother, John, I hear, writes letters for persons in legal troubles. – I don't know whether he has special knowledge or gift or what, – & this may be a *harmless* defect in my brother – but he writes such letters. Not long after the teacher came to Mr ____'s house & they saw John passing on foot with his coat on his back. They called to him & he came in, & Malcolm told John about the errant [sic]. John listened intently, & betimes sniffed & snorted. This meant that he was amused. – He wouldn't laugh 'out.'

Well said John to Malcolm you sit down & I'll tell you what to write, & you may polish or correct. The letter was sent. Down came the Grant with warm blue & red large seals like a circular saw.

After some years, the Engineer came down. 'Who wrote the last letter for the Grant?' he asked. The grantee replied 'I wrote it myself.' The engineer was irate and said only that my question was careless & defective, I would arrest you, I should have asked in what University the man passed? Only for that, I wouldn't let such a foul lie go unpunished.

1 Journalist and poet (1892–1974) born in Pictou, Nova Scotia. He became editor of the New York *Protestant* and won the Governor-General's Poetry Award for *By Stubborn Stars and Other Poems* (1938).
2 A wonder of height (7'9") and strength, MacAskill (1825–63) became an international attraction with P.T. Barnum. Known as 'The Cape Breton Giant,' he was the subject of Gillis's book by that title.
3 James Gay (1810–91), self-proclaimed 'Poet Laureate of Canada and Master of All Poets,' lived in Guelph, Ontario, and was one of the subjects of *The Four Jameses*.

---

## From Lorne Pierce

'South Ridge' #309
49 Glen Elm Avenue
Toronto
December 15, 1956

My dear Bill:

This morning, as on so many week-end mornings, I rolled out of bed, had a quick cup of coffee, and in pajamas and bath-robe stretched out to read your pages.

I want to tell you this morning, as I have so often wanted to say, how magnificent your service to letters in Canada, and to Canadian letters, has been this long generation. The work of planning the pages during the past weeks, and executing them, is enormous. The routine weekly pages, and the numerous specials, demand a physical stamina few could command, while the other and continuous expenditures make a man old.

You have been very kind and helpful to Ryerson. This morning I was especially thankful to you for giving Bruchési a top placing in spite of his late arrival. The Paris publishers were impossibly slow. However it is an attractive book, and, as you point out, the French Canadian point of view is well worth understanding.

I would like to think of some souvenir that you would like, that would remind you of our long association. Before long I shall be out of a job no doubt, and my association with you will no longer be that of critic and editor but critic and long-time subscriber. If you can think of something you would like as an old colleague will you not be candid and let me know?

My very best to Sally and you.

Lorne

## To Lorne Pierce

January 8, 1957

Dear Lorne,

Your typically kind letter did not cause my ego to inflate and burst because I feel it founded on a set of misapprehensions; and these I tried to state logically in long epistles I wrote you on Dec. 21 and 26. Neither satisfied me so here I am again with a final try.[1]

I do appreciate your considerate regard for me – based on wholly wrong premises. As I understand it, your thought was: Poor old Bill, working his guts out, thinking of everybody except himself, getting old and tired and infirm and lonely and discouraged, with no honors, only dark thoughts of soon struggling over the hill to the Poor House. What can we do for Bill to lighten his discouragement?

Oh, Lorne, it is so wrong! I'm the happy man – as near as may be to complete human happiness and satisfaction with my lot.

Of course I work like a horse; and, not being very bright, I have to work longer and harder than better endowed men. But I LOVE my chosen work; and love is not conspicuous among the causes of death.

First, you must remember that nobody asked me to be a writer; that was my own idea. Nobody compelled me to slavery in the galleys. I desired it and my many wise friends of 36 years ago did their utmost to dissuade me from being such a fool; for I was doing well as a young lawyer in the biggest and best firm in Manitoba.[2] My Mother died at 86 mourning my wasted life; she wanted me to duplicate my father's brilliant career in law – and I couldn't. In me too much love of books from my Welsh grandfather Davies, the printer turned Wesleyan missionary to Canada, too much of my great-grandfather John Smith, captain and ship-owner out of Liverpool, who regarded a storm or mutiny as a welcome opportunity to exercise his skill in handling a ship. When he picked up a marlin spike and knocked the six members of the press gang off his deck, the judge said: 'Any captain who can do this to six men is entitled to his crew. Case dismissed.'

Law was in the blood also: I inherit from judges and the like but could not stand the life for specific reasons. In the humbler but very profitable branch of office work – wills, mortgages etc – there was fearful monotony because meanings of words and phrases had been fixed by 1,000 years of court decisions. The clause for 'quiet enjoyment' in your lease has back of it a whole library of definition, so it is now exact; and those words must be used and none other. Boring, I calls it.

On the other side there is pleading. I don't think fast enough for court work; but I could have learned if I had been able to read cases every night. What irked me was the hair-splitting, worse than theologians of the Middle Ages. Some slight, insignificant word or phrase or circumstance, invoking the famous decision of Hodges vs the Queen, and what Jones, J., said in another case in 1882 etc, etc. Hell! man; it was bloody nonsense. I had no respect for it. There was nothing of humanity in it. Never were truer words said than 'The Law is an ass.'

So I was reading poetry, essays, novels, biography, etc; and I was stupid enough to send a review to *N.Y. Times*. They printed it and sent me a cheque. For the four years after my graduation I was slipping out of law into literature. All writing on the side and at first only for New York papers; but Dafoe discovered me and I was T.B. Roberton's assistant. He taught me and told me to go East. Sandwell, for whom I had written, told Paul of *Saturday Night* to hire me. You know the rest. I took the one chance in a thousand. THANK GOD I DID!

Of course, as you say or imply, my job is a humble one. Like all middlemen, I perform a necessary service. I am paid for it but the money is secondary. I am doing the work I feel I am fitted for; and it takes all the brains I have and all the knowledge I've acquired in the nearly 40 years I've been at it, as amateur and pro. Luckily, I came in when Canada could use a guy like me.

Never get the idea that I'm a frustrated poet or envious of successful novelists. What I do takes all the skill I have. Don't imagine some great genius has been wasted. Reviewing demands all my powers; and I'm grateful to have found my right place, doubly grateful that men like you think my product good enough for the time and place.

Don't imagine I suffer from lack of appreciation. From time to time I am surprised to receive compliments. Happily, I don't get a swelled head because I can't take much time out to gloat because xxx has made flattering remarks. I have had all the evidence of approval it is healthy for a fellow to receive – more than I deserve by a ton.

I am a proud man, hence grateful to the gods that I have only worked for top papers. (Nobody else would have me for a gift.) But it is a deep satisfaction that, when I approach a stranger with: 'I'm Deacon of *The Globe*,' I get instant, respectful attention, not a snarl. Even among the French of Montreal, I hear them say: 'That's a *Globe and Mail* man'; and it evidently means something.

What man could be happier in his home and family life?

Money? Of course in early years there wasn't much. Nobody had any experience of what to pay an industrious reviewer; but that has all changed. I'm among the higher rather than lower paid staff writers. I have no real doubt that my pension will be adequate.

That eliminates everything except the honors business and I'm too old to get any satisfaction out of mere vanity. You spoke once of trying to wangle me into the Royal Society. Please desist. I am now getting out of all organizations and embroilments. I don't need it for prestige; its only function would be an extra line in the obit.

So, my dear and thoughtful friend, we reach the conclusion that there isn't anything in particular that you can do for me. I come from folk of great stamina. My youngest uncle died last year at 92. Of course I'm tired now, not so resilient; but I'm due for retirement in three years at 70; and I shall last because I hire more work done, try to do less myself.

I've been more successful than I ever dreamed I would be and I still love my work.

Now I'm going to use a bad metaphor. Dreiser opened the last paragraph of *Jenny Gerhardt* with the sentence: 'Shall you say to the full-blown rose, 'well done'?' Now as the mother said to the teacher: 'My boy Bill ain't no rose; larn him, don't smell him.' It is true that I'm no rose; but I'm full blown, all right. I suppose it would be more exciting if I were yearning for something I haven't got; but I can't imagine what it would be. So the (to me) most wonderful career imaginable is drawing slowly and peacefully to its close; and I think I'm the luckiest fellow in the whole world.

There hasn't been time for social life; but friendships have been rich and valued – by no means least valued yours.

Good luck my friend. Thanks for thinking of me so warmly and generously.

1 Deacon did not send these, but kept copies for his files.
2 From 1917 to 1922, Deacon worked for the Winnipeg law firm of Pitblado, Hoskin.

---

## From James D. Gillis

Alderwood R. Home
Beddeck, Nova Scotia
May 1957

D. Sir:

I appreciate the magazine, newsp. & the Note you sent.[1] I am grateful to you & to Mr. Robbins,[2] the editor of the forthcoming Cyclo'dia.

I am mailing you a copy of three of my efforts, and I'm sorry I haven't a copy of *The Great Election*. In the latter there was one Lyric (Air: Green grow the Rushes O) which with 'Bonnie Birdie' to the tune 'Daintie Davie.' I believe 'Daintie or Daenty Davie' is an old tune. In the Highlands it was long known as 'Sud an ga l a bhagad rm &c.' i.e. 'Such was the love thou had'st for me: – the crave for sleep – the warmth of the blankets – That was your love & it's now evaporated.' But *re* the Lyric & B. Birdie, I judge it & them the best of my 'poetries.'

Before Burns' time there was a song in Broad Scotch or English beginning 'Being pursued by the Dragoons' &c. &c. to that tune.

Perhaps, if you see Mr. Robbins, it might be appropriate to show or give him those books with my sincere thanks for his condescension.

I wish him success in his heavy undertaking. It must have been a ponderous task to collect, collate & arrange & present to the people in readable style, as it were, a Dictionary of our past, present & future requirements. – There is much Knowledge today, but unfortunately much of it is not set before the young or adults in an understandable manner. For instance 'Graphs' in Algebra &c. illustrated by misleading & inaccurate prints or drawings, are a useless fake. No subject is hard, if logically taught. People don't expend on Schools to read riddles or puzzles or to spend years on negative equations.

Thanking you again & your friend, Mr. Robbins, I am, yours &c.

James D. Gillis

1 Deacon's note has not survived.

2 John Everett Robbins (b. 1903), editor-in-chief (1952–60) of the *Encyclopedia Canadiana*, the first edition of which appeared in 1957

---

## To Mazo de la Roche May 14, 1957

Dear Mazo,

How kind of you to write! But you should not have done it when suffering such pain. We all missed you last Friday at the branch annual dinner; and Claude Lewis spoke so warmly of you.

I think our Weekly is nice; but its toll in labor is much more than outsiders could guess.[1] I could not stand the hours some of the younger men put in – say from 10:30 a.m. till 4:30 a.m. Even so, I had to work approx 10 hours a day for 21 consecutive days, and have just taken my first Saturday and Sunday off. And I am so busy editing my contributors' reviews that I have almost ceased to be a writer. (Maybe that's for the best, at that.)

From a reader's standpoint, *Ringing the Changes* was weak on references to the calendar. Sometimes you state your then age, and naming events helps older people like me to judge when things happened; but sometimes chronology was very vague. There was the prize you tried for at nine. Other matters intervened and then, on page 96: 'I was so very young, so ignorant. I am sure that most twelve-year-olds of to-day are more knowledgeable than I was at that time.

In secrecy then the story was finished. In secrecy it was posted to *Munsey's Magazine* ...'

Interpretation depends on what you mean by 'at that time.' Eighteen is precocious for writing adult short stories; but the logic of the thing seemed to me: 'most 12–year-olds today are more knowledgable than I was at 12 years of age.' My credulity was stretched but the best I could make of it was that you, at 12, were unsophisticated. And in the next sentence you have sent the story; within 8 printed lines you have sold it for $50.

On page 238 you say: 'on the twentieth of May we sailed from Southhampton.' You do not state the year.

You are without the journalist's training in pinning facts down concretely. Your publisher's editor must have noted lack of clear definition of time periods. But you are so famous he probably didn't like to suggest that some readers would wish you had been more specific.

Because you and your career are going to be studied in the future, it might be a good idea if you annotated *Ringing the Changes* by jotting dates in the margins. Or Caroline might, and your children could be custodians.

With love to you both from us both –

1 On 4 May 1957 the regular Saturday *Globe and Mail* expanded to an eight-section edition called 'The Weekly,' which began appearing every Saturday.

---

## To Lorne Pierce

September 10, 1959

Dear Lorne,

My apologies for not writing my thanks earlier for the luncheon. It was kind of you to introduce me to Dr. Grant.[1]

Everybody is asking me questions about Graphic, about the workings of which I do not know much. My life has been too busy reading and writing to keep files. Of recent years when my desk gets too smothered with papers Sally just brushes them off into waste baskets and I begin afresh.

I have no catalogue but my memory is that Graphic during 7 years published 98 titles, of which the top 14 were important additions to Can. lit; the bottom 14 were just waste of paper; the others just middling. Percy Gomery's *The Red Circle* is, I think, the worst Canadian book I ever read.[2]

I had no contract with Grove at that time but can tell you the tale of *My Search for America*. That summer [1926] I spent my vacation in Pratt's cottage at Bobcaygeon. Art and Lal Phelps were next door in their cottage. Art had this cart-load of ms. with him and was bound I should read it. I declined to spend my two weeks of freedom reading any ms – always hate reading ms. We compromised. I was to sit one evening before Phelps's fire while he read aloud one single chapter. I sat, smoked, listened. Art tried to cheat by reading a second chapter; but I stopped him. I wanted to talk and swap intelligence with Art.

He said: 'You don't understand. This man is desperate. Can't get a publisher anywhere; and I think this novel worthy of print.'

'Ease up,' I said. 'I don't have to swallow the whole thousand pages to recognize quality. This is good stuff; and I'll get you a publisher. Just leave everything to me.'

That shut Art up; and we got on to other items on the agenda. But he had to get Grove's permission to let me have possession of the script. He and Watson Kirkconnell had a hell of a battle with Grove getting permission to express me the ms. I don't know what argument Art used. Grove was a miserable man to get on with. But I did get the ms. I wrote Miller[3] a letter as short as the shortest sentence in the Bible: 'Jesus wept.' I said: 'Publish this.'

He did and you know the rest. Grove, the conceited, ungrateful bastard never wrote me the one word 'thanks' for getting him into print. Nor, when I met him years later, did he ever mention it.

You know me too well to imagine I wanted thanks. My business is to see that the right books are published and I've been midwife to a good many. Then my business is to see they are properly presented to the reading public. I just mention this lack of manners because that surly fellow was no good as a human being – for all his self-pity.

I never heard of Miller's wish to continue to publish Grove's other books, though *In Search of America* was financially successful. I can well imagine Hugh's [Eayrs] attempt to take a successful author away from another publisher. Grove would have done better to stay with Miller, who was a bright lad.

I have no idea who made the editorial decisions. I saw Miller in Ottawa once only; and he called me at my Toronto [office] once only.

Jim Pedley is a veteran officer of the First World War, the laziest man I ever knew. If still living, he will be found living somewhere around Belleville, perhaps as far east as Kingston. Haven't seen him in 20 years.

I knew his uncle, a Congregational minister [and] was at school with his cousin Hilton Pedley. The Pedleys who came from around Montreal were very clever, charming, allergic to hard work.

Jim was a young lawyer, who graduated at Osgoode just before leaving for overseas or just after he got back. He had desk space at $5 a month at 85 Richmond St. West; and his practice was too small to matter. Luck rode on his shoulder. An aunt died and left him a small legacy – say $1,500 or $4,500 or something like that. This lazy bum was very shrewd and the time was the post-war boom, when some mining stocks soared. Jim got a tip to buy some shares, which he did on margin. The stock rose like a balloon. Jim sold out at the top of the market; and, on another tip, invested the whole works in another wild-cat mine that was about to hit the roof. It did. He retired from business worth $125,000 and said he would never work again. He married and had a family and I heard somewhere that he was very cautious in subsequent sound (conservative) investments. He was a militia commander of an Eastern Ontario regiment, which can hardly be called work.

Jim wrote a bang-up war novel, which Graphic published and I reviewed. Forget the title but you can find that in Reginald Watters' ridiculous *Check List of Canadian Literature*. Maybe called *Only This*.[4] Just look for Pedley in the name index.

I knew Louis Carrier of Montreal but never knew he had anything to do with Graphic.

I never heard of Burland.[5] While Miller published three books of mine,[6] I never had anything to do with the company. I only heard of Miller because Madge [Macbeth] told me the secret of *The Land of Afternoon*.

Burpee presumably you knew. He was an amiable, quiet fellow, very pleasant. His real job was secretary of The International Joint Commission. He was so easy-going that, if he had money in it, he would not worry about the business.

From what I saw, I should not imagine that adequate records survive. Of this I am sure. Whatever went wrong was not Miller's fault. He was perfectly straight, hard-working, ambitious. But he lacked capital and that is the ultimate secret of most business failures. Others come in and the active man loses control.

Oh, yes, when I ran the special sections for books in *Saturday Night*, Graphic and Macmillan were the chief advertisers. Tor. Pub. Library will have those files – years 1925/28. Look at Graphic ads and you will find the titles.

Sorry not to be more help.

1 John Webster Grant (b. 1919), professor and theologian, became editor-in-chief of Ryerson Press in 1960 and remained there until 1963, when he was appointed

Professor of Church History at Emmanuel College, University of Toronto. Presumably Pierce was responding to Deacon's earlier allusion to his own non-membership in the Royal Society.

2 Percy Gomery (1881–1960) was a Canadian banker and writer. Deacon was recalling the title of his science fiction novel about psychic phenomena, *End of the Circle* (1929).

3 Henry C. Miller, an Ottawa printer, founded Graphic Publishers in 1924 and was President and Managing Editor until 1928, when financial difficulties forced the reorganization of the company.

4 *Only This: A War Retrospect* was published in 1927.

5 George H. Burland, who in 1927 became manager of Graphic Press. Deacon had, in fact, corresponded with him.

6 *Poteen* (1926), *The Four Jameses* (1927), *Open House* (1931)

---

## From Peter Newman[1]

The Press Gallery
House of Commons
December 7, 1959

Dear Mr. Deacon;

As you well know, writing books is the loneliest of occupations. You spend countless nights sitting before a typewriter picking your nose, and wondering why you're not doing something productive like bowling, watching television or playing poker, instead of juggling words around. Then, finally, your book comes out. The majority of the critics cut out the worst parts of your publisher's blurb, run the rest as a review, and within weeks, the whole adventure is forgotten by everyone except the author who's back behind his typewriter, still picking his nose, and still juggling words, certain that the next book really *will* shake up the world.

Fortunately, the publication of a book sometimes produces a little more than the above procedure. You meet sympathy, understanding from one or two people, and you realize that the sweaty midnights have not all been wasted. You suddenly are aware that someone understands all that you tried to accomplish, and even more important, appreciates it.

The letter from you which I found waiting for me when I returned to Ottawa[2] is the nicest thing that has happened to me as a result of FLAME OF POWER. I particularly appreciate it, because you took the time to write this letter personally during your busiest season.

Later in the winter when you have some time, I would so much like to have a long conversation with you. Meanwhile, a heartfelt thank you for a gracious and inspiring letter.

Yours sincerely,
Peter

1 Peter Charles Newman (b. 1929), journalist and writer, had worked for *The Financial Post* from 1951 to 1956, the year he joined *Maclean's* and became, in turn, assistant editor (1956–60), Ottawa editor (1960–3), and national editor (1963–4). He went on to work for *The Toronto Star* as Ottawa editor (1964–9) and Editor-in-chief (1969–71) and then returned to *Maclean's* as Editor-in-chief (1971–82). It was during his first period with *Maclean's* that he began to correspond with Deacon, warming to the older man's encouragement, which came with the publication of Newman's first book, *Flame of Power: Intimate Profiles of Canada's Greatest Businessmen* (1959).

2 Neither the letter nor a copy of it has survived.

---

## To Peter Newman

Home midnight
December 15, 1959

Dear Peter,

I wasn't going to send you my ill-typed, ill-constructed letter of the 10th. Intended to edit, re-write, etc. I was too tired, and of course, I'm an old man. But the hell with that. Life's too short. In essence I have nothing to retract. (Though as a writer I'd like to re-phrase.) Make what you can of it.

Meanwhile, my friend Wilf Eggleston,[1] Journalism, Carleton University, made a silly speech at Montreal deploring the alleged fact that Canadian writers can't make a living – true 50 years ago, false now. My older friend, Leslie Roberts of Montreal,[2] wrote a long letter to the *Gazette* deploring Wilf's out-dated remarks. Except for his RCAF service in First World War, Les has been a writer all his life. He has raised a family, is doing better all the time.

You may have noted in last Saturday's Fly Leaf that I cut comment on the Eggleston speech to a short paragraph. The real reply was to cite a young man, a first-book author and, as a critic of 40 years, say: 'Keep your eye on this fellow. He has begun a great career.'

One thing I have learned. I have a peculiar faculty, maybe psychic, for judging writing capacities. There are a dozen books in existence, all successful, which I suggested to their authors. Why didn't I write them myself? I didn't have interest in the subjects, nor the specialized knowledge. It would have bored me to write any one of these books; therefore I should not have done it well. But I knew what books would succeed and who should write them.

Case in point. On my way to Kingston about four years ago to a Writers' Conference, a man came over and asked if he could talk to me. I said: 'Sit down; it's a free country; who are you?' He said he was Frank Panabaker,[3] a professional painter who had earned a better living than most, but he wanted to write. Could he write? We had about 20 minutes before I got off at Kingston. I engaged him in general conversation for that period. Got his address and said I'd write him.

My conclusion was that he was the only articulate painter I had ever met, and I know a few, including some famous. So I told him yes, but not to lean on me. I'm busy. I'd look at his first chapter; otherwise he was on his own. The first chapter was charming and next I saw the completed book. He now writes an occasional piece for me. His first book was commercially successful. The Women's Canadian Club of Toronto gave it their cash prize for a beginning writer. His proposal for a second book fell on the deaf ears of six major publishers. I know what his ranking book is going to be. We shall meet in January and I shall tell him. That's the thing you partly know by reason, mainly in your bowels – intuition.

For you, my lad, the future is writing and more writing. I don't give a damn whether it is reporting, feature writing, book authoring or whatever; but WRITE. Don't go into business (you will have chances). Don't edit. Both will pay well but you, Peter C. Newman, will be nobody. Just a high-priced son of a bitch, if I make my meaning clear.

You see, Peter, my people have been here 150 years. We were farmers and lumbermen, for four generations now lawyers. My great-uncles were judges, my father a brilliant court man. I went into law only because it was easy – anybody can learn it – and in youth I couldn't earn a living, bare living, any other way. But, in 1922, with wealth and success before me, I just couldn't take it. I was a fucking writer. But, at first, 50 years ago, writers like us simply couldn't make a living in Canada. Hence I had to go into law to eat. Of course my friends and relatives did their best to prevent me from committing suicide. The idea of refusing a senior law partnership in a major firm was fantastic. But like a lunatic I rejected all that and, by a fluke of luck, got a $40 a week job as lit. ed. *Saturday Night*, which really did not want a critic at all. I swindled them into it.

After a trial 6 months, my boss said: 'I don't understand what you are doing. In-so-far as I understand it, I don't approve of it. But our readers like it and that is all that counts. I give you $50 a week and ask you to stay on.' Thus virtue triumphed.

You, my young friend, will write and write and write, as long as you can punch keys. If you do not, God have mercy on your soul; and you will be miserable. Men like us can't live on dollars.

I shall not be here, Peter at the hour of your great triumphs; but I take satisfaction in them now. Canada will exert power utterly beyond its population. Speak out; the world will hear.

Finally, one caution. This correspondence is private. I own copyright to the contents of these letters and you may not quote them, even when I am dead.

Who I am and what I am is nobody's business but mine. My words are legally my words for all time. Legally, the period is my life plus 50 years. As I expect to live at least 15 years more, that means 2025 – perhaps even longer.

Good luck, fellow. I've no doubt of your complete success. Only remember that you are a writer first, a money-maker second.

Your friend Carol Chapman has given me your address.

One further point. In the weekly issue of our Magazine, July 4, 1959, I made a prediction of the course of Canadian literature 1960–2000. I presume this document is in the Library of Parliament. It will save us time when we meet if you have read it. My statement occupies one page only.[4]

There is no use wishing you success because I *know* you will have it.

Your audience is, of course, not just Canada. You will be speaking out of Canada to the world. You will be heard, far, far from here.

About New Year's you will get a Christmas card. The N's are far down the list.

Regards –

Addendum.

A. I enclose our Overseas edition with my review of *Flame of Power* in it. I have nothing to do with this selection. It is done in our office by a senior man, who picks the most important items from the previous six daily issues. But a Canadian Communist writer in Peking, correspondent for *Canadian Tribune*, recently wrote me commending our editorials.[5] So your book has already been heard of in many countries.

B. For a fair hunk of my life I thought of my law career as 'the 10 lost years.' Only lately did I realize the absurdity of that. I absolutely needed the discipline of the law, the mental discipline. Your client is sunk if you haven't grasped the precise facts of his situation; also if you haven't grasped the exact law applicable thereto. I learned to think straight. Without that discipline, I should have been a vague, idealistic, windy poet, of no significance to God nor man. With that hard-won discipline, I have been able to make fairly sensible judgments; and to that extent have helped Canada find its authentic voices.

My hope is that I have served a pioneer Canada reasonably well. Because, if so, I have served the world. Canada is crucial in the next 50 years. Our position is uniquely detached and central.

I hope to see you in 1960. Your friend Carol Chapman has given me your home address.

1 Wilfrid Eggleston (1901–86), journalist, writer, teacher, a past president of the Parliamentary Press Gallery, and currently Professor Emeritus, Carleton University School of Journalism. Among his books are *The Frontier and Canadian Letters* (1957) and *The Green Gables Letters* (1959).

2 Author, lecturer, broadcaster (b. 1896), for many years associated with Montreal's radio station CJAD. A war veteran and correspondent, Roberts wrote numerous books about Canada at war.

3 Frank Shirley Panabaker (b. 1904), artist and landscape painter, published his memoirs, *Reflected Lights*, in 1957.

4 In 'World Vogue for Canadian Books, Perhaps?' Deacon predicted that in the third forty-year period of Canadian literature, beginning in 1960 and stimulated by the prospect of the centennial year, 'the Canadian book will become and remain in active demand in world markets.' He predicted 'an increasing use of the nation's own story as basic material' and stressed the need for 'factual writing.'

5 Sydney Gordon (1915–85), who was also co-author with Ted Allan of *The Scalpel, the Sword: The Story of Dr Norman Bethune* (1954). Gordon's letter has been lost.

## From Peter Newman

The Press Gallery
House of Commons
December 20, 1959

Dear Mr. Deacon;

First, let me thank you for writing me at such length, and so wisely. I agree with all you say, with one exception. I will not be your guest at our Toronto dinner; you must be mine.

I have, incidentally, joined the Ottawa branch of the Canadian Authors Association, and expect to attend my first meeting in January.

You write that I will have chances to go into business. I have had some offers, and I have turned them down without any trouble. It's not that I believe I have any special message as a writer, but I would far rather earn a less profitable living doing something I like, and something that I can believe in. I can well appreciate your own feelings about the law, and I am sure that I am only the latest of many Canadians who have been glad that you took the course in life that you chose to take.

I seem to keep thanking you all the time, but I really am most grateful that you sent me the Overseas *Globe* containing your review which I would otherwise have missed, and I also thank you for the note about my book being sold out, in your Flyleaf of last Saturday. The publisher has ordered another run of 3,000 for January, and I've had a nibble for translation rights. There is also a possibility that *Flame of Power* will go into paperback form sometime in 1960, but nothing has been decided on that, and to reveal it now might discourage hard-cover sales.

I must admit that the reception of *Flame of Power* has been very exciting. I am, for some reason, reminded of a statement in one of Faulkner's novels. 'No man,' he writes, 'has courage, but any man can blunder into valour, blindly, as one stumbles into an open man-hole.' *Flame of Power* took three years, three hundred interviews, and three revisions of a first draft that ran close to half a million words. Then, almost suddenly, I had a book in my hands, and people have actually paid money to read it.

But all these things are better left for personal conversation. I do not yet know when I'll be in Toronto, but as soon as I have a date of departure, I'll let you know and hope that you will be free for a dinner.

With best wishes.

Peter Newman

---

## From Gabrielle Roy

Quebec
January 8, 1961

Dear Bill,

All my congratulations on your life's achievement so far, your beautiful sympathy for writers, in which, for my part, I found comfort, help, warmth and such it should be, I think. What is the value of critic [sic] if it doesn't contain something of the heart as well as of the intellect! I know that you will continue to read, write, gather and give, even though you are retiring from active – so-called – journalism. I wish you joy in this other form of living – who knows, perhaps even more active than the demanding years.

I would have loved to join your friends on this day, to have been present around the table, and with others who love you drink to your health, to your future writing and happiness. Dear Bill, from Marcel and from myself, affectionate memories and affectionate wishes.

Gabrielle Roy

---

## From Lorne Pierce[1]

January 11, 1961

WILLIAM ARTHUR DEACON

Authors, publishers and readers of Canadian books in all the land owe a vast debt to William Arthur Deacon, one that can scarcely be measured and never adequately paid. How does a young nation go about it, if it wishes to recognize its debt to one who has served this country with complete devotion for four decades? There must be some suitable way.

Born in the same year, and commencing our literary careers in

Toronto at the same time, I have followed the achievements of Bill Deacon year in and year out.

By his articles and reviews, his books and brochures, his wide variety of services on behalf of aspiring writers as well as established authors, he has performed a prodigious service. We are profoundly grateful to him, and want him to know that, in retiring, he receives the accolade of the whole country. It is given to few men to serve their homeland for so long a time, and with such unflagging zeal and dedication. We give him our profound gratitude and our warmest good wishes.

1 This tribute was read *in absentia* at Deacon's retirement dinner.

---

## From A.R.M. Lower

R.R. 3
Collins Bay, Ontario
January 12, 1960 [1961][1]

Dear Bill: –

I had intended to get a word up to your retirement dinner,[2] there to be read, but as I am at the moment confined, for a few days, to barracks, that is, temporarily in hospital, I did not manage it. So please take this scrawl in lieu.

I would put your book page right up among the top of our Canadianizing institutions – along with the CBC, *Maclean's*, the Ryerson Press, etc. Doesn't it seem both tragic and ridiculous that one of our big jobs, perhaps our biggest, is to make Canadians out of Canadians? It may be that Dutch immigrants are more likely material.

I am doing another book for L.G. & Co [Longmans Green] this one on my impressions of 'The Commonwealth' as I saw it last year.[3] My kindest regards & good wishes.

Arthur Lower

1 Lower had misdated the letter.
2 It had taken place the previous evening at the Royal York Hotel in Toronto.
3 The book was never published.

From Hugh MacLennan

McGill University
Montreal
May 24, 1961

Dear Bill:

All this past winter and spring I was so overwhelmed with work and various commitments (the price of letting oneself become un homme engagé) that I had a pile of unanswered correspondence half a foot high on my desk. It had to wait until I finished my book on the rivers of Canada and the marking of a deluge of exams at McGill. One of the letters I wanted to write, and should have written despite all, was to you on your retirement as literary editor of the G&M. So far as I have since been able to see, the retirement has been at best partial.[1] May it stay no more than that.

For in all the growing years of writing here, Bill, you have played a role that was absolutely invaluable. You were a voice crying in the wilderness for years. You were an encouragement to all of us who tried to break the long winter of our literary discontent. You were virtually the ONLY critic in the whole country, and invariably were a constructive one. I still have in my files valued, and very valuable, letters to me about my own work in my earlier days. I think it was probably you, though also my own compulsions, who more than any other individual made me realize that I must ground all my best work in this peculiar country of ours, and that at a time when one almost had to apologize for finding Canada an interesting country to live in.

Truly I can think of hardly anyone who has done more than you to bring about this birth of literature, especially prose literature, in Canada. This I wanted to write to you last January, but I was frantic for time to finish a book for a fall deadline – which finally I did with only a couple of days to spare. At least you recognize that the excuse is as good a one as anyone could offer to a man like yourself.

My warm affection, and my appreciation of what you have done for myself, as well as for many others.

Sincerely,
Hugh MacLennan

1 Deacon continued his 'Fly Leaf' column until 6 July 1963.

---

## To Hugh MacLennan May 28, 1961

Dear Hugh,

I am most grateful to you for your letter of the 24th and deeply appreciate both your kindness in writing and reassurance that my life has not been wholly misspent. I'm still suffering from shock and, as yet, only hoping to get re-organized.

Our pension plan was set up in 1954. This gave me 6 years to contribute; and law trained me in prudence. Hence, I contributed maximum permitted and also negotiated with the proper executive permission to extend employment to 1964, which would involve yielding a sort-of minimum income thereafter – which is important because my family has a nasty habit of living into their 90's.

When this executive was shifted to other work, I paid no attention. Hence one day last November I was involuntarily retired, over my loud protests. These only resulted in upping my pension by $10 a week plus permission to continue the old column at 40% of former wordage. Provided I'm not physically or mentally incapacitated, this provides a bare living if costs do not rise (as, of course, they will).

I had no option. For 40 years I've been lit. ed. and know no other trade. 'Our' paper, of which I am still proud, has become Big Business, object profit – 900 regular employees, capitalization can't be less than $20 million. Sentiment is out. Old hands discarded. Foolishly, I didn't think this meant me – partly because columnist J.V. McAree was on the strength [sic] till he died at 83, when his output had dwindled to a single col. a week.

So out I was on my backside and the only people who realized the personal disaster were the Toronto publishers. In December a committee phoned they were getting up a memorial dinner but, during the pre-Christmas season, they were busy and would I mind waiting. I thanked them, dreaded this sort of public funeral of a living corpse, and suggested early in 1961.

I came off Jan. 11, 1961. There were 400 present from a wide geographical area – and hundreds of wires from all over this continent. It was by all means the most spectacular demonstration any

Canadian literary man has received. Nearest to it was our party for C.G.D. Roberts when he was knighted – no dinner, about 250 turned up at a room holding 150. During my dinner 85 telegrams were delivered, of which the chairman had only time to read 35. Hundreds of letters subsequently reached me.

This was the third great shock. The second was the obituary published by my paper, which certainly suggested my retirement was voluntary. You see, Hugh, the greater part of my life has been spent alone in a silent room, reading and writing. Personal contacts with Canadian authors, as with you, had been infrequent but intense. Now they were before me, a sea of faces. I'd been prudent enough to write my acknowledgement speech; and with a glass of whiskey I read it with the appearance of sanity.

But I only dimly perceived. My son-in-law [Lloyd] Haines valiantly stood by in case. My degree of imperception may be measured by the fact that later I congratulated three couples on their wisdom 'in staying away from the damned dinner.' In each case they said: 'We were there; you shook hands with us; you spoke to us.' After that I never assumed anybody was present or absent. The whole thing was a shock.

The fourth shock was the private parties. These came two to four a week for two months. We had to be polite and accept, though earlier we had had no social life whatsoever for obvious reasons – no time. Our social life had been zero because I was always reading or writing.

Hundreds of letters came, some from readers I didn't know. Many I've answered – some not yet. (I feel defeated.)

Hugh, my friends were magnificent, vocal and generous. The cash presentation amounted to a quarter of a year's salary.

Further, some individual publishers have propositioned me about writing books at high pay – mostly histories written in a fictional style. Extra good pay but I've never written fiction and can't learn now. Last offer was for $2,500 in advance and guarantee of $7,500 total. But I've never written fiction nor history. To hell with that. Some offers were higher. I'm just a book reviewer without any chance of reviewing a book.

Your wood-chopper essay in *Scotchman's Return*[1] touched me because (a) it led me to believe this was Hatley and I lived at Stanstead between ages 5 and 17; (b) I'm also a wood-chopper on my

Lake Couchiching acre just north of Orillia, Ont., (Leacock's Mariposa.) I, too, am a wood chopper. As a forest Canadian from 1800, Ottawa Valley, I can't live without water, trees and rocks. My 12 Manitoba years, 1911–22, were invaluable.

I'm still shattered but hope that physical work on my summer home at Lake Couchiching will restore me to mental health. (Right now I just refuse every offer.) I've astonished Canadian Writers Foundation by increasing my annual contribution. They have graciously offered to make me a beneficiary whenever I say. I hope this day never comes.

Hugh, I'm not quite sane but hope to return to that status.

You know, Hugh, at 71, however misguided the life, it is a great satisfaction to be able to say: 'Fuck you.' It's not my privilege, like you, to point to a series of masterly books. I wasn't a creative but a derivative writer. I just hope I helped.

My hope is that in the three months of wood chopping I may return to normal mentally and get some job that enables me to provide for us for the next 10 years.

Canada owes me nothing. Canadian writers owe me nothing. I've had a wonderful time – doing exactly what I liked. How many Canadians can say that?

I didn't do this for Canadian writers; I did it for myself. I'm the most selfish person I know.

Sally shrinks from living all year at Orillia, which is the logical solution. We may have to. Well what? Simply this: I led exactly the life I wanted. What more can man ask?

I'm a free lance now, not on staff at all – have not even the slightest influence on book page. Sometimes they cut down or cut out what I say, sometimes change it. Hope by fall to connect with something more satisfactory.

Your career, of course, has been a great gratification to me. Especially the nice upward curve in your artistry. I've read the Rivers stuff in *Maclean's* and shall be glad to see the book.[2] Hope it will be illustrated.

I really don't think your teaching interferes. I think the slower production yields you more power. During past two years I've made gifts of several copies to friends, who were always pleased. Last was in April when I sent six books to my sister-in-law in San Francisco. She wrote enthusiastically about yours, didn't mention the others specifically. *Scotchman's Return* is also grand stuff. I'll hope for more essays. I'm still delighted with your friend who shot the horn-blower in the ass.[3]

Don't worry about me. I've always enjoyed the luck of the Irish and expect I'll find a raft by the end of the year.

Best wishes,

1 'Confessions of a Wood-Chopping Man' in *Scotchman's Return and Other Essays* (1960) contrasted the landscape of Quebec's Eastern Townships with that of Nova Scotia.
2 MacLennan's article, 'The Rivers of Canada,' appeared in *Maclean's Magazine* on 28 May 1961 and was based on his *Seven Rivers of Canada* (1961).
3 'A Disquisition on Elmer' in *Scotchman's Return*

---

## From Thomas Costain

50 Riverside Drive
New York
September 23, 1961

Dear Bill:

Thanks for your interesting long letter. Needless to state, I am glad that you have signed a contract with George Nelson for your history of Canadian literature. You have a good contract and I don't think you should worry about the matter of time. Once you get into it the stuff will flow along and you will be through with it before reaching the deadline. Of course, it is never necessary to hit the exact date named in the contract.

I am relieved to learn you are not going to write with an eye over your shoulder for the professorial group. You have really been mild in dealing with them to my notion. I blame them for the situation which we now face with reference to the slump of interest in novels on the part of the public. For the last two generations the worthy professors have been preaching the relative unimportance of story. The men who come out of college and become critics are almost exclusively convinced that there is something vulgar or something wrong about telling stories and that an author's concern must be exclusively in his characters. Stream of consciousness, symbolism, the study of the mind and the heart; these are all important but to consider the story as of no consequence has changed the whole face of things. Now the booksellers are inclined to think they have to sell the more popular type of novel from under the counter. It is my firm conviction that between the lot of them they have taken away any appetite that readers had for the more popular type of novel. We have now reached the inevitable consequence. The Golden Goose has been killed and the public are not keen for the addled eggs that are being offered.

In a quiet way I have been doing what I can to provide stories for people who want them. I do not mean in connection with my own historical novels. It was to give them a chance to read the great stories which history offers that I took the plunge into that field. Then I got started on the preparation of anthologies where the first consideration was that each selection should have a story to tell. The sale of these anthologies has been almost exclusively in book clubs but they have been distributed in the millions. In other words, there is still a great desire for fiction if the professors will only gain some breadth of viewpoint.

Don't worry about the market for your book. You have a wide open field and it will sell as readily in the colleges as in the bookstores.

Yours,
Tom

---

## To Thomas Costain September 26, 1961

Dear Tom,

Receipt of your kind and valuable letter of the 23rd coincides with (a) receipt of contract signed by George [Nelson] and (b) end of cleaning up my study sufficiently so that I'll turn from this letter directly into the mechanical job of listing Canadian authors and their books since 1880.

Prof. Watters of U.B.C.[1] lists 5,986 authors, incl. 1,991 poets. *The Canadian Who's Who* lists 350 – all now living; and my own records show every book reviewed in *G & M* in the past 25 years. How many are worth mentioning is something else again.

Your encouragement and advice has been invaluable and one of the main factors in inducting me into this new life. The alternative was to rust away. This is the logical chore; afterwards the Memoirs, which will be great fun.

As you know, there was no precedent for me in Canada. I took them seriously, read each carefully and judged them as faithfully as I could. The result was a working week of 80 hours for 40 years. When the Newspaper Guild was formed I couldn't join it because members were only permitted to work 40 hours – double pay for overtime. And if management had realized how long I worked they would have discharged me for incompetence.

Result was I was dog-tired at the end of last year when they fired me for old age. I was hurt and angry, believing I deserved better and not realizing that I was coming to a stand-still.

The shock was worse because of the kindness of friends in arranging the big dinner, to say nothing of hundreds of letters and wires, gifts and what-not. To me, all this just signified I was through. And I was quite a wreck.

A visit in San Francisco in March (gift of the G & M staff) was pleasant and healing. We saw our daughter and son-in-law, whom we had never met, and their children – to say nothing of Sally's 24 other Townsend relatives in the environs. But the good effects soon wore off and answering all those messages was like thanking them for sending flowers to my funeral.

As summer came on I pined for the cottage. For years we'd only been able to stay there week-ends (I couldn't take my vacations because I had no replacement, not even a secretary) and I decided we'd spend most of this summer there come what may. I recalled my fire-ranging days in Temagami 1907, '08 & '09, and believed that outdoor physical work was the right medicine. Rooting out briar, killing poison ivy, chopping out surplus trees was great fun and I had good long sleeps. I was really cured and saw that what I thought was disaster was really a merciful release.

When you and George came along with the Toronto book suggestion I shunned it from lack of interest. That was a lucky decision; half a dozen people are now writing Toronto books.

The Crowell mix-up led to your and George's suggestion for the Can. Lit. effort – a topic on which I have considerable knowledge and really deep interest. What finished my hesitation was (a) encouragement from both of you, (b) final realization that this year off duty has left me more able than I've been for quite a while.

I'm deeply grateful to both of you. Shall, of course, do my best.

What you say about the professors lousing up creative literature, esp. the novel, is true in the main. Certainly the tale is the core of the art of writing – from Homer. In fact, I've lately read *The Epic of Gilgamesh*; and this yarn must date back at least as far as Abraham, possibly older.

But I think you overlook what you have accomplished remedially. Your Canadian History Series has revolutionized the writing of biography in Canada. Kilbourn's *The Firebrand* (Wm Lyon Mackenzie); Roger Graham's *Arthur Meighen*; Hutchison's *The Incredible Canadian* (W.L.M. King) are life-*stories* of these men – no footnotes, no listing of sources at the bottom of every page. These are human interest narratives. These are stories, true stories of actual men; but minus the dry-as-dust. Consequently, they are popular reading.

If you will pardon a disagreement, I decline to accept the death of the novel. Publishers now want international readership – at least big circulations. A lot of fictional crap will no longer find publishers. That may not be a bad thing. And I'm sure the novel that appeals strongly to one sort of taste will come back.

As you say, the taste for the story is basic in mankind. I don't think anything can eradicate it. What has happened is that the story technique has been employed in history and biography, even in the histories of industries.

Now, Mr. Costain, you must excuse me because I have work to do, namely, writing a book. For your sake I hope it will be good because George is going to be very sad if it isn't.

Best wishes and a ton of gratitude.

I've sent carbon of this to George –

1 Reginald Eyre Watters (1912–79), professor of English at the University of British Columbia (1946–61), then at the Royal Military College at Kingston, and author of *A Checklist of Canadian Literature and Background Materials 1628–1950* (1959, 1972), to which Deacon is referring here

---

## From E.J. Pratt

5 Elm Avenue
Toronto 5
[16 March 1963][1]

Dear Bill:

I was glad that my brother Cal was here from Ottawa and had the chance to read your heart-warming article in *The A & B*.[2] It was another evidence of the unwavering loyalty existing between us for more than thirty years. That's what gives immortality to friendship. When we returned to the house we talked, long and tenderly of our associations, for richer for poorer, in sickness and in health (to paraphrase the sacred ritual). God bless you & Sal and the rest of the family. Vi calls out – give Sal a second blessing for me. There will always be a second loaf of bread for the Deacon clan when flour turns into dough.

Yours
Ned

1 On the holograph letter is Deacon's typed notation 'Received March 16, 1963.'
2 'Laureate Uncrowned: A Personal Study of E.J. Pratt,' *Canadian Author and Bookman*, 38, 3 (Spring 1963) 2, 20

---

## To E.J. Pratt

March 16, 1963

Dear Ned,

So glad you are so much better. Thanks for your letter. Evidently you went out somewhere when your brother was here. That is good news because I gathered that you were pretty sick at the year-end.

Of course I'm glad that you like my *Author & Bookman* piece. The editor was disappointed that I didn't write a greater length; but more than 40 years of journalism gradually taught me that (a) concision lends strength; and (b) that 10 times as many people will read a short piece as a long one. You yourself are a fine exponent of the merits of brevity. This is what made your poetry powerful.

I was much attracted to you when we were freshmen in the fall of 1907, though of course I knew you much better after 1923 when you published *Newfoundland Verse*. That happened to be the year of publication of my own first book.

Last summer we had a fine visit with Art Phelps when he presented the Leacock Medal for Humor at Orillia. He now lives at Kingston and gets his chief income from doing CBC's Neighborly News every Sunday morning at 10 or 10:30. Lal has been seriously ill for years and requires three practical nurses for eight hours each around the clock.

Sally fell a year ago when getting off a bus, twisted a knee no medical aid has yet done any good. This is our main problem which, so far, we have not solved.

Warm regards from both of us to both of you,

---

## To Peter Newman April 12, 1964

Dear Peter,

*Our National Mess*

Your broadcast today on the general Canadian mess was excellent. But, regarded historically, isn't it logical?

New France was a product of 1534. After Wolfe so gloriously captured Quebec in 1759, the generous British victors following the custom of the time offered to ship the colonists back to France; and the professional class (priests excluded) took advantage and left. The bulk of the people were farmers and prosperous for those days. Most of them were Canadian natives of three or four generations – nothing to go 'back' to. Besides, the aristocratic gentlemen in Paris had been affronted that the Canadian farmers (not being 'gentlemen') kept saddle horses for their pleasure and spent most of the winters in an unending round of house-parties at each others' homes. The French officials in Canada had been unable to prevent this winter social life. So the bulk of the French stayed here and continued to have big families.

After the American Revolution many British types came here for all sorts of reasons, mainly economic. I'm 100% British by blood. Three Deacon brothers migrated – the eldest as a result of a feud in Ireland. His younger brothers were veterans of Waterloo and could get extensive free lands in Ontario. My Welsh grandfather came as a Methodist missionary with the laudable object of saving the Canucks from no sin; but he was prudent enough in Liverpool to marry the daughter of a rich English sea captain who owned six ships. My Scottish grandmother died when I was a small child and I never learned why she migrated.

As I heard your wise words on the air re the weakness of Mike[2] (a diplomat who wants to agree with everybody) and the occasional irrationality and inconsistency of Dief, I wondered why these things should surprise you. Just who in hell are we – the Canadians?

Only answer is a polyglot people, especially today. When I was young the Russians were settling on the prairies in vast numbers – people minus any experience of democracy. Alderman Pichinini [sic] is the leader of the Toronto Italians, who are numerous enough to form a city of fair size.[3]

There was French Canada, a reality; and then British Canada in the 19th century. But today who are we? Where do we want to go? Nearly all the answers are negatives. I'm pretty sure that a plebiscite would show that the majority of us don't want to be absorbed into the United States. But what a hell of a conclusion! We can only agree on a negative!

Mike became a sort of international man at the U.N. A man who only wants warm relations with everybody can't lead a nation – certainly not our nation with its thousand divisions on everything from A to Z. John A. Macdonald was a perfect P.M. because he had (a) no principles at all; and (b) be had something like a dog's sense of smell in knowing what measures to put forward to keep himself in power. He supplied government, kept the nation steady. He kept us united and reasonably steady. Mackenzie King, whom I disliked, had something like the same a-moral political instinct. I can't think of any practising politician today able to give us even this false sense of unity.

Now we have no sense of national unity, joint ambitions, etc. I was born in Ontario, grew up mostly in Quebec, spent early adult life in Manitoba. At 18 I visited Saint John, N.B., and the first night was taken to a Five Hundred party. My partner, daughter of the mayor, said brightly: 'You come from Canada, don't you?' A solar plexus blow. Maritimers are a sort-of northern extension of New England. The Pea Soups are now separatists. I'd say Ontario, Manitoba & Saskatchewan are recognizably Canadian provinces. I don't know Alberta; but the closest friends of the Vancouverites live in Seattle. An extended visit to San Francisco in 1961 brought quite a shock. These people are wholly regional. They have a fine daily paper but the interest of readers stops dead at the Rockies. Generally but not always, there was a half-column on something Pres. Kennedy had said or done; but no news of any kind from New York, let alone Chicago, Boston, Philadelphia.

My sister-in-law's TV programs were lousy. An ex-Winnipegger, she spent most of her time doing cross-word puzzles. Being rich and lonely she had bought the Encyc. Brit. to help her do the puzzles.

There was one TV program she liked – about popular science. When I saw it I laughed. Here was Prof. Ivey and his pal from U. T.[4] Marg was surprised it was of Canadian origin and seen here weekly coast-to-coast. They didn't even carry good programs from New York.

It was spring and the climax came. I searched the sports pages every day to find out which teams were in the Stanley Cup play-offs. One day it was there – one column-inch in agate type, just the finishing order of the regular schedule. I read it three times before I realized what was wrong with it: there were only five teams, Detroit didn't exist. During an 8–hour wait in Vancouver for a plane, I read all the papers just to find what had gone on in the world since I left B.C.

As I see it, Peter, there are several of our French politicians, who, if they could forget about being French, are capable of being Canadian prime ministers of the stature of Laurier. I don't give a damn whether a P.M. is personally or politically crooked, or both; but he must have an in-built sure knowledge for what Canadians, as a whole, will go for. Neither the Maritimes nor the Far West can give us that man. Between Ontario and Quebec, the latter has far better chance of producing the man. In this phase, English-speakers will follow a Frenchman; the French simply will not rally round an English-speaker.

I suppose this is all silly to you; but I'm bloody scared. We're being Balkanized, hence emasculated as a nation. Sending more troops to Cyprus than anybody else does us no good, however it may be to Europe. If another Great Depression catches us before [we] unite nationally on the political front we may get into deep trouble.

The only hope I see is to persuade Dief to make the supreme sacrifice by handing Conservative leadership over to a Frenchman. He might rise to the bait: 'A man should lay down his life for his friends. And not just his friends; the real stake is the triumph of a united Canada. An appeal to his Christian instincts might work.

Socialism isn't going to work here because we're all capitalists. Even a poor book-reviewer can own his home, subject to a mortgage. Labor itself is a vested interest. The strength of Sir. John A. was the C.P.R. station with one exception. Gen. Mgr. wired the Div. Supt.: 'How Come?' Answer: 'It was an oversight.'

Too long a letter. My apologies.

And regards,

1 The date of Jacques Cartier's first voyage to Canada
2 Lester Bowles Pearson (1897–1972), public servant, diplomat, and 14th Prime Minister of Canada (1963–8)
3 Joseph Piccininni (b. 1922) was elected to Toronto's City Council in 1960.
4 Donald Glenn Ivey (b. 1922) and James Nairn Patterson Hume (b. 1923) of the Department of Physics, University of Toronto, were involved in the preparation and presentation of educational television programs for the CBC, among them 'The Nature of Things' (1960–5).

---

## From Peter Newman

Parliamentary Press Gallery
April 27, 1964

Dear Bill,

I was showing a very close and confidential friend of mine all the letters I'd received on my Diefenbaker book the other day. We came across your original note and my friend, who happens to be one of the most original thinkers in Ottawa, said: 'That's the best letter you got. Deacon judges this man and his actions in the historical context. That doesn't make Diefenbaker any better a man, but it does at least partly explain his failure.'

Your April 12 letter is in the same category, and I thank you for it. You're quite right, of course, I do not have any background in Canadian history. I came here as an immigrant and I had to learn about this country's history in a way which stresses success rather than difficulty. Because I wanted Canada to become a great and unified power at the same time. (If you look at the roster of rabid nationalists in this country, you'll see that with the exception of Walter Gordon, most of them are foreign-born.)

I agree with everything you say and I suspect that you're right about the next effective leader coming from Quebec. The trouble with most of the people in Ottawa, I find, is that they still regard Canada as an economy, not a society. This is an important distinction to my mind and really is the key to our future.

I, too, fear for national unity and Pearson's appeasement tactics certainly won't carry the day.

I'm now deep into the research for my next book. It's an examination of the power structure of Canada – political, economic, religious, etc. A really tough job, but one worth trying. I hope you're progressing well with your labors and send you my fondest regards,

Peter

1 Walter Lockhart Gordon (1906–87), politician, nationalist, author of *A Choice for Canada: Independence or Colonial Status* (1966). He was appointed Minister of Finance in the Liberal government of Lester Pearson in April 1963 and was a co-founder with Peter Newman and Abraham Rotstein (b. 1929) of the Committee for an Independent Canada (1970–81).
2 Newman's next book was, in fact, *The Distemper of Our Times: Canadian Politics in Transition 1963–1968* (1968). His research on the power structure in Canada emerged as the two-volume *The Canadian Establishment* (1975, 1981).

---

## To J.A. Flaherty September 5, 1964

Mr. J.A. Flaherty
District Director of Postal Service
London, Ontario

Dear Mr. Flaherty,

Your File 5–2/11–12–16
*Dr. W. Sherwood Fox*[1]

Thanks for your kind letter of August 28; but there was no need to apologize for a clerical error. Our postal service is excellent and as a professional writer I depend heavily on the mails.

I was puzzled when my letter addressed to Harrison Crescent came back as improperly addressed. I knew Bill Fox at 87 and almost blind would not have eloped with a young blonde; if he had died the fact would have been in *The Globe & Mail*. So I appealed to H.Q., Ottawa; and sent my letter in a new envelope to Harrison Crescent, adding a note about the postal blockage.

The second attempt was successful; and Fox replied that he had had a lot of trouble with his mail since moving to Richmond St. It is 14 years since he concluded his 20–year presidency of the University of Western Ontario, which he built almost unaided. Many regarded him as London's first citizen; and, as author, he is still active. One of his books was published a month ago[2] and I believe there is another to come.

I think you should also know that this slight error has been of real value to me. My first 10 adult years were spent as a lawyer in Manitoba. Then I became a book-reviewer in New York, Winnipeg, Toronto. My final 25 years as book-reviewer were spent as literary editor of *The Globe & Mail*, which involuntarily retired me at 70 – 5 years ago. Now I'm just an author. So my wife and I decided that, as author, our sensible course was to turn our summer home at Orillia into an all-year home and work from that basis.

Apparently, that involves the risk of my being 'lost' on Lake Couchiching, which I can't afford. Therefore I'll remain as at Toronto 17. Which is Leaside and very pleasant; and our local postman is not only efficient but a good friend – and highly intelligent. I discuss my plans with him.

It is vital to my work that I be available not only by mail but by long distance phone also. If Bill Fox could get lost by moving to another street in London, I might cease to belong to the human race if I moved to Orillia. We'll remain here.

Thanks for the courtesy of your letter; but there is no need to apologize for a clerk's error. It has been wisely said that the man who never makes a mistake never makes anything else either.

Sincerely,

1 Both Fox and Deacon were greatly entertained by Deacon's correspondence with the Post Office over the return of a letter he had addressed to Fox in London, Ontario.
2 *Sherwood Fox of Western* (1964).

---

## From Thomas Raddall

Liverpool, Nova Scotia
January 25, 1965

Hello Bill:

Delighted to hear from you again, and to know that you are doing a history of Canadian literature – 'opinionated' as you say.[1] I've always liked Van Wyck Brooks' definition: – 'How does a bookman differ from a critic? He differs in that he assumes as given the whole sphere of values. The bookman does not judge, nor is he asked to judge. He appreciates, he enjoys, he communicates pleasure. In the world of the bookman, taste is the main affair, enthusiasm, gusto, relish.'

I have had no book published since *The Governor's Lady* in 1960. *GL* had taken a long effort, with research in New Hampshire, England and Belgium. (I had previously researched the Nova Scotia period in the Wentworths' lives.) After the book finally came out I asked myself the inevitable question 'what shall I do next?' and there was no answer. I had now published sixteen books of various kinds and I felt that I should pause and take stock. What did I really want to do? Two things had been nagging at my mind for a long time – and long put aside because I had to earn a living and these things weren't the kind that enrich publishers or authors. One was the story (call it history) of Sable Island – the so-called 'Graveyard of the Atlantic' – where as you know I spent a year in my sea-wandering youth.[2] The other was a collection of true stories of men and things connected with Nova Scotia – all the way from the whole story of the famous mystery ship Mary Celeste (not just the episode of her abandonment off the Azores) to the real story of 'Grey Owl,' who spent more time amongst the Micmacs than he ever did amongst the Ojibways. (When he enlisted in the Canadian army he was living with Micmacs at Bear River, N.S.) This would include the real story of his army career and his wounds – he was an artful dodger in these as he was in everything else.[3]

So I took off on a wonderful Sabbatical, riding in all directions – everything from pulling up sunken tombstones in a search for the grave of the first captain of the Mary Celeste, at a place called (believe it or not) Economy, N.S. – to hunting up Archie Belaney's former platoon commander and one of his fellow snipers in the Ypres salient, vintage 1915. (I located these in Montreal and Saskatchewan!)

Meanwhile Doubleday was getting worried because I wasn't working on another novel. At their urging I went to New York for a chat with their top men and with Tom Costain. They wanted me to start another costume novel right away, and Tom suggested one written about the central figure of Frontenac or of Champlain. I said No.

Both Frontenac and Champlain have been written to death, and in any case I preferred to stick to my chosen theme – people in the Nova Scotia scene, past and present. I thought there might be a novel in the story of Charles and Madame La Tour, and the Doubleday men were quite happy about it. So I came home and spent most of a year digging up all I could about the La Tours. But in the end I gave it up. Madame was a magnificent creature, but unfortunately after her death in the hands of Charnisay's men the story was one long anticlimax, because La Tour was just a weak shifter.

Then I spent months revising and bringing up to date my *Halifax, Warden of the North*, originally published in 1948. (Doubleday is publishing the new edition this year.) Also I went on gathering material for the collection of true stories.

Then I got the notion for a novel based on Halifax during the Napoleonic wars, when hundreds of French prisoners were kept there in hulks and on Melville Island. I had always been intrigued with the history of the McNabs, of McNab's Island at the harbor mouth. Old Peter McNab bought the island in the early days of Halifax and lived there like a Highland laird, with a little clan of servants and retainers about him. The French prisoners were allowed parole to work in and about Halifax – everything from pick-and-shovel on the roads to teaching French and dancing in the homes of the gentry. I began to see a plot involving the McNabs with one of the French officer-prisoners. Followed a long job of research, including every detail of the old Melville Island prison, and of the McNab *menage*. McNab's Island had a stony point sticking out into the main harbor channel, and the Admiral used to hang the bodies of mutineers on gibbets there, within sight of Peter McNab's house – much to McNab's disgust. So that circumstance gave me the title of the book, *Hangman's Beach*.[4]

I'm well into the job and hope to finish it in time for publication this Fall. After that I'll finish the book of true stories – no title for that yet. After that the Sable Island book, though George Nelson thinks I should do yet another novel after the true story collection. That remains to be seen.

*Governor's Lady* was not used as a play on radio or TV, so I can't think where you saw or heard Lady Wentworth's journey cut out.

As they say in Newfoundland, 'Oi drinks an' looks t'ards ye!'

Cheers,
Tom

1 Raddall was likely responding to a Christmas card from Deacon.

2 Raddall broke his contract with Doubleday for a history of Sable Island. He did,

however, write the foreword to Bruce Armstrong's *Sable Island,* published by Doubleday in 1981.

3 Raddall's *Footsteps on Old Floors: True Tales of Mystery,* which included 'Grey Owl' and '*Mary Celeste,*' was published in 1968 by Doubleday.

4 Published in 1966 by Doubleday

---

## To Thomas Raddall October 16, 1965

Dear Tom,

My apologies to you for (a) not acknowledging your most helpful letter of January 25th nor (b) your kindness in August in becoming one of my referees.[1] George Nelson forwarded a copy to me of your letter to him about it. Also I'm looking forward to *Hangman's Beach* this fall because I haven't read a new Canadian book in a long time. Nor any other new book.

When I retired George kept at me to write my autobiography, which I refused because my life has been uninteresting ... except that I got a thrill out of seeing all you new Can. authors come on to supply me with fascinating reading. I enjoyed seeing Can. lit. grow in power as well as in quantity. That was my happy life. I wasn't sure I could do it – but I ought to be doing something and, God knows, I was no good for anything else. So I weakened and signed.

I've written a lot but it is a very slow business. I hadn't realized how much I had forgotten of what I had read. A fellow reads a lot in 40 years when that is his business. To give you an idea of the scope, this year *Literary History of Canada* was published. Written by 15 professors who, between them, filled 945 extra large pages; and the thing sells for $18. I suppose it will be good for class-room use. Mine will be nothing like that – more sketchy, concentrating on highlights both as to authors mentioned and individual books. When I began with the first book of C.G.D. Roberts in 1880, I had no conception of what I'd be faced with in dealing with authors who published between 1945 and 1965.

Now at age 75 my memory isn't what it was. Fortunately most of your books are on my shelves at home; and I'm looking forward to *Hangman's Beach* this fall. It will be a great relief to read a new book for a change; and of course I'm sold on you anyway. As reviewer, I've always been sold on you anyway and you, as author, probably had my reviews and understand how highly I regard you. But all I have room for is a summary. I'll see that *Hangman's Beach* gets in; but *History of the West Nova Scotia Regiment* (1948) may not be mentioned. I think it would be effective to begin with *Halifax: Warden of the North* (1948).

Happily, as I say, copies of most of your books – not all – are on a special shelf in my study; and there is not much point in mentioning those out of print. I think I'll ask Ethel Blais[2] here.

I was tremendously pleased when you brought Mrs. Raddall to the Toronto Convention. I'm just an hon. mem. now. Nobody is deader than an ex-president. But I'm grateful to you. As to Can. Lit., you brought the Maritimes into Confederation.

I'll never forget the trip from Bedford Basin, across Halifax to the south. I could not remember half the history you told me in that hour; but I did get a lasting impression. Especially of your courtesy. I had a hell of a time getting aboard, from ship to ship. I wanted to get down and crawl on my hands and knees. Somebody kindly gave me a hand.

Well, Tom, you as a writer and I as a reviewer have played our parts. You will go on but I'm on my last lap. I'm trying now to sum up; but it doesn't really matter whether I do. Canadian authorship is accepted and each of us has played our parts. I think it was worth doing.

Warm regards,

1 Deacon was working on a history of Canadian literature for George Nelson of Doubleday. Nelson applied in Deacon's name to the Canada Council for a centennial grant to finish the job and wrote for letters of support to Raddall, Northrop Frye, and George Hardy.

2 George Nelson's administrative assistant for over twenty years

---

## From Al Purdy[1]

R.R. 1
Ameliasburg, Ontario
June 21, 1966

Dear Mr. Deacon:

I am hoping you would be good enough to sign and return the copy of *The Four Jameses* which I have? Of course I'll send along postage. It's one of my most treasured books, one I've turned back to many times over the past few years. And such is my bibliophiliac nature, I'd like it signed.

Only, of course, if it seems no bother to you.

Sincerely,
Al Purdy

1 Alfred Wellington Purdy (b. 1918) was already well established as a poet and recipient of the Governor-General's Award for *The Cariboo Horses* (1965) when he wrote requesting Deacon's autograph on a copy of *The Four Jameses*. Not aware of Purdy or his work, Deacon was none the less flattered. His delight and Purdy's appreciation indicate the degree to which the cycle of literary growth had entered a new stage and re-expressed Deacon's ideal of 'craft solidarity' across the generations.

---

## From Al Purdy

R.R. 1
Ameliasburg, Ontario
July 5, 1966

Dear Mr. Deacon,

Thanks much for your letter.[1] Just to identify myself: no I am not the Purdy who lived in your house previously: I'm the Purdy that recently received the Governor General's Award for poetry – for 1965. The book was *The Cariboo Horses* –

I might say that I've read your columns for many years, and it is very pleasant to have a letter from you. *The Four Jameses* is the only book of yours I have, the others being quite scarce, tho I intend to pick them up when I see copies. I am an inveterate habitue of used book stores. Incidentally, I did recently live in Toronto, where my wife was going to Teacher's College. We lived in 'Cabbagetown,' on Sackville St., that is, two blocks east of Parliament, quite a rough district now. But my wife has got her certificate, so we moved away. Besides, I am on the last half of a Canada Council fellowship, whereby I go to Newfoundland for the summer, having bought a pickup truck and camper to go with it.

Anyhow, I'd like to say again how much I've enjoyed *The Four Jameses* over the years. It is much better known since Ryerson's re-published it, but there is the occasional literary person who hasn't heard of it. For instance, I showed it to a young poet name Lionel Kearns[2] about a month ago. Came across James McIntyre's poems[3] in the Village Book Store some time back. I didn't buy it, for they wanted $25. or $30. or some such fabulous price. And you, Mr. Deacon, are largely responsible for such literary inflation. I first bought the book, say 10 years ago, then gave my copy to Louis Dudek (McGill English Dept.) on his solemn promise to return it. But he forgot. So I bought another in Vancouver a year or so ago.

I haven't read your *Peter MacArthur*. Tho I remember giving my mother a MacArthur book as a Christmas or birthday present many years ago (I'm now 47 years old.) His name immediately brings to mind the poem about the stone in the middle of the road, which nobody would move. I suppose I write very different things than that myself, but I still enjoy many of the older poets, even if labeled somewhat modern and avant garde. For instance, I teethed on Bliss Carman in high school. When I read his poem A Beginning: Arnoldus Villanova/Many years ago/Said peonies have magic/And I believe it so – when I read that I started to write the stuff myself, at the age of 13, and haven't stopped since.

I hesitate to mention it, for you might not care at all for the sort of poems I write, but I'd love to send you along a copy of my own book. Please ignore the suggestion if you like. I don't think you'd want to read my stuff –

I did want to say this: I think if you had written no other book but *The Four Jameses* you'd still be remembered for a very long time. I suppose you're used to compliments and such outright flattery as this, but I can't help doing it, since I've so enjoyed and laughed over your book and recommended it to so many people who agreed with me. Please believe this, for I have no earthly reason for such outrageous flattery unless it were the truth as it is. But I'll stop before you find me quite sickening. Will be here for about 2 weeks more.

Best Wishes,
Al Purdy

1 Deacon did not keep a copy of his letter.

2 Vancouver poet (b. 1937) and one of the founders of *Tish* magazine (1961–9).

3 McIntyre was the author of *Musings on the Banks of the Canadian Thames* (1884) and *Poems of James McIntyre: Fair Canada Is Our Theme, Land of Rich Cheese, Milk and Cream* (1889).

## To Al Purdy August 1, 1966

Dear A. Purdy,

No, of course you did not live in this house. His name was Firby.

I see the last sentence of your letter of July 5th reads: 'I shall be here about 2 weeks more.'

I took along your book and letter when my wife and I went to our cottage on Lake Couchiching near Orillia. I'd expected that you would send a forwarding address; but no luck. Do tell me where you are and I'll mail the book.

Oddly, I'm having a variant of the same problem with a man, whom I've never met, but who wants me to go to St. John's, Nfld., to see him installed as president of the university there.[1]

Well, Al Purdy, God bless you. Just tell me where to mail the book and it will be put in the mails. I'm proud to have an appreciative reader 39 years after publication.

Warm regards,

1 These details remain confused and unverifiable. M.O. Morgan was President *pro tem* of Memorial University from 1 March 1966 to 31 May 1967 when Lord Stephen Taylor, MD, FRCP, became President.

## From Al Purdy August 1 [1966]

Dear Mr. Deacon,

Thank you for writing. The book may be sent to my address at R.R. 1, Ameliasburg, Ont. – where it will be held until I return.

On my way thru Montreal a week ago I picked up your collection of essays, 'Open House' which pleased me. I have no books of my own with me, so will have to wait until I go back to Ameliasburg before sending you the book.

My wife & I are now parked in our camper-truck in Cape Breton, and will take the ferry to Nfld. Thurs. I quite agree about this retiring business maybe a man at a hard physical job would want to retire, but not a writer and journalist. Books & writing have been my own life, and I couldn't give them up at any age. Do have a good summer.

Best wishes,
Al Purdy

---

## To Al Purdy

August 10, 1966

Dear Al,

Writing *The Four Jameses* was the hardest job I ever tackled. They published at various times; and I would not, for the world, hurt any of them – and did not. They were all pleased as anything. One came to Toronto to thank me and to request that I supply a preface to his next volume. I complied, using the same technique as in *The Four J*'s.[1] He was very pleased. I was surprised that none saw through my spoofing; but such is human vanity.

Then there were the general readers of *The Four J*'s. Those who knew me well, as a writer, caught onto the jest and enjoyed my mock-serious presentation. But a surprising number took me seriously and thought I had just gone off my head. Some just threw my book away in disgust. 'How could Deacon really admire such stuff?' I have no way of knowing how many, like you, got the message as I had intended. The book is rather rare today and no publisher suggested a re-print.[2]

I fear a large proportion of my readers just threw the book away in disgust. But I did achieve my twin objectives – not to hurt the feelings of these poetasters and also to bring their effusions to the attention of a good many readers, who shared the joke with me. A few used readings from it to entertain guests in their homes.

Too bad I haven't one in hard covers to send you.

Hope you are enjoying your trip. It sounds wonderful.

With warm regards,

1 *Poems and Essays* by John J. MacDonald (1849–1937), who also wrote under the pseudonym James MacRae, was published by Graphic Press in its Ru-Mi-Lou Imprints series in 1928 with a foreword by Deacon.

2 In fact, Ryerson had published a revised edition in 1953 which was reprinted by Macmillan in 1974. In his introduction to the Macmillan edition, Doug Fetherling described *The Four Jameses* as an 'underground classic.'

# Index

Page numbers in bold type indicate main references in the annotations.

www.ingramcontent.com/pod-product-compliance
Lightning Source LLC
Chambersburg PA
CBHW060615100726
47907CB00006B/1625